Computational Intelligence in Analytics and Information Systems

Volume 1

Data Science and AI, Selected Papers from CIAIS-2021

Computational Intelligence in Analytics and Information Systems, 2-volume set

Hardback ISBN: 978-1-77491-142-6
Paperback ISBN: 978-1-77491-143-3

Volume 1: Data Science and AI, Selected Papers from CIAIS-2021

Hardback ISBN: 978-1-77491-144-0
Ebook ISBN: 978-1-00333-231-2
Paperback ISBN: 978-1-77491-145-7

Volume 2: Advances in Digital Transformation, Selected Papers from CIAIS-2021

Hardback ISBN: 978-1-77491-146-4
Ebook ISBN: 978-1-00333-236-7
Paperback ISBN: 978-1-77491-147-1

Computational Intelligence in Analytics and Information Systems

Volume 1

Data Science and AI, Selected Papers from CIAIS-2021

Edited by
Hardeo Kumar Thakur, PhD
Manpreet Kaur, PhD
Parneeta Dhaliwal, PhD
Rajeev Kumar Arya, PhD
Joan Lu, PhD

First edition published 2024

Apple Academic Press Inc.
1265 Goldenrod Circle, NE,
Palm Bay, FL 32905 USA
760 Laurentian Drive, Unit 19,
Burlington, ON L7N 0A4, CANADA

CRC Press
6000 Broken Sound Parkway NW,
Suite 300, Boca Raton, FL 33487-2742 USA
4 Park Square, Milton Park,
Abingdon, Oxon, OX14 4RN UK

Library and Archives Canada Cataloguing in Publication

Title: Computational intelligence in analytics and information systems / edited by Hardeo Kumar Thakur, PhD, Manpreet Kaur, PhD, Parneeta Dhaliwal, PhD, Rajeev Kumar Arya, PhD, Joan Lu, PhD.
Names: Thakur, Hardeo Kumar, editor. | Kaur, Manpreet (Lecturer in computer science), editor. | Dhaliwal, Parneeta, editor. | Arya, Rajeev, 1985- editor. | Lu, Zhongyu, 1955- editor.
Description: First edition. | Includes bibliographical references and index. | Contents: Volume 1. Data Science and AI, Selected Papers from CIAIS-2021
Identifiers: Canadiana (print) 20230146627 | Canadiana (ebook) 20230146694 | ISBN 9781774911426 (set ; hardcover) | ISBN 9781774911433 (set ; softcover) | ISBN 9781774911440 (v. 1 ; hardcover) | ISBN 9781774911457 (v. 1 ; softcover) | ISBN 9781003332312 (v. 1 ; ebook)
Subjects: LCSH: Computational intelligence. | LCSH: Information technology.
Classification: LCC Q342 .C66 2023 | DDC 006.3—dc23

Library of Congress Cataloging-in-Publication Data

....

CIP data on file with US Library of Congress

....

ISBN: 978-1-77491-144-0 (hbk)
ISBN: 978-1-77491-145-7 (pbk)
ISBN: 978-1-00333-231-2 (ebk)

About the Editors

Hardeo Kumar Thakur, PhD, is working as an Associate Professor in the Department of Computer Science and Technology of Manav Rachna University (MRU), Faridabad, India. He has more than 10 years of teaching and research experience in leading institutions of India. He earned his PhD (Computer Engineering) from the University of Delhi in 2017 in the field of data mining. His current research interests are data mining, dynamic graph mining, machine learning and big data analytics.

Manpreet Kaur, PhD, is working as an Associate Professor in the Department of Computer Science and Technology, Manav Rachna University, India. She has more than 14 years of teaching and research experience. She is currently working in the domains of machine learning, deep learning, and natural language processing. She is a Senior Member, IEEE (USA).

Parneeta Dhaliwal, PhD, has over 16 years of experience in teaching and research. Presently, she is working as Associate Professor in the Department of Computer Science and Technology, Manav Rachna University, India. She is also working as Head of the Research Cluster of Computing (RCC) to facilitate students in their research and innovative projects.

Rajeev Kumar Arya, PhD, is currently an Assistant Professor with the Department of Electronics and Communication Engineering at National Institute of Technology, Patna, India. His current research interests are in wireless communication, soft computing techniques, cognitive radio, signal processing, communication systems, and circuits design.

Joan Lu, PhD, is a Professor in the Department of Computer Science and the Research Group Leader of Information and System Engineering (ISE) in the Centre of High Intelligent Computing (CHIC) at the University of Huddersfield, United Kingdom, having previously been team leader in the IT Department of the publishing company Charlesworth Group.

Contents

Contributors

Ankur Kumar Aggarwal
Manav Rachna University, Faridabad, Haryana, India

Himanshu Aggarwal
Computer Science and Engineering Department, Punjabi University, Patiala 147002, Punjab, India

Sagar Aggarwal
Department of Computer Science & Technology, Manav Rachna University, Faridabad, Haryana, India

Apresh Agrawal
Amity University Haryana, Haryana, India

Parikansh Ahluwalia
Computer Science and Engineering Department, Netaji Subhas University of Technology (Formerly NSIT), Delhi, India

Md Asrar Ahmed
Department of Computer Science and Engineering, Osmania University, Hyderabad 500007, Telangana, India

Syed Heena Andrabi
Department of Computer Science and Engineering, Islamic University of Science and Technology, Jammu and Kashmir, India

Mamta Arora
UIET, Kurukshetra University, Haryana, India
Manav Rachna University, Haryana, India

Shweta Bali
Department of Computer Science and Engineering, Faculty of Engineering & Technology, Manav Rachna International Institute of Research & Studies, Faridabad, India

Srikanth Bethu
Department of Computer Science and Engineering, Gokaraju Rangaraju Institute of Engineering & Technology, Hyderabad, Telangana, India

Shubham Budhiraja
Department of Computer Science & Engineering, Manav Rachna University, Faridabad, Haryana, India

Deepa Bura
Manav Rachna International Institute Research and Studies, Faridabad, Haryana, India

Satish Chand
School of Computer and Systems Sciences, Jawaharlal Nehru University, New Delhi, India

Gunjan Chandwani
Department of Computer Science & Technology, Manav Rachna University, Faridabad, India

Ram Chatterjee
Department of Computer Science and Technology, Manav Rachna University, Faridabad, India

Meena Chaudhary
Department of Computer Science & Technology, Manav Rachna University, Faridabad, India

Priyanka Chawla
Department of Computer Science Engineering, Lovely Professional University, Punjab, India

B. Chitra
Department of Electronics and Communication Engineering, Noorul Islam Centre for Higher Education, Kanyakumari, Tamil Nadu, India

Ankit Dagar
Department of Computer Science & Technology, Manav Rachna University, Faridabad, Haryana, India

Parneeta Dhaliwal
Department of Computer Science & Technology, Manav Rachna University, Faridabad, Haryana, India

Sanjeev Dhawan
Department of CSE, UIET, Kurukshetra University, Haryana, India

Rishabh Dhiman
Department of Computer Science & Technology, Manav Rachna University, Faridabad, Haryana, India

Mohit Gambhir
Director, Innovation cell, Ministry of Education, Government of India, India

Vaishali Garg
Department of Computer Science, Amity University, Gurugram, India

Garima
Final Year Student, Amity University Haryana, Haryana, India

Sarika Gaind
Department of Computer Science & Engineering, Manav Rachna University, Faridabad, Haryana, India

Deepak Gauba
Department of Computer Science & Engineering, Manav Rachna University, Faridabad, Haryana, India

Gitika
Final Year Student, Amity University Haryana, Haryana, India

Abhyuday Gupta
Department of Computer Science & Technology, Manav Rachna University, Faridabad, Haryana, India

Sandeep Gupta
Department of Computer Science and Engineering, JIMS Engineering Management Technical Campus, Noida, Uttar Pradesh, India

Sumita Gupta
Amity School of Engineering and Technology, Amity University, Noida, Uttar Pradesh, India

Akshat Jain
School of Computer Science, University of Petroleum & Energy Studies, Dehradun, Uttarakhand, India

Manjula Jain
Department of Management, Teerthanker Mahaveer University, Moradabad, Uttar Pradesh, India

Junali Jasmine Jena
School of Computer Engineering, Kalinga Institute of Industrial Technology (Deemed to be University), Odisha, India

Sathya K.
Department of Computer Science and Engineering, Coimbatore Institute of Technology, Coimbatore, Tamil Nadu, India

Manpreet Kaur
Department of Computer Science & Engineering, Manav Rachna University, Faridabad, Haryana, India

Preeti Kaur
Computer Science and Engineering Department, Netaji Subhas University of Technology (Formerly NSIT), Delhi, India

Vandana Dixit Kaushik
HBTU, Kanpur, India

P. Gopala Krishna
Department of Information Technology, GRIET, Hyderabad, Telangana, India

Vempati Krishna
Department of Computer Science and Engineering, TKR College of Engineering & Technology, Hyderabad, Telangana, India

Rajiv Kumar
Department of Computer Science and Engineering, Chandigarh University, Punjab, India

S. S. Kumar
Department of Electronics and Communication Engineering, Noorul Islam Centre for Higher Education, Kanyakumari, Tamil Nadu, India

Vidit Kumar
Department of Computer Science and Engineering, Graphic Era (Deemed to be University), Dehradun, Uttarakhand, India

Rajalakshmi M.
Department of Information Technology, Coimbatore Institute of Technology, Coimbatore, Tamil Nadu, India

Anamika Maurya
School of Computer and Systems Sciences, Jawaharlal Nehru University, New Delhi, India

Anjali Mehta
Manav Rachna International Institute Research and Studies, Faridabad, Haryana, India

Preeti Mishra
School of Computer Engineering, Kalinga Institute of Industrial Technology (Deemed to be University), Odisha, India

Shambhavi Mishra
Amity School of Engineering and Technology, Amity University, Noida, Uttar Pradesh, India

Usha Mittal
Department of Computer Science Engineering, Lovely Professional University, Phagwara, Punjab, India

Subrajeet Mohapatra
Department of Computer Science and Engineering, Birla Institute of Technology, Mesra, Ranchi, India

Diana Nagpal
Department of Computer Science and Engineering, Chandigarh University, Gharuan, Punjab, India
Guru Nanak Dev Engineering College, Ludhiana, Punjab, India

Sarika Narender
Department of Computer Science & Technology, Manav Rachna University, Faridabad, India

Ramesh Narwal
Computer Science and Engineering Department, Punjabi University, Patiala, Punjab, India

Ritu Pal
Department of CSE, Dev Bhoomi Institute of Technology, Dehradun, Uttarakhand, India

Mrinal Pandey
Department of Computer Science and Technology, Manav Rachna University, Faridabad, India

Bhaskar Pant
Department of Computer Science and Engineering, Graphic Era (Deemed to be University), Dehradun, Uttarakhand, India

Aditya Pathak
Department of Computer Science & Technology, Manav Rachna University, Faridabad, Haryana, India

Archit Prashant Patil
Computer Science and Engineering Department, Netaji Subhas University of Technology (Formerly NSIT), Delhi, India

Jagdish Chandra Patni
School of Computer Science, University of Petroleum & Energy Studies, Dehradun, Uttarakhand, India

Urmila Pilania
Department of Computer Science & Technology, Manav Rachna University, Faridabad, Haryana, India

P. Vara Prasad
Department of Computer Science and Engineering, Gokaraju Rangaraju Institute of Engineering & Technology, Hyderabad, Telangana, India

Pooja Rana
Department of Computer Science Engineering, Lovely Professional University, Phagwara, Punjab, India

Damarla Lakshmi Rohita
Department of Computer Science and Engineering, ACE Engineering College, Hyderabad, Telangana, India

Sahil
Department of Computer Science and Engineering, Guru Nanak Dev University Regional Campus, Gurdaspur, Punjab, India

Riya Sapr
Department of Computer Science & Technology, Manav Rachna University, Faridabad, Haryana, India

Krishan Kumar Saraswat
Department of Computer Science and Engineering, JIMS Engineering Management Technical Campus, Noida, Uttar Pradesh, India

Deepthi Sehrawat
Department of Computer Science, Amity University, Gurugram, India

Utpal Shrivastava
G L Bajaj Group of Institution, Uttar Pradesh, India

Boda Sindhuja
Department of Computer Science and Engineering, GRIET, Hyderabad, Telangana, India

Dilpreet Singh
Department of Computer Science Engineering, Lovely Professional University, Phagwara, Punjab, India

Kulvinder Singh
Department of CSE, UIET, Kurukshetra University, Haryana, India

Niraj Kumar Singh
Department of Computer Science and Engineering, Birla Institute of Technology, Mesra, Ranchi, India

Shekhar Singh
Department of Computer Science and Engineering, JIMS Engineering Management Technical Campus, Noida, Uttar Pradesh, India

Vaibhav Sinha
School of Computer Engineering, Kalinga Institute of Industrial Technology (Deemed to be University), Odisha, India

Vineeta Singh
GLA University, Mathura, Uttar Pradesh, India

Shrikant V. Sonekar
Department of Computer Science & Engineering, JD College of Engineering & Management, Nagpur, Maharashtra, India

Sandeep Kumar Sood
Department of Computer Applications, National Institute of Technology, Kurukshetra, Haryana, India

Seeripi Naga Surya
Amity School of Engineering and Technology, Amity University, Noida, Uttar Pradesh, India

Vikas Thada
Amity University Haryana, Haryana, India

Milind Tote
Department of Computer Science & Engineering, JD College of Engineering & Management, Nagpur, Maharashtra, India

Khushboo Tripathi
Department of Computer Science, Amity University, Gurugram, India

Vikas Tripathi
Department of Computer Science and Engineering, Graphic Era (Deemed to be University), Dehradun, Uttarakhand, India

Nitin Tyagi
Department of Electronics and Communication Engineering, JIMS Engineering Management Technical Campus, Noida, Uttar Pradesh, India

S. S. Tyagi
Department of Computer Science and Engineering, Faculty of Engineering & Technology, Manav Rachna International Institute of Research & Studies, Faridabad, India

Devesh Kumar Upadhyay
Department of Computer Science and Engineering, Birla Institute of Technology, Mesra, Ranchi, India

D. Ushasree
Department of Computer Science and Engineering, Gokaraju Rangaraju Institute of Engineering & Technology, Hyderabad 500090, Telangana, India

Sanjana Vasireddy
Department of Computer Science and Engineering, Gokaraju Rangaraju Institute of Engineering & Technology, Hyderabad, Telangana, India

Siddharth Yadav
Computer Science and Engineering Department, Netaji Subhas University of Technology (Formerly NSIT), Delhi, India

Abbreviations

AAL	active and assistive learning
AC	accent conversion
AE	auto encoder
AI	artificial intelligence
AM	acoustic mechanism
AMP	articular marginal plane
ANN	artificial neural network
APDS	adaptive primal-dual splitting
ARC	activity recognition chain
ASL	American Sign Language
ASR	automatic speech recognition
AUC	area under the curve
AUC-ROC	area under the receiver-operating characteristic curves
BCE	binary cross-entropy
BI-RADS	reporting and data system for breast imaging
CAD	computer-aided diagnosis system
CBE/SBE	clinical/self breast examination
CBI	computer-based intelligence
CCC	concordance correlation coefficient
CDC	Centers for Disease Control and Prevention
CHT	circular Hough Transform
CIN	cervical intraepithelial neoplasia
CNN	cascading neural network
CNN	convolutional neural networks
CRBM	Conditional Restricted Boltzmann Machines
CRFs	conditional random fields
CSSE	Center for Systems Science and Engineering
CSN	convolution similarity network
CSV	comma separated values
CUFS	CUHK Face Sketch
CV	Chan-Vese
CV-APDS	Chan-Vese-based adaptive primal-dual splitting algorithm
DBN	deep belief network
DCNN	deep convolutional neural networks

DCT	discrete cosine transform
DePA	decision propagation and adaptation
DIP	digital image processing
DPFL	deep pyramid feature learning
DRNs	dilated residual networks
DSI	data source identity
DT	decision table
DTs	decision trees
DWT	discrete wavelet transform
ELM	extreme learning machine
END	ensemble of nested dichotomies
EQ	emotional intelligence
ERD	emotion recognition and detection
ERS	emotion recognition system
ER-EST	eigen region-based eigen subspace change
EV	electric vehicles
FBP	filtered back projection
FC	frequency count
FCN	fully convolutional network
FER	facial emotion recognition system
FFT	fast Fourier transform
FN	false negative
FP	false positive
FS	feature selection
GAD	generalized anxiety disorder
GAN	generative adversarial network
GAP	global average pooling
GLCM	gray level co-occurrence matrix
GMM	Gaussian mixture model
GPU	graphics processing unit
HADS	hospital anxiety and depression scale
HAR	human action recognition
HDPS	heart disease prediction system
HIRIS	high-resolution imaging spectrometer
HPV	human papillomavirus
HSIL	high-grade squamous intraepithelial lesion
HVS	human visual system
IDD	Indian Driving Dataset
IHS	intensity hue saturation

ILD	interstitial lung disease
iLIDS-VID	iLIDS video reidentification
IoT	internet of things
IQA	image quality assessment
IR	infrared
IR	iterative reconstruction
ISR	in-schedule reachability
IT	information technology
ITS	intelligent transport system
KL	Kullback-Leibler
KMC	K-means clustering
KNN	k-nearest neighbor
LBP	local binary pattern
LDW	loop detectors for the waiting vehicles
LN	lymph nodes
LR−	Negative likelihood ratio
LSA	Latent Semantic Analysis
LSI	latent semantic indexing
LSIL	low-grade squamous intraepithelial lesion
LSTM	long short-term memory
MFCC	mel-frequency cepstral coefficients
MI	multispectral images
mIoU	mean Intersection over Union
ML	machine learning
MLP	multilayer perceptron
MPSNR	mean peak signal-to-noise ratio
MRI	magnetic resonance imaging
MS	multispectral image
MSAM	mean unearthly point mapper
MSIC	multispectral image compression
MSE	mean square error
MSS	multispectral scanner
NBC	Naïve Bayesian Classifier
NCC	normalized correlation coefficient
NCI	National Cancer Institute
NNge	non-nested generalized examples
NNs	neural networks
NPV	negative predictive value
NRC	not reaching

NRFML	natural random forest machine learning model
ODANB	One Dependency Augmented Naïve Bayes Classifier
OOB	out-of-pack bumble
PAP	Papanicolaou
PC	principal component
PCA	principal component analysis
PET	positron emission tomography
PLS	partial least squares regression
PMED	Program for Monitoring Emerging Diseases
POMS	profile of mood states
PPV	positive predicted value
PRID	person R-ID dataset
PSNR	signal to noise ratio
RBFN	radial basis neural network
RBM	restricted Boltzmann machines
RC	rotator cuff
ReLU	rectified linear unit
ReNN	recursive neural networks
RF	random forest
RFTs	random forest trees
RGB	red green blue
ROIs	regions of interest
RNN	recurrent neural networks
RSUs	road side units
rTSA	reverse total shoulder arthroplasty
SARS-CoV-2	severe acute respiratory syndrome coronavirus 2
SAS	speed advisory system
SB	sub-bands
SER	speech emotion recognition system
S-G-D	stochastic/gradient/descent
SGGNN	Similarity Guided Graph Neural Network
SN	speaker normalization
SOM	soil organic matter
SPB	spectral bands
SPECT	single-photon emission computed tomography
SRU	signal regulating unit
SSIM	structural similitude
STFT	short-term Fourier transform
SVD	singular value decomposition

SVM	support vector machine
TBG	time before the start of green phase
TM	Thematic Mapper
TN	true negative
TP	true positive
TSA	total shoulder arthroplasty
TSCT	traffic at signal clearing time
TTS	text-to-speech
UGC	uterine cervical cancer
VIPeR	visual person detection made reliable
WAC	weighted association classifier
WSN	wireless sensor networks
ZSI	Zijdenbos similarity index

Preface

Data science is a multidisciplinary domain composed of scientific techniques, computer algorithms, and real-time systems to generate knowledge and hidden patterns in data. It is an amalgamation of data mining, deep learning, and also big data. The data science domain includes theories from mathematics, statistics, and knowledge of computer science with the respective domain knowledge. An important field that covers a maximum part of data science is artificial intelligence (AI). AI is human intelligence that is demonstrated by machines, while handling real-time situations. With the help of AI, machines are enabled and trained enough to take appropriate actions while handling any kind of problem statement.

Machine learning provides a link between data science and AI. Machine learning (ML) is the study of computer techniques that learn and train themselves implicitly through experience, based on the dataset in question. These algorithms generate a model using the sample dataset, referred to as "training data," so as to perform effective decision-making. AI provides the tool for data science, generating solutions for real-time problems. Machine learning provides support in achieving that goal.

Machine learning has its applications in various domains such as healthcare, mail filtering among various folders, and computer vision, where conventional approaches are ineffective in performing the desired tasks. Machine learning helps in predictive analytics, giving futuristic projections for business profitability. The extension of machine learning is deep learning. It is basically applied for handling unstructured data such as image, audio, and video surpassing human expertise.

This book widens its scope by discussing new technological advancements in various application areas using the concepts of AI and machine learning. The predictive analytics of the data from various application domains have helped to ease the life of humans and provide timely solutions to various problems.

THE PURPOSE OF THE BOOK

The book focuses on research developments, limitations, and management of real-time problems using computational intelligence. It covers empirical research, prospects covering theoretical research and applications in data science and AI. It helps in assisting in reviews, proposing optimized techniques using latest technologies for effective operations.

The book provides knowledge in the form of surveys and critical reviews of the state-of-the-art techniques, by identifying benefits and limitations and developments for future adaptability. Various novel approaches covering the domains of healthcare, natural language processing, and smart cities are shared. The book has collected vast experience of many stakeholders, researchers, decision makers, and smart cities management officials in identifying applicable approaches in order to enhance, automate, and develop effective solutions to resolve critical problems.

WHO SHOULD READ THE BOOK

The audience for the book includes researchers working in interdisciplinary or multidisciplinary areas of healthcare, image analysis, natural language processing, and smart cities. The researchers may be academicians, people from industry, or may be students with an engineering background with research interest in these varied domains. The book would be highly beneficial because, in addition to the review papers, it also discusses novel approaches for handling the COVID-19 pandemic. It discusses various advanced technologies to handle text and voice data. The book also provides vital information for researchers working to develop smart cities. It would be of interest to researchers focusing on applications of data science and AI in varied domains.

ORGANIZATION OF THE BOOK

This volume contains 31 chapters authored by researchers with expertise in their field of work. These chapters are selected papers presented at the International Conference on "Computational Intelligence in Analytics and Information Systems (CIAIS-2021)," held on April 2–3, 2021 at Manav Rachna University, Faridabad, India. The papers were selected based on the double-blind review process through the Easy-chair Conference Management System.

This book has been organized into four sections, with each section focusing on a different domain of research work. Broadly, the book has been fragmented as follows:

- Section A: Computational Intelligence in Image Processing which includes seven chapters.
- Section B: Computational Intelligence in Healthcare, which includes 10 chapters.
- Section C: Techniques for Natural Language Processing, which includes eight chapters.
- Section D: Computational Intelligence in Smart Cities, which includes six chapters.

A brief introduction to each of the chapters is as follows.

In Chapter 1, Urmila Pilania et al. present a study showing that with the growth of computer and internet, image processing also experienced an intensive progress in the recent years. It also discusses that image processing has many applications in various fields such as research, pattern recognition, communication, remote sensing, medical, and so on. The main objective of digital image processing (DIP) is to produce a more suitable image than the original image for some specific application. This chapter provides an overview of different issues and challenges associated with image-processing techniques.

In Chapter 2, Vineeta Singh and Vandana Kaushik discuss that while designing a fusion-based model, a researcher has to keep in mind generic prerequisites. This chapter also discusses how an image-fusion scheme along with various image-processing techniques enhance face recognition, feature extraction, object detection as well tracking, moving object identification, and so many advanced leading application areas contributing toward smart cities, ubiquitous computing, as well as hassle-free big data handling.

In Chapter 3, Ankur Aggarwal and Mrinal Pandey outline the self-examination related methods, that is, BSE and CBE, and traditional methods for breast cancer early detection. Several emerging techniques are discussed in order to improve regularities. While mammography has been used for the past several years, the findings are not accurate for some female patients. It is demonstrated that MRI is a safer choice than mammography where radiation exposure is less.

In Chapter 4, B. Chitra and S. S. Kumar propose three main phases of Pap Smear Segmentation, namely the preprocessing phase, segmentation phase as well as morphological operation. The input cervical cancer datasets are preprocessed in the initial phase. In phase two, an appropriate segmentation is conducted by constructing a Chan-Vese-based adaptive primal-dual splitting algorithm (CV-APDS) to obtain an optimal segmented image set. In the third step, the morphological operation is carried out to obtain the segmentation results more accurately. In addition to this, the segmentation performance of the proposed approach is validated by employing various kinds of evaluation metrics.

In Chapter 5, Srikanth Bethu et al. propose the NRFML technique for multispectral model image compression. The wavelet transformations are used for effectively coding the picture with Huffman coding. A 3D-DWT decomposes the image, and after thresholding the wavelet, coefficients are encoded using Huffman encoding. NRFML performs compression of the multispectral images and extract the force of assault.

In Chapter 6, Vidit Kumar et al. present an unsupervised video representation learning approach for the movie scene retrieval problem, where convolutional autoencoder is exploited to learn features. To encode the spatial-temporal features, 3D convolution is used in the encoder and decoder. The learned features are matched using cosine distance for retrieval. The experimental results demonstrate the effectiveness of the proposed methodology.

In Chapter 7, Parneeta et al. discuss various techniques for person reidentification. There has been an increase in demands to implement systems that can ensure public safety. Today person reidentification through image capturing or by video surveillance has become the foremost and the most popular way to ensure safety. Combining the above process with convolutional neural networks and deep-learning mechanisms has helped to improve current technology far beyond and help us tackle various challenges that come with it.

In Chapter 8, Anjali Mehta and Deepa Bura review work done by researchers in the field of healthcare with the help of data-mining techniques. The authors give a brief introduction with background study, techniques of data mining, and factors of cardiac arrest. Accuracy and performance are two important measures for any algorithm. With the help of this study, it is proved to achieve better and accurate prediction of diseases, to decrease death rate, and to avoid many other problems, various methods of data mining must be used in a hybrid approach.

In Chapter 9, Milind Tote and Shrikant V. Sonekar present a comprehensive review of the prediction of shoulder arthroplasty by using various deep-learning techniques. It was observed that in different scenarios, different algorithm approaches are used and accordingly performance varies but dataset and feature selection is very significant to get better predictions.

In Chapter 10, Sandeep Gupta et al. present an early assessment of computer-based intelligence (CBI) against nCOVID-19 virus. The fundamental territories where CBI can add to the battle against the nCOVID-19 virus are examined. It is presumed that CBI does not prove to be significant against this virus. Its utilization is obstructed by an absence of information, and by excess information.

In Chapter 11, Jagdish Chandra Patni et al. depict various upgrades for helping in the arrangement of new strategies, techniques, and conventions over a social insurance framework in light of the COVID-19 pandemic. Their study toward the possible solution to deal with this kind of pandemic is based on the clinical data using machine learning that helps us to early diagnosis and treatment of critically ill patients without failure that definitely reduces the mortality rate.

In Chapter 12, Vaishali Garg et al. review a machine learning approach for the prediction analysis of COVID-19 and the results showed an upward curve in the number of cases. One way as perceived in China, the number of COVID-19 cases were minimized by keeping sensitive people away from infected people which included senior citizens and infants.

In Chapter 13, Devesh K. Upadhyay et al. focus on the behavioral aspects of the automatic detection of mood and anxiety disorders. The behavioral characteristics are fed as an input to K-Nearest Neighbors Algorithm (KNN), Support Vector Machine (SVM), Radial Basis Neural Network (RBFN), Naïve Bayesian Classifier (NBC), and Multilayer Perceptron (MLP) classifier as an input, for the assessment of mood disorders among students. It is observed that SVM performed better with accuracy of 93.91% as compared to RBFN with 90.43%.

In Chapter 14, Shweta Bali and S. S. Tyagi work to find a model suitable for achieving highly accurate results on small dataset of medical tools. The study focuses on various aspects of the CNN architecture as the backbone. The authors successfully find that the InceptionV3 architecture has proved to be useful in the process of classifying different medical tools.

In Chapter 15, Mamta Arora et al. review the taxonomy of cervical cancer screening and commonly used ML techniques in the prognosis of cervical cancer. The usage of MLA in cancer prognosis has been depicted in the form of a chart that shows the rapidly increasing demand of ML in healthcare. The models used for prediction of cervical cancer are classified in two major categories on the basis of input fed to the model. One type of model takes input as test screening images and the other that uses clinical numerical values.

In Chapter 16, Srikanth Bethu et al. propose a versatile computer-based intelligence calculation for the early figure of sickness with higher exactness to spare human life and to reduce the treatment cost. The motivation behind this structure is to look at and clarify how ANN works and decide to break faith check together, offer a superior reaction, then see breast risky advancement, notwithstanding how the segments lessened. The neural system also persuades human urgent information assessment, and we can do preconfirmation with no astounding medicinal learning.

In Chapter 17, Ram Chatterjee et al. use various mining classification techniques for data such as Multi-Layer Perceptron, Bagging, Boosting, Voting, MLP, SVM, Naïve Bayes, and proposed ensemble technique, that is, ADABOOST with MLP for heart disease prediction. The classification techniques are then applied on the dataset and are validated using 10 cross-fold technique, and the results are finally compared based on accuracy, specificity, sensitivity, recall, and precision levels, respectively. The results conclude that ADABOOST with MLP has outperformed other classification techniques by having the highest accuracy rate of 92.96%.

In Chapter 18, Sumita Gupta and Mohit Gambhir describe the solution to skim through the data for distilled and appropriate information using the automatic text summarization method. A text summarizer extracts relevant information that intends to meet the standards of human-produced summary but comparatively in much less time. The only goal of automatic text summarizer is to produce such concise text that fits the human proximity of summarization. The authors focus on discussing and comparing the implementation of various extractive techniques for text summarization in detail.

In Chapter 19, Gunjan Chandwani et al. propose a novel algorithm for document indexing. Indexing is particularly important for unstructured data, such as emails, market research reports, correspondence, etc. Structured data such as sales invoices of a business are stored in databases that have their own document-retrieval algorithms. Document indexing is a powerful technique that retrieves documents from repositories containing millions of documents. Documents are indexed by their content or by metadata attached to the document. In this chapter, they propose a new document-indexing algorithm and its comparative analysis with the traditional indexing algorithm approach.

In Chapter 20, Priyanka Chawla et al. discuss their research on recognizing musical instruments. Deep neural networks are great at working with noisy data and for musical instrument classification or for classifying human voice from rest of the musical instruments. So, using deep neural networks one can separate a single sound wave from all the rest of the sound waves or noise. The authors explain the various approaches for instrument recognition using machine learning and compared them to identify the approach that gives the best results.

In Chapter 21, Preeti Kaur et al. discuss shifting speech to the native accent after detecting "foreign" accents. Their objective is to give accurate classification of a given speech clip into a native or a nonnative accent. The authors propose a methodology to perform the task of accent conversion by the usage of multiple methods: neural style transfer applied to audio fragments and recurrent neural networks with training labels as the native accent.

In Chapter 22, Sarika Gaind et al. propose a model by applying deep learning to analyze the emotional state through speech and improve the performance of virtual personal assistants. The analysis of voice samples is done on features like amplitude, frequency, and Mel-Frequency Cepstral Coefficients (MFCCs). Datasets with six emotions are used to get better insights on emotion analysis using the Recurrent Neural Networks (RNN) classifier.

In Chapter 23, Vikas Thada et al. develop a serverless, highly available, highly scalable, high-performance application using deep learning and Amazon Web Services (AWS) cloud that would interpret signs in real time and translate them for those who don't know the sign language. In the analysis, based on the American Sign Language (ASL), MNIST dataset from Kaggle sign language, a convolutional neural network is trained, and 100% test accuracy is achieved.

In Chapter 24, Shambhavi Mishra et al. present an extensive study of various methods that are utilized for emotion recognition using speech, body postures with facial expressions, and other body movements. A comparative study of existing technologies based on databases used in every research, how emotions are extracted, their advantages, and limitations is discussed.

In Chapter 25, Ramesh Narwal and Dr. Himanshu Aggarwal propose a model to solve the challenging problem of ambiguity in sentences interpretation by machine learning algorithms while doing text-based emotion recognition due to lack of voice modulation and facial expressions.

In Chapter 26, Diana Nagpal and Rajiv Kumar provide a brief understanding of human action recognition (HAR), that is, sensor-based and vision-based HAR. The best in time techniques of machine learning such as decision trees, K-nearest neighbors are reviewed for HAR. Also, deep learning neural network strategies are depicted, for example, artificial NN, RNN, and CNN and the results obtained by these methods are discussed.

In Chapter 27, Sahil and Sandeep K. Sood propose an intelligent framework using Fog-Cloud centric Internet of Things (IoT) for traffic management in urban spaces. Their system initially monitors vehicle mobility in real-time at the fog layer and immediately classifies the in-schedule reachability (ISR) of the vehicles. The framework uses the J48 decision tree for ISR classification at the fog layer and a proposed approach for traffic prediction at the cloud layer. The result analysis acknowledges the efficiency of J48 as compared to other employed classifiers viz. accuracy, sensitivity, specificity, and F-measure.

In Chapter 28, Vikas Thada et al. implemented a traffic signs recognition algorithm using a CNN, and it's done using python and the deep learning framework Keras. Training of 43 traffic signs is done using CNN and Keras and is tested under various parameters and scenarios, such as network depth, filter size, dropout rate, preprocessing, and segmentation techniques were used for training. The research work reached test accuracies above 95%, and the experimental results confirmed high efficiency.

In Chapter 29, Anamika Maurya and Satish Chand propose an atrous pyramid pooling mechanism along with layers of pretrained ResNet-50 model to capture details of small objects in complex unstructured road scenarios in the encoder part. The newly proposed approach demonstrate its superiority over state-of-art-models by achieving 0.623 mean Intersection over Union (mIoU) on the validation set of Indian Driving Dataset (IDD).

In Chapter 30, Vaibhav Sinha et al. focus on deriving the best possible methodology to help farmers in choosing the most profitable crop. The dataset is taken on the basis of the required parameters for a particular crop like temperature and rainfall suitable for crop growth and is derived and integrated in from of various authentic sources. Random forest and artificial neural networks have been used for prediction of profitable crops and ANN with Adam optimizer gives 95% accuracy.

In Chapter 31, Sathya Kand Rajalakshmi M proposes CapGAN for identifying a cropping patterns recommendation system in which farmers are able to monitor the soil data, predict, and recommend suitable for cultivation resulting in high yield. CapGAN uses Generative Adversarial Network (GAN) for data augmentation and Capsule Networks for crop prediction. Furthermore, GAN generates more soil features from historical cultivation and yield data. The proposed system implements an Android-based user interface for helping the farmers to track the cropping patterns more efficiently and periodically.

Committees of the International Conference on "Computational Intelligence in Analytics and Information Systems (CIAIS-2021)," April 2–3, 2021, Manav Rachna University, Faridabad, India

Chief Patrons
Dr. Prashant Bhalla,
President, Manav Rachna Educational Institutions

Dr. Amit Bhalla,
Vice President, Manav Rachna Educational
Institutions

Patron
Prof. I. K. Bhatt,
Vice Chancellor, Manav Rachna University

Executive Chairs
Prof. Sangeeta Banga,
Dean Academics, Manav Rachna University

Prof. Pradeep K. Varshney,
Dean Research, Manav Rachna University

Prof. Shruti Vashisht,
Dean Students Welfare, Manav Rachna
University

General Chairs
Prof. Anjana Gosain,
University School of Information Communication
Technology, Guru Gobind Singh Indraprastha
University, New Delhi, India

Prof. Rajkumar Buyya,
The University of Melbourne, Australia

Prof. Joan Lu,
School of Computing and Engineering,
University of Huddersfield, London, UK

Organizing Chair
Prof. Hanu Bhardwaj,
Head, Department of Computer Science &
Technology, Manav Rachna University

Dr. Jyoti Pruthi,
Associate Head, Department of Computer
Science & Technology, Manav Rachna University

Secretary
Prof. Susmita Ray,
Professor, Department of Computer Science &
Technology, Manav Rachna University

Dr. Rajeev Arya,
Assistant Professor, NIT, Patna

Convener
Dr. Hardeo Kumar Thakur,
Associate Professor, Department of Computer
Science & Technology

Dr. Manpreet Kaur,
Associate Professor, Department of Computer
Science & Technology

Dr. Parneeta Dhaliwal,
Associate Professor, Department of Computer
Science & Technology

ADVISORY BOARD

Dr. Gurpreet Singh Lehal, Head, AI and Data
Science Research Centre, Punjabi University,
Punjab, India

Joan Lu, Prof. Department of Computer Science
School of Computing and Engineering Centre
for Planning, Autonomy and Representation of
Knowledge, University of Huddersfield, London

Dr. Nathaniel G Martin, Emiretus Faculty,
University of Rochester, New York, USA

Prof.(Dr.) S. S. Aggarwal, Emiretus Scientist CEERI/CSIR, Advisor CDAC-Noida, Director General KIIT Group of Colleges, India

Dr. Dvln Somayajulu, National Institute of Technology, Warangal 506004, Telangana, India

Prof. S.C. Sharma, IIT Roorkee, India

Dr. Upasana Singh, University of Natal, South Africa

Dr. A R Abdul Razak, BITS Pilani, Dubai Campus, Dubai

Dr. Bhanu Prasad, Florida A&M University, USA

Dr. Abhinav Dhall, Associate Professor, IIT Ropar, Punjab, India

Rajkumar Buyya, The University of Melbourne, Australia

Dr. Anand Gupta, Associate Professor, Netaji Subhas Institute of technology, Dwarka, New Delhi, India

Dr. MPS. Bhatia, Professor, Netaji Subhas Institute of Technology, Dwarka, New Delhi, India

Dr. Satish Chand, Professor, Jawahar Lal Nehru University, New Delhi, India

Dr. Alok Gupta, Founder & CEO, Pyramid Cyber Security & Foresnsic (P) Ltd. New Delhi, India

Dr. Anjana Gossain, Professor, Indraprastha University, New Delhi, India

Dr. Saurabh Pandey, IIT Patna, India

Dr Vasudha Bhatnagar, Professor, Delhi University, India

Dr. Kiran Kumar Pattanaik, Associate Professor Department: Information Technology, IIIT Gwalior, India

Prof. Sanjay Kumar Dhurandher, Professor and Head IT, NSUT, India

TECHNICAL PROGRAM COMMITTEE

Dr. Xiao-Zhi Gao, School of Computing, University of Eastern Finland, Kuopio 70210, Finland

Dr. Sansar Singh Chahuan, Professor, Galgotias University, Greater Noida, Uttar Pradesh, India

Dr. Sanjeev Pippal, Professor, Galgotias University, Greater Noida, Uttar Pradesh, India

Dr. Sapna Gambhir, JC BOSE YMCA University, India

Dr. Neelam Duhan, JC BOSE YMCA University, India

Dr. Samayveer Singh, Assistant Professor, NIT, Jalandhar, Punjab, India

Dr. Rashmi Agarwal, JC BOSE YMCA University, India

Dr. Sudhanshu Kumar Jha, Assistant Professor, Allahabad University, Uttar Pradesh, India

Dr. Sirshendu Sekhar Ghosh, Assistant Professor, NIT, Jamshedpur, Jharkhand, India

Dr. A.K. Mohapatra, Associate Professor, Indira Gandhi Delhi Technical University, Delhi, India

Dr. Vimal Bibhu, Associate Professor, Amity university, Uttar Pradesh, India

Dr. Suneet Gupta, Assistant Professor, Bennett University, Noida, Uttar Pradesh, India

Dr. Geeta Rani, G.D. Goenka University, Gurugram, Haryana, India

Dr. Vidhi Khanduja, Sal Educational Campus, Saltier, Gujarat, India

Dr. V Kumar Assistant Professor, NIT Jamshedpur, Jharkhand, India

Dr. Niraj Kumar Singh, Assistant Professor, BIT Jagdeep Kaur Meshra, Ranchi, Jharkhand, India

Dr. Durgesh Singh, Assistant Professor, BIT Meshra, Ranchi, Jharkhand, India

Dr. Anil Kumar Yadav, Assistant Professor, Jaypee University, Guna, Madhya Pradesh, India

Dr. Shiv Prakash, Assistant Professor, Allahabad University, Uttar Pradesh, India

Dr. Vishal Goyal, Associate Professor, Punjabi University Patiala, Punjab, India

Dr. Vishal Gupta, Assistant Professor, Punjab University, Chandigarh, India

Dr. Parminder Singh Professor and Head, Guru Nanak Engineering College, Ludhiana, Punjab, India

Dr. Akashdeep, Assistant Professor, Punjab University, Chandigarh, India

Dr. Vinay Chopra, Associate Professor, DAV Institute of Engineering and Technology, Jalandhar, Punjab, India

Dr. Ashima Assistant professor, Thapar Institute of Technology, Patiala, Punjab, India

Monika Oberoi Application Development Lead, Shell, Bangalore India

Dr. Ashish Payal Assistant Professor, USICT, Guru Gobind Singh Inderprastha University, Delhi, India

Jaspreeti Singh Assistant Professor, USICT, GGSIPU, Delhi, India

Dr. Manuj Assistant Professor, University of Delhi India

Dr. Pinaki Chakraborty Assistant Professor, Netaji Subhas Institute of Technology, Dwarka, New Delhi, India

Dr. Badal Soni Assistant Professor, NIT Silchar, India

Dr. Sunil Kumar Singh, Assistant Professor, Mahatma Gandhi Central University, Bihar, India

Dr. Vipin Kumar, Assistant Professor, Mahatma Gandhi Central University, Bihar, India

Dr. Jagdeep Kaur, Assistant Professor, NIT Jalandhar, India

Mohit, PhD research scholar, Dayalbagh University, Uttar Pradesh, India

Mala Saraswat, Associate Professor, ABES Engineering College, Ghaziabad, Uttar Pradesh, India

Priti Bansal, Assistant Professor, Netaji Subhas Institute of Technology, Dwarka, New Delhi, India

Rohit Beniwal, Assistant Professor, Delhi Technological University, New Delhi, India

Dr. Dileep Kumar Yadav, Assistant Professor, Galgotia University, Greater Noida, Uttar Pradesh India

Dr. Pranav Dass, Assistant Professor, Galgotia University, Greater Noida, Uttar Pradesh, India

Dr. Arun Kumar, Assistant Professor, Galgotia University, Greater Noida, Uttar Pradesh, India

Dr. Navjot Singh, Assistant Professor, NIT, Allahabad, Uttar Pradesh, India

Sh. Nitin Gupta, Assistant Professor, NIT Hamirpur, Uttar Pradesh, India

Dr. Lokesh Chouhan, Assistant Professor, NIT Hamirpur, Uttar Pradesh, India

Dr. Amit Gaurav, Assistant Professor, Galgotia College of Engineering and Technology, Greater Noida, Uttar Pradesh, India

Dr. Lokesh Kumar Sharma, Assistant Professor, Galgotia College of Engineering and Technology, Greater Noida, Uttar Pradesh, India

Dr. Vikram Bali, Professor, J.S.S. Academy of Technical Education, Noida, Uttar Pradesh, India

Nemi Chandra Rathore, Assistant Professor, Central University of South Bihar, India

Dr. Rajeev Kumar Arya, Assistant Professor, NIT, Patna, Bihar, India

Dr. Vivek Sharma, Assistant Professor, Amity School of Engineering and Technology, Delhi, India

Dr. Aruna Malik Assistant Professor, Galgotia University, Greater Noida, Uttar Pradesh India

Dr. Vikas Chaydhary NIT, Kurukshetra, Haryana India

Dr. Rajeev Garg Cpa Global, Noida, Uttar Pradesh India

Deevyankar Agarwal Assistant Professor, HCT, Muscat, UAE India

Dr. Manish Kumar Singh Associate Professor, GCET, Greater Noida, Uttar Pradesh India

Dr. Satyajee Srivastava Assistant Professor, Galgotias University, Greater Noida, Uttar Pradesh India

Dr. Rishav Singh, Assistant Professor, Bennett University, Noida, Uttar Pradesh, India

Dr. Upasana Pandey, Associate Professor, IMS Engineering College, Ghaziabad, Uttar Pradesh, India

Dr. Anshu Bhasin, Assistant Professor, I. K. Gujral Punjab Technical University, Punjab

Dr. Abhilasha Singh, Assistant Professor, Amity University Noida, Uttar Pradesh

Dr. Yogesh Kumar, Associate Professor, Chandigarh Group of Colleges, Landran, Punjab

Dr. Amit Singhal, Professor-Department of CSE, RKGIT Ghaziabad Uttar Pradesh

Dr. Navneet Kaur, Assistant Professor, Baba Banda Singh Bahadur Engg College Fatehgarh Sahib

Dr. Bharti Sharma, Associate Professor and Academic Head Department of Computer

Application, DIT University, Dehradun Uttarakhand, India

Ms. Poonam Chaudhary, Assistant Professor, North Cap University, Gurugram, Haryana

PUBLISHING COMMITTEE

Dr. Mrinal Pandey (Chair)
Dr. Sachin Lakra (Co chair)
Dr. Sanjay Singh
Ms. Mamta Arora
Ms. Riya Sapra
Mr. Ram Chatterjee
Ms. Anupriya Sharma
Ms. Alpana

Session Track Committee:
Dr. M. Thurian Pandian, Associate Professor (Chair)
Ms. Gunjan Chindwani
Ms. Urmila Pilania
Ms. Gaganjot Kaur
Ms. Priyanka Gupta

Sponsorship Committee:
Dr. Parneeta Dhaliwal (Chair)
Ms. Hanu Bhardwaj (Co-Chair)
Dr. Susmita Ray
Mr. Ankur Kumar Aggarwal
Ms. Priyanka Gupta

Media and Marketing Committee:
Dr. Prinima Gupta (Chair)
Ms. Nikita Taneja (Co-Chair)
Ms. Gunjan Chindwani
Ms. Bharti Jha
Mr. Manoj Kumar
Ms. Anupriya Sharma
Ms. Shreya Malhotra

Finance Committee:
Dr. Jyoti Pruthi (Chair)
Mr. Agha Imran Hussain (Co-Chair)
Mr. Narender Gautam
Ms. Priyanka Gupta
Mr. Anup Singh Khuswaha

Program Committee:
Ms. Neelu Chaudhary (Chair)
Ms. Gaganjot (Co-Chair)
Ms. Meena Chaudhary
Ms. Sarika Gambhir
Ms. Shailja Gupta
Mr. Narender Kumar

Student Committee:
Ravi Prakash (Developer)
Parikshit Sharma (Designer)
Sanchit Bajaj (Developer & Designer)
Harsh Mittal (Developer & Designer)

PART I
Computational Intelligence in Image Processing

CHAPTER 1

A Study of Issues and Challenges with Digital Image Processing

URMILA PILANIA, ANKIT DAGAR, SAGAR AGGARWAL, and
ADITYA PATHAK

*Department of Computer Science & Technology, Manav Rachna University,
Faridabad, Haryana, India*

ABSTRACT

With the growth of computer and Internet, image processing also experienced
an intensive progress in recent years. Development in computer technology
improves the growth of image processing tools in many fields. Image
processing has many applications in various fields like research, pattern
recognition, communication, remote sensing, medical, etc. Every application
has different requirements and concerns. Image quality assessment has
become the subject of current research because of its effectiveness in many
applications. The main objective of digital image processing is to produce a
more suitable image than the original image for some specific application.
This paper provides an overview of different issues and challenges associated
with image processing techniques.

1.1 INTRODUCTION

Digital image processing (DIP) techniques have their applications in various
fields like in the medical, military, object detection and recognition, traffic

Computational Intelligence in Analytics and Information Systems, Volume 1: Data Science and AI,
Selected Papers from CIAIS-2021. Hardeo Kumar Thakur, Manpreet Kaur, Parneeta Dhaliwal,
Rajeev Kumar Arya, and Joan Lu (Eds.)

control schemes, communication, robotics, etc.[5] But still, digital images are under development in many aspects. For DIP improvement, various methods already exist. With the help of graphical software, digital images could be produced, reformed, and various visual effects can be added.[1] By converting an image into digital code, it can be compressed without any loss of information and transmitted through digital media. In machine visualization, instinctive examination schemes and robots could create some conclusions depending on the digitized input by the TV camera.[6] Some of the limitations of image processing systems are costly hardware, complexity, poor quality, loss of information during compression,[31] etc.

Image is processed with the help of a computer device. Image processing system utilizes many different algorithms for its processing. Components of the DIP system are shown in Figure 1.1 with their working.

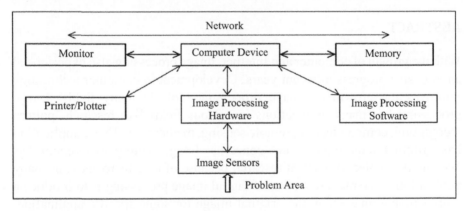

FIGURE 1.1　Image processing components.

1.1.1　IMAGE PROCESSING COMPONENTS

- *Image Sensors*: Image sensors comprise problem area. It can sense illumination, phase, generosity, coordinates, color, and many more characteristics of images and then send the recorded results to image processing hardware. It senses, detects, and transfers recorded information to hardware device for further processing of an image.[7]
- *Image Processing Hardware*: It communicates the information received by image sensor to computer device. It is the main part of the image processing system.

- *Computer*: It is an electronic device that we use in our daily life. The general purpose computer system's actual image processing is done on it.
- *Image Processing Software*: It is the set of rules that contain all the necessary algorithms to process an image.
- *Memory*: It contains all the pixels of the image under process.
- *Printer/Plotter*: When processing of an image is completed then it can be stored temporarily in memory and can be taken as hard copy with the help of printing device.
- *Monitor*: It acts as the output device with the help of monitor screen image can be viewed.
- *Network*: It provides communication between all the devices required to process an image.

1.1.2   CLASSIFICATION OF IMAGE PROCESSING

DIP techniques are useful in object counting and it also decreases time of counting efficiently. For effective counting of objects, technique needs correct recognition of these objects.[3] The precision of technique depends on many factors, such as the size of object, brightness conditions, type of camera used, intensity of object, color of object, etc. DIP techniques are expanding compression of image, recognition of image, and subdivision delivers good compression ratio and precision of the image. Image development processes provide many methods for altering images to obtain visually satisfactory images. The choice of these methods is a function of a particular task, image gratified, viewer appearances, and viewing situations.[4] Some of the DIP techniques are given in Figure 1.2.

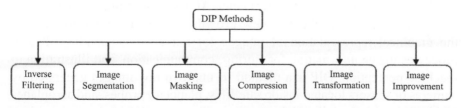

FIGURE 1.2   Classification of image processing techniques.[9]

First, images are converted into digital form with the help of a scanner digitizer. By using all these DIP techniques basically image properties are enhanced for use in digital communication systems or in medical, etc. Whole the process of enhancing image properties is done by a computer system.

1.2   LITERATURE

DIP is the procedure to improve the quality of digital images with the help of computer algorithms. In this section, the overview of some of the DIP techniques is explored to understand these techniques as follows.

The author in this paper reviewed many local and global contrast improvement methods for images. DIP has an exciting problem of image development with low-level image handling. Basically, image development is done for improving image visual quality. Contrast improvement is also a significant feature for image development. Histogram and frequency spectrum-based methods are significant image processing methods that are applied to improve the quality of image. The histogram is an efficient method for contrast and brightness of an image.[17,18]

The author in this paper reviewed many noise and denoising models. From the study, it has been found that noise is always there in digital images during image procurement, encoding, communication, and processing. It is challenging to eliminate noise from digital images without knowing the noise model. That is why the noise model is reviewed first and then tried to remove or reduce noise from digital images.[7] Author reviewed about 200 models of NN in image processing and also discussed its role in the present and future. These models are characterized into a new 2D nomenclature for image processing methods. First dimension points to the kind of assignment completed by the method: preprocessing, information reduction, feature retrieval, subdivision, object identification, etc. The second dimension focuses on input information handled by method: pixel level, local feature level, structure level, object level, etc. At last, the author discussed its application and relates them to new growth.[8] DIP is a method to enhance the graphical representation of images for human understanding. It also processes image information for storing, communication, and illustration to machine perception. DIP is a method to improve raw images generated by cameras or sensors located inside satellites, planetary probes, and aeroplanes and images taken in daily life for many applications. DIP is growing continuously in current years and has many applications in medical and science. DIP basically provides image procurement, image development, image subdivision, feature retrieval, image ordering, etc.[19] Author in this paper explored the method of identifying the mango from the mango tree. For identifying mango, the author used color processing to filter the unrelated color. Along with this color model, they also used a shape identification technique to identify edges that is circular Hough transform (CHT). CHT technique finds candidates of mango and discovers round design with predefined radius. This technique efficiently identifies the mango and also counts the number of mangos present.[20]

An adaptive integrated technique for identification and elimination of cracks inside digitized paintings is proposed by the author. These cracks inside digital painting are identified with thresholding which is the o/p of morphological top-hat transform. This technique also enhances the quality of digital media.[21] In the past three decades, a lot of research has been done by researchers for the extraction of images. Currently, research in these areas demonstrates that a wide gap is present among content-based image extraction and image semantics understood by human beings. Author in this paper focuses on development in image retrieval and also delivers a complete review on image processing. Author analyzed important features of the many AIA techniques, comprising retrieval and semantic learning of image processing. The authors also give a report of their outcomes and suggest direction for future research in AIA field.[22] This paper evaluated the current development of lossy and lossless radiologic image compression and also illustrated legal problems of lossy compression for medical registers. For illustrating the lossy compression, author defined essential ideas of radiologic imaging and digitization. After that, the author inspected current compression methods in the arena of medical imaging and digitization. Author considered significant controlling rules and legal queries fronting the usage of compression in this area. We conclude with a summary of future challenges and research directions.[23]

In various DIP techniques, it is necessary to selectively use DIP for detecting construction of images. For detecting the construction of image grey level, thresholds among structures are located for finding respective peaks in histogram of image. The paper delivers techniques for mechanically identifying the peaks and chosen grey level thresholds for dividing an image into distinct constructions containing steps of identifying peaks in a grey level histogram of image by using flattening and differencing operatives.[24] Noise is the essential part in an image but it causes disturbance in image or degradation in image quality. To remove unnecessary noise from the image and to improve image quality, some methods are used such as frequency spectrum, histogram, entropy graph, Laplacian and Harr filtering. Clustering techniques are convenient for image reorganization, information retrieval, pattern analysis, decision-making, etc.[25] A novel hybrid technique is used for image segmentation in this paper. The hybrid technique is the combination of morphological machinists, watershed procedure, and threshold. Mainly work is done on the one most important feature that is thinning. The thinning procedure is used to recognize the internal processing of image and feature retrieval at a lower level. For doing thinning on images, following operations need to be done: median filters are used to do preprocessing of image, watershed and morphological machinists are applied to identify edges, selection of suitable region, threshold calculation, and calculation of distance for detection of feature point.[26]

Table 1.1 shows the literature summary based on different challenges associated with DIP for the two decades.

1.3   ISSUES AND CHALLENGES WITH DIP TECHNIQUES

There are many issues and challenges with DIP, as discussed below:

- In the 1950s, some work was done on parallel image processing systems. While in the 1970s, it was soon comprehended that to do parallel processing what programmers need is more than one identical local computation unit.[2]
- For working with a parallel image processing system, one of the constraints is time. It consumes a lot of time to do parallel processing. So it is a challenge for researchers in this field to limit this time constraint.[10]
- Multimodality includes image smoothness and separation of multimodal, multichannel, multiscale images obtained from the matching samples. For dealing with such type of information, some actions like registering, denoising, image merging, etc., need to be done. For retrieving related data from complicated dataset need to integrate many acquisition methods.[11,12]
- One more challenge with DIP among researchers is colorimetric record of image detail and precise regeneration. This issue plays an important role in the case of art objects. The process of digitizing should not damage artwork but the damage might happen by extreme supervision and radioactivity by highly illuminated light bases. Artwork needs to be digitized for providing various applications. Because of this, it executes very challenging requests on the attainment procedures and approaches.[13]

TABLE 1.1 Literature Summary.

Authors	Year	DIP method	Issue/challenge
Caroline Chaux, Laurent Duva and Amel Benazza-Benyahia	2008	Nonlinear stein-based estimator	Noise in image processing
Shefali Gupta andYadwinder Kaur	2014	Histogram-based techniques	Brightness and contrast improvement
Barbora Zahradnikova, Sona Duchovicova and Peter Schreiber	2015	Image mining and classification techniques	Issues in storing, processing, and retrieval of image
Kede Ma, Zhengfang Duanmu Zhou Wang	2016	Review of image quality assessment (IQA)	Background condition of image
Nitesh Kumar1, Deepak Kourav2	2018	Wavelet and contoured transform	Large memory requirement
Chitra P.L and Bhavani P	2019	SVM and K-nearest neighbor (KNN) classifier methods	Images processing attacks like sharpening, clipping, rotation, transform, etc.
Gurlove Singh and Amit Goel	2020	Eigen face method	Different image formats
Yuanjin Xu and Xiaojun Liu	2020	Wavelet method	Statistical properties of image

- Connecting conflicting data in different kinds of medical images is a stimulating work for multimodal image registering. In IGS, the patient's organ is looked over at several intervals with the help of different kinds of imaging modalities that cause problems in identifying patient position and alignment with respect to many different types of imaging methods.[32]

- Medical images having noise and some misplaced information causes problems in feature-based registration. Also, this registration method is not much robust during retrieval of features and does not provide a satisfactory feature matching.[14]

- Image coding has worked with various new techniques like spatial temporal, object-oriented coding, consistency coding, fovea coding, etc. As the region of interest has already been assigned many bits at the time of coding so graphical representation is very important for measuring quality. Texture resemblance also plays an important role, as the original matrix could barely evaluate quality of the textured area.[15]

- Watermarking also plays an important role in image processing. Watermarking means concealing secret information in LL and HH frequency coefficients. Due to concealing of some extra information in the image, some features of the image got altered. It results in disturbance in very bright or dark areas of image; along with this it causes nonuniformity in other features of image which is sensitive to human visual system.[15]

- The Web is the massive source of different types of images having different formats. An image database carries unlimited data. Examining the web and extracting specific information from these images denote key challenges for image processing.[16]

- Moving from high-level to low-level pixel demonstration of images is natural. For effective image processing, researchers should be able to extract background details of concealed messages and it is very crucial.[31]

- Because of the floating-point calculation, performance of DIP techniques degrades. Operations like image transforms, sifting, image restore, and statistical property need floating-point calculation and also floating-point execution units.[27]

- There are many masking models that exist to determine if distortions are noticeable or not. But a very well-known problem with these models is that they are not valid for distortions that are outside a given threshold of perceptibility.[28]

- These geometric attacks cause low influence on the visual quality of image. But these minor geometric alterations can cause huge changes in pixel brightness and illumination.[29]
- Successive use of different DIP techniques needs more memory to store the intermediate results. Also requires a lot of calculation to perform alteration on the host image.[30]

A summary of challenges associated with DIP techniques is shown in Figure 1.3. A lot of research has already been done on DIP techniques but still many challenges are associated. These issues need to be recovered for better results in this field.

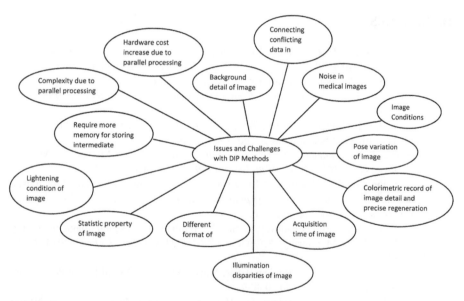

FIGURE 1.3   Issues and challenges associated with DIP.

1.4   CONCLUSION

Image quality measurement has become an important topic of current research because of its utilization in various applications. In this paper, some issues and challenges associated with DIP techniques are discussed. Many image processing techniques already exist to enhance the image quality but still further improvement is required to handle all these issues and challenges. By using artificial intelligence systems, further improvement can be achieved to get better results.

KEYWORDS

- **digital image processing**
- **image sensor**
- **image compression**
- **image enhancement**
- **image segmentation**

REFERENCES

1. Akram, S.; Dar, M.; Quyoum, A. Document Image Processing—A Review. *Int. J. Comput. Appl.* **2010,** *10* (5), 35–40. Sivappriya, T., and Muthukumaran, Kumar (2014).
2. Unger, S. H. A Computer Oriented Toward Spatial Problems. In *Proceedings of the May 6–8, 1958, Western Joint Computer Conference: Contrasts in Computers*, 1958, May; pp 234–239.
3. Adelson, E. H.; Anderson, C. H.; Bergen, J. R.; Burt, P. J.; Ogden, J. M. Pyramid Methods in Image Processing. *RCA Eng.* **1984,** *29* (6), 33–41.
4. Lehmann, T. M.; Gonner, C.; Spitzer, K. Survey: Interpolation Methods in Medical Image Processing. *IEEE Trans. Med. Imag.* **1999,** *18* (11), 1049–1075.
5. Sharma, D.; Jindal, G. Identifying Lung Cancer Using Image Processing Techniques. In *International Conference on Computational Techniques and Artificial Intelligence (ICCTAI)*, Vol. 17, 2011; pp 872–880.
6. Dutta, S.; Pal, S. K.; Mukhopadhyay, S.; Sen, R. Application of Digital Image Processing in Tool Condition Monitoring: A Review. *CIRP J. Manuf. Sci. Technol.* **2013,** *6* (3), 212–232.
7. Boyat, A. K.; Joshi, B. K. A Review Paper: Noise Models in Digital Image Processing, 2015. arXiv preprint arXiv:1505.03489.
8. Egmont-Petersen, M.; de Ridder, D.; Handels, H. Image Processing with Neural Networks—A Review. *Pattern Recognit.* **2002,** *35* (10), 2279–2301.
9. Akram, S.; Dar, M.; Quyoum, A. Document Image Processing—A Review. *Int. J. Comput. Appl.* **2010,** *10* (5), 35–40.
10. Seinstra, F. J.; Koelma, D. User Transparency: A Fully Sequential Programming Model for Efficient Data Parallel Image Processing. *Concurr. Comput. Pract. Exp.* **2004,** *16* (6), 611–644.
11. Chaux, C.; Duval, L.; Benazza-Benyahia, A.; Pesquet, J. C. A Nonlinear Stein-Based Estimator for Multichannel Image Denoising. *IEEE Trans. Signal Process.* **2008,** *56* (8), 3855–3870.
12. Duval, L.; Moreaud, M.; Couprie, C.; Jeulin, D.; Talbot, H.; Angulo, J. Image Processing for Materials Characterization: Issues, Challenges and Opportunities. In *2014 IEEE International Conference on Image Processing (ICIP)*; IEEE, 2014; pp 4862–4866.

13. Barni, M.; Pelagotti, A.; Piva, A. Image Processing for the Analysis and Conservation of Paintings: Opportunities and Challenges. *IEEE Signal Process. Mag.* **2005**, *22* (5), 141–144.

14. Alam, F.; Rahman, S. U.; Ullah, S.; Gulati, K. Medical Image Registration in Image Guided Surgery: Issues, Challenges and Research Opportunities. *Biocybern. Biomed. Eng.* **2018**, *38* (1), 71–89.

15. Zhang, F.; Li, S.; Ma, L.; Ngan, K. N. Limitation and Challenges of Image Quality Measurement. In *Visual Communications and Image Processing 2010*, Vol. 7744; International Society for Optics and Photonics, 2010; p 774402.

16. Zahradnikova, B.; Duchovicova, S.; Schreiber, P. Image Mining: Review and New Challenges. *Int. J. Adv. Comput. Sci. Appl.* **2015**, *6* (7), 242–246.

17. Kathiravan, S.; Kanakaraj, J. A Review on Potential Issues and Challenges in MR Imaging. *Sci. World J.* **2013**, *2013*.

18. Gupta, S.; Kaur, Y. Review of Different Local and Global Contrast Enhancement Techniques for a Digital Image. *Int. J. Comput. Appl.* **2014**, *100* (18), 18–23.

19. Chitradevi, B.; Srimathi, P. An Overview on Image Processing Techniques. *Int. J. Innov. Res. Comput. Commun. Eng.* **2014**, *2* (11), 6466–6472.

20. Hussin, R.; Juhari, M. R.; Kang, N. W.; Ismail, R. C.; Kamarudin, A. Digital Image Processing Techniques for Object Detection from Complex Background Image. *Procedia Eng.* **2012**, *41*, 340–344.

21. Giakoumis, I.; Nikolaidis, N.; Pitas, I. Digital Image Processing Techniques for the Detection and Removal of Cracks in Digitized Paintings. *IEEE Trans. Imag. Process.* **2005**, *15* (1), 178–188.

22. Zhang, D.; Islam, M. M.; Lu, G. A Review on Automatic Image Annotation Techniques. *Pattern Recognit.* **2012**, *45* (1), 346–362.

23. Wong, S.; Zaremba, L.; Gooden, D.; Huang, H. K. Radiologic Image Compression—A Review. *Proc. IEEE* **1995**, *83* (2), 194–219.

24. Sezan, M. I.; Schaetzing, R. *U.S. Patent No. 4,731,863.* U.S. Patent and Trademark Office: Washington, DC, 1988.

25. Chithra, P. L.; Bhavani, P. A Study on Various Image Processing Techniques. *Int. J. Emerg. Technol. Innov. Eng.* **2019**, *5* (5).

26. Grau, V.; Mewes, A. U. J.; Alcaniz, M.; Kikinis, R.; Warfield, S. K. Improved Watershed Transform for Medical Image Segmentation Using Prior Information. *IEEE Trans. Med. Imag.* **2004**, *23* (4), 447–458.

27. Chandler, D. M.; Alam, M. M.; Phan, T. D. Seven Challenges for Image Quality Research. In *Human Vision and Electronic Imaging XIX*, Vol. 9014; International Society for Optics and Photonics, 2014; p 901402.

28. Larson, E. C.; Chandler, D. M. Most Apparent Distortion: Full-Reference Image Quality Assessment and the Role of Strategy. *J. Electron. Imag.* **2010**, *19* (1), 011006.

29. Chandler, D. M. Seven Challenges in Image Quality Assessment: Past, Present, and Future Research. *Int. Sch. Res. Notices* **2013**, *2013*.

30. Ma, K.; Duanmu, Z.; Wu, Q.; Wang, Z.; Yong, H.; Li, H.; Zhang, L. Waterloo Exploration Database: New Challenges for Image Quality Assessment Models. *IEEE Trans. Imag. Process.* **2016**, *26* (2), 1004–1016.

31. Lu, W.; Varna, A.; Wu, M. Secure Video Processing: Problems and Challenges. In *2011 IEEE International Conference on Acoustics, Speech and Signal Processing (ICASSP)*; IEEE, 2011; pp 5856–5859.

32. Singh, G.; Goel, A. K. Face Detection and Recognition System using Digital Image Processing. In *2020 2nd International Conference on Innovative Mechanisms for Industry Applications (ICIMIA)*; IEEE, 2020; pp 348–352.

33. Sharma, S. K.; Wang, X. Live Data Analytics with Collaborative Edge and Cloud Processing in Wireless IoT Networks. *IEEE Access* **2017,** *5,* 4621–4635.

CHAPTER 2

A Methodical View of Prerequisites of Picture Combination, Strategies, and Key Indicators with Usage in Real Life and Scientific Domains Facilitating Smart Ubiquitous Environment

VINEETA SINGH[1] and VANDANA DIXIT KAUSHIK[2]

[1]GLA University, Mathura, Uttar Pradesh, India

[2]HBTU, Kanpur, India

ABSTRACT

Since images leveraged with pertinent information demonstrate a promising involvement in many fields of research, such as medical imaging, microscopic imaging, soft computing, smart cities, network transmission, military areas, feature extraction, object identification and tracking, remote sensing, geographical areas, classification, and so on. Whereas an image fusion scheme yields an informative image via integration of two or more than two partly focused images. Image fusion scheme comes under the basic research fields of image processing. Image fusion is a procedure to amalgamate two or more images of the same scene in such a way so that the final fused image includes the required information from the point of view of researcher, observer, and study. Image fusion is beneficial for object identification, facial features extraction, object tracking, as well movement, visual perception,

Computational Intelligence in Analytics and Information Systems, Volume 1: Data Science and AI, Selected Papers from CIAIS-2021. Hardeo Kumar Thakur, Manpreet Kaur, Parneeta Dhaliwal, Rajeev Kumar Arya, and Joan Lu (Eds.)

video surveillance, medical imaging (multimodal image fusion for tumor detection, skin cancer, etc.), machine learning, human perception, network transmission, smart ubiquitous environments, computer vision, and so on. Fused images are enriched with focused objects, optimal brightness, sharpness, and contrast as well. In this chapter, the author has studied a number of image fusion methodologies from the traditional level to advanced level, their pros and cons with different evaluation metrics and various application areas. This chapter is organized in the following way: Section 2.1 illustrates related work in the field while Section 2.2 involves a description about prerequisites for image fusion techniques, Section 2.3 elucidates the kind of levels at which the image fusion technique relies. Section 2.4 demonstrates image techniques description while Section 2.5 illustrates different performance metrics, while Section 2.6 demonstrates various application areas and Section 2.7 concludes the paper and illustrates limitations with future scope.

2.1 INTRODUCTION AND BACKGROUND OF THE WORK

The word fusion illustrates the merging of information. Thus image fusion refers to the merging pertinent information extracted from the input images so that the purpose of study, research, and observation may be fulfilled. There are different kind of image fusion, multisensor image fusion, multifocus image fusion (see Figure 2.1 for demonstration), and multimodal image fusion. One of the promising targets of image fusion is to generate a quality fused image with sharp content and uniform focus. Fusing various features of images to produce a solitary image is known as the image fusion procedure. The fused images are better utilized in computer vision, robotics, and medical imaging.[19] The main aim of image fusion is basically to produce very clear images.[2] There is an issue of inadequate depth of field due to an elevated degree of intensification in optics of lenses. An increase in focal length and magnification of lens is subject to a decrease in depth of field. Thus fewer objects in the image are included for consideration.

A focused image will include all the objects of image-focused and clear. A fused image will possess all the pertinent information extracted out of the input images and with an extension in-depth field and widely applicable to biomedical imaging, as well as computer vision research field.[10,11,22] The process of integration of various features of images to produce a solitary image is known as image fusion model. Recently, it is highly applicable to medical imaging as well due to its accurate results along with potential in diagnostic purposes. The fused images obtained via numerous modalities of images and tools are utilized for different application fields like medical imaging, robotics, military field, microscopic imaging, and computer vision.[20]

(a)   (b)   (c)

FIGURE 2.1 A sample diagram of multifocus image fusion. (a) and (b) input images. (c) Fused output image.

The image fusion procedure must retain important information of source images via eliminating unnecessary components out of the fused image. The image fusion procedure does not put off any simulated details such as human observer distraction or advanced tasks of image processing. These processes have to be very efficient in avoiding shortcomings, such as misregistration.[9]

Various pertinent image fusion models are proposed in the research field that relied on multiscale decomposition. Mainly three kinds of methodologies exist as depicted in Figure 2.2, that is, decision level, feature level, and pixel level.[5,13] Pixel level fusion models can be further classified in two subcategories, that is, spatial domain as well as transform-domain methods. Spatial domain based methods include principal component (PC) analysis.[5,24] Feature and human perception based methods include guided filtering.[5,10,11]

Transform domain based methods include multiresolution geometric analysis tools and are known for fusion models like ripplet, shearlet, contourlet, trained dictionaries: wavelets and discrete cosine transform local energy functions.[5,26] Various deep learning classifiers are utilized for image fusion procedures.[13] A PC analysis, that is, principal component analysis (PCA) as well as the discrete wavelet transform (DWT) based image fusion model was proposed by[3] to fuse CT and PET images in the medical field. Content adaptive blurring technique based multifocus image fusion algorithm was proposed.[2]

Clustering PCA along with joint dictionary learning, a hybrid approach was devised for the image fusion technique by Yang et al.[24] An image fusion model was proposed that relied on sparse representation and geometric dictionary construction methodology.[21] An image fusion model was proposed by Farid et al.[2] based on PCA with a hybrid of DWT for medical images mainly for CT and PET images. A model based on end-to-end multifocus image fusion with the help of a deep convolutional neural network was developed by Wenda[27]. There were several convolutional neural network (CNN) models used for fusion. In addition, during training to improve performance, the results were simultaneously tracked. However, by fusing multifocused images and CNN, the approach struggled to improve performance.[27]

Image fusion focused on the high pass filter, that is, HPF and key component analysis, that is, KCA was part of the research.[15] A study of image fusion algorithms was proposed[20,25] an image fusion strategy but was unsuccessful to include Bayesian theory for performance improvement.

Devised an image fusion strategy via morphological decomposition. Here images were decomposed into different layers via morphological components as a result of which it was protected from different layers. After getting feature vectors from different layers, it was trained via a support vector machine. Finally, the fusion of coefficients was fulfilled with the help of decision matrix sets but the method was unsuccessful to fused color images.[12]

In the case of underwater spontaneous operation, the involvement of intelligence in computer vision technique is commendable. Due to the under-water area, lack of illumination as well as less quality images need to be rectified/enhanced in the preprocessing step, which is ultimately a prominent requirement for the vision under the sea. In the context of deep-sea resources, effective use as well as growth of development and exploring under the sea autonomous operations are an essential way. A hybrid of max-red, green, and blue (RGB) technique along with gray technique shaded was consumed for the underwater enhancement of vision devised by Han et al. Further a CNN was utilized to solve weak illumination issues in the context of underwater pictures for getting a connection for mapping to generate maps of illumina-tion. A deep CNN scheme was devised for the achievement of identification as well as the classification for marine organisms using the speedy technique for detection of objects, which ultimately solved the issues of weak illumina-tion as well as lesser contrast, as features of underwater vision.[4]

Jung et al. devised a new technique to detect the objects in motion via dynamic camera image series with the help of an inertial measurement unit (IMU) sensor. It is a tedious task to identify dynamic objects via dynamic (in motion) cameras and this is a crazy research area in the globe. The technique devised by researchers in this chapter involves extraction of targeted points with the help of Harris detector, whereas classification in between foreground and background is accompanied via epipolar geometry. Here the utilization of IMU takes place for computation of the fundamental matrix. Further feature points at the background are matched to generate a transformation matrix. Moreover, image registration is utilized for series images and further extraction of difference maps takes place to obtain the region of foreground. At last, to locate, identified "in motion" object minimum bounding box is utilized. Experimental results demonstrated the superiority of the devised technique as compared to different real-time/world driving videos.[7]

Rai et al. devised a technique for extraction of human facial features to identify the feelings such as sorrow, rejoice, anger, smile, etc., in the case of noisy scenarios. Recognition of facial features involves a vital role in many research areas and has a wider role in applications like human–computer connection, security features. For example, biometric devices capture the facial features or thumb impression structures to authorize the entry, similarly in the case of smartphone access, computer access, and so on. In the technique devised, the use of formulae was done relied on HSV model, that is, hue, saturation, value; for demonstration of skin color models to identify as well as extract features of face. An HSV model suits the perception of human color as well as it is fast too. Moreover, probability neural network (PNN) increases effectiveness of the surveillance model since PNN has the capability to produce the yield image, whereas information image may contain noise in it. Experimentation work was accompanied via MATLAB as well as with relevant IPT, that is, image processing toolbox.[16]

Yadav and Singh (2016) devised a new robust model to identify a moving object in thermal video frames that relied on threshold technique based on Kullback–Leibler divergence (KLD) as well as background subtraction, that is, BGS scheme. A background model was implemented, relied on, trimmed-mean, which is strong enough to limit the noise level as well as dynamic elements existing in the background. Here the distribution of all pixels is normally placed, it was assumed. With the utilization Gaussian mixture technique as well as KLD, computation between the current pixel and background pixel was fulfilled. The devised threshold is effectively capable of classifying every pixel state. Further, to complete edge linking the use of morphological technique was accompanied. Moreover, to fill holes flood-fill technique was used. At last, the generation of silhouette for targeted object was accompanied. The devised technique is speedy and outperformed other real-time/world-thermal video series.[23]

Identifying a moving object in a video sequence is a complex as well as a tough task. This moving object may be a moving human being in thermal video. Video surveillance involves such video sequences where detection of moving objects becomes essential. In this case, relevant information is extracted while redundant information is filtered out. But to accompany all this, researchers require efficient techniques. Mainly challenging task in the case of the thermal video sequence, to recognize the moving object is variation at intensity levels as well as moving scenarios of the background. Sharma et al. devised a novel technique that relied on a background subtraction model with the help of a threshold based on Fisher's linear discriminant ratio and this threshold is checked spontaneously at the run-time for every pixel in each of the series frames. Since this works spontaneously that reveals no human intervention (like user or programmer) at the time of selection of threshold. During run-time with the help of this threshold pixel classification is accompanied effectively. Devised technique resolves the issues originated out of the dynamic behavior of the background with the help of the Fisher's ratio. With the help of this, there is maximization of separation in between background pixels as well as foreground pixels. The experimentation outcomes demonstrated the better effectiveness of the devised technique as compared to other considered peer techniques.[18]

In the presence of a complex background, it is a very tedious task to identify a moving object. Here moving objects refer to any vehicle, human being, animal, patient, or it may be a tissue of the body moving inside the body in the case of medical field. In such a scenario, Sharma and Yadav devised a strong background subtraction technique to resolve issues relied on motion as well as variation in illumination. At first, in the training stage, with the help of starting frames, a background modeling technique was devised. Further, at the testing stage, a technique was devised to identify moving objects (in video frames) named as foreground modeling technique. In the testing phase, with the devised technique, classification of moving pixels takes place via a fitting threshold as well as further updating of background takes place via suitable learning rate. Updating of learning rate is accompanied via histogram; here histogram will be calculated for classified frame output as well as for background technique. At last, for improvement of identification quality, image processing schemes along with morphological filters were utilized. Here utilization of two schemes, that is, controlling technique relied on adaptive learning rate as well as updating scheme relied on feedback-based technique makes the devised model enhancement. With the help of devised scheme variation issues of illumination as well as dynamic background effects issues were resolved.[18,23]

Lochab et al. illustrated the strong bond in between the emergence of IoT along with cloud computing. IoT application areas include a number of domain areas as well as services areas for much more efficiency as well as performance. Authors studied various associated possibilities along with shortcomings; issues meanwhile resolution techniques were also demonstrated. With the passing of time, the future will be like the "Internet of Everything." Researchers also devised a technique to be utilized in various areas such as defense areas like the Indian military, navy, army, as well as air force, and so on.[14]

Alam et al. have done a literature survey to fulfill the purpose of data fusion in the case of IoT along with a specific attention toward mathematical models like the theory of belief, artificial intelligence, as well as probabilistic models as well as with particular IoT scenarios, such as object tracking environments, nonlinear environments, distributed environments, as well as heterogeneous environments. The authors have illustrated scopes as well as difficulties in relation with all studied mathematical models as well as included IoT scenarios. Further a possible future trend as well as scope was predicted on the basis of study done by the researchers involving future trends, evolving areas benefited via IoT as well as data fusion, smart vehicles, data fusion, as well as smart cities relied on deep learning techniques.[1]

Kaur et al. have done an assessment of fusion dataset with the help of different schemes relied on extraction methods. Further, for the selection of potential characteristics, selection methods relied on features selection consumed. At last, with the utilization of deep belief network, the construction of machine learning model for the purpose of image fusion was accompanied.[8]

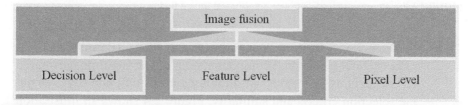

FIGURE 2.2   Levels of image fusion.

2.2   PREREQUISITES OF IMAGE FUSION

After a serious evaluation of the literature review, it can be inferred that the following requirements must be fulfilled while designing an effective image fusion technique. The final fused image must include all the pertinent information from the source images. There must not be any loss of pertinent information in fused image. It must be free from avoiding flaws like misregistration. A fused image must be free from any irrelevant information. During the fusion procedure, there must not be any kind of introduction of inconsistencies or artifacts which may lead to inaccurate result or may affect badly the fusion procedure.

2.3 LEVELS FOR IMAGE FUSION METHODOLOGIES

Basically at three levels, image fusion procedure is accompanied:

 a) **Pixel Level Fusion:** One of the easiest procedures and is implemented at lower level that means integrate pixels where processing of pixels is minimum and the pixels with in input image determine each pixel in the final used image, for instance, the method of averaging. Figure 2.3 shows an illustration diagram for pixel-based image fusion.

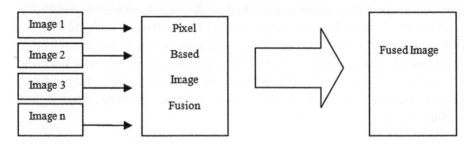

FIGURE 2.3 Representation diagram: pixel-based image fusion.

 b) **Feature Level Fusion:** As name suggests here fusion is accompanied by fusing extracted components out of the input images based on the features like texture information, intensities, and edges as per the selection criteria and similarity. Figure 2.4 shows an illustration of feature-based image fusion.

 c) **Decision Level Fusion:** At the decision level, integrating the information is unified by a more elevated measure of thought, combining the outcomes of various techniques to obtain an accurate decision on blended information, working with the input image mostly for the retrieval of information, and then incorporating the acquired information, applying decision rules to reinforce standard insight. In the final moment, the result is the identification and aggregation of important objects with the aid of source images. Figure 2.5 shows an illustration of decision-based image fusion.

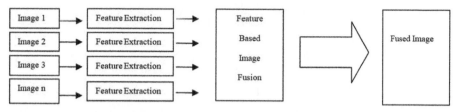

FIGURE 2.4   Representation diagram: feature-based image fusion.

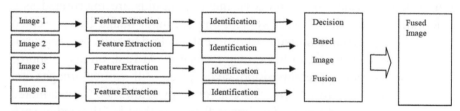

FIGURE 2.5   Representation diagram: decision-based image fusion.

2.4   CONTEMPORARY FUSION METHODS

2.4.1   *INTENSITY HUE SATURATION (IHS) TRANSFORM MODEL*

In the area of image fusion, intensity hue saturation (IHS) is a typical technique. The whole IHS model operates on the basis that the individual intercept visual e plan of all these three segments as asymmetrical perceptual central core, the major obstacle of this system is that only three classes were used, the IHS fusion model is generally on the actual nature space of the RGB wherein the input images are converted to the IHS color space from RGB color space. The hue (H) as well as immersion (S) bands are improved in the merge, and the opposite transformation is imposed to recreate the resulting RGB image.

2.4.2   *BROVEY TRANSFORM MODEL*

The fundamental process of the Brovey transform initially multiplies every multispectral image (MS) band with the high-resolution pan band, further divides every product by the sum of the MS bands.

$$R_{new} \frac{R}{(R+G+B)} \times PAN \tag{2.1}$$

$$G_{new} = \frac{G}{(R+G+B)} \times PAN \tag{2.2}$$

$$B_{new} = \frac{B}{(R+G+B)} \times PAN \tag{2.3}$$

2.4.3   PYRAMID METHODS

Within the binocular fusion process, image pyramids are interpreted as a blueprint for the human visual system, and the input image is represented by framing the pyramid structure at different levels. The selective approach to the pattern contributes to fused image creation. At first, on every source image, the pyramid decomposition takes place. All source images are combined to get the fused image, the inverted pyramid method is adopted to achieve the desired image. The image fusion method is followed at each stage of decomposition and it is possible to acquire a blended image out of this.

2.4.4   PRINCIPAL COMPONENT ANALYSIS

PCA may be considered a mathematical tool by which numerous correlated variables are converted to uncorrelated variables. It produces a new set of orthogonal axes. PC at first is carried toward the maximum variance direction. PC at second place is restricted to be present in the subspace which is perpendicular to the first PC and so on. In MS, spatial components are replaced by panchromatic image ultimately the algorithm incorporates panchromatic image (pan) spatial details in the MS. The steps are given below.

PCA transforms multispectral resample bands to the same resolution, as of panchromatic image.

To compensate for spectral differences between two of the images (that may occur as a result of different image acquisition angles and dates or due to different sensors), the first PC and panchromatic image histogram are matched.

The final fused multispectral is produced by calculating inverse transformation of PCA.

2.4.5   DISCRETE WAVELET TRANSFORM

In DWT, here two input images are taken, wavelet transform is applied, further coefficients are generated, and inverse of DWT is applied to produce a final fused image. Refer Figure 2.6 to have an understanding of DWT steps. In DWT, mainly two parts are generated, the approximation part and the detailed part. Example: [cA, cH, cV, cD] = dwt2(X, wname), it computes the single-level 2-D DWT of the input data X using the wname wavelet, dwt2 returns the approximation coefficients matrix cA, and detail coefficients matrices cH, cV, and cD (horizontal, vertical, and diagonal, respectively), as shown in Figure 2.7.

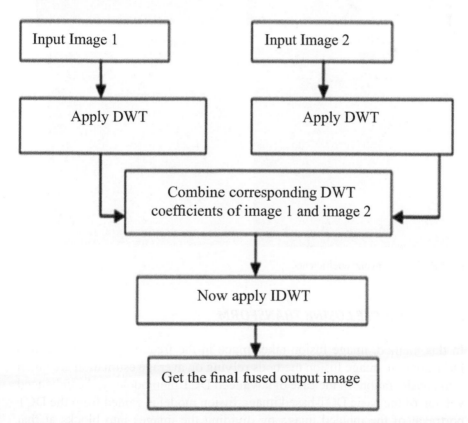

FIGURE 2.6   A sample diagram for DWT-based image fusion.
Source: Adapted from Ref. [6].

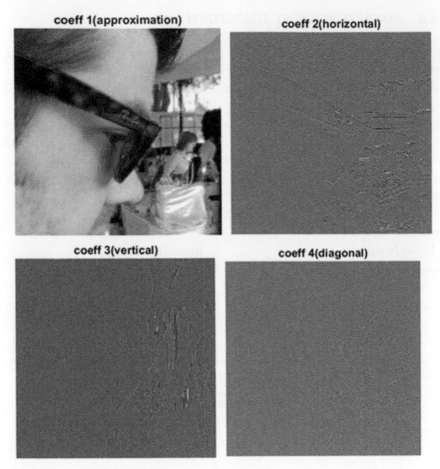

FIGURE 2.7   Wavelet coefficients.

2.4.6   *DISCRETE COSINE TRANSFORM*

In this method, image fusion takes place in the frequency domain. In this DCT domain, image fusion methods relying on average estimation are taken into consideration. In the case of advanced DCT methodology, the enhanced version of the basic DCT-based image fusion model is gained from the DCT portrayal of the melded image by dividing the images into blocks at that point and computes portrayal of the DCT via calculating average of all the DCT portrayals for respective blocks. At last, by incorporating the reverse discrete cosine transform the fused image is obtained. This image fusion strategy is termed as modified or "enhanced" DCT technique.

2.4.7 CURVELET TRANSFORM

Curvelet transform is an extension of wavelet transform. Image fusion process by curvelet transform for fusing image involves the following stcps:

- Register input images.
- Analyze each of the input images and generate the curvelet coefficients.
- Use the maximum frequency rule to fuse the curvelet coefficients.
- Apply inverse curvelet transform to obtain the final fused image.

2.4.8 GENETIC ALGORITHM BASED METHODS

Genetic algorithm (GA) is used to address problems such as classification as was optimization, although no investigation has indeed been motivated by classification-dependent image fusion through GA, taking into account the way that the selection problems are not overly confusing in image fusion evolved from classification and therefore can be effectively resolved with the aid of important different classifiers. For image fusion calculations, which involve some kind of parameter upgrades, GAs will support anyway, or in some other way, GA may be used to overhaul the process and efficiency of image fusion by assessing the best algorithmic parameter measurement.

2.4.9 NONSUBSAMPLE CONTOURLET TRANSFORM

In this technique, each image is broken into low-frequency components as well as high-frequency components. As per the frequency components, two input images are melded with each other via directive contrast in the case of high frequency, moreover, stage congruence in the case of low frequencies for the purpose of the fusion process. The final fused image is yielded after implying inverse nonsubsampled contourlet transform.

2.5 PERFORMANCE METRICS

Fusion metrics work as performance indicators for the image fusion algorithms. Some of the metrics are discussed below.

2.5.1   MI

MI stands for mutual information and it is a quantity of mutual dependence of two images in between two images and it is given by:

$$MI = \frac{1}{2}\Big[MI\big[A(g,h),T(g,h)\big] + MI\big[B(g,h)T(g,h)\big]\Big] \qquad (2.4)$$

where *A(g, h)* and *B(g, h)* depict two source images and *T(g, h)* shows the produced fused image.

2.5.2   PSNR

The ratio of maximum signal power with the noise that affects the fidelity is calculated using PSNR and given below:

$$PSNR = \frac{1}{2}[PSNR[A(g,h),T(g,h)] + PSNR[B(g,h),T(g,h]] \qquad (2.5)$$

where *A(g, h)* and *B(g, h)* denote two input images while *T(g, h)* shows the final fused image.

2.5.3   RMSE

Root mean square error is a measurement for calculating the error of a fusion method to estimate quantitative data. It is given by the following equation:

$$RMSE = \frac{1}{2}[RMSE\,[A(g,h),T(g,h)] + RMSE\,[B(g,h),T(g,h)]] \qquad (2.6)$$

where *A(g, h)* and *B(g, h)* demonstrate two source images, whereas *T(g, h)* depicts the final fused image.

2.5.4   CORRELATION COEFFICIENT

The correlation extent between two images is demonstrated by the performance metrics correlation coefficient (CC). The CC for two images is given by the following equation:

$$C(g,h) = \frac{\sum_{i,j}\left[\left(g_{i,j} - m_g\right) \times \left(h_{i,j} - m_h\right)\right]}{\sqrt{\sum_{i,j}\left[\left(g_{i,j} - m_g\right)^2\right] \times \sum_{i,j}\left[\left(h_{i,j} - m_h\right)^2\right]}} \qquad (2.7)$$

Where $g_{i,j}$ and $h_{i,j}$ illustrates the gray value in the position (i, j) of two images. m_g and m_h denote the mean of two images, consecutively. The CC should be high for a good image fusion method.

2.5.5   DEVIATION INDEX

Computation of deviation index is done by the following equation:

$$\frac{1}{PQ}\sum_{i=1}^{P}\sum_{j=1}^{Q}\frac{\left|I(i,j) - \dot{I}(i,j)\right|}{I(i,j)} \qquad (2.8)$$

where I illustrates the intensity *value for* the source image and $\dot{I}$ represents the intensity *value for* the final fused *output* image in the position *(i, j)*, respectively. The deviation index should be the least for an effective image fusion algorithm.

2.5.6   UQI

To calculate first- and second-order statistic of two images UQI is taken and is given by the following equation:

$$U = \frac{4\mu_G\mu_D\mu_{G,D}}{\left(\mu_G^2 + \mu_D^2\right)\left(\sigma_G^2 + \sigma_D^2\right)} \qquad (2.9)$$

Where, μ_G and μ_D indicate the mean value of two images, and $\sigma_G\sigma_D$ are the variance of two images. UQI value closer to +1 denotes an effective algorithm.

2.5.7   SSIM

SSIM is utilized to compute the comparison between two images. The SSIM value is maximal of the effective method.

$$SSIM(K,H) = \frac{\left(2\eta_K\eta_H + \varphi_1\right)\left(2\xi_{KH} + \varphi_2\right)}{\left(\eta_K{}^2 + \eta_H{}^2 + \varphi_1\right)\left(\xi_K{}^2 + \xi_H{}^2 + \varphi_2\right)} \qquad (2.10)$$

where the terms K and H denote the pixels. The terms η_K and η_H depict the mean pixel value, and the variance of pixels is denoted as ξ_K and ξ_H. The term ξ_{KH} denotes the covariance of pixels, and the terms φ_1 and φ_2 are the variables used for stabilization purposes.

2.6   APPLICATIONS OF IMAGE FUSION METHODS

Various applications of image fusion techniques are listed below:

A. Remote and satellite area: To properly view remote or satellite region image fusion technique is a boon.

B. Image fusion technique is used for enhancement of spatial resolution for an image by fusing images.

C. Classification: In remote sensing applications, the main task is classification. In the presence of more than two images, the efficient classification is enhanced for remote sensing images.

D. Medical field: In medical imaging, image fusion plays a vital role in the case of analysis for disease via image vision, spatial resolution, as well as through frequency point of view.

E. Artificial neural network: In the case of 3D focal length changes as per the wavelength use of image fusion plays a vital role.

F. Robotics: In the field of robotics research, the concept of image fusion is utilized for the location as well as object detection in parallel with guidance for navigating the robot.

G. In machine vision, the image fusion technique is utilized effectively for the visualization of two states. At that point of time, the conclusion for the image is perfect from the perspective of human vision.

H. Facial recognition: To identify and verify a person effectively via fusion technique is accompanied efficiently via fusing the descriptions out of different images.

I. Object identification: For maximization of information, derived out of the images produced by satellite, the concept of image fusion has a prominent role in optimizing the process.

J. Object detection: To boost up the situational awareness, the concept of image fusion technique is utilized in the detection of typical object classes as compared to other object classes in varying environmental situations.

K. Optimization and pattern recognition: GA is used in image fusion to optimize and identify pattern problems, such as optimization of functions, identification of systems, facial recognition, identification of systems, and control.

L. For monitoring of natural resources and also tracking of the natural resources by analysis after a particular time gap. Other areas include urban development. So a change is detected with the help of the aforementioned technique.

M. Surveillance of the oceans: inspection, tracking, and identification of ships and submarines.

N. Strategic vigilance and defense: It is possible to identify signs of approaching critical activities.

O. Awareness of the battlefield, reconnaissance, and mission acquisition: future ground objectives are identified and detected.

P. Medical diagnosis: To identify the location and detection of tumors, diseases, and abnormalities, image fusion is used.

Q. Data transmission in network: To reduce the network traffic utilization of fused images in spite of multiple images of the same scene demonstrates the better utilization of image fusion technique. Subsequently, it reduces the time of transmission and amount of network traffic, ultimately less use of memory.

2.7 CONCLUSION, LIMITATIONS, AND FUTURE SCOPE

Finally, it can be concluded while designing a fusion-based model; a researcher has to keep in mind about the generic prerequisites. Image fusion scheme along with various image processing techniques will enhance the face recognition, feature extraction, object detection, as well tracking, moving object identification, and so many advanced leading application areas contributing toward smart cities, ubiquitous computing, IoT, cloud computing, as well as Big data handling hassle-free. Techniques elaboration involves IHS model, PC analysis, DWT, discrete cosine transform, curvelet transform, nonsubsampled contourlet transform, deep belief network, deep CNN, threshold based on Fisher's linear discriminant ratio, etc. Seven quality parameters for assessing the quality of the fused resultant image, that is, MI, PSNR, RMSE, CC, DI, UQI, and SSIM are summarized here. Image fusion scheme plays a vital role in object identification, tracking, and movement in many application fields, such as military, defense, sea, remote sensing, geographical estimation, earthquake-prone areas to measure the amount of damage done, to estimate the damage done in field crops via satellite images while in the medical field for tumor detection, multimodal image fusion is very helpful. In the future, studies for data fusion as well as image fusion involving hybrid approaches may be done. Only seven image fusion quality metrics have been reviewed in this paper due to space constraints, in future a wider variety of quality metrics may be introduced.

KEYWORDS

- **image fusion prerequisites**
- **essentials of image fusion**
- **fusion metrics**

REFERENCES

1. Alam, F.; Mehmood, R.; Katib, I.; Albogami, N. N.; Albeshri, A. *Data Fusion and IoT for Smart Ubiquitous Environments: A Survey. IEEE Access* **2017**, *5*, 9533–9554. doi:10.1109/access.2017.2697839.
2. Farid, M. S.; Mahmood, A.; Al-Maadeed, S. A. Multi-Focus Image Fusion Using Content Adaptive Blurring. *Inform. Fusion* **2019**, *45*, 96–112.
3. Guruprasad, S.; Kurian, M. Z.; Suma, H. N. A Medical Multi-Modality Image Fusion Of CT/PET With PCA, DWT Methods. *J. Dental Mater. Tech.* **2013**, *4* (2).
4. Han, F.; Yao, J.; Zhu, H.; Wang, C. Underwater Image Processing and Object Detection Based on Deep CNN Method. *J. Sens* **2020**, *2020*.
5. Jing, Z.; Pan, H.; Li, Y.; Dong, P. Evaluation of Focus Measures in Multi-Focus Image Fusion. In *Non-Cooperative Target Tracking, Fusion and Control*; Springer: Cham, 2018; pp 269–281.
6. Jinju, J.; Santhi, N.; Ramar, K.; Bama, B. S. Spatial Frequency Discrete Wavelet Transform Image Fusion Technique for Remote Sensing Applications. *Eng. Sci. Technol. Int. J.* **2019**, *22*(3), 715–726.
7. Jung, S.; Cho, Y.; Kim, D.; Chang, M. Moving Object Detection from Moving Camera Image Sequences Using an Inertial Measurement Unit Sensor. *Appl. Sci.* **2020**, *10* (1), 268.
8. Kaur, M.; Singh, D. Fusion of Medical Images Using Deep Belief Networks. *Cluster Comput* **2020**, *23*, 1439–1453.
9. Li, H.; Chai, Y.; Li, Z. Multi-Focus Image Fusion Based on Nonsubsampled Contourlet Transform and Focused Regions Detection. *Optik* **2013**, *124* (1), 40–51.

10. Li, S.; Kang, X.; Hu, J. Image Fusion with Guided Filtering. *IEEE Trans. Image Process.* **2013,** *22* (7), 2864–2875.

11. Li, S.; Kang, X.; Hu, J.; Yang, B. Image Matting for Fusion of Multi-Focus Images in Dynamic Scenes. *Inform. Fusion* **2013,** *14* (2), 147–162.

12. Li, X.; Wang, L.; Wang, J.; Zhang, X. Multi-Focus Image Fusion Algorithm Based on Multilevel Morphological Component Analysis and Support Vector Machine. *IET Image Process.* **2017,** *11*(10), 919–926.

13. Liu, S.; Wang, J.; Lu, Y.; Li, H.; Zhao, J.; Zhu, Z. Multi-Focus Image Fusion Based on Adaptive Dual-Channel Spiking Cortical Model in Non-Subsampled Shearlet Domain. *IEEE Access* **2019,** *7*, 56367–56388.

14. Lochab, K.; Yadav, D. K.; Singh, M.; Sharmab, A. Internet of Things in Cloud Environment: Services and Challenges. *Int. J. Database Theory Appl.* **2017,** *10*, 23–32.

15. Metwalli, M. R.; Nasr, A. H.; Allah, O. S. F.; El-Rabaie, S.; Abd El-Samie, F. E. Satellite Image Fusion Based on Principal Component Analysis and High-Pass Filtering. *JOSA A* **2010,** *27* (6), 1385–1394.

16. Rai, M.; Yadav, R. K.; Husain, A. A.; Maity, T.; Yadav, D. K. Extraction of Facial Features for Detection of Human Emotions under Noisy Condition. *Int. J. Eng. Manuf.* **2018,** *8* (5), 49.

17. Sharma, L.; Yadav, D. K. Histogram-Based Adaptive Learning for Background Modelling: Moving Object Detection in Video Surveillance. *Int. J. Telemed. Clin. Pract.* **2017,** *2* (1), 74–92.

18. Sharma, L.; Yadav, D. K.; Singh, A. Fisher's Linear Discriminant Ratio Based Threshold for Moving Human Detection in Thermal Video. *Infrared Phys. Technol.* **2016,** *78*, 118–128.

19. Tian, J.; Chen, L.; Ma, L.; Yu, W. Multi-Focus Image Fusion Using a Bilateral Gradient-Based Sharpness Criterion. *Optics Commun.* **2011,** *284* (1), 80–87.

20. Venkatrao, P. H.; Damodar, S. S. HW Fusion: Holoentropy and SP-Whale Optimisation-Based Fusion Model for Magnetic Resonance Imaging Multimodal Image Fusion. *IET Image Process.* **2017,** *12* (4), 572–581.

21. Wang, K.; Qi, G.; Zhu, Z.; Chai, Y. A Novel Geometric Dictionary Construction Approach for Sparse Representation Based Image Fusion. *Entropy* **2017,** *19* (7), 306.

22. Wang, Z.; Ma, Y.; Gu, J. Multi-Focus Image Fusion Using PCNN. *Pattern Recognition* **2010,** *43* (6), 2003–2016.

23. Yadav, D. K.; Singh, K. A Combined Approach of Kullback–Leibler Divergence and Background Subtraction for Moving Object Detection in Thermal Video. *Infrared Phys. Technol.* **2016,** *76*, 21–31.

24. Yang, Y.; Ding, M.; Huang, S.; Que, Y.; Wan, W.; Yang, M.; Sun, J. Multi-Focus Image Fusion via Clustering PCA Based Joint Dictionary Learning. *IEEE Access* **2017,** *5*, 16985–16997.

25. Zafar, R.; Farid, M. S.; Khan, M. H. Multi-Focus Image Fusion: Algorithms, Evaluation, and a Library. *J. Imag.* **2020,** *6* (7), 60.

26. Zhang, Y.; Liu, Y.; Sun, P.; Yan, H.; Zhao, X.; Zhang, L. IFCNN: A General Image Fusion Framework Based on Convolutional Neural Network. *Inform. Fusion* **2020,** *54*, 99–118.

27. Zhao, W.; Wang, D.; Lu, H. Multi-Focus Image Fusion with a Natural Enhancement via a Joint Multi-Level Deeply Supervised Convolutional Neural Network. *IEEE Trans. Circ. Syst. Video Technol.* **2018,** *29* (4), 1102–1115.

CHAPTER 3

A Study of Emerging Issues and Possibilities for Breast Cancer Diagnosis Using Image Modalities

ANKUR KUMAR AGGARWAL and MRINAL PANDEY

Manav Rachna University, Faridabad, Haryana, India

ABSTRACT

Breast cancer becomes the world's alarming health problem, which is the most prevalent malignancy among females. In the medical domain, the analyses of digital images are somewhat amenable in various field of applications. The quality of images and dense breasts may result in misinterpretation by radiologists and lead to reduce the accuracy of diagnosis. In developing an up-to-date prognosis process that can effectively reduce disease complications with higher recovery, early intervention is critical. The radiologist will analyze and perform the diagnosis of numerous tumors in terms of the digital images created by such techniques, and using the computer-aided diagnostic algorithm with the high level of performance. Early diagnosis is the safest approach to strengthen breast cancer prognosis. The research study conducted in this paper mainly reflects the current challenges and future directions to the researchers to intervene and erect a system as early as possible to diagnose breast cancer.

Computational Intelligence in Analytics and Information Systems, Volume 1: Data Science and AI, Selected Papers from CIAIS-2021. Hardeo Kumar Thakur, Manpreet Kaur, Parneeta Dhaliwal, Rajeev Kumar Arya, and Joan Lu (Eds.)

3.1   INTRODUCTION

Cancer is a category of the disease that initially induces the cells of the body to differ and encourages them to expand uncontrollably.[1] Breast cancer was identified among women worldwide as a solemn threat in women, it rates as the principal malignant disease after lung cancer. Breast cancer screening is an asymptomatic procedure, apparently an effort to classify healthier people for breast cancer diagnosis early (if a woman is a carrier of deficient genes but has no noticeable symptoms).[2] Screening and early detection are crucial to optimizing any modality's efficiency. Large numbers of cases can be identified at an early stage to reduce the mortality rate. We will also review the prevailing along with new tumor detection modalities utilized to perform screening and diagnosis to determine possible areas for research growth.

With an aid of performance, the radiologist may analyze and even diagnose the tumor in terms of an image rendered by such approaches, before biopsy and surgery. Mammography is the earliest step of the most common cancer screening strategy. It fits seamlessly in postmenopausal patients, but not for patients who are in premenopausal condition, and often X-ray exposures can also be the cause of cancer.[3] Both the true-positive rate and the spatial image of the patient's breasts MRI are strong, and more precise images can be given. But MRI still has disadvantages: poor precision, interpretative difficulty, costly, and unstandardized. High intensity, appropriate precision, duration, simple to enforce, occurrence rate, and economical are the essential standards for a successful breast cancer screening technique.

This research is structured as follows: Section 3.2 addresses different modalities of imaging for breast cancer and their diagnostic potential. The evolving trends for the diagnosis of cancer are covered in Section 3.3. In Section 3.4, the present state of breast cancer imaging is addressed. Finally, in Section 3.5, the findings of this work are outlined.

3.2   IMAGING MODALITIES FOR BREAST CANCER DIAGNOSIS

In 1993, the reporting and data system for breast imaging (BI-RADS) served as the standard by various radiologists and researchers to categorize the outcome of assessment between the radiologist and patient.[4] The initial phase of the assessment showed no significant abnormality and required to apply other imaging modality to confirm the same. And later the phases go from negative to benign and to more probably benign which would require the patient to undergo biopsy. In the phase of malignancy, the stage could be from suspicious to highly malignant which requires further investigation and biopsy has proven malignancy to the patient. In this section, we will discuss various image modalities that can be used at an early stage of abnormality. Comparative study of numerous breast malignancy detection modalities is discussed in Table 3.1.

3.2.1 CLINICAL/SELF BREAST EXAMINATION (CBE/SBE)

Note that breast examinations, that is, CBE and BSE, are mainly prescribed but often dangerous approaches for cancer screening. CBE offers 97.11% high specificity, though sensitivity is marginally smaller, that is, 57.14%.[5] It is mainly effective for the identification of suspected breast lesions since it cannot yet assess malignancy. Additional studies indicate that young people particularly those who do not go for routine medical examinations are still using CBE and BSE. With self-examination, there are various issues that need to be addressed by a physician; in most cases, this practice is not recommended as lacking sufficient knowledge of examination, lower mortality rates, and high health risks could occur as patients cannot identify any lump by performing BSE or CBE; and this could lead to increased chances of infection in healthy tissues. Various challenges of performing self-examination are that the sensitivity of CBE and BSE is very low, may not even determine malignancy in women, and are harmful if a cancer diagnosis is delayed and further biopsy procedure is required.

3.2.2 MAMMOGRAPHY

It is a low radiation X-ray test for evaluating and identifying breast disorders. The X-ray devices used currently for mammography that actually are exposed to less radiation than those previously used. It is indeed fairly rapid and broadly accessible, so considered as the first-hand cancer detection technique. It often applies perfectly well with postmenopausal females, but not well for young women under the age of 40, and prolonged X-ray exposures could be a trigger for growth of cancer in women. Its shortcomings are related to the small dynamic range, low contrast, and grainy frame. It is difficult to visualize very small lesions in patients with implants or severe surgical marks.[6] In digital mammography, instead of video, the image is documented in an electronic format. Digital mammographic images may indeed be conveyed through tele-mammography, enabling the radiologist to

TABLE 3.1　Breast Malignancy Detection Modalities Comparative Analysis.

Imaging modality	Sensitivity	Specificity	Benefit	Drawback
Mammography	Low (<40) High (>40)	High	Efficient model with high true (positive/ negative) rate, portable, high-digital image to analyze dense breast	High rate of false-positive, low contrast images, discomfort, and radiation to patient
MRI	High	Low	No radiation, little discomfort, high resolution, and relevant contrast image, detection of intraductal extent, and good sensitivity	Costly, heavy device, and not portable, low specificity, only lateral scanning is possible
Ultrasound	Low	Moderate	Portable device, as almost no gap between device and skin surface applicable to patients with dense/fatty breast	Very low contrast in output image, and high rate of false positives
Nuclear medicine	High	Moderate	High true positive rate, good contrast, image registration, and fusion is accurate	Expensive, heavy, and nonportable device, exposure to radiation due to use of ionized/ radioisotope and low-quality images
Electrical impedance	Low	Moderate	Noninvasive, no radioactive element, and low cost of device	Device is in contact with patient, poor resolution, electrical fluctuation due to surrounding, discomfort to patient
Thermography	High	Low	Non (invasive and contact) modality, no radioactive/radiation exposure, can be applied at early stage of screening	Low true negative rate, impact of surrounding temperature, high false (positive/negative) rate
Optical imaging	—	—	Noninvasive, no radioactive element, and low cost of device, images with good contrast	Contrast decreases with high scattering, low spatial resolution of image, potential to combine with other modalities

analyze the pictures even from distant locations. The effectiveness of visual mammography among patients with dense breast tissue, and even among young adults, is comparatively higher than that of film mammography.[7] The drawbacks are its poor spatial resolution and highly trained radiologist to analyze the mammography.[8] The breast tissues are squeezed at a weight of up to 42 pounds during the screening process. This explodes a cancerous tumor cell's mutability and releases malignant cells into the bloodstream.

3.2.3 MAGNETIC RESONANCE IMAGING

The American Cancer Society recommends screening of patient breasts using MRI alongside with an annual mammography who are at high risk.[10] New research has demonstrated that MRI is a better screening alternative because it does not entail exposure to radiation and so there are no substantial safety risks, and it also operates reasonably well for both pre- and postmenopausal patients. Breast MRI is perhaps the most active tool for the detection of breast anomalies. Probably the most active instrument for the identification of breast abnormalities is the breast MRI. It is possible to use breast MRI to extensively examine suspected lesions or to look at previously diagnosed cases. In order to change the position of hydrogen nucleus protons, breast MRI uses radio signals and a magnetic field and thus produces a very detailed cross-section image of this tissue modification. Known for its high spatial resolution, MRI screening delivers further detailed images. MRI has some drawbacks, too little precision that contributes to more screening or biopsy, being costly and not systematic, of all its extremely distinct benefits.[11] MRI time can be productive with a modern, versatile, and screen-printed MRI coil.[12] Applying a coil to a syringe that takes a blood sample at a lower cost and also decreases the high magnetic field effect. There are numerous difficulties, the MRI specificity is low and it takes time to produce visuals even in a situation where there is metallic implantation in a patient this technique could not be used.

3.2.4 BREAST ULTRASOUND

It is sometimes referred to as sonography which feeds the sound waves to the patient body to examine the internal organ defects. In general, it acts as a follow-up test following a mammogram for abnormality and offers guidance for a needle biopsy of the lump. On the upper surface of the breast, a portable device called a transducer is located, where the gel will be spread and transferred over the breast, exposing the upper surface to the structure of the underlying tissues. The low soundwaves are then released, and the produced echoes are nabbed by a transducer that reflects the underlying breast tissues. The echoes are then transformed into a picture that requires to be labeled with respect to the direction and position of the breast lesion.[13] It traces the movement of blood and even recites the physical behavior of the tissue. It is commonly used over the years as a consequence of the sturdy rise in image feature.[14] Both ultrasound and mammography are covered by a singular module, which can boost screening and also enhance detection.[15] The three factors mainly affect the overall accuracy of the ultrasound; performance rate of the transducer used, competence by pathologist to analyze image, and use of a multidisciplinary approach. Ultrasound requires little exposure to radiation and is, therefore, a painless process. And, it is also less sensitive to the detection of micro-calcification.[16]

3.2.5   NUCLEAR MEDICINE TECHNIQUE FOR BREAST CANCER

This creates realistic pictures that are focused on the molecular properties of tissues. The course of the inserted nuclear compounds was examined by special cameras. Nuclear medicine technologies are costly and their sensitivity to radiation is heavy. Nuclear medicine scans are tissue metabolism dependent because on tumor modifications induced by other imaging techniques in the body. By comparison to other imaging approaches, the neural role of the organ should be studied. It may be referred to as cancer therapy and cellular or molecular imaging.[17] A few of the popular techniques for nuclear medicine are discussed below.

- **Positron emission tomography (PET):** A section image is generated using a wave called tomograph. The reconstruction algorithms to create tomographs are filtered back projection that requires less computation resources and iterative reconstruction (IR) requires heavy computation and results in high accuracy of PET images.[18]
- **Single-photon emission computed tomography (SPECT):** This depicts a picture in 3D by way of a tomographic reconstruction. SPECT device captures the flow of induced radionuclides into the bloodstream as it is uniformly distributed in tissues. Various radioisotopes have been discussed in literature[19] that are used to generate SPECT images by inserting radio elements in the bloodstream.

- **Scintimammography:** The images are generated by capturing the radiation released by radionuclides to the external detectors, such as gamma cameras.[20] For the test, a small amount of radioactive tracer is injected into the vein. The tracer is then added to the breast cancer cells and a special detector will classify them. This technique could detect such irregular lesions that, as per some radiologists, mammography may not detect. But some earlier experiments indicate that, unlike MRI for cancer diagnosis, it is not even applied by radiologists to breast cancer diagnosis. Table 3.1 details the comparative analysis of breast malignancy detection modalities.

3.3 EMERGING MODALITIES

In recent decade, various other techniques were devised to perform diagnosis of cancer with the advancement of technology and availability. A few of such emerging techniques are discussed in this section.

3.3.1 ELECTRICAL IMPEDANCE SCANNING

It is performed to check the electrical conduct on the surface of breast, the conductivity of normal tissue is different as compared to cancer tissue. An image based on the current difference is generated by passing low current to the breast area and observed using electrodes over the complete breast surface. It is less risky, noninvasive, and also relatively inexpensive.[21,22] Due to a small amount of calculated data, its main concern is the lower visual resolution image.[23]

3.3.2 THERMOGRAPHY

With the assistance of a heat-sensing camera, the skin of the breast is first measured and plotted by this technology. The infrared test shows the fluctuation of the temperature around the breasts. While the temperature of the tumor cell region and internal blood vessels frequently varies greatly relative to the surrounding healthy tissue temperature.[24] The scanning duration is sluggish as a series of infrared images of one breast are carried out while another is cooled and conversely. Afterward, by processing the results, a computer model provides the evaluation of patterns in infrared images. Infrared (IR) thermography is noninvasive and has a fast time to generate the images. Infrared radiation, as per the constitution, has a fixed wavelength of 0.7–300 Â μm, that is, IR quickly detects large-sized tumors. One disadvantage is that both the procedural errors and the placement of the breast significantly impact the IR image for further analysis.[25] However, because the body temperature is asymmetrical, the findings of the experiment could lead to false (positive/ negative) situations. Additional infrared imaging drawbacks are the location of the tumor and the differences associated with age, or even analyzing the large scale of the IR images. Even due to the presence of various limitations, the analysis results of cancer detection using IR are promising for patients with dense breasts and tumor size-position.[26]

3.3.3   OPTICAL IMAGING

Optical imaging seems to be a very viable technique for imaging that uses near-infrared light to test tissue optical properties and is intended to play an important role in the diagnosis of breast cancer.[27] It functions in the concept of reflection but is limited to the process of tissues with the superficial surface.[28] The procedure does not involve squeezing of the breast. To help diagnose cancer, research is also underway to get this method paired with MRI or three-dimensional mammography. As for data, diffuse optical spectroscopy, diffuse optical tomography, and diffuse optical imaging may be investigated. A crucial prerequisite for the use of optical imaging is precise measurement of breast size and optical properties.[29]

3.3.4   FUSION METHODOLOGY FOR BREAST CANCER DIAGNOSIS

There are several variations of various imaging modalities required to create mixed medical imaging techniques which can improve the performance of fused models. Various literature discuss the use of combined imaging modalities like MRI and sonography fusion[30] which showed the improvement of model sensitivity of 98% after performing fusion, 3D ultrasound with digital tomosynthesis fusion,[31] tomography and ultrasonography fusion,[32] MRI navigated with ultrasound[33] showed the sensitivity of 96.3%, digital mammography and ultrasound,[34] US and CAD and mammograms and infrared fusion.[35] It is also worth noting that leading to the maturity, availability, and cost-effectiveness of the technology, clinical image fusion has shown to be helpful in enhancing the clinical efficacy of diagnostic imaging for diagnostic purposes and research.[36,37] The study of various fusion or multimodalities for breast cancer screening and diagnosis are studied in Table 3.2.

3.4   VARIOUS OPPORTUNITIES IN BREAST CANCER DIAGNOSIS

Like for certain medical applications, some forms of diagnostic modalities might be inadequate or inept to include the required source of knowledge, which in effect limits the reliability of the appropriate processes. This challenge can be addressed through other forms of medical imaging that can provide reasonable and sufficient information. The use of fused methodology can give better result for performing breast cancer diagnosis. Combining databases from various regions could give better sensitivity. The concerns regarding such alternate modalities are as follows: economic initiatives, in addition to the susceptibility to patients to radiation that is detrimental to public health.[38]

3.5   CONCLUSION

Breast cancer is a worldwide challenge and the major cause of mortality for women. Death rate can be improved by a simple early stage diagnosis phase. Self-examination-related methods, that is, BSE and CBE, and traditional methods for breast cancer early detection have been outlined. Several emerging techniques have already been discussed in order to improve regularities. The primary method used to diagnose cancer at an early stage is mammography. While mammography is an important screening method used for the past several years, the findings are not accurate for female patients with fatty or dense breasts and even with the patients who have surgical history. Recently, it has been demonstrated that MRI is a safer choice than mammography where radiation exposure is less. The MRI's key limitations are that specificity is too poor and analysis is subjective and not systematic, which means screening only for women at high risk. Often used for breast cancer screening is other diagnostic methods such as Ductogram, nuclear medicine dosage, PET scan, molecular breast diagnostic, EII, IR-thermography, optical imaging research, microscopic imaging, and PEM. The role of imaging techniques will continue to evolve with the advancement in hardware and algorithms that have the main goal of decreasing the mortality rate as the strategies for diagnosis of breast cancer are more developed. High level of sensitivity (true positive rate)

TABLE 3.2 Study of Fused Modalities for Breast Cancer Detection.

Fused modalities	Individual sensitivity	Fused sensitivity	Limitation
MRI and sonography[30]	MRI—85% Sonography—91%	RVS system—98%	Synchronization of data due to body movement
3D ultrasound with digital tomosynthesis[31]	Not available	Fusion-X-US system—29 lesions identified	Limited region capture by ultrasound with low spatial images
Tomography and ultrasonography[32]	Not available	100% with AUS dual positive	Radiation exposure with PET/CT and high-cost device
MRI with ultrasound[33]	MRI—94% Ultrasound—87%	96.3%	Challenging to accurate coregistration of MRI and ultrasound data
Digital mammography followed with ultrasound[34]	Digital Mammography—76% Ultrasound—87%	Sensitivity—97.37% Specificity—99%	Total time for data capture is more due to follow-up of ultrasound with mammography
Multimodality fusion[35]	Not available	98%	

and specificity (true negative rate) may be reached to a significant degree with the usage of fused techniques and emerging modalities such as thermography to identify lesions at earlier stages.

KEYWORDS

- **breast cancer diagnosis**
- **thermography**
- **infrared imaging**
- **MRI**
- **thermal imaging**
- **mammography**
- **early detection**

REFERENCES

1. Bandyopadhyay, K.; Maitra, I. K.; Banerjee, S. Digital Imaging in Pathology Towards Detection and Analysis of Human Breast Cancer. In *2010 2nd International Conference on Computational Intelligence, Communication Systems and Networks*, Liverpool, 2010; pp 295–300
2. https://en.wikipedia.org/wiki/Breast_cancer_screening (accessed 10 Jan, 2021).
3. Nover, A. B.; Jagtap, S.; Anjum, W.; Yegingil, H.; Shih, W. Y.; Shih, W. -H.; Brooks, A. D. Modern Breast Cancer Detection: A Technological Review. *Int. J. Biomed. Imag.* **2009,** *2009*, 14. Article ID: 902326.
4. Obenauer, S.; Hermann, K. P.; Grabbe, E. Applications and Literature Review of the BI-RADS Classification. *Eur. Radiol.* **2005,** *15*, 1027–1036.
5. Ratanachaikanont, T. Clinical Breast Examination and Its Relevance to Diagnosis of Palpable Breast Lesion. *J. Med. Assoc. Thai.* **2005,** *88* (4), 505–507. PMID: 16146255.
6. Yang, N.; Muradali, D. The Augmented Breast: A Pictorial Review of the Abnormal and Unusual. *Am. J. Roentgenol.* **2011,** *196*, W451–W460.
7. Köşüş, N.; Köşüş, A.; Duran, M.; Simavlı, S.; Turhan, N. Comparison of Standard Mammography with Digital Mammography and Digital Infrared Thermal Imaging for Breast Cancer Screening. *J. Turk. Ger. Gynecol. Assoc.* **2010,** *11* (3), 152–157. Published 2010 Sep 1.
8. Planche, K.; Vinnicombe, S. Breast Imaging in the New Era. *Cancer Imag.* **2004,** *4* (2), 39–50. DOI: 10.1102/1470-7330.2003.0033. PMID: 18250006; PMCID: PMC1434581.
9. Heywang-Köbrunner, S. H.; et al. Advantages and Disadvantages of Mammography Screening. *Breast Care (Basel)* **2011,** *6* (3), 199–207.

10. El-Gamal, F. E. Z. A.; Elmogy, M.; Atwan, A. Current Trends in Medical Image Registration and Fusion. *Egypt. Inf. J.* **2016,** *17* (1), 99–124. ISSN: 1110-8665.

11. Sehgal, C. M.; Weinstein, S. P.; Arger, P. H.; Conant, E. F. A Review of Breast Ultrasound. *J. Mammary Gland. Biol. Neoplasia.* **2006,** *11* (2), 113–123.

12. Corea, J.; Flynn, A.; Lechêne, B.; et al. Screen-Printed Flexible MRI Receive Coils. *Nat. Commun.* **2016,** *7,* 10839.

13. Kapur, A.; et al. Combination of Digital Mammography with Semi-Automated 3D Breast Ultrasound. *Technol. Cancer Res. Treat.* **2004,** *3* (4), 325–334.

14. Saini, P. K.; Singh, M. Brain Tumor Detection in Medical Imaging Using Matlab. *Int. Res. J. Eng. Technol.* **2015,** *02* (02), 191–196.

15. Cunitz, B.; et al. Improved Detection of Kidney Stones Using an Optimized Doppler Imaging Sequence. *IEEE Int. Ultrason. Symp.* **2014,** *2014,* 452–455.

16. Kennedy, D. A.; Lee, T.; Seely, D. A Comparative Review of Thermography as a Breast Cancer Screening Technique. *Integr. Cancer Ther.* **2009,** *8* (1), 9–16.

17. James, A. P.; Dasarathy, B. V. Medical Image Fusion: A Survey of the State of the Art. *Inform. Fus.* **2014,** *19,* 4–19. ISSN: 1566-2535.

18. Herman, G. T. *Fundamentals of Computerized Tomography: Image Reconstruction from Projection*, 2nd edn; Springer: Berlin, 2009.

19. Elangovan, A.; Jeyaseelan, T. Medical Imaging Modalities: A Survey. In *2016 International Conference on Emerging Trends in Engineering, Technology and Science (ICETETS)*, Pudukkottai, 2016; pp 1–4.

20. Scintigraphy definition in the Medical dictionary by the Free Online Medical Dictionary. https://medical-dictionary.the freedictionary.com/scintigraphy (accessed 10 Jan, 2021).

21. Brown, B. H. Electrical Impedance Tomography (EIT): A Review. *J. Med. Eng. Technol.* **2003,** *27* (3), 97–108.

22. Stojadinovic, A.; Moskovitz, O.; Gallimidi, Z.; Fields, S.; Brooks, A. D.; Brem, R.; Mucciola, R. N.; Singh, M.; Maniscalco-Theberge, M.; Rockette, H. E.; Gur, D.; Shriver, C. D. Prospective Study of Electrical Impedance Scanning for Identifying Young Women at Risk for Breast Cancer. *Breast Cancer Res. Treat.* **2006,** *97* (2), 179–189.

23. Zhang, X.; Liu, J.; He, B. Magnetic-Resonance-Based Electrical Properties Tomography: A Review. *IEEE Rev. Biomed. Eng.* **2014,** *7,* 87–96.

24. Yahara, T.; Koga, T.; Yoshida, S.; Nakagawa, S.; Deguchi, H.; Shirouzu, K. Relationship Between Microvessel Density and Thermographic Hot Areas in Breast Cancer. *Surg. Today* **2003,** *33* (4), 243–248.

25. Parisky, Y. R.; Sardi, A.; Hamm, R.; Hughes, K.; Esserman, L.; Rust, S.; Callahan, K. Efficacy of Computerized Infrared Imaging Analysis to Evaluate Mammographically Suspicious Lesions. *Am. J. Roentgenol.* **2003,** *180* (1), 263–269.

26. Arora, N.; Martins, D.; Ruggerio, D.; Tousimis, E.; Swistel, A. J.; Osborne, M. P.; Simmons, R. M. Effectiveness of a Noninvasive Digital Infrared Thermal Imaging System in the Detection of Breast Cancer. *Am. J. Surg.* **2008,** *196* (4), 523–526.

27. Herranz, M.; Ruibal, A. Optical Imaging in Breast Cancer Diagnosis: The Next Evolution. J. Oncol. **2012,** *2012,* 10. Article ID: 863747.

28. Kamkaew, A.; et al. An Agent for Optical Imaging of TrkC-Expressing. Breast Cancer. *MedChemComm.* **2017,** *8* (10), 1946–1952.

29. Walsh, A. J.; et al. Quantitative Optical Imaging of Primary Tumor Organoid Metabolism Predicts Drug Response in Breast Cancer. *Cancer Res.* **2014,** *74* (18), 5184–5194.

30. Nakano, S.; Yoshida, M.; Fujii, K.; Yorozuya, K.; Mouri, Y.; Kousaka, J.; Fukutomi, T.; Kimura, J.; Ishiguchi, T.; Ohno, K.; Mizumoto, T.; Harao, M. Fusion of MRI and Sonography Image for Breast Cancer Evaluation Using Real-Time Virtual Sonography with Magnetic Navigation: First Experience. *Jpn. J. Clin. Oncol.* **2009**, *39* (9), 552–559.

31. Schaefgen, B.; Heil, J.; Barr, R. G.; et al. Initial Results of the FUSION-X-US Prototype Combining 3D Automated Breast Ultrasound and Digital Breast Tomosynthesis. *Eur. Radiol.* **2018**, *28*, 2499–2506.

32. Ueda, S.; Tsuda, H.; Asakawa, H.; et al. Utility of 18F-Fluoro-Deoxyglucose Emission Tomography/Computed Tomography Fusion Imaging (18F-FDG PET/CT) in Combination with Ultrasonography for Axillary Staging in Primary Breast Cancer. *BMC Cancer* **2008**, *8*, 165.

33. Park, A. Y.; Seo, B. K. Real-Time MRI Navigated Ultrasound for Preoperative Tumor Evaluation in Breast Cancer Patients: Technique and Clinical Implementation. *Korean J. Radiol.* **2016**, *17* (5), 695–705.

34. Giuliano, V.; Giuliano, C. Improved Breast Cancer Detection in Asymptomatic Women Using 3D-Automated Breast Ultrasound in Mammographically Dense Breasts. *Clin. Imag.* **2013**, *37* (3), 480–486. ISSN: 0899-7071.

35. Arena, F.; DiCicco, T.; Anand, A. Multimodality Data Fusion Aids Early Detection of Breast Cancer Using Conventional Technology and Advanced Digital Infrared Imaging. In *The 26th Annual International Conference of the IEEE Engineering in Medicine and Biology Society*, 2004

36. James, A. P.; Dasarathy, B. V. Medical Image Fusion: A Survey of the State of the Art. *Inform. Fus.* **2014**, *19*, 4–19. ISSN: 1566-2535.

37. Vaughan, C. L. Novel Imaging Approaches to Screen for Breast Cancer: Recent Advances and Future Prospects. *Med. Eng. Phys.* **2019**, *72*, 27–37. ISSN: 1350-4533.

38. El-Gamal, F. E. Z. A.; et al. Current Trends in Medical Image Registration and Fusion. *Egypt. Inf. J.* **2015**, *17*, 99–124.

CHAPTER 4

Pap Smear Image Segmentation Using Chan-Vese-Based Adaptive Primal Dual Splitting Algorithm

B. CHITRA and S. S. KUMAR

Department of Electronics and Communication Engineering, Noorul Islam Centre for Higher Education, Kanyakumari, Tamil Nadu, India

ABSTRACT

Cervical cancer is a deadly disease and it must be identified at an early stage for survival. The computer-aided screening process provides an early detection and analysis of cervical cancer is the precise cell segmentation. An automatic and accurate cervical pap smear image segmentation is considered an evergreen research problem. To address such shortcomings, this paper comprises three main phases, namely, the preprocessing phase, segmentation phase, as well as morphological operation. The input cervical cancer datasets are preprocessed in the initial phase. In phase 2, an appropriate segmentation is conducted by constructing a Chan Vese based adaptive primal-dual splitting algorithm to obtain an optimal segmented image set. In the third step, the morphological operation is carried out to obtain the segmentation results more accurately. The method used in this paper is computed by employing the dataset called the Herlev Pap smear dataset. The performance analysis and the comparative analysis are conducted and the results reveal that the proposed approach provides a high accuracy rate and efficiency when compared with other methods.

Computational Intelligence in Analytics and Information Systems, Volume 1: Data Science and AI, Selected Papers from CIAIS-2021. Hardeo Kumar Thakur, Manpreet Kaur, Parneeta Dhaliwal, Rajeev Kumar Arya, and Joan Lu (Eds.)

4.1   INTRODUCTION

Cervical cancer is considered as the deadliest disease all over the world. Every year, about 266,000 people pass away due to this deadly disease. But the early diagnosis of these types of cervical cancer cells was not perceptible. Uterine cervical cancer (UGC) is more common in women and every year about 250,000 women die from cervical cancer. The medical process of UGC depends upon the prognostic factor-like nodal status and tumor volume. The pathologist normally monitors the cervical cytology smears via the microscope. It detects the abnormal cell where the cervical cell morphologies and its nucleus needs Papanicolaou (PAP) test. Here, the PAP test identifies early cervical carcinogenesis via manual screening.[1] Magnetic resonance imaging (MRI) is the most prescribed modality for assessing the soft tissue details more clearly than tumor identification. Particularly, MRI assists in the evaluation of tumor extension in the uterus, parametrium, rectal wall, vagina, and urinary bladder wall. The process of diagnosis and treatment is speed up by assisting the multiorgan segmentation.[2]

PAP screening is the cyclical time-consuming task and needs more concentration. After the prolonged work period, the experienced pathologists in the screening region shall generate some errors because of the decreased attention as well as fatigue. Hence, the computer-aided diagnosis system (CAD) is necessary in helping the pathological segmentation and detection of cervical cancer cells. Thus, it enhances the accuracy of cervical cancer identification and decreases the mortality and occurrence of cervical cancer.[3] So the researchers focused on the automated cervical cell image examinations that are developing globally. In the entire automated analysis system, the segmentation of nuclei is the most significant schemes. The accurate location as well as the contour recognition of nuclei contributes to several follow-up works like quantitative and qualitative cell image analysis, cell segmentation. The traditional segmentation scheme consists of morphological methods, threshold algorithm methods, and active contour models.[4]

Cervical cancer deaths shall be avoided if efficient screening programs take place and lead to a decrease in mortality and morbidity. The success of screening depends on various factors such as screening test quality, access to facilities, diagnosis and lesions treatment, and adequacy of follow-up. The screening of cervical cancer is not much severe in Middle East countries because of the deficiency of skilled and trained health workers and restricted healthcare resources to maintain screening programs.[5,6]

The most significant factor in image segmentation is the CAD progression of cervical cancer that depends on MRI. It is the basic step in image interpretation and analysis. Normally, image segmentation schemes shall be classified into low- and high-level methods. High-level segmentation does not depend on the grey-level information. They integrate human skills as the aforementioned knowledge in the segmentation.[7,8] The segmentation process is the main step in the screening process because it will enhance the efficiency of the system. The number of segmentation algorithms is circulated and employed for the cervical image screening and can be broadly classified into three major categories: characteristic feature, region extraction, and edge detection.[9,10]

This paper proposes three main phases, namely, the preprocessing phase, segmentation phase, as well as morphological operation. The input cervical cancer datasets are preprocessed in the initial phase. In phase 2, an appropriate segmentation is conducted by constructing a Chan Vese based adaptive primal-dual splitting algorithm (CV-APDS) to obtain an optimal segmented image set. In the third step, the morphological operation is carried out to obtain the segmentation results more accurately. This paper fulfills the following objectives:

➢ Employing three phases, namely, the preprocessing, CV-based APDS for cervical image segmentation, as well as morphological operation.
➢ Proposing CV-based APDS for cervical image segmentation and morphological operation thereby obtaining segmentation results more accurately.
➢ Comparing our proposed approach with other existing approaches to determine the system efficiency.

The rest of the paper is organized as follows: Section 4.2 describes the review of past literature works regarding the segmentation of the cervical cancer cell. The proposed approach containing three major phases is described in Sect. 4.3. In Sect. 4.4, the performance analysis and the comparative results are discussed. Section 4.5 concludes the chapter.

4.2 RELATED WORKS

The method for the segmentation of the cervical image is proposed by the previous information for recognizing the defect of cervical cancer cell image in the finest manner.

Rajarao et al.[11] proposed to improve the kernel graph cuts and continuous max-flow optimization for the improved segmentation in the cervical cancer detection process. This method used error and absolute deviation for enumerating its accurate degree in noise elimination from the input Pap smear image when compared with other baseline methods.

Devi et al.[12] developed neutrosophic graph-based cut-based segmentation approach and was utilized in examining the overlapping of preprocessed images to enhance the recognition accuracy. In this process, the preprocessed input image is converted to the neutrosophic set that depends on the calculated values which combine the spatial information and intensity of the preprocessed image. The result provides improved accuracy, recall, sensitivity, precision, and specificity. In the future, the proposed method is combined with any of the graphic cut schemes for cervical cancer detection.

An optimal weight updating with the multilevel set was proposed by Taneja et al.[13] to estimate the segments and ROI. This method provides enhanced prediction performance and cervical image handling of biological applications. This method is difficult in segmenting the folded and colliding cells in cervical images.

Song et al.[14] proposed the learning-based scheme for cell segmentation in Pap smear image for sustaining regular observation of change in cell which was the important requirement of recognition of cervical cancer to overcome the cytoplasm overlapping. This provides better segmentation accuracy. The method is efficient in the abnormal cell segmentation for the images consisting of high degrees of overlapping and a large number of overlapped cells.

4.3   PROPOSED METHODOLOGY

Figure 4.1 describes the flow diagram of the proposed approach based on lesion segmentation for the diagnosis of cervical cancer. The proposed methodology is mainly divided into three main phases, namely, the preprocessing phase, segmentation phase, as well as morphological operation. The input cervical cancer datasets are preprocessed in the initial phase. In phase 2, an appropriate segmentation is conducted by constructing a CV-APDS to obtain an optimal segmented image set. In the third step, the morphological operation is carried out to obtain the segmentation results more accurately.

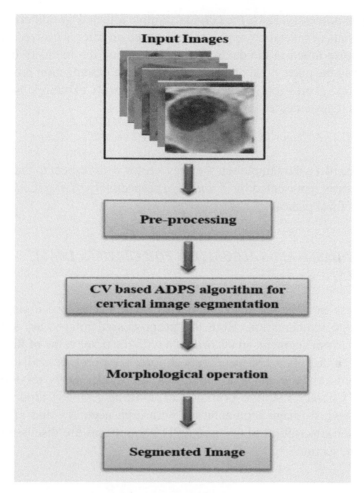

FIGURE 4.1   Structure of the proposed methodology.

4.3.1   DATA ENHANCEMENT OR PREPROCESSING

Image enhancement or preprocessing is the preliminary stage involved in the proposed method. Here, the cervical screening data are attained in two various forms, namely, the images and spectrum. In general, the input images consist of a few redundant signals like noise, unwanted data, blurry boundaries, intensity homogeneity, etc., and it needs to be removed. The main intention of the data enhancement or preprocessing phase is to enhance the images from various distortions and unnecessary features thereby drafting for the subsequent processes. Here, the cervical sample affected by numerous noise signals results in several noise points, and a median filter is utilized to eradicate the noise found in the dataset thus minimizing the intensity deviation by replacing the pixel value of the image. After the deionization process, the mathematical expression for the grey vector in terms of sample and index position is represented as follows.[15]

$$Y\_G_{(J)}\_Median = \left[G_{(J)}^1\_Median,\ G_{(J)}^2\_Median, \dots G_{(J)}^n\_Median \right] \qquad (4.1)$$

From eq (4.1), the sample set, the grey vector with respect to the position of the index is represented by Y *and* $G_{(J)}$, respectively. N signifies the total number of focal planes.

4.3.2   CV-BASED APDS ALGORITHM FOR CERVICAL IMAGE SEGMENTATION

The process next to the data enhancement or the preprocessing phase is the image segmentation. Here the preprocessed images are split into multiple parts or segments in accordance with the pixel value of the image. Here, few image data are inaccurate among the preprocessed image set and it needs to be enhanced. Therefore, this paper proposes the Chan Vese (CV) based Adaptive primal-dual splitting (APDS) algorithm for optimal cervical image segmentation with high accuracy and efficiency. The detailed description of CV and APDS algorithms are discussed in the subsequent section.

4.3.2.1   CV ALGORITHM

An active contour design in terms of functional level set and simplified Mumford shah is referred to as the CV algorithm which was proposed by Chan and Vese in 2001.[16] Let us consider an input image J and a closed contour C is formulated in eq (4.2),

$$J : \delta \rightarrow R$$
$$C : \{ y \in \delta : \omega(y) = 0 \} \qquad (4.2)$$

From eq (4.2), $\omega(y)$ signifies the level set function. Then the mathematical formulation for the section found interior and exterior of the contour is represented as follows:

$$Inside : \delta_{IN} : \{y \in \delta : \omega(y) > 0\}$$
$$Outside : \delta_{OUT} : \{y \in \delta : \omega(y) < 0\} \tag{4.3}$$

a) Energy function equation

Therefore, the energy function equation with respect to the level function of the CV algorithm is formulated in eq (4.4). Hence,

$$E_{CV}[\delta, p, q] = \lambda \int_{\delta} \nabla \left| h_f \left(\delta(y) \right) dy \right| + \alpha_1 \int_{\delta} \left(J - p^2 \right) h_f \left(\delta(y) \right) dy + \alpha_2$$

$$\int_{\alpha} \left(J - q^2 \right) h_f \left(\delta(y) \right) dy \tag{4.4}$$

From eq (4.4), the fixed positive constant values are represented by λ, α_1 and α_2. The intensity average found inside and outside of the contour is represented by p and q, respectively. The Heaviside function is represented by $h_f(\delta(y))$.

b) Heaviside function equation

The mathematical expression and its derivative involved in the Heaviside function are represented in eqs (4.5) and (4.6).

$$h_f\left(\delta(y)\right) = \begin{cases} 1 & \delta(y) > f; \\ 0 & \delta(y) < -f; \\ 0.5\left[1 + \dfrac{\delta}{f} + \dfrac{1}{\pi}\sin\left(\dfrac{\pi\delta(y)}{f}\right)\right] & otherwise \end{cases} \tag{4.5}$$

Then, the derivative value of $h_f(\delta(y))$ is represented by:

$$h_f\left(\delta(y)\right) = \begin{cases} 0 & |\delta(y)| > f; \\ 0.5f\left[1 + \cos\left(\dfrac{\pi\delta(y)}{f}\right)\right] & |\delta(y)| \le f; \end{cases} \tag{4.6}$$

c) Evolution function equation

The mathematical relation in terms of evolution function is expressed as follows:

$$\frac{\partial \delta}{\partial T} = \lambda \vartheta_f(\delta) div\left[\frac{\nabla \delta}{|\nabla \delta|}\right] - \vartheta_f(\alpha)\left[(J(x)-p)^2 - (J(x)-q)^2\right] \qquad (4.7)$$

On the other hand, the energy function equation of the CV model to be minimized consists of local minimum values that results in suboptimal segmentation and are sensitive to δ. Therefore, the stationary solution for eq (4.7) is represented in eq (4.8).

$$\frac{\partial \delta}{\partial T} = div\left[\frac{\nabla \delta}{|\nabla \delta|}\right] - (\alpha)\left[(J(x)-p)^2 - (J(x)-q)^2\right] \qquad (4.8)$$

d) Gradient descent flow equation

The gradient descent flow equation for the above-mentioned energy equation is represented as follows:

$$= \int_\delta |\nabla \delta| dy + \alpha \int_\delta (J-p^2)(J-q^2)\delta dy \qquad (4.9)$$

For solving the problem based on minimization, the global minimization function is evaluated from eq (4.9), therefore,

$$= \underset{0 \le \delta \le 1}{Min} \int_\delta |\nabla \delta| dy + \alpha \int_\delta (J-p^2)(J-q^2)\delta dy \qquad (4.10)$$

Thus the minimizer δ is obtained by solving the minimization issue and the threshold level is set for $\beta \in [0,1]$. Therefore,

$$\begin{aligned} Inside &: \delta_{IN} : \{y, \delta(y) \ge \beta\} \\ Outside &: \delta_{OUT} : \{y, \delta(y) \le \beta\} \end{aligned} \qquad (4.11)$$

Then, the energy function equation in terms of the active contour model is represented as follows:

$$E = \lambda \int_\delta \nabla \left| h_f(\delta(y)) dy \right| + \alpha_1 \int_\delta E_N D_1 h_f(\delta(y)) dy + \alpha_2$$

$$\int_\delta (1-E_N) D_2 h_f(\delta(y)) dy \qquad (4.12)$$

From eq (4.12), the normalized Euclidean distance and data fitting terms are represented as E_N, D_1, and D_2, respectively. Then the simplified energy flow equation with respect to the convex energy is represented in eq (4.13).

$$E = \lambda \int_{\delta} |\nabla \delta| dy + \alpha_1 \int_{\delta} E_N D_1 - \alpha_2 \int_{\delta} (1 - E_N) D_2 h_f \delta dy \qquad (4.13)$$

4.3.2.2 APDS ALGORITHM

The adaptive primal-dual splitting algorithm is employed extensively for the segmentation of cervical images and its variants were developed by Yuan and He.[17] The convergence equation for the primal-dual splitting gradient algorithm is measured by the residual size or gradient. In addition to this, the PDS algorithm is employed in solving the problem based on saddle point for two convex points' u and v. Thus,

$$\underset{X \in x}{Min} \underset{Y \in y}{Max} u(X) + Y^t BX - v(Y) \qquad (4.14)$$

The primal and the dual gradient with respect to the variables X and Y is represented in eq (4.15).

$$P_{I+1} = \partial u(X_{I+1}) + B^t Y_{I+1}$$
$$D_{I+1} = \partial v(X_{I+1}) + B^t Y_{I+1} \qquad (4.15)$$

From eq (4.15), the subdifferential equation of u and v is represented by ∂u and ∂v, respectively. Then on substituting the optimal condition on eq (4.14), the resultant equation is determined as follows:

$$P_{I+1} = \frac{1}{\alpha_I}(X_I - X_{I+1}) - B^t(Y_I - Y_{I+1})$$
$$D_{I+1} = \frac{1}{\beta_I}(Y_I - Y_{I+1}) + B^t(X_I - X_{I+1}) \qquad (4.16)$$

From eq (4.16), the trade-off among the primal and the dual residuals are represented by α_I and β_I, respectively. To attain residual balancing, it is essential to verify the back-tracking conditions followed by every iteration. Thus,

$$\frac{K}{2\alpha_I}\|X_I - X_{I+1}\|^2 - 2(Y_I - Y_{I+1})^t B(X_I - X_{I+1}) + \frac{K}{2\beta_I}\|Y_I - Y_{I+1}\|^2 > 0 \quad (4.17)$$

From eq (4.17), the constant term is represented by $K \in [0,1]$ and in most experiments, the value of K is assumed to be 0.9. Thus, by employing the CV-based APDS algorithm, cervical image segmentation is done.

4.4   MORPHOLOGICAL OPERATION

The third step involved in the proposed approach is the morphological operations or the postprocessing approach. In order to perform an efficient segmentation approach, a few morphological operations are employed. The morphological operations perform logical operations[18] and are easy to use. Dilation, erosion, opening, and closing are the few morphological operations employed in the proposed approach. The detailed description and their operations of each operation are employed in the following section.

a)   Dilation

In general, the dilation approach employs filling the missed pixels or holes in an image. The dilation operation helps an object to grow and the growth depends on the size, shape, and nature of an image. The image dilation P consisting of the structural element Q is represented as follows:

$$P \oplus Q = \{x \mid (Q_z) \cap P \neq \theta\} \tag{4.18}$$

These dilations provide smooth spatial low pass filters in linear image filtering.

b)   Erosion

The complement of the dilation process is the erosion operation. The image with less size and the noises among various images are eliminated. The logical operation employed in the erosion phase is represented as follows:

$$P - Q = \{x \mid (Q_z) \in P\} \tag{4.19}$$

These dilations provide sharp spatial high pass filters in linear image filtering.

c)   Opening

The combination of both erosion and dilution is the opening operation. The image opening P consisting of the structural element Q is represented as follows:

$$P - Q = \{(P - Q) \oplus Q\} \tag{4.20}$$

d) Closing

The combination of both erosion and dilution is the opening operation. The closing operation varies from the opening operation where the image closing P consisting of the structural element Q is represented as follows:

$$P - Q = \{(P \oplus Q) - Q\} \qquad (4.21)$$

4.5 RESULTS AND DISCUSSIONS

The proposed segmentation of the cervical cancer cell was conducted on Pap smear image with lesions obtained from Herlev dataset. Here, the performance metrics such as dice, Jaccard, precision, recall, accuracy, specificity, and sensitivity were evaluated for the performance of the segmented results. The comparative analysis of the proposed CV-based ADPS algorithm for the cervical image segmentation is compared with other methods is also explained in this section.

4.5.1 DESCRIPTION OF DATASET

The database employed here is the Herlev Pap dataset. Here, the database was gathered from the institution of Denmark as well as Herlev. It comprises a 917 image set that has a single Pap cell. In addition to this, the Herlev database images were attained at the intensification of 0.211 µm/pixel containing the average size of the image as 156 × 140. While considering all the images, the longest side length is 768 pixels, as well as short length is 32 pixels, and thus side lengths of the database become wider. The dataset image is broadly classified into seven major categories that are discussed in Table 4.1. Figure 4.2 provides the image sample of various classes.[19]

TABLE 4.1   Cell Distribution of the Herlev Database.

Set	Types	Type of the cell	Total number of the cell	Grand total
I	Normal	Columnar	99	243
II		Transitional squamous	75	
III		Superficial squamous	69	
IV	Abnormal	Severe dysplasia	193	675
V		Carcinoma in situ	151	
VI		Mild dysplasia	184	
VII		Moderate dysplasia	147	

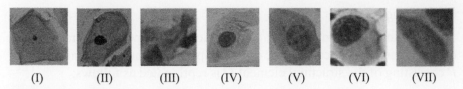

(I)   (II)   (III)   (IV)   (V)   (VI)   (VII)

FIGURE 4.2   Image sample of seven classes from the Herlev database.

4.5.2   PERFORMANCE METRICS

The segmentation performance of the proposed approach is validated by employing various kinds of evaluation metrics, such as precision, accuracy, recall, Jaccard coefficient, dice coefficient, and Zijdenbos similarity index (ZSI) were explained in below equations.

$$Precision = \frac{t_p}{t_p + f_p} \tag{4.22}$$

$$Accuracy = \frac{t_p + t_n}{t_p + t_n + f_p + f_n} \tag{4.23}$$

$$Recall = \frac{t_p}{t_p + f_n} \tag{4.24}$$

$$Dice\ coefficient = 2 \times \frac{t_p}{t_p + t_n + f_p + f_n} \tag{4.25}$$

$$Jaccard\ coefficient = \frac{t_p}{t_p + f_p + f_n} \tag{4.26}$$

$$ZSI = \frac{2t_p}{2t_p + f_p + f_n} \tag{4.27}$$

In eqs (4.22–4.27), t_p indicates the total number of true distinguished pixel, f_p represents the number of pixels detected perfectly, and f_n indicates the total number of pixels that are not detected.

4.5.3   PERFORMANCE ANALYSIS

This section provides the experimental analysis as well as the comparisons. The predominance of the proposed CV-based ADPS algorithm for cervical image segmentation scheme is examined using MATLAB 2013a by using the Herlev database for computing its performance over the other cervical cancer detection schemes. The segmentation outcomes achieved with respect to the Herlev database are described in Figure 4.3. The initial line describes the original images and the last line describes the segmented image. The model is trained on the single NVIDIA GTX 1080ti GPU.

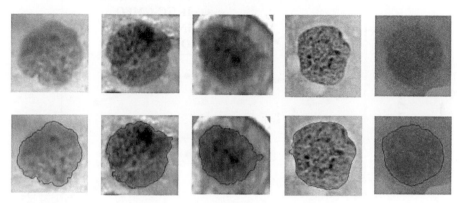

FIGURE 4.3 Segmentation results of Herlev dataset. First row: original image. Second row: segmented image.

Table 4.2 provides the quantitative comparisons of published results with other approaches regarding precision, recall, as well as ZSI for the image of the Herlev database.

TABLE 4.2 Comparative Analysis of Various Approaches.

Method	Precision	Recall	ZSI
Proposed CV-based ADPS	0.98 ± 0.12	0.97 ± 0.05	0.98 ± 0.11
Mask RCNN+ LFC-CRF[10]	0.96 ± 0.05	0.96 ± 0.11	0.95 ± 0.10
D-MEM[11]	0.946 ± 0.14	0.984 ± 0.00	0.933 ± 0.14
RGVF[12]	0.83 ± 0.20	0.96 ± 0.13	0.87 ± 0.19

Figure 4.4 describes the importance of the proposed CV-based ADPS segmentation algorithm. The proposed approach is compared with the benchmarked IKGC-CMFO, INGC-GDES, and OWU-ML[20] segmentation schemes. The accuracy achieved by the proposed CV-ADPS approach is about 99.74% which is high when compared with all other approaches like IKGC-CMFO, INGC-GDES, and OWU-ML. The sensitivity value of the proposed segmentation approach is 99.42% which is optimal for all the other

approaches and is described in Figure 4.5. Finally, the specificity of the proposed method is 98.94% which is better than all the other approaches and is described in Figure 4.6.

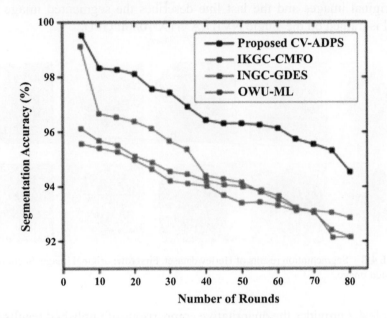

FIGURE 4.4   Comparison of accuracy with number of round.

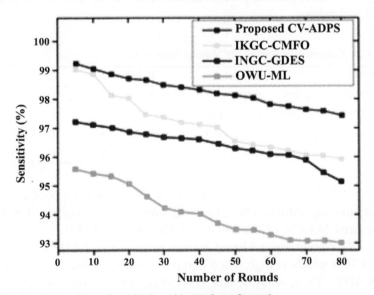

FIGURE 4.5   Comparison of sensitivity with number of round.

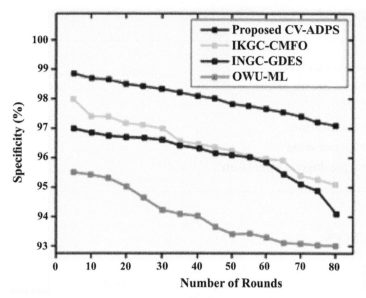

FIGURE 4.6   Comparison of specificity with number of round.

4.6   CONCLUSION

In this paper, three main phases, namely, the preprocessing phase, segmentation phase, as well as morphological operation are proposed. The input cervical cancer datasets are preprocessed in the initial phase. In phase 2, an appropriate segmentation is conducted by constructing a CV-APDS to obtain an optimal segmented image set. In the third step, the morphological operation is carried out to obtain the segmentation results more accurately. The method used in this paper is computed by employing the dataset called the Herlev database. In addition to this, the segmentation performance of the proposed approach is validated by employing various kinds of evaluation metrics, such as precision, accuracy, recall, Jaccard coefficient, dice coefficient, and ZSI. Finally, performance analysis and the comparative analysis are conducted and the results reveal that the proposed approach provides a high accuracy rate and efficiency when compared with other methods.

KEYWORDS

- **cervical cancer**
- **Chan-Vese algorithm**
- **APDS**
- **segmentation**
- **preprocessing**
- **morphological operation**

REFERENCES

1. Hollandi, R.; Szkalisity, A.; Toth, T.; Tasnadi, E.; Molnar, C.; Mathe, B.; Kovacs, M. nucleAIzer: A Parameter-Free Deep Learning Framework for Nucleus Segmentation Using Image Style Transfer. *Cell Syst.* **2020.**
2. Bnouni, N.; Rekik, I.; Rhim, M. S.; Amara, N. E. Context-Aware Synergetic Multiplex Network for Multi-Organ Segmentation of Cervical Cancer MRI. In *International Workshop on PRedictive Intelligence in Medicine*; Springer: Cham, 2020; pp 1–11.
3. Martins, G. L.; Ferreira, D. S.; Medeiros, F. N.; Ramalho, G. L. Ensemble of Algorithms for Multifocal Cervical Cell Image Segmentation. In *Brazilian Conference on Intelligent Systems*. Springer: Cham, 2020; pp 271–286.
4. Wang, R.; Kamata, S; I. Nuclei Segmentation of Cervical Cell Images Based on Intermediate Segment Qualifier. In *2018 24th International Conference on Pattern Recognition*; IEEE, 2018; pp 3941–3946.
5. Wang, H.; Jiang, C.; Bao, K.; Xu, C. Recognition and Clinical Diagnosis of Cervical Cancer Cells Based on Our Improved Lightweight Deep Network for Pathological Image. *J. Med. Syst.* **2019,** *43* (9), 301.
6. Sarwar, A.; Sheikh, A. A.; Manhas, J.; Sharma, V. Segmentation of Cervical Cells for Automated Screening of Cervical Cancer: A Review. *Artif. Intell. Rev.* **2019,** 1–39.
7. Daly, A.; Yazid, H.; Solaiman, B.; Essoukri Ben Amara N. Multiatlas-Based Segmentation of Female Pelvic Organs: Application for Computer-Aided Diagnosis of Cervical Cancer. *Int. J. Imag. Syst. Technol.* **2020.**
8. William, W.; Ware, A.; Basaza-Ejiri, A. H.; Obungoloch, J. A Review of Image Analysis and Machine Learning Techniques for Automated Cervical Cancer Screening from Pap-Smear Images. *Comput. Methods Prog. Biomed.* **2018,** *164,* 15–22.
9. Liu, Y.; Zhang, P.; Song, Q.; Li, A.; Zhang, P.; Gui, Z. Automatic Segmentation of Cervical Nuclei Based on Deep Learning and a Conditional Random Field. *IEEE Access.* **2018,** *6,* 53709–53721.
10. Rajarao, C.; Singh, R. P. Improved Normalized Graph Cut with Generalized Data for Enhanced Segmentation in Cervical Cancer Detection. *Evol. Intell.* **2020,** *13* (1), 3–8.
11. Rajarao, C.; Singh, R. P. Improvised Kernel Graph Cuts and Continuous Max-Flow Optimization Scheme-for Enhanced Segmentation in Cervical Cancer Detection.

12. Devi, M. A.; Sheeba, J. I.; Joseph, K. S. Neutrosophic Graph Cut-Based Segmentation Scheme for Efficient Cervical Cancer Detection. *J. King Saud Univ. Comput. Inform. Sci.* **2018**.

13. Taneja, A.; Ranjan, P.; Ujlayan, A. Multi-Cell Nuclei Segmentation in Cervical Cancer Images by Integrated Feature Vectors. *Multimed. Tools Appl.* **2018**, *77* (8), 9271–9290.

14. Song, Y.; Tan, E. L.; Jiang, X.; Cheng, J. Z.; Ni, D.; Chen, S.; Lei, B.; Wang, T. Accurate Cervical Cell Segmentation from Overlapping Clumps in Pap Smear Images. *IEEE Trans. Med. Imag.* **2016**, *36* (1), 288–300.

15. Huang, J.; Wang, T.; Zheng, D.; He, Y. Nucleus Segmentation of Cervical Cytology Images Based on Multi-Scale Fuzzy Clustering Algorithm. *Bioengineered* **2020**, *11* (1), 484–501.

16. Li, X.; Li, C.; Liu, H.; Yang, X. A Modified Level Set Algorithm Based on Point Distance Shape Constraint for Lesion and Organ Segmentation. *Phys. Med.* **2019**, *57*, 123–136.

17. Goldstein, T.; Li, M.; Yuan, X. Adaptive Primal-Dual Splitting Methods for Statistical Learning and Image Processing. *Adv. Neural Inform. Process. Syst.* **2015**, *28*, 2089–2097.

18. Ravi, S.; Khan, A. M. Morphological Operations for Image Processing: Understanding and Its Applications. In *Proceedings of the 2nd National Conference on VLSI, Signal processing & Communications NCVSComs-2013*, 2013.

19. Zhao, J.; Li, Q.; Li, X.; Li, H.; Zhang, L. Automated Segmentation of Cervical Nuclei in Pap Smear Images Using Deformable Multi-Path Ensemble Model. In *2019 IEEE 16th International Symposium on Biomedical Imaging*; IEEE, 2019; pp 1514–1518.

20. Li, K.; Lu, Z.; Liu, W.; Yin, J. Cytoplasm and Nucleus Segmentation in Cervical Smear Images Using Radiating GVF Snake. *Pattern Recognit.* **2012**, *45*, 1255–1264.

12. Devi, M. A., Sheeba, J. I. (eds.) In: A. N., S. Nighthawking GraphThe Blast Segmentation Scheme for Effective Cervical Cancer Detection. J. King Saud Univ. Comput. Inform. Sci. 2015.

13. Jantzen, A., Bjerrum, E., Dilhuan, A. Multi-Cell nuclei Segmentation in Cervical Cancer Images by Interaction Feature Vectors. Multimedia. Tools Appl. 2018, 78(8), 9521–9540.

14. Song, Y., Tan, E. L., Jiang, X., Cheng, J. Z., Ni, D., Chen, S., Lei, B., Wang, T. Accurate Cervical Cell Segmentation from Overlapping Clumps in Pap Smear Images. IEEE Trans. Med. Img. 2016, 36(1), 288–300.

15. Zhang, L., Wang, H., Zhou, D., He, Y. Nucleus Segmentation of Cervical Cytology Images Based on Multi-Scale Fuzzy Clustering Algorithm. Bioinformatics 2020, 17(1), 345–461.

16. Li, C., Li, C., Fan, H., Yuan, X. A Multi-Plane Level Algorithm Based on Point Distance Shape Constraint for Lesion and Tissue Segmentation. Proc. Artif. 2019, 22, 123–136.

17. Guo, Jun., Li, M., Yuan, X. A Novel Thread Total Splitting Methods for Statistical Learning and Image Processing. Adv. Neural Inform. Process. Syst. 2018, 25, 2080–2097.

18. Ravi, S., Khan, A., T. Graph Neural Networks for Image Processing: Understanding and Its Applications. In: Proceedings of the 27th European Conference on AI, Signal Processing & Communication (eds.), MCP, Croatia, 2015, 2015.

19. Zhao, Y. J., Qi, J., Y., C. H., Zhang, F. Automated Segmentation area of Cervical Nuclei in Pap Smear Images Using Deformable Model and Ensemble Method. In: 2018 IEEE 15th International Symposium on Biomedical Imaging (ISBI) 2018, pp. 1514–1518.

20. Li, K., Lu, Z., Liu, W., Yin, J. Neoplasm and Nucleus Segmentation in Cervical Smear Images Using Watershed. SVR. Statist. Pattern Recogn. 2012, 45, 1255–1264.

CHAPTER 5

Satellite Image Compression by Random Forest Optimization Techniques and Performance Comparison Using a Multispectral Image Compression Method

SRIKANTH BETHU[1], SANJANA VASIREDDY[1], D. USHASREE[1], MD ASRAR AHMED[2], and P. VARA PRASAD[1]

[1]*Department of Computer Science and Engineering, Gokaraju Rangaraju Institute of Engineering & Technology, Hyderabad, Telangana, India*

[2]*Department of Computer Science and Engineering, Osmania University, Hyderabad, Telangana, India*

ABSTRACT

Multispectral image compression is a current dominating challenge topic in research attention. Satellite communications, radars, and sensing area technologies are continuously monitoring the earth, space, and environment. In competitive world sources, like power consumption, storage is available with more economy. Also, performance capability remains limited. In this process, multispectral image processing techniques and its usage requirements are compulsory. The related geographical information, optical information, disaster monitoring water wells, etc., are monitored by satellite

Computational Intelligence in Analytics and Information Systems, Volume 1: Data Science and AI, Selected Papers from CIAIS-2021. Hardeo Kumar Thakur, Manpreet Kaur, Parneeta Dhaliwal, Rajeev Kumar Arya, and Joan Lu (Eds.)

cameras. So, image quality compression, attacks, histogram equalization, machine learning statistical parameters need to be improved. Existing methods are mainly based on matrix-based modeling, discrete wavelet transform techniques segmentation, low-rank tensor decomposition, but they fail to discover the different strip components and have more limitations. Machine learning also can solve the problems of spectral redundancy, sub-bands removing models. In this research, we are using the natural random forest machine learning model (NRFML). This model compresses and trains the multispectral image for various application usage, at final comparison the parameters like MSE, peak signal-to-noise ratio, NCC, and structural similitude with existing methods conclude that the proposed NRFML is competing with previous methods.

5.1   INTRODUCTION

Remote sensing technologies consist of different multispectral images (MI).[26] These MIs consist of thousands of spectral bands (SPB)[25] and sub-bands (SB), we need to train these SPB and SB in a systematic manner. MI is very useful for many practical applications. Because of this, spatial and spectral information is necessarily improved. Apart from sensing technologies, these MIs are inevitably generated from environment monitoring, military surveillance, urban planning devices, etc. At that time, generating MIs consist of different types of noises being added to spectral and spatial data. There are two kinds of wireless image sensing technologies, that is an active sensible image and passive image remote image identifying.[13]

Multispectral image pressure distant detecting needs low trouble, high strength, yet in addition raised effectiveness since it for the most part works on satellite, radar, just as clinical applications where capacities, similar to vitality, memory, and preparing capacity are limited. So mean square error (MSE),[7] top signal-to-noise ratio (PSNR),[13] and normalized correlation coefficient (NCC),[14] are used for performance investigations. Until we investigate the PSNR, structural similitude (SSIM) is used for investigations.

Excess and expelling subgroups before pressure ideas are not secured at this point. These two boundaries definitely diminish the memory (pressure). So powerful multispectral pressure[27] is accomplished and PSNR, NCC, SSIM, MSE boundaries are improved.

Dynamic sensors produce essentialness in order to clear articles and zones whereupon a sensor by then perceives and measures the radiation that is reflected or backscattered from the target. RADAR and LiDAR[22] are occasions of dynamic far-off distinguishing where the time delay among transmission and return is assessed, developing the zone, speed, and course of a thing. Inactive sensors collect radiation that is released or reflected by the thing or incorporating locales. Reflected sunshine is the most notable wellspring of radiation evaluated by inert sensors. Examples of idle distant sensors are consolidate film photography, infrared, charge-coupled devices, and radiometers.

A code is a plan of pictures including letters, numbers, bits, etc., which are used to address a combination of information or set of events. Each serenity of information or event has consigned a gathering of code pictures called code words a comparative thought is used to give code words for the grayscale estimations of the image to lessen the proportion of data used to address it.

A discrete subjective variable *rk* meanwhile 0,1 addresses the diminished degrees of an image and that each *rk* occurs with probability pr(rk). The estimation of *pr(rk)* can be constrained by the following equation:

$$pr\,(rk) = nk/n \qquad\qquad (5.1)$$

where $k = 0,1,2,3 \dots L\text{-}1$, L is the number of gray levels
nk is the occasions, the *k*th dim level shows up in the picture, and *n* is the all-out number of pixels in the picture. On the off chance that the quantity of bits used to speak to each estimation of *rk* is *l(rk)*, at that point the normal number of bits required to speak to every pixel is. The typical length of the code words selected to various diminish level characteristics is found by adding the consequence of the quantity of bits used to address every dull level and the probability of occasion of that diminish level. As such, the all dwarf of bits required to code an $M \times N$ picture is MNLavg. Addressing the diminished degrees of an image with a trademark m-bit twofold code reduces the right-hand side of eq 5.2. to m-bits. That is Lavg = *m* when m is fill in for *l(rk)* at that point the steady m might be taken 1, which is equal-L $\leq k \leq$ outside the summation, exit basically the aggregate of the *pr(rk)* for 0–1. This view of coding repetition is executed in the ensuing occurrence of variable length coding:

Step 1: Define the Objective—Before plunging into the test and building a random forest (RF) AI model, one must have an unmistakable, well-characterized objective, or a true objective at the top of the priority list. This may fluctuate contingent upon what the association is attempting to accomplish. Powerful objectives are given below.

Objectives

1. Image compression on the satellite image.
2. Image quality assessment.
3. PSNR calculation.
4. MSE, SSIM, NCC calculation.
5. Multispectral image compression such that calculating the compression ratio.
6. Different types of attacks.
7. Rotation attack.
8. Histogram equalization.
9. Color improvement.
10. Mosaicking.

Step 2: Levers—Switches are the information sources that can be controlled or a few changes the model can make, to drive the target characterized in Stage 1. For example, to guarantee that the clients are fulfilled:

• A method container provides superior benefits to existed model.
• Give free proposed model and design in a right manner.

An AI model cannot be a switch; however, it can enable the association to distinguish the switches. It is essential to comprehend this differentiation unmistakably.

Step 3: Data—The following stage is to discover what information can be useful in recognizing and setting the switch that the association may have. This can be not the same as the information previously given or gathered by the association before.

Step 4: Predictive models—When we have the required information that can be useful in accomplishing the above-characterized objective, the last advance is to fabricate a re-enactment model on this information. Note that a recreation model can have different prescient models. For instance, building one model distinguishing what things ought to be prescribed to a client, and another model foreseeing the likelihood that a client handles a specific parameter on a proposal. The thought is to make an improvement model, instead of a prescient model.

Common characteristics of most MI consist of neighboring pixels, they are correlated. Such redundant information exists. Redundancy and irrelevancy reductions are two essential modules of compression.

a) Redundancy decline:
   This is the method of removing duplicate information from the image from the source.

b) Irrelevancy reduction:
   It is a part of the system but not manual. This will not be noticed by the receiver.

Again redundancy is three types.

1. Spatial redundancy: in this, a correlation exists amongst neighboring pixel standards.
2. Spectral redundancy: this model consists of correlation flanked by dissimilar color planes or SPB.
3. Temporal redundancy: correlation between adjacent frames in the sequence of pictures.

5.2 LITERATURE SURVEY

Satellite imaging has its range of usages that reaches from earth perception, logical research, military applications, regular asset the executives, worldwide ecological checking, and to the endless of uses. The obtaining of these pictures is done through remote detecting sensors situated from the satellites. It catches the earth with various wavelengths and produces a huge measure of data as various groups. The multispectral scanner[15] produces the four groups of information, the thematic mapper (TM)[8] intended to secure picture with seven groups and the high-resolution imaging spectrometer[18] produces the information with 192 groups.[5]

These pictures have to chronicle for learning and further preparation with numerous applications.[8] The chronicling and transmission of the multispectral picture are not the simple errands on account of the size factor. Henceforth, it needs more measure of memory space and high data transfer capacity run for capacity and transmission separately because of its high level of conveying data. Numerous methodologies are proposed for packing multispectral pictures. A vector quantization based strategies,[12] embraces the square-based coding procedures wherein squares are worked in spatial space and a nondirect square forecast is utilized to accomplish the unearthly relationship.

Another lossless strategy called mean-standardized vector quantization is likewise proposed for compacting multispectral pictures.[20] An all-encompassing vector quantization based technique that speaks to the three-dimensional square utilizing Kronecker product with littler vectors is proposed in.[21] Despite these methodologies, change-based techniques are viable with multispectral pictures.[4] A pressure calculation utilized Eigen region-based Eigen subspace change (ER-EST)[16] for multispectral pictures that are worked dependent on the choice standard that is determined to utilize the head relationship of a picture connection framework. At that point, the Eigen districts are ordered utilizing the choice standard and the Eigen areas are compacted utilizing ER-EST. A quadtree-based KLT change[24] and wavelet put together approaches with respect to 3D area[11,17] are additionally proposed for multispectral pictures.

With this writing study, we can reason that the wavelet-based techniques make ready to produce multispectral picture pressure, particularly with the 3D space. In addition, these techniques might be irreversible and yield better pressure execution.[19,10] As quality is the principle viewpoint in the multispectral pictures, an ideal pressure codec is required that protects both pressure and quality variables. Thus, in this broadsheet, we projected a close lossless multispectral picture pressure strategy that uses the three-dimensional discrete wavelet transform (3D-DWT) and Huffman coding for encoding wavelet recurrence coefficients. The staying of this chapter is composed as follows: coming section portrays the essential foundation information for our proposed technique. The strategy and working standard of our proposed technique are outlined in methodology, implementation contains the assessed outcomes, and talk lastly, we finished up the chapter in results discussion.

5.2.1   METHODOLOGY

Its portrayal where the arrangement of information esteems is meagre, in this way compacting the data substance of the sign into a more modest number of coefficients. A decent quantizes attempts to allocate additional bits on behalf of coefficients through extra data content or perceptual importance, also smaller amount bits for coefficients with fewer data substance bases on a specified stable piece spending entropy coding which expels repetition commencing the yield of the quantizes appeared in Figure 5.1.

The designing of the arranged dehazing structure has shown up in Figure 5.2, where *n* CNN individuals with the waiting structure are related in corresponding to take in the backslide from the dim picture to the indisputable picture. Getting ready with different degrees of obscurity tests, these CNNs have assorted dehazing limits and can deliver different yields. These yields are expanded by their looking at weight maps and merged through a convolutional layer to make the last clear picture.

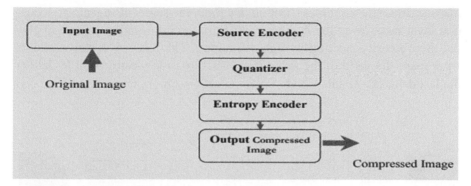

FIGURE 5.1 Lossy compression system.

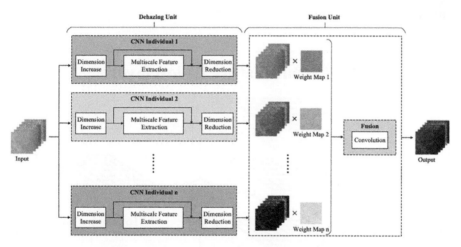

FIGURE 5.2 Dehazing network.

The structure of the arranged CNN individual has showed up in Figure 5.3. In addition, A 3 × 3 convolutional layer with 16 channels is first used to diagram information picture to high estimation. It is then followed by an extra structure with two multiscale convolutional layers, a part mix layer, and a segment-wise deduction layer. Each multiscale convolutional layer includes three resembled convolutions with different part estimates {1 × 1, 3 × 3, 5 × 5}, to expel multiscale features of darkness. To save size invariant for the three scales, paddings are set to {0, 1, 2} and advances are {1, 1, 1}. The component blend layer is used to interweave the multiscale feature maps, which find out the ordinary characteristics among the contrasting feature guides of the three scales, pixel by pixel, see Figure 5.4. The merged feature maps address the cloudiness section. By then, the segment sagacious deduction layer takes away the darkness part from the information picture to play out the obscurity ejection in high estimation. The last 3 × 3 convolutional layer maps the yield of the rest of the structure to low estimation to deliver the last dehazing result.

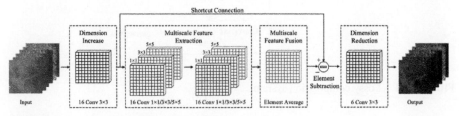

FIGURE 5.3   CNN individual.

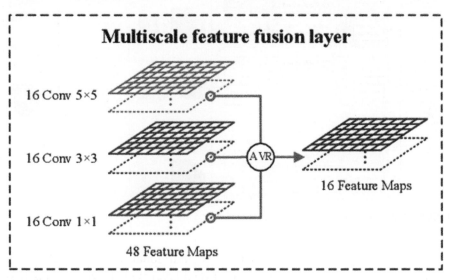

FIGURE 5.4   Multiscale feature fusion layer.

Figure 5.5 demonstrates the procurement procedure and handling of the pictures in the analysis. The pictures are taken by a 13 Mpx camera on XiaomiRedmi 3S telephone and by a multispectral RedEdge camera. Information from the multispectral camera was prepared in the MATLAB program and various kinds of pictures were made, for example, weighted pictures by the vegetative record (see part C) and RGB composite pictures that were contrasted and the pictures from an ordinary camera.

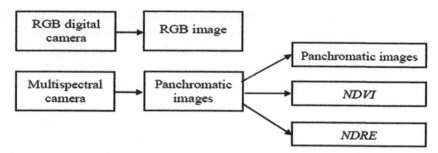

FIGURE 5.5   Block diagram of image processing.

Figure 5.6 depicts the making of consolidated pictures in more detail. An enlistment procedure must be taken after panchromatic picture catching. From that point onward, the consolidated pictures can be determined (RGB—utilizing making out of spectra in MATLAB).

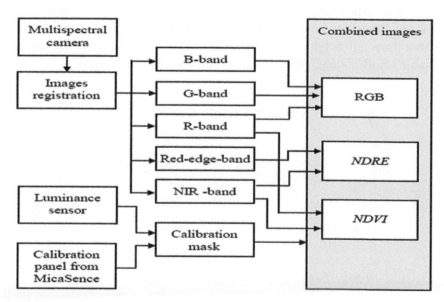

FIGURE 5.6   Band model.

5.3   MULTISPECTRAL IMAGES USING WAVELET TRANSFORM

A pixel-level wavelet-based way to deal with circuit engineered opening radar (SAR) symbolism with multispectral (MS) symbolism. Picture combination consolidates data from at least two pictures to create another picture, which is wealthy in data. Because of the integral idea of SAR as well as multispectral symbolism, a combination of these pictures is of huge enthusiasm for the field of remote detecting. The essential target of this effort is to improve spatial data in multispectral pictures by infusing auxiliary data obtained from the SAR picture. Because of the negative relationship between SAR and multispectral information, traditional segment substitution techniques face the issue of otherworldly mutilation in the melded picture. Wavelet-based combination methodologies conquer this issue because of phenomenal restriction in the spatial and recurrence area. Here, various wavelet-based combination principles are connected for the combination of SAR and multispectral pictures. Combination guidelines connected to breaker estimated subgroups also part of subgroups of these pictures deliberate ghostly dis-closeness amongst them. Consequences are assessed outwardly, just as utilizing regular superiority measurements also be situated contrasted and part replacement combination procedures to be specific, head segment examination, and summed up IHS change. The exchange between the phantom and spatial nature of the intertwined picture has been watched while combining SAR and multispectral pictures. Figure 5.7 illustrates the data compression through variable-length coding. Table 5.1 details the rank-based analysis.

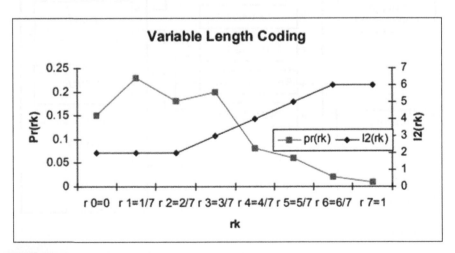

FIGURE 5.7   Data compression through variable length coding.

5.4   IMPLEMENTATION METHOD

After full exploitation of literate survey using prior knowledge like components of SPB, SB, spatial parameters, image components, and dataset designings is corresponding regularizations. We can instantiate the destriping objective functions. Apply the model which we proposed at final improving the parameters and objectives, as shown in Figure 5.8.

TABLE 5.1 Rank-based Analysis.

r_k	$p_r(r_k)$	Code 1	$l_1(r_k)$	Code 2	$l_2(r_k)$
$r_0 = 0$	0.15	000	3	11	2
$r_1 = 1/7$	0.23	001	3	01	2
$r_2 = 1/7$	0.18	010	3	10	2
$r_3 = 3/7$	0.2	011	3	001	3
$r_4 = 4/7$	0.08	100	3	0001	4
$r_5 = 5/7$	0.06	101	3	00001	5
$r_6 = 6/7$	0.02	110	3	000001	6
$r_7 = 1$	0.01	111	3	000000	6

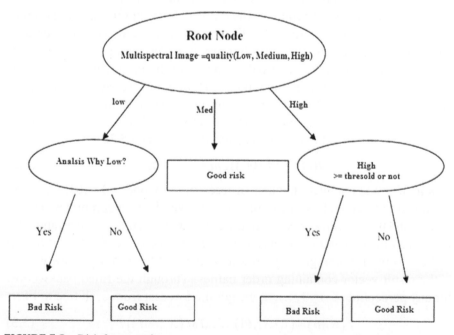

FIGURE 5.8 Risk factor analyses.

Here I am always calculating the risk of statics. If the risk is good, the process will move to the right way if the not bad risk is in front. Depending upon this strategy decisions will take and divert to a good risk way. Here threshold concept is introduced, fixing the T_h values if T_h > risk value being to be good risk. If T_h < risk value being to be a bad risk. Estimating potential or counterfactual outcomes is often of interest to researchers. When using the potential outcome framework, the outcome under each possible value of a predictor, say ×1, must be observable. However, only the outcome under the actual value for ×1 is observed, whereas the potential outcomes under the other possible values for ×1 are considered to be missing data.

The proposed model development gives accurate results. Here, the number of samples (n) is much less than the volume of features (p) "$n <<$ p." The development of the model RF is integrated with machine learning. The demonstrated model is very useful, adding to present models in which improved classification, improved presentation also meant full selection compared to ordinary RF. Figure 5.9 shows that application purpose and design purpose blocks are aligned. There are several tuning parameters that can affect the construction of a RF including mtry, ntree, and node size. The mtry parameter controls the number of randomly selected predictors used to determine the best split at each node, and typically remains constant throughout the tree building process. The parameter ntree specifies the number of trees to be used to construct the forest, and node size is the minimum size of the terminal nodes. Here, node size acts as a stopping criterion, meaning that once a minimum node size is achieved, no further splits will be performed on this node, as shown in Figures 5.9 and 5.10.

A forest FF is a collection of decision trees from eq 5.3:

$$\mathcal{F}(\Theta) = \{\mathcal{J}_m(\Theta_m)\}, \; m = 1,...,M, \tag{5.2}$$

Where M is the complete number of trees in the woods, $\Theta = \{\theta 1, ..., \Theta M\}$ speaks to the parameters in FF. In irregular woods, Θ incorporates parting factors and their parting esteems. In the component identification arrange, FF is fitted by the preparation information X and y, where $X \in Rn \times pX \in Rn \times p$ is the info information grid with n tests and p highlights and $y \in Rn \; y \in Rn$ is the result vector containing order names. Through the fitted backwoods, for any perception X_i, $i = 1, ..., n$, we get the forecast from each tree in FF:

$$f(X_i;\theta) = \left(T_1(X_i;\theta 1).......TM(X_i;\theta M)\right)T \tag{5.3}$$

where $TM(X_i; \theta M) = y{\char`\^}im$ is the parallel expectation of perception x_i given by J_m. Consequently, mean $f_i := f(X_i; \theta)$ for effortlessness, for a perception x_i, f_i is a double vector abridging the sign recognized from the woodland and later on fills in as the new information highlights to be nourished into the DNN.

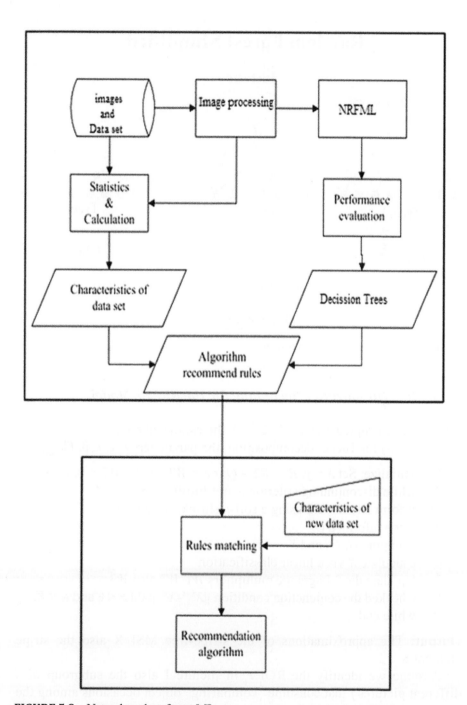

FIGURE 5.9 Natural random forest ML.

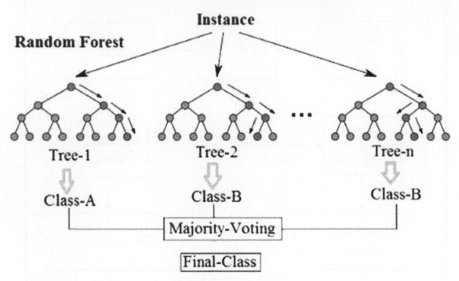

FIGURE 5.10   Decision trees adjustment.

Algorithm: Optimization Technique for the NRFML Model.

Input: The corrupted image y $\in$ R^{MXNxB}. the estimated rank
  $(ri, r2, r3)$ for Tucker decomposition, the parameters $\lambda_1\lambda_2, \lambda_3, \beta$, $\in$k$_{max}$.

I: Initialize: Set $X = y$, R, $= R2 = Q = S = W1 = W2 = W2 = 0$, $k = O$.
2:   while discontinuing criterion is not fulfilled do
3:   Inform $R1$, also $R2$ using a soft-t_h shrinkage scheme.
4:   Keep informed Q
5:   Compute G, U_i, and S
6:   Calculate X via a linear classification
7:   Up_date the 3 Lagrange multipliers $W1$. $W2$ also $W3$.
8:   Checked the conjunction condition $||X^{k+1}-X^k|| \, ||X^k|| \, F < \in$ and $K < K_{MAX}$
9:   while end

Output: The approximations of the stripe-free MSI X also the stripe element S.

Assume we identify the ROI r_i in picture I also the subgroup of s different pictures j that consume "comparing" object occasions among the arrangement of preparing pictures aimed at that class. At that point we might decide the relating ROIs r_j of pictures j by advancing the accompanying cost work:

$$\mathcal{L}_i = \underset{\{r_j\}}{Max} \sum_{j=1}^{8} K\left(D(r_i), D(r_j)\right) \tag{5.4}$$

where $D(r_i)$ and $D(r_j)$ are the descriptors for the ROIs r_i and r_j individually The trees at this point are parallel also are developed in a top-down way The twofold test at every hub can be picked in one of two different ways: (1) haphazardly, for example, information autonomous; otherwise (2) through a covetous calculation which picks the test that greatest isolates the assumed preparing models. "Best" here is estimated through the data gain

$$\Delta E = -\sum_i \frac{|Q_i|}{|Q|} E(Q_i) \tag{5.5}$$

brought about by dividing the set Q of models into two subsets Q_i concurring the assumed test. At this point $E(Q)$ is the entropy—PN j=1 pj log2(p_j) with p_j the extent of models in q having a place with class j, and $|$. $|$ the size of the set

$$p_i = g(\mu_{i1}) = \frac{e^{\mu_{i1}}}{e^{\mu_{i0}} + e^{\mu_{i1}}} \tag{5.6}$$

Where $i = 1, \ldots, n$.

$p_i \quad := \quad Pr(y_i = 1 | \mathbf{f}_i)$

$\mu_{i0} \quad := \quad [\mathbf{z}_i^{(out)}]^T \mathbf{w}_0^{(out)} + \mathbf{b}_i^{(out)}$

$\mu_{i1} \quad := \quad [\mathbf{z}_i^{(out)}]^T \mathbf{w}_1^{(out)} + \mathbf{b}_i^{(out)}$

The limitations to remain assessed in the DNN are along these lines every one of the loads and predispositions. The model can be prepared to utilize a stochastic/gradient/descent/(S-G-D) founded Algorithm 21 by limiting the cross-entropy misfortune work.

$$\mathcal{L}(\Psi) = -\frac{1}{n} \sum_{i=1}^{n} \{y_i log\,(\hat{p}_i) + (1 - y_i)\,log\,(1 - \hat{p}_i)\} \tag{5.7}$$

where again Ψ indicates totally the model limitations, and $p^\wedge p^\wedge{}_i$ is the fitted estimation of p_i. Additional insights regarding DNN containers be found in normal profound knowledge.

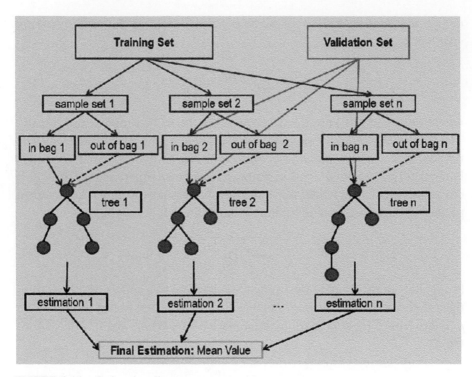

FIGURE 5.11   Estimation diagram.

The RF count[2] is immediately depicted. Discretionary forest is an outfit information method subject to Uchiyama's pressing idea.[23] A RF includes CART-like decision trees that are uninhibitedly based on a bootstrap test. Appeared differently in relation to additionally assembling information figurines, for instance expanding[3] that amass a level tree course of action of decision stumps, an RF uses a social affair of decision trees, is multiclass gifted likewise has a few best qualities.[6] Figure 5.11 detailed the estimation diagram.

- Similar or favored precision over RF.
- Robust to clatter and abnormalities.
- Faster getting ready than pressing or boosting.
- Useful internal evaluates: screw-up, quality, relationship, and variable hugeness.

A tree is developed expending the following calculation:

- Select ntree tests through M factors beginning N showing tests indiscriminately.

- The remainder of the models is used to figure the out-of-pack bumble (OOB-botch).
- At each center point decide m try$<< M$ factors unpredictably reliant on a best split.
- Thoroughly build up the tree without pruning.

A completed RF contains a couple of collection trees $1 \leq t \leq T$ in which the class probabilities, evaluated by larger part throwing a voting form, are used to figure the model's imprint $y(x)$ with respect to a segment vector x:

$$y(x) = \operatorname*{argmax}_{c} \left(\frac{1}{T} \sum_{t=1}^{T} I_{h_t(x)=c} \right) \tag{5.8}$$

The judgment function $h_t(x)$ offers the organization of one tree to a class c through the indicator function I:

$$I_{h_t(x)=c} = \begin{cases} 1, & h_t(x) = c, \\ 0, & \text{otherwise.} \end{cases} \tag{5.9}$$

Train RF course with weighted democratic:

- Select the most extreme number of stages S and the number of trees per arranged T.
- Select genuine positive t_p and genuine negative t_n target rates per organizing.

  "For $(0 < s \leq S)$"
  "For $(0 < t \leq T)$"
  "Train single tree"
  "if $(t_{ps}, t > t_p \ \& \ t_{ns}, t > t_n)$"
  "Stage completed"

- "Calculate $\alpha s = \exp(f$ measure)."
- "Delete true-negatives."
- "Refill with false-positives,"
- "Normalize weights α to a range of 0 and 1."

5.5 RESULTS AND DISCUSSION

In Figure 5.12, MI received from different types are satellites, types of satellites generate different types of MI. These images contain special spectral bands and SB; these information should be controlled with the proposed natural RF machine learning model (NRFML).

FIGURE 5.12   Multispectral image from satellite.

In Figure 5.13, MI received from different types are satellites, types of satellites generate different types of MI. These images contain special spectral bands and SB; these information should be controlled with the proposed NRFML.

Figure 5.13 also shows that geographical land using latitudinal and longitudinal values selection will be done with setup of experiment. Using these values, selection land can be processed.

In Figure 5.14, NRFML part of the picture, here we can alter the choice trees with legitimate estimations of N and R esteems. In the recreated analyses, the accessible land which can be downloaded on the Google site and MIT information base is chosen as the ground truth picture. The first satellite land picture contains 191 ghastly groups through 1208×307 pixels in every group, and we separate a subimage of size $256 \times 256 \times 10$ in our examination. In our investigations, we mimic two sorts of stripes as per the dissemination of the stripe area in various groups.

To improve the numerical calculation likewise portrayal, the diminish estimations of the MSI are scaled to [0, 1] prior to including stripes. Places of stripes are randomly distributed in every band in this sort of investigation, we pick the satellite image of the subpicture as the ground certainty to incorporate stripes. In distant recognizing imaging structures, there are generally two kinds of stripe racket in an image: periodic stripes in cross-track imaging devices likewise nonintermittent stripes in push-floor brush imaging devices. Figure 5.15 explains that the selection zoomed part from selected land and gives these values from simple images and datasets.

FIGURE 5.13 Selected multispectral satellite image.

FIGURE 5.14 Random forest with segmentation.

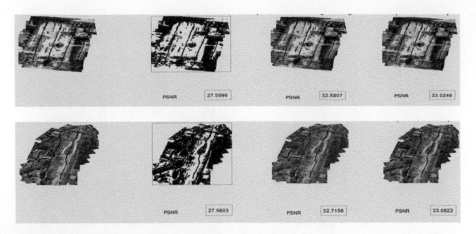

FIGURE 5.15   PSNR values for without process images.

Figure 5.16 shows that the RGB-colored image says that original properties versus trained properties. Also, Figure 5.16b explains the error between original and recovery image.

To reproduce these effects, we, exclusively, consciously the discontinuous additionally nonincidental stripes to the ground-truth picture, likewise the territories of stripes are subjectively circled in each band. To make the situation progressively tangled, the corruption planes of the assorted stripe lines are also exceptional. Together with the intermittent also no occasional stripes are remembered for the going with model subject to the defilement model (5.1). Stripe uproar age: addition stripes to an image is no ifs, ands, or buts an uncovered issue, in the meantime, there is no bound together system, thus we could made stripes ensuing the continuous stripe upheaval ejection composing previously addition bands to the image, we need to choose two pointers: the degree of the stripe an area inside the image (imply r), likewise the force (mean preeminent estimation of pixels) of each stripe line (demonstrate I). The rate r of stripes in the course of action of {0.2, 0.5, 0.8, 0–1} are estimated in our assessment. At that point, the force I of each stripe line in the plan of {0.2, 0.5, 0.8, 0–1} is added to the image. It is critical that $r = 0–1$ addresses that the corruption level of the stripe lines is differing in each band. So additionally, $I = 0–1$ implies that the intensity of each stripe line is randomly passed on. For the benefit of imitating irregular stripes, $r \times 10$ stripe lines in each 10 lines are found at times included into the image, and the power estimation of each stripe line proportional to I. Figure 5.17 details the background and foreground threshold.

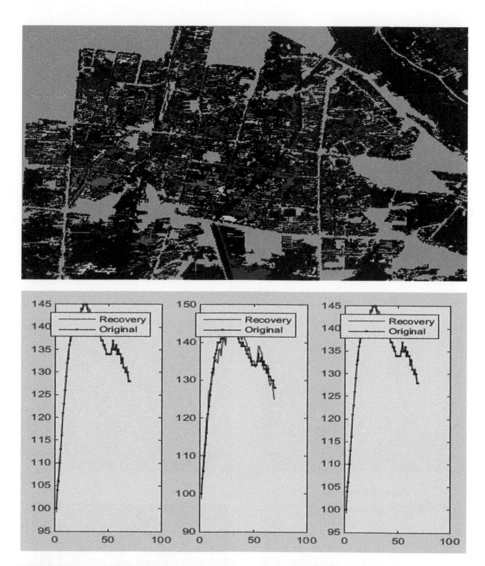

FIGURE 5.16 (a) RGB values applied, (b) recovery and original comparison.

Figures 5.17 and 5.18 explain that original image versus the grayscale image using this we filtered the image using a mean filter adjust the coefficients to sharpen the image properties.

Figure 5.19 explains that locating the road from a satellite multispectral image and highlights the image with color margin manner.

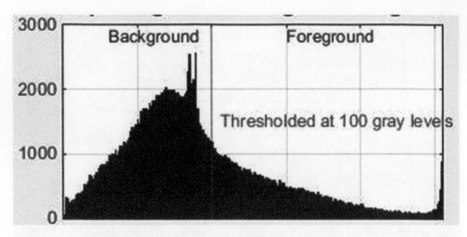

FIGURE 5.17   Background versus foreground threshold.

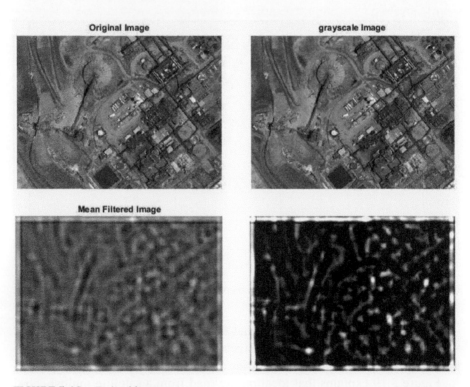

FIGURE 5.18   Trained image.

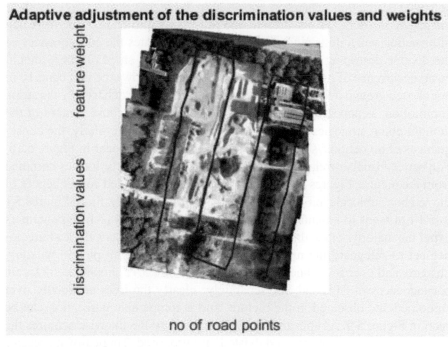

FIGURE 5.19 Road point marking.

$$\text{MPSNR} = \frac{1}{B} \sum_{i=1}^{B} \text{PSNR}_i$$

$$\text{MSSIM} = \frac{1}{B} \sum_{i=1}^{B} \text{SSIM}_i$$

$$\text{MSAM} = \frac{1}{MN} \sum_{i=1}^{MN} \arccos \frac{(\chi^i) \cdot (\hat{\chi}^i)}{\|\chi^i\| \cdot \|\hat{\chi}^i\|}$$

We haphazardly choice $r \times N$ lines in the picture to include stripes aimed at recreating no periodic stripes. Hence, we, individually, reproduce 16 unique belongings for intermittent nonperiodic stripes, which varieties the circumstance progressively convoluted. Visual excellence examination: subsequently there are several corrupted circumstances in our reproduced test, we pick one situation commencing the intermittent stripes also no periodic stripe test on behalf of correlation, separately appeared in Table 5.2. Besides, as a result of the page constraint, we just present one run-of-the-mill band of the recreated information when destriping. Figure 5.11 demonstrates the consequences of the diverse destriping techniques with the occasional stripes if there should be an occurrence of $r = 0.5$ and $I = 0.2$. Figure 5.13 shows the first band 10 in our chosen ground information. The picture is genuinely debased by the stripe commotion, as appeared in Figure 5.14. The destriping consequences of the thought about strategies have appeared in Figure 5.15. Similarly, the consequences of no periodic stripe case ($r = 0.5$ and $I = 0.2$) appear in Figure 5.16. For better visual correlation, we amplify some nitty-gritty locales trimmed from the picture. Figures 5.12 and 5.14 present the amplified consequences of the red box sublocale in Figures 5.15 and 5.17, individually. From Figures 5.1 to 5.14, it tends to remain understood that SPB, SB, also TREES containers expel the majority of the undeniable stripes. Be that as it may, these strategies neglect to safeguard the nitty-gritty data, which results in picture twisting, obscure, and over smoothness. For instance, Figure 5.12 shows the sublocale consequences of SPB and SB, separately; clearly the trees are totally over smoothed and obscured in the picture, and a comparable perception can be seen in Figure 5.9. As appeared in Figures 5.2–5.4, RF likewise acquires the minor mutilation contrasted and existed and proposed. Tragically, it presents some stripe-like relics as appeared in Figure 5.7.

Table 5.2 details the PSNR SSIM ZC values from simulation results. From the consequences of the proposed technique that appeared in Figures 5.11–5.14, it can be obviously observed that the anticipated NRFML model accomplishes the greatest destriping recreation consequences. Specifically, we container watch the prevalence of RF since amplified outcomes, which demonstrate that the proposed NRFML can adequately evacuate stripes and safeguard picture subtleties and structures. The quantitative correlation has appeared in Table 5.3 to further assess the general execution of the proposed technique, we give a quantitative examination for every exploratory case. Meanwhile the ground-truth picture subsists, three measureable files, that is, the mean pinnacle mean peak signal-to-noise ratio, mean spectral angle mapper,[15] and mean unearthly point mapper[16] are utilized in our reproduced trials.

5.6   CONCLUSION

The NRFML technique for multispectral model image compression was suggested in this document. The wavelet transformation is used for effectively

TABLE 5.2 PSNR SSIM ZC Values from Simulation.

Dataset	Threshold value	CR	BPP	PSNR (db)	SSIM	ZC %
Dataset 1	5	3.97	2.24	49.80	0.9998	58.38
	10	4.67	1.87	43.15	0.9971	73.32
	15	4.98	1.27	39.19	0.9962	79.86
	20	5.89	1.16	37.52	0.9860	85.96
	25	5.74	1.11	35.54	0.9852	88.25
Dataset 2	5	4.88	1.72	49.74	0.9975	72.74
	10	5.48	1.43	43.93	0.9968	86.14
	15	5.59	1.39	40.69	0.9957	89.49
	20	5.64	1.37	38.24	0.9906	90.57
	25	5.79	1.29	38.22	0.9887	92.24
Dataset 3	5	4.79	1.89	49.91	0.9993	78.95
	10	4.89	1.72	45.12	0.9966	86.15
	15	5.25	1.48	44.18	0.9943	87.47
	20	5.78	1.43	40.27	0.9915	90.63
	25	5.89	1.39	39.99	0.9883	92.62
Dataset 4	5	4.80	1.97	49.57	0.9985	77.93
	10	4.92	1.76	46.50	0.9956	84.24
	15	5.32	1.67	44.20	0.9934	87.72
	20	5.45	1.58	42.82	0.9901	89.69
	25	5.68	1.34	40.82	0.9864	90.97
Dataset 5	5	4.98	1.77	49.66	0.9982	81.34
	10	5.29	1.66	44.10	0.9965	87.96
	15	5.68	1.56	42.12	0.9944	92.94
	20	5.89	1.49	40.96	0.9923	91.82
	25	5.93	1.37	39.98	0.9902	92.62

TABLE 5.3 Final Comparison.

Dataset	Huffman coding			3-DWT ($T_h = 15$)					Proposed ($T_h = 15$) NRFML			
	CR	BPP	MSE (with PSNR = ∞)	SSIM	CR	BPP	PSNR	SSIM	CR	BPP	PSNR	SSIM
Dataset 1	1.15	6.93	0	1	4.64	1.72	37.18	0.9902	4.98	1.29	39.19	0.9962
Dataset 2	1.33	5.98	0	1	5.47	1.46	40.68	0.9937	5.59	1.39	40.69	0.9957
Dataset 3	1.34	5.96	0	1	5.31	1.50	40.73	0.9946	5.25	1.48	44.18	0.9943
Dataset 4	1.34	5.95	0	1	5.22	1.53	40.20	0.9930	5.32	1.67	44.20	0.9934
Dataset 5	1.41	5.65	0	1	5.48	1.46	41.09	0.9945	5.68	1.56	42.12	0.9944
Avg.	1.31	6.09	0	1	5.22	1.53	39.98	0.9932	5.364	1.47	42.076	0.9948

coding the picture with Huffman coding. A 3D-DWT is used to decompose the image, and after thresholding, the wavelet coefficients are encoded using Huffman encoding. NRFML is used to compress multispectral image and remove the force of the assault. The findings indicate that our suggested technique reduces the complexity of space and spectral redundancy, SB as well as better performance, very effectively. Compression efficiency is ensured by the use of wavelet and Huffman encoding. Our NRFML method has therefore accomplished our goal of near-lossless ownership and therefore our technique boosts the ease of various apps using satellite imagery.

KEYWORDS

- **multispectral image**
- **natural random forest ML (NRFML)**
- **spectral redundancy**
- **sub-bands removal**

REFERENCES

1. Beaumont, G. P. Bivariate Distributions. In *Probability and Random Variables*, 2005. DOI: 10.1533/9780857099471.146.
2. Breiman, L.; Friedman, J. H.; Olshen, R. A.; Stone, C. J. *Classification and Regression Trees. Classification and Regression Trees*, 2017. DOI: 10.1201/9781315139470.
3. Canta, G. R.; Poggi, G. Compression of Multispectral Images by Address-Predictive Vector Quantization. *Signal Process. Imag. Commun.* **1997**. DOI: 10.1016/s0923-5965 (96)00043-4.
4. Chang, L.; Cheng, C. M. Multispectral Image Compression Using Eigen-Region-Based Segmentation. In *International Geoscience and Remote Sensing Symposium*, 2001. DOI: 10.1109/igarss.2001.977091.
5. Daschiel, H.; Datcu, M. Information Mining in Remote Sensing Image Archives: System Evaluation. *IEEE Trans. Geosci. Remote Sens.* **2005**. DOI: 10.1109/TGRS. 2004.838374.
6. Ferecatu, M.; Boujemaa, N. Interactive Remote-Sensing Image Retrieval Using Active Relevance Feedback. *IEEE Trans. Geosci. Remote Sens.* **2007**. DOI: 10.1109/TGRS. 2007.892007.
7. Fürnkranz, J.; Chan, P. K.; Craw, S.; Sammut, C.; Uther, W.; Ratnaparkhi, A.; Jin, X.; et al. Mean Squared Error. In *Encyclopedia of Machine Learning*, 2011. DOI: 10.1007/ 978-0-387-30164-8_528.

8. García, M. J. L.; Caselles, V. Mapping Burns and Natural Reforestation Using Thematic Mapper Data. *Geocarto Int.* **1991**. DOI: 10.1080/10106049109354290.

9. Gleason, S.; Ferrell, R.; Cheriyadat, A.; Vatsavai, R.; De, S. Semantic Information Extraction from Multispectral Geospatial Imagery via a Flexible Framework. In *International Geoscience and Remote Sensing Symposium*, 2010. DOI: 10.1109/IGARSS.2010. 5649141.

10. Heideman, M. T.; Johnson, D. H.; Burrus, C. S. Gauss and the History of the Fast Fourier Transform. *IEEE ASSP Mag.* **1984**. DOI: 10.1109/MASSP.1984.1162257.

11. Jayakar, M.; Anand Babu, K. V. S.; Srinivas, K. Color Image Compression Using SPIHT Algorithm. *Int. J. Comput. Appl.* **2011**. DOI: 10.5120/2023-2728.

12. Jégou, H.; Douze, M.; Schmid, C. Product Quantization for Nearest Neighbor Search. *IEEE Trans. Pattern Anal. Mach. Intell.* **2011**. DOI: 10.1109/TPAMI.2010.57.

13. Johnson, B.; Xie, Z. Unsupervised Image Segmentation Evaluation and Refinement Using a Multi-Scale Approach. *ISPRS J. Photogramm. Remote Sens.* **2011**. DOI: 10.1016/j.isprsjprs.2011.02.006.

14. Johnson, D. Signal-to-Noise Ratio. *Scholarpedia* **2006**. DOI: 10.4249/scholarpedia.2088.

15. Koutsoudis, A.; Vidmar, B.; Ioannakis, G.; Arnaoutoglou, F.; Pavlidis, G.; Chamzas, C. Multi-Image 3D Reconstruction Data Evaluation. *J. Cult. Herit.* **2014**. DOI: 10.1016/j. culher.2012.12.003.

16. Lee, J. Optimized Quadtree for Karhunen-Loeve Transform in Multispectral Image Coding. *IEEE Trans. Imag. Process.* **1999**. DOI: 10.1109/83.753734.

17. Mulla, A.; Baviskar, J.; Baviskar, A.; Warty, C. Image Compression Scheme Based on Zig-Zag 3D-DCT and LDPC Coding. In *Proceedings of the 2014 International Conference on Advances in Computing, Communications and Informatics*, 2014. DOI: 10.1109/ICACCI.2014.6968373.

18. Römpp, A.; Spengler, B. Mass Spectrometry Imaging with High Resolution in Mass and Space. *Histochem. Cell Biol.* **2013**. DOI: 10.1007/s00418-013-1097-6.

19. Shapiro, J. M. An Embedded Hierarchical Image Coder Using Zerotrees of Wavelet Coefficients. In *Data Compression Conference Proceedings*, 1993. DOI: 10.1109/DCC. 1993.253128.

20. Thigpen, J.; Shah, S. K. Multispectral Imaging. In *Microscope Image Processing*, 2008. DOI: 10.1016/B978-0-12-372578-3.00013-1.

21. Tong, X. –Y.; Xia, G. –S.; Hu, F.; Zhong, Y.; Datcu, M.; Zhang, L. Exploiting Deep Features for Remote Sensing Image Retrieval: A Systematic Investigation. *IEEE Trans. Big Data* **2019**. DOI: 10.1109/tbdata.2019.2948924.

22. Tupin, F.; Inglada, J.; Nicolas, J. M. *Remote Sensing Imagery*. Remote Sensing Imagery, 2014. DOI: 10.1002/9781118899106.

23. Uchiyama, T.; Yamaguchi, M.; Ohyama, N.; Mukawa, N.; Kaneko, H. Multispectral Image Retrieval Using Vector Quantization. In *IEEE International Conference on Image Processing*, 2001. DOI: 10.1109/icip.2001.958945.

24. van der Meer, F. D.; van der Werff, H. M. A.; van Ruitenbeek, F. J. A.; Hecker, C. A.; Bakker, W. H.; Noomen, M. F.; van der Meijde, M.; Carranza, E. J. M.; de Smeth, J. B.; Woldai, T. Multi- and Hyperspectral Geologic Remote Sensing: A Review. *Int. J. Appl. Earth Obs. Geoinform.* **2012**. DOI: 10.1016/j.jag.2011.08.002.

25. Verrelst, J.; Rivera, J. P.; Gitelson, A.; Delegido, J.; Moreno, J.; Camps-Valls, G. Spectral Band Selection for Vegetation Properties Retrieval Using Gaussian Processes Regression. *Int. J. Appl. Earth Obs. Geoinform.* **2016**. DOI: 10.1016/j.jag.2016.07.016.

26. Yi, Z.; Zhiguo, C.; Yang, X. Multi-Spectral Remote Image Registration Based on SIFT. *Electron. Lett.* **2008**. DOI: 10.1049/el:20082477.
27. Zheng, Q.; Weng, Q.; Huang, L.; Wang, K.; Deng, J.; Jiang, R.; Ye, Z.; Gan, M. A New Source of Multi-Spectral High Spatial Resolution Night-Time Light Imagery—JL1-3B. *Remote Sens. Environ.* **2018**. DOI: 10.1016/j.rse.2018.06.016.

CHAPTER 6

Learning Spatiotemporal Features for Movie Scene Retrieval Using a 3D Convolutional Autoencoder

VIDIT KUMAR, VIKAS TRIPATHI, and BHASKAR PANT

Department of Computer Science and Engineering, Graphic Era (Deemed to be University), Dehradun, Uttarakhand, India

ABSTRACT

Every year hundreds of TV shows, films, and documentaries with many genres and languages are produced worldwide. Shooting an impressive film scene or TV serial scene for the audience is a challenging task for the director. Having a database of videos from various entertainment sources can help a director or actor to watch similar scenes before the final shooting of their scene. However, searching similar scenes from this database can be a laborious work and time-consuming, even if the database is labeled with some semantic tags. On the other hand, from the users (audiences) point of view, the user can generate a query in form of video to obtain similar scenes he/she wishes to view. In this chapter, we tend to address these problems through content-based search technique using deep learning. Specifically, we propose a convolutional autoencoder deep learning approach to learn the visual features without requiring the labels. We used the Hollywood-2 dataset for evaluation purposes and achieved better results.

Computational Intelligence in Analytics and Information Systems, Volume 1: Data Science and AI, Selected Papers from CIAIS-2021. Hardeo Kumar Thakur, Manpreet Kaur, Parneeta Dhaliwal, Rajeev Kumar Arya, and Joan Lu (Eds.)

6.1 INTRODUCTION

With the technological advances in the entertainment industry, hundreds of TV shows and movies are made every year. Making film is a complex process that involves multiple stages from initial thought to writing, shooting and editing, and other development stages. After the script of the film is written, a director is assigned to direct the film. The director is the person most responsible for the film's productivity on the set as the director is the only person who imagines the story and works with the actors and technical staff accordingly.[1] When shooting a particular scene, directors usually adopt a dynamic script as the scene may change with the available budget or other environmental factors. Making a scene original while making it effective for the audience is a challenging task for a director. By looking at scenes similar to those from previous sources, directors can adapt it to their scene to create impressive scene. However, searching similar scenes from unlabeled database is a time-consuming and laborious task. Furthermore, creating a database of such videos with appropriate labels is expensive because it requires labeling each scene of the film. On the other hand, when the users wish to watch other similar clips related to a particular clip, they can generate a query to retrieve similar scenes. To solve these problems, a robust content-based search technique is required and an unsupervised methodology is also needed to learn visual features. To this end, in this paper, we propose a deep learning based framework for movie scene retrieval (see Figure 6.1). More specifically, we propose a 3D convolutional autoencoder to learn visual features from unlabeled movies clips. After that these features are used for scene representation and retrieval of similar videos. Our main contributions are as follows:

- We propose an unsupervised learning approach to learn spatiotemporal features for movie clips.
- We design an efficient 3D convolutional autoencoder for fast encoding.
- We validate the learned features in the Hollywood-2 dataset via the nearest neighbor task.

6.2 RELATED WORK

Image retrieval has received a lot of research in past decades,[2,3] but not enough attention has been paid to video retrieval. There are some efforts done related to recommendation and genre classification, like Zhou et al.[4] proposed the framework for movie genre classification which is based on bag of visual word model. Yang at et al.[5] used a fusion of multiple features (such as textual, visual, and auditory) for video recommendation. Rasheed et al.[6] exploit visual cues in the form of color variance and motion for the movie genre classification task. Deldjoo et al.[7] proposed a recommender system based on visual cues (lighting, color, and motion). Wang Fangshi et al.[8] compute features based on feature differences between adjacent two frames. Yoo et al.[9] exploit various dynamic and visual features with a genetic algorithm for interactive movie scene retrieval. Muneesawang et al.[10] proposed the fusion-based approach to retrieval of movie clips. They exploit both audio and visual features. However, all these techniques rely on hand-design features. Further, Deldjoo[11] used deep features along with hand-crafted features based on color and texture. Portillo-Quintero et al.[12] exploit image-text model to extract video representation. Bain et al.[13] presented the text to video retrieval approach that combines the speech, text, and visual clues to represent the video. In addition, Kumar et al.[14,15] exploit CNN and LSTM in supervised way for video representation. There is also work on movie clip retrieval[16] which is based on unsupervised approach. However, they used pretrained CNN for feature extraction. These CNNs are trained on large-scale dataset (e.g., Imagenet). When considering videos, massively labeled datasets can be expensive to create (requiring high labor cost). One effective solution is to learn representation from freely unlabeled videos in an unsupervised way. In this regard, the author of ref.[17] deals with unsupervised learning of video features. Further[18] use proxy-based task to learn video representations.

6.3 METHOD

The proposed framework is illustrated in Figure 6.1. First unlabeled training video sequences are sampled from the training set and fed to the network to learn encodings. After that indexing is done based on learned features. Then retrieval is done by matching query features to a gallery set of features using cosine distance. Next, we first describe the basics of autoencoder then we will discuss our method to learn features.

6.3.1 PRELIMINARIES

Autoencoder is the type of neural network that consists of encoder and decoder, which aims to learn low-dimensional encoding in unsupervised manner. It works by encoding the data to some low dimensional and then decoding back to match the input. Let x be the input, the encoder E encodes the input x as $h = \delta\,(W_E x)$, where h is low-dimensional feature, W_E refers to weights of the encoder, and δ is a activation function. Then, the decoder D reconstructs the input from h as $x' = \delta'\,(W_D h)$. Then the autoencoder is trained to minimize the loss $L(x, x') = \|x' - x\|^2$. The vanilla autoencoder works well with $1 \times N$ vectors but it is difficult to extract discriminative features from $M \times N$ images with basic autoencoder. One method is to stretch out $M \times N$ matrix to obtain $1 \times MN$ vector, and fed to autoencoder. However, this loses the spatial information contained in the image. This issue can be resolve by using convolutions in the encoder and decoder. Further, to encode a variety of features, multiple convolutional layers can be added to the encoder.

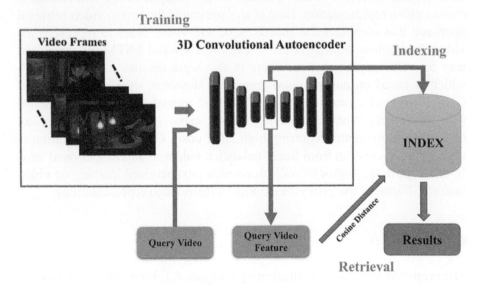

FIGURE 6.1   Overview of the proposed framework for movie scene retrieval.

6.3.2   3D-CONVOLUTIONAL AUTOENCODER (3D-CA)

With the similar motive of autoencoder, the convolutional autoencoder consists of convolutional layers for encoding and transposing convolutional layers for decoding. Convolutional layers are responsible for extracting spatial features while reducing spatial resolution of the input using a kernel with some stride, whereas transpose convolutional layers are responsible for upscaling the input while reconstructing the ground truth spatial content.

Figure 6.2 depicts the general convolutional autoencoder architecture. To learn unsupervised spatiotemporal features, we design our network as input, conv3d_1 (3,3,3/64), conv3d_2 (3,3,3/128), conv3d_3 (3,3,3/256), fc-1024, fc-25088, reshape, Tconv3d_1 (3,3,3/128), Tconv3d_2 (3,3,3/64), Tconv3d_3 (3,3,3/3). The layer conv3d_1 (3,3,3/64) represents the 3d convolutional layer with a kernel size of $3 \times 3 \times 3$ with 64 kernels. The Tconv3d_1 (3,3,3/128) represents the 3d transpose convolutional layer with a kernel size of $3 \times 3 \times 3$ with 128 kernels. Table 6.1 reports the parameter details of our 3D-CA. Each convolutional and transpose convolutional layer is followed by batch normalization and leaky relu. Each convolutional layer in encoder downsamples its input by half reaching to $7 \times 7 \times 256 \times 2$ size. And, in similar way each transpose convolutional layer in decoder upsamples its input by double reaching back to network's input size. All upsampling and downsampling are done with appropriate padding. We train our 3D-CA with back-propagation with a mean square error objective as follows:

$$L(I,I') = \frac{1}{K}\sum_{k=1}^{K}\frac{1}{M \times N \times C \times F}\sum_{f=1}^{f=F}\sum_{c=1}^{c=C}\sum_{n=1}^{n=N}\sum_{m=1}^{m=M}\left(I_{ijk} - I'_{ijk}\right)^2, \qquad (6.1)$$

where $I \in R^{M \times N \times C \times F}$ is input, $I' \in R^{M \times N \times C \times F}$ is reconstructed version, M is height, N is width, C is channel, F denotes the number of frames, and K is minibatch size.

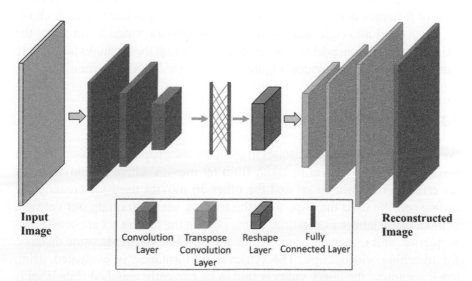

Input Image

Convolution Layer

Transpose Convolution Layer

Reshape Layer

Fully Connected Layer

Reconstructed Image

FIGURE 6.2 General convolutional autoencoder network architecture.

TABLE 6.1   3D-CA Architecture and Parameters.

Layer	Kernel size/stride	Output size
Input	–	$56 \times 56 \times 3 \times 8$
Conv3d_1	3,3,3/2,2,2	$28 \times 28 \times 64 \times 4$
Conv3d_2	3,3,3/2,2,1	$14 \times 14 \times 128 \times 4$
Conv3d_3	3,3,3/2,2,2	$7 \times 7 \times 256 \times 2$
Fc1	1024	$1 \times 1 \times 1024$
Fc2	25088	$1 \times 1 \times 25088$
Reshape	–	$7 \times 7 \times 256 \times 2$
Tconv3d_1	3,3,3/2,2,2	$14 \times 14 \times 128 \times 4$
Tconv3d_2	3,3,3/2,2,1	$28 \times 28 \times 64 \times 4$
Tconv3d_3	3,3,3/2,2,2	$56 \times 56 \times 3 \times 8$

6.3.3   IMPLEMENTATION

Training deep autoencoders is time-consuming task. To speed up the learning of 3D-CA, the input size is set to $56 \times 56 \times 3 \times 8$, where 56×56 is spatial resolution, 8 is number of frames, and 3 is channel representing an RGB frame. We set the temporal stride 2. For data-augmentation, we perform random cropping and random horizontal flipping to the sample resized to 64 (to shorter side) from 240×320 sized clip. Learning rate set to 0.001 for 70 epochs and thereby decrease with factor 1/2 every 40 epochs. Minibatch size is set to 64 clips of 8 frames and Adam optimizer is used. During inference, each clip is evenly divided into eight frames chunks with temporal stride 2 and fed to the trained model, the encoder outputs are averaged across these chunks to compute feature for the complete video. Figure 6.3 shows the loss during training.

6.4   EXPERIMENTAL SETTINGS

We choose Hollywood-2[19] dataset to evaluate the proposed approach, which consists of 1707 video clips taken from 69 movies where 33 movies used for creating the training set and the other 36 movies used for creating the testing set. We used the clips from the training set for training our network without using labels. For testing, all the clips in the testing set are considered as queries, and retrieval is done on the training set. We used cosine distance for matching video clips. The retrieval performance is evaluated using top-k accuracy: the query video is said to be correctly matched if its label is matched within top-k nearest neighbor's labels. Then mean over all queries is computed to output final accuracy. The proposed approach is evaluated on MATLAB with Nvidia tesla k40c gpu.

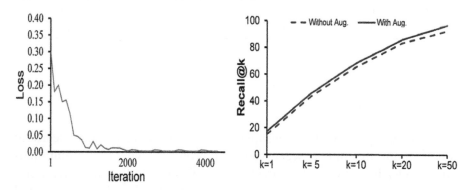

FIGURE 6.3   (Left) Training loss curve. (Right) Effect of data augmentation on retrieval accuracy.

6.5   RESULTS

First, we analyze the effect of data augmentation on retrieval accuracy. For this, we test the system under two variations: with augmentation (spatial and temporal cropping, flipping; refer to Section 6.3.3) and without augmentation. The result is depicted in Figure 6.3, where we can see a slight improvement with data augmentation. Next, we compare our 3D convolutional autoencoder with its 2D variant of input size of 56 × 56 × 3. We report the results in Table 6.2, where we can see that 3D variant is more powerful to represent the videos than 2D variant. From $k = 1$ to 50, 3D-CA performance is far higher than 2D-CA.

TABLE 6.2   Top-k Accuracy (%) on Hollywood-2.

	$k = 1$	$k = 5$	$k = 10$	$k = 20$	$k = 50$
2D-CA	14.54	43.54	64.54	79.54	94.83
3D-CA	17.18	45.68	68.31	85.80	96.48

We also compare our method with other unsupervised methods, that is, 3dRotNet[20] and reported in Table 6.3. 3dRotNet was build using resnet architecture to learn spatiotemporal features by predicting rotations. For fair comparison, we make 3dRotNet using encoder part of 3D-CA and learn features by predicting four rotations: 0°, 90°, 180°, and 270°. It can be notice that our method performs better than[20], which proves the effectiveness of our approach.

TABLE 6.3   Comparison with 3dRotNet.

	$k = 1$	$k = 5$	$k = 10$	$k = 20$	$k = 50$
3dRotNet[20]	16.15	44.12	65.74	83.43	95.19
3D-CA	17.18	45.68	68.31	85.80	96.48

6.6   CONCLUSION

This chapter presented an unsupervised video representation learning approach for the movie scene retrieval problem, where convolutional-autoencoder is exploited to learn features. To encode the spatialtemporal features 3d convolution is used in the encoder and decoder. The learned features are matched using cosine distance for retrieval. The experimental results demonstrated the effectiveness of the proposed methodology. This also suggests that learning unsupervised features from cheap unlabeled videos are a promising approach to deal with the need of large labeled data. Future works will include to make network deeper, using larger dataset, and exploring other unsupervised ideas in context of movie clip representation.

KEYWORDS

- **convolutional autoencoder**
- **movie clip search**
- **unsupervised learning**
- **video retrieval**

REFERENCES

1. Mackendrick, A; Cronin P. On Film-Making: An Introduction to the Craft of the Director. *Cinéaste* **2005,** *30,* 46–54.
2. Zhou, W.; Li, H.; Tian, Q. Recent Advance in Content-Based Image Retrieval: A Literature Survey, 2017. arXiv preprint arXiv:1706.06064
3. Kumar, V.; Tripathi, V.; Pant, B. Content Based Fine-Grained Image Retrieval Using Convolutional Neural Network. In *7th International Conference on Signal Processing and Integrated Networks (SPIN)*, 2020; pp 1120–1125.

4. Zhou, H.; Hermans, T.; Karandikar, A. V.; Rehg., J. M. Movie Genre Classification via Scene Categorization. In *Proceedings of the 18th ACM International Conference on Multimedia*, 2010; pp 747–750.

5. Yang, B.; Mei, T.; Hua, X. S.; Yang, L.; Yang, S. Q.; Li, M. Online Video Recommendation Based on Multimodal Fusion and Relevance Feedback. In *Proceedings of the 6th ACM International Conference on Image and Video Retrieval*, 2007; pp 73–80.

6. Rasheed, Z.; Sheikh, Y.; Shah, M. On the Use of Computable Features for Film Classification. *IEEE Trans. Circ. Syst. Video Technol.* **2005**, *15*, 52–64.

7. Deldjoo, Y.; Elahi, M.; Cremonesi, P.; Garzotto, F.; Piazzolla, P.; Quadrana, M. Content-Based Video Recommendation System Based on Stylistic Visual Features. *J. Data Semant.* **2016**, *5*, 99–113.

8. Fangshi, W.; De, X.; Weixin, W. A Cluster Algorithm of Automatic Key Frame Extraction Based on Adaptive Threshold. *J. Comput. Res. Dev.* **2005**, *10*.

9. Yoo, H. W. Retrieval of Movie Scenes by Semantic Matrix and Automatic Feature Weight Update. *Expert Syst. Appl.* **2008**, *34*, 2382–2395.

10. Muneesawang, P., Guan, L.; Amin, T. A New Learning Algorithm for the Fusion of Adaptive Audio–Visual Features for the Retrieval and Classification of Movie Clips. *J. Sig. Process. Syst.* **2010**, *59*, 177–188.

11. Deldjoo, Y.; Quadrana, M.; Elahi, M.; Cremonesi, P. Using Mise-En-Scene Visual Features Based on Mpeg-7 and Deep Learning for Movie Recommendation, 2017. arXiv preprint arXiv:1704.06109.

12. Portillo-Quintero, J. A.; Ortiz-Bayliss, J. C.; Terashima-Marín, H. A Straightforward Framework for Video Retrieval Using CLIP, 2021. arXiv preprint arXiv:2102.12443.

13. Bain, M.; Nagrani, A.; Brown, A.; Zisserman, A. Condensed Movies: Story Based Retrieval with Contextual Embeddings. In *Proceedings of the Asian Conference on Computer Vision*, 2020.

14. Kumar, V.; Tripathi, V.; Pant, B. Content Based Movie Scene Retrieval Using Spatio-Temporal Features. *Int. J. Eng. Adv. Technol.* **2019**, *9*, 1492–1496.

15. Kumar, V.; Tripathi, V.; Pant, B. Learning Compact Spatio-Temporal Features for Fast Content Based Video Retrieval. *Int. J. Innov. Technol. Explor. Eng.* **2019**, *9*, 2402–2409.

16. Zou, L.; Jin, X.; Wei, B. Film Clips Retrieval Using Image Queries. *Multimed. Tools Appl.* **2020**, *79*, 14725–14732.

17. Buchler, U.; Brattoli, B.; Ommer, B. Improving Spatiotemporal Self-Supervision by Deep Reinforcement Learning. In *Proceedings of the European Conference on Computer Vision (ECCV)*, 2018; pp 770–786.

18. Xu, D.; Xiao, J.; Zhao, Z.; Shao, J.; Xie, D.; Zhuang, Y. Self-Supervised Spatiotemporal Learning via Video Clip Order Prediction. In *Proceedings of the IEEE Conference on Computer Vision and Pattern Recognition*, 2019; pp 10334–10343.

19. Marszalek, M.; Laptev, I.; Schmid, C. Actions in Context. In *2009 IEEE Conference on Computer Vision and Pattern Recognition*, 2009; pp 2929–2936.

20. Jing, L., Yang, X., Liu, J., Tian, Y. Self-Supervised Spatiotemporal Feature Learning via Video Rotation Prediction, 2018. arXiv preprint arXiv:1811.11387.

CHAPTER 7

Person Reidentification Using Deep Learning and Neural Networks

PARNEETA DHALIWAL, RIYA SAPR, RISHABH DHIMAN, and
ABHYUDAY GUPTA

*Department of Computer Science & Technology, Manav Rachna University,
Faridabad, Haryana, India*

ABSTRACT

In today's society, safety and security have become an indispensable suite
of services for our lives. In this paper, we introduce a significant topic
of research which is Person Re-Identification (Re-ID) that might play an
important role in forensic and security applications. Person Re-ID is the task
of retrieving the identity of an individual from a given gallery of images
that are captured by multiple surveillance cameras employed across different
locations forming a wide disjoint view. Despite many progressive works
already being accomplished in this field, it remains an open-world problem
due to difficulties like lighting, occlusion, background clutter. Our research
focus is on studying the use of deep learning techniques like Neural Nets or
Conv Nets to help in Person Re-ID. We will review the various state-of-the-
art methods that use deep learning techniques for Person Re-ID.

7.1 INTRODUCTION

Person Re-identification (Re-ID) refers to matching together identity classes
of individual images from disjoint camera views employed in public open

Computational Intelligence in Analytics and Information Systems, Volume 1: Data Science and AI,
Selected Papers from CIAIS-2021. Hardeo Kumar Thakur, Manpreet Kaur, Parneeta Dhaliwal,
Rajeev Kumar Arya, and Joan Lu (Eds.)

areas for surveillance purposes.[1] It is a highly challenging task owing to factors like body pose, illumination, background clutter, angle of images, etc. that can change the visual appearance of a person drastically.[2]

During Person Re-ID, a camera captures an image of an individual whose identity needs to be matched. A Re-ID system performs person segmentation and then symmetrically partitions the image of the person, extracting important appearance signatures. These extracted signatures are matched with those found in other images that either be captured from a different camera or might be part of a gallery setting. The signature-matching system successfully identifies the captured individual.

The Person Re-ID systems provide us with a lot of forensic and security applications involving from multi-camera tracking of suspected persons to tacking down their possible trajectories of motion.[5] It can help authorities to identify run-away criminals or even match those trying to flee the crime scene.

Present ways to deal with the Re-ID problems depend on either the extraction of features that are invariant to the normal wellsprings of variety[6,7] or the utilization of supervised learning to find the most important data for matching images.[8,9] Each one of these methodologies has its downsides: invariant element extraction algorithms might be planned depending on instinct[10] or utilizing a material science-based model[11] of the anticipated variety. As both physically based models and hand-created feature extraction algorithms depend on human judgment, they might not be able to catch a portion of the unpretentious, yet conceivably essential, parts of the information. Also, with learning-put together methodologies that depend on pre-set-up features, a substantial number of parameters may be gotten the hang of, prompting overfitting, because of the little size of the training sets accessible for this issue.[12,13] Their execution may likewise be unequivocally identified with the picked pre-set-up features and not be reproducible with other types of potentially informational collections.[14]

In the paper, we provide a literature or background review of the existing techniques for Person Re-ID in Section 7.2. In Section 7.3, we have performed a comparative analysis of various Person Re-ID techniques. Section 7.4 deals with the advantages and disadvantages of using CNN for Person Re-ID. Various applications of Person Re-ID are explored in Section 7.5. In the following section, we conclude the paper and present ideas for future research work.

7.2 RELATED WORK

Our problem statement is to identify a single person from a gallery of images of supposedly the same individuals captured by different cameras. Various types of state-of-the-art techniques have been worked upon to solve the Re-ID problem. Some notable works include the use of deep learning techniques to tackle the situation. These include the use of Deep Neural Networks or Deep Convolutional Networks for matching purposes. Convolutional neural networks (CNN) are a class of deep neural networks most commonly applied for analyzing visual imagery.[15] CNNs use a variation of multilayer perceptron designed to require minimal preprocessing.[16,17] Some works also put forth the idea of using Convolutional Similarity Networks and Similarity Guided Graph Neural Network.

ConvNet, the deep learning architecture of convolutional neural networks, is made of input, output, and many hidden layers. These hidden layers comprise activation function, pooling layers, fully connected layers, and normalization layers.[18,19] Following are several works related to our problem statement based on deep learning.

7.2.1 DEEP LEARNING MULTI-SCALE REPRESENTATIONS

Yanbei Chen et al's research put forth DPFL (Deep Pyramid Feature Learning) CNN architecture that implements a closed-loop design.[20] It contains m number of scale-specific feature learning branches and also consists of one multi-scale feature fusion branch. Each branch is trained simultaneously by the same id class label. In the end fusion branch tries to learn consensus on identity taking into account all m scales. This approach is called consensus learning. The learning is then back propagated to every scale branch simultaneously to control iterative learning behavior.[20]

7.2.2 DEEP CONVNETS WITH MULTI-TASK LEARNING

Niall McLaughlin, Jesus Martinez del Rincon, and Paul Miller put forth Siamese network architecture[23,24] for a Deep CNN training to extract useful features for the task of Person Re-ID. The system implemented multi-task learning. The proposal works by training CNN to produce a low-dimensional representation of person input pictures wherein the images belonging to the same person are located closely in feature-space, whereas those of dissimilar or different persons are mapped onto a different location. The model is trained using a wide set of images to let the NN learn cues indicating whether the concerned person in an image is the same or not.[14] The system used SoftMax classification.

7.2.3   MULTI-INSTANCE LEARNING

Domonkos Varga and Tamás Szirányi's work proposed a model which consisted of two Convolutional Neural Networks having similar structure and also sharing the same parameters.[27] The architecture comprises five convolutional layers following which we have a max-pooling operator, Then, we have a single concatenation layer succeeded by two fully connected layers. Convolution layers utilize filters of sizes 5×5 and 3×3 respectively. The model uses ReLU[28] as an activation function. The overall structure of the proposed work is a Siamese structure using two CNN incorporating multi-scale convolution.[29]

7.2.4   INEXACT MATCHING IN DEEP NN

A. Subramaniam, M. Chatterjee, and A. Mittal put forth two novel CNN-based models for Person Re-ID, respectively.[32] Both have Sia-mese architecture that takes as input two images and output probability of both beings of the same individual.

The Normalized X-corr model consists of tied conv layers followed by a normalized corr layer that captures the similarity of two input images. Following up we have cross patch feature aggregation layers that are used to take into account extra information from local neighborhood pixels. In the end, we have fully connected layers, the output of the model is given by two SoftMax units, one indicating the likelihood of similarity and later for dissimilarity.

In the second CNN-based fused model, the idea fuses state-of-the-art matching techniques[33] with normalized X corr. The idea of the motivation behind this was to reap benefits from both models. With effective training, both the fused components can learn complementary patterns from data.[32]

7.2.5   MASK-BASED DEEP RANKING NEURAL NETWORK

Work by Lei Qui, Yinguan Shi, Yang Gao et al proposed for an image segmentation deep NN to be utilized to extract person foreground removing the background. Following which model has a feature-fusing layer that is used to merge and capture robust person representation. In the end, it has a ranking loss used to optimize the network. It is used to rank images of a person with a matching identity at the top of the training batch.[35]

7.2.6   MULTI-LEVEL SIMILARITY USING CSN

Yiluan Guo and Ngai-Man Cheung put forth the idea of using a CSN (Convolution Similarity Network). CSN so proposed is used to measure similarity between two inputs.[37] Suppose two images namely I1 and I2 are fed to 3 successive convolution layers. The outputs from the second and third are further input to two CSNs. The CSN has two output-sets—one is a similarity score and the other is a feature map for captured/extracted local parts of two original input images.[37] There are three more conv layers that further process similarity score maps. The idea here is to place identical pair of images closer in embedding space.

7.2.7   RE-ID USING DEEP SGGNN

Yantao Shen et al put forth an approach of using an SGGNN (Similarity Guided Graph Neural Network)[40] for person Re-ID task. Given a test picture and a few gallery pictures, SGGNN[40] makes a graph representing the pairwise connections between the test display sets (nodes) and uses such connections to refresh the test-gallery connection in an end-to-end manner. Exact likeness estimation can be accomplished by utilizing such updated relations for future predictions.[25]

7.2.8   PEDESTRIAN MONITORING USING DEEP NN

Wenzheng Qu et al put forth a six-component scalable network architecture.[25] Firstly, there is a 2-layer-tied conv structure that uses 20 of 5*5*3 filters for calculating high-order features. It is followed by a second-tied conv structure that uses 25 of 5*5*20 filters for obtaining the feature maps. Both tied-layers are followed by max-pool layers. After this, there is a cross input neighborhood difference structure[25] that compares between adjacent feature maps. In success to this, there is a patch summary feature whose function is to obtain the overall difference. The penultimate component focuses on the learning of neighborhood difference spatial relationships. At the end we get a full connection.

7.2.9   ATTENTION DRIVEN PERSON RE-ID

The proposed methodology by Fan Yang et al was to use an attention-driven network.[4] With a person's image as an input, using pose estimation they determined an aligned complete body image along with four body part images. Further five intra-attention networks having shared lower convolutional layers map input image to differentiating features supervised by independent SoftMax classification loss. After this, an inter-attention module is trained that fuses the outputs from the previous five nets under relevancy in feature matching.[4]

7.2.10   JOINT VERIFICATION AND IDENTIFICATION OF IDENTITY ATTRIBUTE LABELS

Shun Zhang et al were inspired by the methodologies that extracted discriminative features of varied body parts of every person, thus they put forth a part-based deep CNN[31] for extracting global and local image features.[31] The backbone of their proposed architecture was the ResNet-50 model. The parts following the block res_conv4_1 were divided into global and part branch, both were trained to learn three functions at the same time: person identification, person verification along with attribute identification.[31] Every connected feature is then joined as a final feature for extracting global and local information.

7.3   COMPARATIVE STUDY

The training was performed with Visual Person Detection Made Reliable (VIPeR)[3] that contains two cameras, each for capturing the viewpoint image per person. CUHK Face Sketch (CUFS)[21] was used for research on face sketch synthesis and face sketch recognition. Person R-ID Dataset (PRID-2011)[22] was used that consists of images extracted from multiple person trajectories recorded from two different, static surveillance cameras. The images from these cameras contain a viewpoint change and a stark difference in illumination, background, and camera characteristics. iLIDS Video re-IDentification (iLIDS-VID)[26] comprises image sequences of distinct individuals, with one pair of image sequences from two camera views of each person's data sets.

In the preparation procedure of the Multi-instance Learning approach,[29] Do-monkos Varga utilized SGD with a starting learning rate of 0.01. On the off chance that the preparation misfortune stops decreasing, we divide the learning rate by 10. Do-monkos experimental results showed that their methodology outperformed state-of-the-art algorithms. From experimental analysis, multi-task learning using deep ConvNets[14] was able to state that a convolutional connect with a basic design can be prepared to perform individual Re-ID at state-of-the-art levels. It also demonstrated that the system can precisely do ordering ascribes identified with apparel, posture, and sex, from a solitary full self-perception, which could have applications autonomous of individual reidentification. The multi-level similarity CSN model[34] accomplishes the best top-1 exactness for CUHK03 recognized datasets, outflanking every one of the techniques by an enormous edge. On the three datasets, this model yields results in execution practically identical to the condition of other state-of-the-art methods with smaller model size and fewer calculations.[34]

Mask-based architecture[35] proved that deep learning techniques have better execution over the existing methods. Performance fluctuates on various datasets with better execution accomplished on a huge scale dataset.[35]

Pedestrian Monitoring[38] using a six-component network by Wenzhung Qu et al was tested using the single-shot setting method on the CUHK03-labeled dataset. The accuracies so obtained by the team are specified in the given table. Attention-driven Person Re-ID architecture[39] accounted for superior robustness and effectiveness.

Table 7.1 lists the comparative study of results achieved by different techniques used in Person Re-ID, frameworks, or methodologies as discussed in the previous section. We will look at the different results achieved on different datasets that we have mentioned above.

7.4 ADVANTAGES AND DISADVANTAGES

Person Re-ID systems with the help of CNN give us major advantages over old techniques that use Neural Nets. It allows us to minimize chances of

TABLE 7.1 Comparative Study of Person Re-ID Techniques.

Technique	Dataset	Result
Deep Learning Multi-Scale Representation[1]	Market-1501	DPFL
		Single Query Multi Query
		rank-1 mAP rank-1 mAP
		87.60 73.50 91.20 79.30
	DukeMTMC-reID	rank-1 mAP
		78.20 62.60
	CUHK03	Labeled Detected
		rank-1 mAP rank-1 mAP
		85.70 80.80 83.00 79.10
Deep ConvNets with Multi-Task Learning[14]	Train Test	CMC
		1 5 10 20
	iLIDS VIPeR	12.51 – 32.42 45.08
	VIPeR PRID	8.80 20.50 24.80 34.40
	PRID VIPeR	11.90 – 27.20 39.69
	CUHK PRID	10.00 22.30 32.30 41.00
Multi-Instance Learning[29]		rank-1 rank-5 rank-10 rank-20
	VIPeR	30.70 59.10 73.30 87.40
	ETHZ	79.90 90.80 92.80 98.80
Inexact Matching in Deep NN[32]		rank 1 rank 10 rank 20
	CUHK03 Fused	71.42 94.50 99.40
	Norm-X-corr	65.83 93.70 95.77

TABLE 7.1 (Continued)

Technique	Dataset		Result		
	CUHK01	Fused	80.22	96.30	99.60
		Norm-X-corr	78.43	95.60	97.40
	QMUL GRID	Fused	18.20	54.60	65.20
		Norm-X-corr	17.00	41.00	54.30
Mask-based Deep Ranking Neural Network[35]	Duke MTMC-reID	rank-1	mAP		
		83.06	78.63		
	Market-1501	Single Query		Multi Query	
		rank-1	mAP	rank-1	mAP
		91.36	87.23	93.60	91.10
Multi-Level Similarity using CSN[37]		CMC			
		top-1	top-1	top-10	
	CUHK03 (detected)	85.42	96.40	98.10	
	CUHK03 (labeled)	86.40	96.85	98.44	
	CUHK01	87.20	99.20	98.34	
	VIPeR	49.11	74.10	85.35	
Re-ID using Deep SGGNN[40]		mAP	top-1	top-5	top-10
	CUHK03	93.30	96.40	98.10	98.50
	Market-1501	81.70	91.20	97.10	98.40
	DukeMTMC	69.30	82.10	89.40	92.30
Pedestrian Monitoring using Deep NN[25]	CUHK03	rank-1	rank-10	rank-20	
		75.00	96.30	98.50	

TABLE 7.1 *(Continued)*

Technique	Dataset	Result		
		R1	R5	R10	mAP
Attention Driven Person Re-ID[4]	Market-1501	93.89	97.23	98.10	85.46
Joint Verification and Identification of Attribute Labels[31]	Duke MTMC-reID	mode	top-1	mAP	
		No re-ranking algorithm	82.20	81.20	
		Best performance	86.70	84.80	

error in confirming the identity of a person thus giving us more success rate in security applications. CNNs are very good feature extractors and are motivated by the fact of feature learning.[36] Another primary element of CNNs is weight sharing. Let's take a guide to clarify this. Let's assume you have a one-layered CNN with 10 filters of size 5×5. Presently, you can just figure parameters of such a CNN, it would be 5*5*10 weighs and 10 biases, that is, 5* 5*10 + 10 = 260 parameters. CNNs[36] thus have less complexity and more memory-saving capacity as compared to the NN.[36]

Apart from various advantages, ConvNets have certain limitations also. CNN requires large training data related to an individual to remember a specific human face,[30,46] thus making deep CNN difficult to train. Another limitation is that pixel-level information can get destroyed because of pooling functions.[42] In the event one does not have a decent GPU, CNN is slow to train (for complex undertakings)[43] and has a higher computational expense.[43]

7.5 APPLICATIONS

Reidentifying individuals deal with matching pictures of the same individual over numerous nonoverlapping camera angles. It is pertinent to follow a specific individual over these cameras, following the direction of an individual, observation, and for legal and security applications.[81] Multi-camera tracking[82] is one of the major applications of CNN. An individual can be identified by a camera using the data it retrieves from another camera, thus making it possible to track down a person using a large number of cameras.[41] Tracking the trajectory[41] is yet another major application, given camera locations, we can redraw an individual movement from place to place. Surveillance and security[41] are the most important application of our problem statement. It can help us to identify suspects or even criminals trying to flee the crime scene.[41]

7.6 CONCLUSION AND FUTURE WORK

In this paper, we have discussed various techniques for Person Re-ID. With increasing demands of public safety, there has been an increase in demands to implement systems that can ensure to do the same. Today Person Re-Identification through image capturing or by video surveillance has become the foremost and the most popular way to ensure safety. Combining the above process with convolutional neural networks and deep learning mechanisms has helped to improve current technology far beyond and help us tackle various challenges that come with it.

In the future, we shall work on a unique methodology to achieve the goal of Person Re-ID. Our idea is to combine the concept of big data along with this task. By using the Hadoop big data framework, we wish to process the data received from camera modules and then use our proposed deep neural network architecture to detect the identity of a captured person. We wish to implement the concept of horizontal scaling to manage our dataset efficiently. Using such a framework will not only make our proposed architecture more scalable, but also make the entire system fault-tolerant. Despite so many works that have already been accomplished in this field, Person Re-ID remains an open area for further research.

KEYWORDS

- **person re-identification**
- **deep learning**
- **pattern recognition**
- **ConvNets**
- **neural network**

REFERENCES

1. Chen, Y.; Zhu, X.; Gong, S. (). Person Re-Identification by Deep Learning Multi-Scale Representations. In *2017 IEEE International Conference on Computer Vision Workshop 2590–2600*, 2017. DOI: 10.1109/ICCVW.2017.304.
2. Gong, M. C.; Yan, S.; Loy, C. C. *Person Re-identification*; Springer, 2014.
3. http://robustsystems.coe.neu.edu/sites/robustsystems.coe.neu.edu/files/systems/projectpages/reiddataset.html#:~:text=VIPeR%20%5Blink%5D,viewpoint%20angle%20of%20each%20image.
4. Yang, F.; Yan, K.; Lu, S.; Jia, H.; Xie, X.; Gao, W. Attention Driven Person Re-identification. *Pattern Recognit.* **2018,** *86.* DOI: 10.1016/j.patcog.2018.08.015.
5. Kviatkovsky, A. A.; Rivlin, E. Color Invariants for Person Re-identification. *IEEE Trans. Pattern Anal. Mach. Intell.* **2013,** *35* (7), 1622–1634. http://rose1.ntu.edu.sg/PersonReId/
6. Land, E. H.; McCann, J. J. Lightness and Retinex theory. *J. Opt. Soc. Am.* **1971,** *61* (1), 1–11.
7. Weinberger, K. Q.; Blitzer, J.; Saul, L. K. Distance Metric Learning for Large Margin Nearest Neighbor Classification. *Proc. Adv. Neural Inf. Process. Syst.* **2005,** 1473–1480.

8. Zheng, W. -S.; Gong, S.; Xiang, T. Reidentification by Relative Distance Comparison. *IEEE Trans. Pattern Anal. Mach. Intell.* **2013,** *35* (3), 653–668.

9. Farenzena, M.; Bazzani, L.; Perina, A.; Murino, V.; Cristani, M. Person Re-Identification by Symmetry-Driven Accumulation of Local Features. In *Proceedings of the IEEE Conference on CVPR*, Jun, 2010; pp 2360–2367.

10. Land, E. H.; McCann, J. J. Lightness and Retinex Theory. *J. Opt. Soc. Am.* **1971,** *61* (1), 1–11.

11. Gray, D.; Brennan, S.; Tao, H. Evaluating Appearance Models for Recognition, Reacquisition, and Tracking. In *Proceedings of the International Workshop Performance Evaluation of Tracking and Surveillance*, 2007.

12. Zheng, W.-S.; Gong, S.; Xiang, T. Associating Groups of People. In *Proceedings of the BMVC*, 2009; pp 23.1–23.11. DOI: 10.5244/C.23.23.

13. McLaughlin, N.; del Rincon, J. M.; Miller, P. C. Person Re-Identification Using Deep Convnets. *IEEE Trans. Circ. Syst. Video Technol.* **2017,** *27* (3).

14. Wikipedia Contributors. Convolutional Neural Network. In Wikipedia, The Free Encyclopedia. https://en.wikipedia.org/w/index.php?title=Convolutional_neural_network&oldid=873543170 (accessed Dec 16, 2018).

15. LeCun, Y. LeNet-5, Convolutional Neural Networks (accessed Nov 16, 2013).

16. Wikipedia Contributors. Convolutional Neural Network. In Wikipedia, The Free Encyclopedia, 2018. https://en.wikipedia.org/w/index.php?title=Convolutional_neural_network&oldid=873543170 (accessed Dec 16, 2018).

17. CS231n Convolutional Neural Networks for Visual Recognition. cs231n.github.io (accessed Dec 13, 2018).

18. Wikipedia Contributors. Convolutional Neural Network. In Wikipedia, The Free Encyclopedia, 2018. https://en.wikipedia.org/w/index.php?title=Convolutional_neural_network&oldid=873543170 (accessed Dec 16, 2018).

19. Chen, Y.; Zhu, X.; Gong, S. Person Re-Identification by Deep Learning Multi-Scale Representations, 2017; pp 2590-2600. DOI: 10.1109/ICCVW.2017.304.

20. http://mmlab.ie.cuhk.edu.hk/archive /facesketch.html#:~:text=CUHK %20Face %20 Sketch%20database%20(CUFS)%20is%20for%20research%20on%20face,synthesis% 20and%20face%20sketch%20recognition.&text=For%20each%20face%2C%20 there%20is,and%20with%20a%20neutral%20expression

21. https://www.tugraz.at/institute/icg/research/team-bischof/lrs/downloads/prid11/#:~:text =Person%20Re%2DID %20(PRID) %20Dataset%202011&text=The%20dataset%20 consists%20of%20images,illumination%2C%20background%20and%20camera%20 characteristics

22. Bromley, J.; et al. Signature Verification Using a 'Siamese' Time Delay Neural Network. *Int. J. Pattern Recognit. Artif. Intell.* **1993,** *7* (4), 669–688.

23. Hadsell, S. C.; LeCun, Y. Dimensionality Reduction by Learning an Invariant Mapping. *Proc. CVPR* **2006,** *2*, 1735–1742.

24. Qu, W.; Xu, Z.; Luo, B.; Feng, H.; Wan, Z. Pedestrian Re-Identification Monitoring System Based on Deep Convolutional Neural Network. *IEEE Access.* **2020,** 1–1. DOI: 10.1109/ACCESS.2020.2986394.

25. http://www.eecs.qmul.ac.uk/~xiatian/downloads_qmul_iLIDSVID_ReID_ dataset.html #:~:text=It%20comprises%20600%20image%20sequences,camera%20views%20 for%20each%20person.&text=The%20iLIDS%2DVID%20dataset%20is,cluttered%20 background%20and%20random%20occlusions

26. Varior, R. R.; Haloi, M.; Wang, G. Gated Siamese Convolutional Neural Network Architecture for Human Re-Identification. *Eur. Conf. Comput. Vis.* **2016,** 791–808.

27. Krizhevsky, I. S.; Hinton, G. E. Imagenet Classification with Deep Convolutional Neural Networks. *Adv. Neural Inform. Process. Syst.* 1097–1105, 2012.

28. Domonkos Varga, T. S. Person Re-Identification Based on Deep Multi-Instance Learning. In *2017 25th European Signal Processing Conference (EUSIPCO)*, 2017.

29. https://www.quora.com/What-are-the-disadvantages-of-applying-convolutional-networks-in-person-re-identification

30. Zhang, S.; He, Y.; Wei, J.; Mei, S.; Wan, S.; Chen, K. Person Re-Identification with Joint Verification and Identification of Identity-Attribute Labels. *IEEE Access.* **2019,** 1–1. DOI: 10.1109/ACCESS.2019.2939071.

31. Subramaniam, A.; Chatterjee, M.; Mittal, A. Deep Neural Networks with Inexact Matching for Person Re-Identification. In *30th Conference on Neural Information Processing Systems NIPS*; Barcelona, Spain, 2016.

32. Ahmed, E.; Jones, M.; Marks, T. K. An Improved Deep Learning Architecture for Person Re-Identification. In *Proceedings of the IEEE Conference on Computer Vision and Pattern Recognition*, 2015; pp 3908–3916.

33. Guo, Y.; Cheung, N. -M. Efficient and Deep Person Re-Identification Using Multi-Level Similarity, 2018. Qi, L.; Huo, J.; Wang, L.; Shi, Y.; Gao, Y. MaskReID: A Mask Based Deep Ranking Neural Network for Person Re-Identification, 2018.

34. Qi, L.; Huo, J.; Wang, L.; Shi, Y.; Gao, Y. MaskReID: A Mask Based Deep Ranking Neural Network for Person Re-Identification, 2018.

35. https://www.quora.com/What-are-the-advantages-of-a-convolutional-neural-network-CNN-compared-to-a-simple-neural-network-from-the-theoretical-and-practical-perspective.

36. Guo, Y.; Cheung, N. -M. Efficient and Deep Person Re-Identification Using Multi-Level Similarity, 2018.

37. Qu, W.; Xu, Z.; Luo, B.; Feng, H.; Wan, Z. Pedestrian Re-Identification Monitoring System Based on Deep Convolutional Neural Network. *IEEE Access.* **2020,** 1–1. DOI: 10.1109/ACCESS.2020.2986394.

38. Yang, F.; Yan, K.; Lu, S.; Jia, H.; Xie, X.; Gao, W. Attention Driven Person Re-Identification. *Pattern Recognit.* **2018,** *86.* DOI: 10.1016/j.patcog.2018.08.015.

39. Shen, Y.; Li, H.; Yi, S.; Chen, D.; Wang, X. Person Re-Identification with Deep Similarity-Guided Graph Neural Network: Proceedings of the 15th European Conference, Munich, Germany, Sept 8–14, 2018. Part XV. DOI: 10.1007/978-3-030-01267-0_30.

40. http://rose1.ntu.edu.sg/PersonReId/

41. https://www.quora.com/What-is-the-disadvantage-of-the-conventional-convolution-neuron-network

42. https://www.quora.com/What-are-some-of-the-limitations-or-drawbacks-of-Convolutional-Neural-Networks

PART II
Computational Intelligence in Healthcare

CHAPTER 8

A Systematic Literature Review in Health Informatics Using Data Mining Techniques

ANJALI MEHTA and DEEPA BURA

Manav Rachna International Institute Research and Studies, Faridabad, Haryana, India

ABSTRACT

Data Mining is a field of finding the useful and important patterns from the huge available data. Data mining is very popular in various research fields such as business, agriculture, weather forecasting. Data mining is very much useful in healthcare also. Clinical decisions are usually made based on the doctor's experience and knowledge rather than the useful knowledge hidden in the patient's database. These decisions can lead to unwanted biasness, error, and more costly treatment and also affect the quality of treatment. Patients will receive better and less expensive services if large clinical data from previous patients will be analyzed and useful knowledge will be interpreted. In this review paper, various data mining techniques are analyzed in the healthcare domain. The knowledge will help to reduce the cost of treatment and help to take accurate decisions from the complex healthcare data.

Computational Intelligence in Analytics and Information Systems, Volume 1: Data Science and AI, Selected Papers from CIAIS-2021. Hardeo Kumar Thakur, Manpreet Kaur, Parneeta Dhaliwal, Rajeev Kumar Arya, and Joan Lu (Eds.)

8.1   INTRODUCTION

World is generating huge amounts of data day by day in various formats such as text, audio, audiovisual, images, numbers. Large organizations in Education, Business, and Healthcare etc. generate huge amounts of data and interpret this data to get useful knowledge. This knowledge is very useful for making right decisions for the growth of that particular organization only when decisions are made at the right time. One of the ways for doing this is data mining, that is, finding useful information or patterns from a bulk amount of data. Data mining is known as the procedure of collection and examination of huge amounts of data to find out unknown patterns with the aim of getting important information or useful results. Many techniques are available in data mining; some of them are classification, clustering, association rules.

Health is an important concept of the human body. Without good health, human beings are useless. Heart is the main part of the human body and according to research most people die due to heart attack. Techniques of data mining are very useful to analyze the healthcare industry. If heart attack is predicted at a very early stage then death of one person can be prevented. Data mining techniques are very helpful to calculate the disease at a very early stage with fewer amounts of data and efforts. The efficiency of the output depends upon the technique used and attributes selected from the available data.

Classification is a supervised learning method in which a classifier is used to predict the label for a class that has an unseen instance. There are various fields in which classification is used. This technique is very useful to analyze healthcare data. A researcher would also analyze the data of patients to predict which method of treatment is beneficial for the patient.

Diabetic patients have high chances of heart disease. The performance of any classification techniques depends upon precision, accuracy, and f-measure. Precision is generally known as the ratio of right predictions for the true class. Accuracy is well defined as the overall number of correct decisions among all the transactions. F-measure is the mean of two terms that are known as precision and recall.

Rich amount of unknown beneficial data is hidden in the record of patients, but doctors make their clinical decisions based on their intuition and experience. Due to this some problems arise like unwanted biasness, error, expensive treatment, and poor quality of treatment. On the other hand, clinical decisions integrated with data mining techniques can lessen the errors in medical field, improve safety of patients, and quality of treatment of patient will be increased.

Data mining permits users to investigate the patient data from various angles or perspectives, sort the data, and summarize it into valuable information. Various methods of data mining are applied on medical data to find valuable information that is called Medical data mining. Patient's data are analyzed on a continuous basis and the outcome is interpreted from time to time. Any changes in the record are monitored and risk level is informed to the patients as well as doctors. With the help of this doctors can calculate heart disease at a very early phase with the help of data mining techniques and computer technology.

8.2 LITERATURE REVIEW

8.2.1 WORK DONE BY RESEARCHERS FOR CARDIAC ARREST

a) Richa Sharma (2019) in her paper discusses various techniques of data mining. The research presented in this paper compares classification algorithms according to their accuracy for cardiovascular disease. C-PLS (Partial Least Squares Regression) and Naïve Bayes achieved maximum accuracy, that is, 84.44% and 83.71% on Tanagra and Weka, respectively.

b) Soni J.[21] in her paper compares various algorithms of data mining for healthcare patients. This paper concludes that Naïve Bayes Algorithm has 86.53% accuracy; KNN has 85.53% accuracy whereas Decision Tree has 89% accuracy on the Intelligent System used to predict Heart disease with the help of .net platform. This paper uses 13 attributes for patient data in which chest pain type, blood sugar level, cholesterol etc. are present.[21]

c) David H.[7] in his work conducts data mining methods on the patients having heart disease. Naïve Bayes, Decision Tree, and Random Forest are used to design a prediction system for heart patients. Data is used from UCI ML repository. This paper concludes that Random Forest is a better technique compared to others with 81% precision by using 14 attributes from patient data.[7]

d) Ordonez C.[17] predicts heart disease in his paper with the help of 13 basic attributes and with the addition of 2 more attributes like smoking and body fat. Neural Network, Decision Tree, and Naïve

Bayes are used to study the precision level for heart patients and results are studied on heart disease patients database.[17]

e) Srinivas et al.[22] studied the various classification techniques in the paper like Neural Network, Decision Tree, Naive Bayes, One Dependency Augmented Naïve Bayes classifier (ODANB) for heart disease patients. Research paper concludes that the ODANB algorithm is better in vehicles, metallurgy but for heart disease prediction Naïve Bayes is better than all and more efficient.[22]

f) Pattekari and Parveen[18] developed a prototype of the Heart Disease Prediction System (HDPS) with the help of Naïve Bayes technique. This system can answer the complex queries of doctors and patients for which traditional systems are not capable. HDPS is web based, user approachable, scalable, consistent, and inflatable. Patient data such as age, sex, BP, blood sugar are used as attributes to predict the heart disease in this system.[18]

g) Sundar et al.[23] studied various techniques like Naïve Bayes, Weighted Association Classifier (WAC), and Apriori algorithm. Simple data set is used and data is categorical not continuous. This paper concludes that Naïve Bayes is more efficient than other algorithms.[23]

h) Kodati[19] studied various tools of data mining in the research paper like Orange and Weka. This paper concludes that finding heart disease from the data of the patient requires a number of tests. Doctors can reduce the number of tests when data mining algorithms are used to identify heart disease that also reduces the cost of the treatment.[15]

i) Shouman et al.[20] finds the research gap of all the techniques of data mining either single or hybrid approach. This paper analyzes the gap in the effort done on the diagnoses of heart disease and the treatment of this disease. This paper also proposes a model to systematically fill those gaps.[20]

8.2.2   WORK DONE BY RESEARCHERS FOR OTHER DISEASES

a) Kaur and Wasan[13] discussed the various uses of data mining in the healthcare industry. Research paper discusses a case study to predict the diabetes in the person by using the basic attributes such as age, sex, previous history, sugar level. Data is collected from the UCL ML database and finally by using classification techniques the data set is classified. Nine attributes are present in the dataset in which only one is a decision attribute, that is, micro-albuminuria.[13]

b) Koh and Tan[14] explore the usefulness of healthcare data in data mining. Data mining can result in useful patterns from the healthcare data if data is clean and noise is removed from the data.[14]

c) Jothi and Husain[12] state that the healthcare industry used data mining methods to identify various diseases such as cancer, heart attack, SCD, thyroid. Various data mining techniques such as anomaly detection, classification, clustering are analyzed in the paper. Advantages and disadvantages of each technique are also explored.[12]

d) Ahmad et al.[2] state that healthcare data is very vast and massive, so the process of extracting beneficial material from this data is difficult with the support of traditional data mining methods. A survey is conducted on various techniques such as classification, regression, and clustering for healthcare data and pros and cons of each technique is described.[2]

e) Liu et al. (2014) used decision table (DT)-based predictive models for breast cancer survivability, concluding that the survival rate of patients was 86.52%. They employed the under-sampling C5 technique and bagging algorithm to deal with the imbalanced problem, thus improving the predictive performance on breast cancer.

f) Delen et al. (2015) had taken 202,932 breast cancer patients' records, which were then preclassified into two groups of "survived" (93,273) and "not survived" (109,659). The results of predicting the survivability were in the range of 93% accuracy[8]

g) Hian Chye (2011) in his paper explores the usefulness of healthcare in data mining. Data mining can result in useful patterns from the healthcare data if data is clean and noise is removed from the data.[17]

h) A. Solanki (2014) in his paper emphasizes on comparison of two classification techniques J48 and Random tree using WEKA. Classification is done with respect to age and blood group. Random trees produce depth decision trees with respect to J48. From tested data it shows that specific blood groups have more chances of SCD.[25]

8.3 TECHINQUES OF DATA MINING

8.3.1 FREQUENT PATTERN MINING AND ASSOCIATION

In this technique, frequent patterns are extracted from the database and association between these patterns is found with the help of association rules. Market Basket Analysis is the most common example of this technique. In this example, the database of a store is analyzed and items that are most likely to be purchased by the customer are extracted depending upon the transactions of past time.

The Association Rule is of the form:

$$\text{Buys (X, Computer)} => \text{buys (Antivirus)}$$
$$[\text{support} = 20\%, \text{confidence} = 60\%]$$

This rule shows that a person who buys a computer also wants to buy antivirus at the same time. The association rules are measured by two parameters: Support and Confidence. These parameters are measured in % term as shown in the above example. From the above rule a support of 20% shows that 20% of customers from the total number of customers buy computer and antivirus together, a confidence of 60% reflects that 60% of the customers who have bought computers are likely to buy antivirus. With the help of these rules, the store manager can enhance the sale by putting these items together. A priori algorithm is the most common technique used to generate frequent patterns from a given database. Figure 8.1 deals with the techniques of data mining.

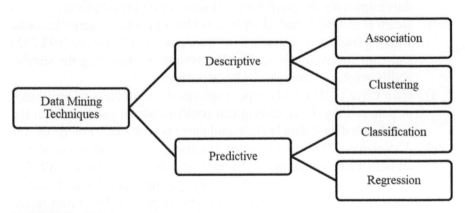

FIGURE 8.1   Techniques of data mining.

8.3.2   CLUSTERING

Clustering is an unsupervised learning technique because input–output patterns are not predefined in this method. Objects with similar properties constitute a cluster and contradictory properties in another cluster and this procedure of grouping is called clustering detailed in Figure 8.2.

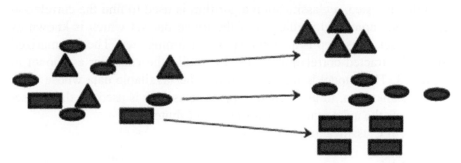

FIGURE 8.2   Clustering technique.

Many types of clustering methods are available. Some of them are:

a)   Partition Method
b)   Hierarchical Method
c)   Density-Based Method
d)   Grid-Based Method

8.3.3   CLASSIFICATION

Classification technique is used to divide the data into groups that are not similar with each other with the help of a classifier. This classification depends upon the attribute that represents the class. This process is done with the help of two steps:

i)   Generate Classification Rules
ii)   Classify the data

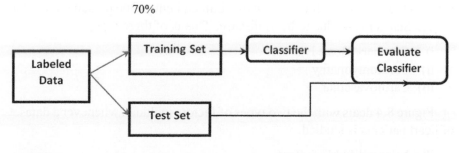

FIGURE 8.3   Classification techniques.

In the first step, a classification algorithm is used to find the correlation between the target and predictors of the given dataset which is known as a training set. This step is also known as a learning step. The summarized report of extracted correlations is used to build the classifier as shown in Figure 8.3. This model is then applied to other available data whose class labels are unknown. In the second step, this classifier is used for the test set and predicts the unknown values for target attributes.

Types of Classification Technique:

1. KNN
2. Decision Tree
3. SVM
4. Neural Network
5. Naïve Bayes

8.3.4   REGRESSION

This is a mathematical tool that is mainly used in statistics. Two variables are there in which one is dependent and the other is independent. The maximum value of a dependent variable can be 1, whereas the value of an independent variable can be greater than 1. Regression can also be divided into two types depending on the count of independent variables that are:

i)   Linear Regression
ii) Multiple Regression

8.4   HEART DISEASE

Heart is the main operating system of a human being. One person died in the United States in 34s due to heart disease. This is of three types:

i)   Coronary Heart Disease
ii)   Cardiomyopathy
iii) Cardiovascular

Figure 8.4 deals with the two types of factors included whenever a dataset of heart patients is studied.

i)   Nonmodifiable factors
     –   Age of the patient
     –   Gender

- Blood pressure details
- Pulse rate details
- Cholesterol level
- Insulin level
- Chest pain type
- ECG report
- Maximum heart rate achieved

ii) Modifiable factors
- Smoking
- Drinking
- Patient previous history

Signs of a heart attack consist of:

Chest pain and uneasiness
Tightness into back, neck, face line, or arms.
Indigestion
Vomiting or sweating
Fatigue or breath problem
Uneven breath

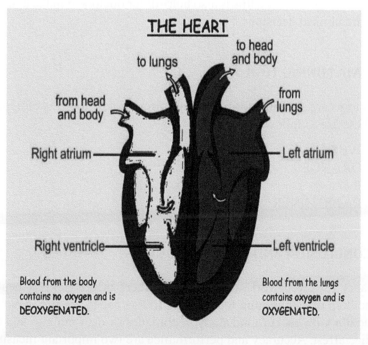

FIGURE 8.4   Two types of factors are included whenever a dataset of heart patients is studied.

8.5   DATA MINING IN HEALTHCARE FOR HEART PATIENTS

The healthcare industry is full of information. It has been possible that very small hospitals may generate data in terabytes in a year. With the help of data mining algorithms, the healthcare industry can utilize the stored patient data. There are several benefits of this that are written below. Various advantages of data mining process in Healthcare:

1.   Provision of safe healthcare treatment.
2.   Reduces the period to delay for the cure of the patient.
3.   Preprocess the noisy data, inconsistent data and also take care of incompleteness of medical data.
4.   Analyzing healthcare hubs for improved health management.
5.   To sense disease epidemics in hospitals.
6.   To detect fraud insurance claims.
7.   To prevent a patient's death.

All the algorithms of data mining are very useful to discover the heart attack at the very primary stage with the help of modifiable and nonmodifiable factors. Doctors can prevent the death of the patient by predicting the heart attack very early and this is also helpful for doctors to make better, safe, and secure clinical decisions.

8.6   DATA MINING TOOLS

Various tools are available for free to interpret the data to get useful information. These are as follows:

i)   WEKA
ii)   ORANGE
iii) R
iv)   RAPIDMINER

8.7   CONCLUSION AND FUTURE WORK

This paper reviewed work done by researchers in the field of healthcare with the help of data mining techniques. In this paper, we first gave a brief introduction with background study, techniques of data mining, and factors of cardiac arrest. Accuracy and performance are two important measures for any algorithm. With the help of this study, we can say that to achieve better and more accuracy to predict diseases, to decrease the death rate and to avoid many other problems, various methods of data mining must be used in a hybrid approach.

KEYWORDS

- **data mining**
- **business**
- **healthcare**
- **treatment**
- **techniques**

REFERENCES

1. Abdallah, S.; Malik, M.; Ertek, G. A Data Mining Framework for the Analysis of Patient Arrivals into Healthcare Centers. In *Proceedings of the 2017 International Conference on Information Technology*, 2017; pp 52–61.
2. Ahmad, P.; Qamar, S.; Rizvi, S. Q. A. Techniques of Data Mining in Healthcare: A Review. *Int. J. Comput. Appl.* **2015,** *120* (15).
3. Anand, R.; Srivatsa, S. K. A Data Mining Framework for Building Health Care Management System. *Int. J. Eng. Res. Technol.* **2013,** *2* (5), 1639–1648.
4. Bhatla, N.; Jyoti, K. An Analysis of Heart Disease Prediction Using Different Data Mining Techniques. *Int. J. Eng.* **2012,** *1* (8), 1–4.
5. Canlas, R. D. *Data Mining in Healthcare: Current Applications and Issues*; School of Information Systems & Management, Carnegie Mellon University: Australia, 2009.
6. Chaurasia, V.; Pal, S. Data Mining Approach to Detect Heart Diseases. *Int. J. Adv. Comput. Sci. Inform. Technol.* **2014,** *2*, 56–66.
7. David, H.; Belcy, S. A. Heart Disease Prediction Using Data Mining Techniques. *ICTACT J. Soft Comput.* **2018,** *9* (1).
8. Diwani, S. A.; Sam, A. Framework for Data Mining In Healthcare Information System in Developing Countries: A Case of Tanzania. *Int. J. Comput. Eng. Res.* **2013,** *3* (10).
9. Huang, F.; Wang, S.; Chan, C. C. August. Predicting Disease by Using Data Mining Based on Healthcare Information System. In *2012 IEEE International Conference on granular computing*; IEEE, 2012; pp 191–194.
10. Ioniță, I.; Ioniță, L. Applying Data Mining Techniques in Healthcare. *Stud. Inform. Control.* **2016,** *25* (3), 385–394.
11. Joshi, S., Nair, M. K. Prediction of Heart Disease Using Classification Based Data Mining Techniques. In *Computational Intelligence in Data Mining-Volume 2*; Springer: New Delhi, 2015; pp 503–511.

12. Jothi, N.; Husain, W. Data Mining in Healthcare—A Review. Proc. Comput. Sci. 2015, 72, 306–313.
13. Kaur, H.; Wasan, S. K. Empirical Study on Applications of Data Mining Techniques in Healthcare. *J. Comput. Sci.* **2006,** *2* (2), 194–200.
14. Koh, H. C.; Tan, G. Data Mining Applications in Healthcare. *J. Healthc. Inform. Manag.* **2011,** *19* (2), 65.
15. Kumar, N.; Khatri, S. Implementing WEKA for Medical Data Classification and Early Disease Prediction. In *2017 3rd International Conference on Computational Intelligence & Communication Technology (CICT)*; IEEE, 2017; pp 1–6.
16. Obenshain, M. K. Application of Data Mining Techniques to Healthcare Data. *Infect. Control Hosp. Epidemiol.* **2004,** *25* (8), 690–695.
17. Ordonez, C. Improving Heart Disease Prediction Using Constrained Association Rules. In *Seminar presentation at University of Tokyo*, 2004.
18. Pattekari, S. A.; Parveen, A. Prediction System for Heart Disease Using Naïve Bayes. *Int. J. Adv. Comput. Math. Sci.* **2012,** *3* (3), 290–294.
19. Kodati, D. R. V. S. Analysis of Heart Disease Using in Data Mining Tools Orange and Weka. *Glob. J. Comput. Sci. Technol.* **2018.**
20. Shouman, M.; Turner, T.; Stocker, R. Using Data Mining Techniques in Heart Disease Diagnosis and Treatment. In *2012 Japan-Egypt Conference on Electronics, Communications and Computers*; IEEE, 2012; pp 173–177.
21. Soni, J.; Ansari, U.; Sharma, D.; Soni, S. Predictive Data Mining for Medical Diagnosis: An Overview of Heart Disease Prediction. *Int. J. Comput. Appl.* **2011,** *17* (8), 43–48.
22. Srinivas, K.; Rani, B. K.; Govrdhan, A. Applications of Data Mining Techniques in Healthcare and Prediction of Heart Attacks. *Int. J. Comput. Sci. Eng.* **2010,** *2* (02), 250–255.
23. Sundar, N. A.; Latha, P. P.; Chandra, M. R. Performance Analysis of Classification Data Mining Techniques Over Heart Disease Database. *Int. J. Eng. Sci. Adv. Technol.* **2012,** *2* (3), 470–478.
24. Thomas, J.; Princy, R. T. Human Heart Disease Prediction System Using Data Mining Techniques. In *2016 International Conference on Circuit, Power and Computing Technologies (ICCPCT)*; IEEE, 2016; pp 1–5.
25. Tomar, D.; Agarwal, S. A Survey on Data Mining Approaches for Healthcare. *Int. J. Bio-Sci. Bio-Technol.* **2013,** *5* (5), 241–266.

CHAPTER 9

Utilization of Artificial Intelligence-Based Methods for Preoperative Prediction in Shoulder Arthroplasty: Survey

MILIND TOTE and SHRIKANT V. SONEKAR

Department of Computer Science & Engineering,
JD College of Engineering & Management, Nagpur, Maharashtra, India

ABSTRACT

In the last few years, rapid acceptance and improvement of technology have been seen in Shoulder Arthroplasty practices. The success rate of Shoulder Arthroplasty can be improved by taking the advantages of artificial intelligence for finding preoperative parameters and better decision-making. In shoulder arthroplasty the common indications are irreparable rotator cuff tears, proximal humerus fractures, osteoarthritis, inflammatory arthritis, and rotator cuff arthroplasty. The primary identification and the selection of which sort of arthroplasty is employed relies on these indications. This paper presents a review for the impact of machine learning and deep learning-based approaches on the prediction of Shoulder Arthroplasty. The brief introduction of various artificial intelligence technique-based approaches used for the prediction of Shoulder Arthroplasty is presented. This paper also presents the summary of results obtained by various researchers available in the literature to predict the Shoulder Arthroplasty. The performance analysis is based on the metrics, for example, accuracy, sensitivity, and specificity.

Computational Intelligence in Analytics and Information Systems, Volume 1: Data Science and AI,
Selected Papers from CIAIS-2021. Hardeo Kumar Thakur, Manpreet Kaur, Parneeta Dhaliwal,
Rajeev Kumar Arya, and Joan Lu (Eds.)

9.1 INTRODUCTION

In the United States every year around 53,000 shoulder replacements are made compared to 900,000 knee replacements and hip replacements, according to the report of Agency for Healthcare Research and Quality. Based on the dysfunction or injury the decision for shoulder arthroplasty can take place which can either be a partial or total replacement. This is mainly due to the relatively complex anatomy and biomechanics of the shoulder joint. Based on the tissues involved and complexities many variations in prosthesis and surgical procedures are present.[1] In shoulder Arthroplasty, pain is the most common indication that has not responded well to severe fracture. The shoulder arthroplasty includes: pseudoparesis occurs due to the lack of rotator cuff and previous unsuccessful shoulder surgery along with some other causes are primary osteoarthritis in which joint pain and stiffness become sever and not able to do daily activities, posttraumatic arthritis occurs after direct physical injury to joint, inflammatory arthritis in which joint inflammation occurs due to overactive of immune system. It is less common than others, and humeral head and neck osteonecrosis in which part of humeral head fails to get blood supply. The shoulder surgery is mainly categorized into three types: Hemi-arthroplasty in which a fractured or injured humeral head is used to replace; total shoulder arthroplasty (TSA) in which a damaged or fractured ball and a socket joint are used to be replaced, and reverse total shoulder arthroplasty (rTSA) that is performed due to failed total shoulder replacement or irreparable cuff tear.[2-6] The success rate of surgery can be improved by taking the advantages of artificial intelligence and its subsets for finding preoperative parameters and better decision-making. Various types of machine learning and deep learning techniques are used for the classification such as Deep-CNN, fast region CNN, unsupervised deep learning, and give different accuracy, precision, and sensitivity.[7-12] In this review paper, Sect. 9.2 describes the basics of various machine learning and deep learning approaches and also the metrics used to calculate and assess the performance of these models. In Sect. 9.3, we present the findings of the systematic literature review which describe the applications of machine learning and deep learning for shoulder arthroplasty. We retrieved the scientific papers that covered the machine learning and deep learning approaches for shoulder arthroplasty from the Scopus and Elsevier databases along with Medline. Almost 30 latest papers were considered for a thorough review and selected papers divided according to the machine learning and deep learning approaches. For each paper we extracted the model and databases used along with the performance. Also performance of each model has been shown in a tabular format in Table 9.1.

9.2 MACHINE LEARNING AND DEEP LEARNING METHODS

9.2.1 MACHINE LEARNING

Machine learning can be categorized into supervised, unsupervised, semi-supervised, and reinforcement learning methods.

1. Supervised Learning: It is a learning method in which we are given a labeled training dataset from which a model can predict labels of unlabeled data points. These unlabeled data points could be either test data points or unlabeled data that we will collect in the future. To validate the model a test dataset is frequently used. Classification (discrete labels) and regression (real values) are the two categories of supervised learning. Neural Net-works, Support Vector Machines (SVMs), and Naive Bayes classifiers are the examples of supervised ML algorithms.

2. Unsupervised Learning: In this learning, the data does not have an output variable or result, only input data is present. The prediction model is constructed based on the prediction of the number of structures present in the input data. In this type of learning method there is no correct answer or no teacher. It is like a self-guided learning method, algorithms are devised by their own about the presence of structure in data. K-means and a priori algorithms are the examples of unsupervised learning.

3. Semisupervised Learning: It is applicable in the situation where the input data has a mixture of labeled and unlabeled examples. This learning method contains both labeled data and unlabeled data. This learning method works better for larger amounts of unlabeled data and fewer amounts of labeled data. If the model needs to make predictions and also to learn the structures that are necessary, then this model is used. The example algorithms include Linear Regression and Random forest.

4. Reinforcement Learning: It takes an appropriate action to maximize reward in a specific context. It is a type of machine learning that is based on the four things, that is, agent, action state, environment, and reward. In particular, the situation is to find the best possible

path or behavior based on reward, it is employed in software or machines.

9.2.2   DEEP LEARNING

Deep Learning is a progressive and promising technology in the area of Machine Learning which has taken many steps forward toward the original goal of machine learning, that is, impersonating the human brain's intelligence. It is an extension of artificial neural net-work with the additional concept of multiple hidden layers. Deep Learning is an area of machine learning that has the capability to learn high-level abstractions from the raw data through multiple layers of processing. Deep learning methods have multiple levels of learning; in each layer, a more abstract representation of the raw data is learned via nonlinear transformations.[13–17] Using such nonlinear modules of transformation, very complex functions can be determined. The critical idea stems from biology, where it is believed that cognition happens through several layers. The basic units of deep learning are CNN, Autoencoder, RBM, and DL.

9.2.3   METRICS

In machine learning one of the important tasks is to measure the performance of a given model. In case of multiclass classification problems for checking the performance, area under the curve (AUC) is a very important evaluation metric. The sensitivity metric measure is used to evaluate actual positive cases, which predict true positive; when the model predicts true positive correctly it means that the value of sensitivity is high and the model is good for use. The specificity metric measure is used to determine actual negative cases; when the model predicts true negatives correctly it means that sensitivity is high and the model is good.

9.3   LITERATURE REVIEW

Paul H. Yi et al.[18] have proposed and measured the performance of deep convolutional neural networks (DCNN) approach to identify and recognize precise Total Shoulder Arthroplasty (TSA) models. The dataset used for the study was publically available image repositories with native shoulders implants, reverse TSA (rTSA) implants, and five different TSA models.

Model performance was calculated based on area under the receiver-operating characteristic curves (AUC-ROC), sensitivity, and specificity. Five prosthesis models performance is given: (1) Biomet Bio-Modular Choice Model had an AUC-ROC of 0.95 with sensitivity of 86%, and specificity of 100%. (2) DePuy Global Model had an AUC-ROC of 0.95 with sensitivity of 92% and specificity of 98%. (3) DePuy HRP Model had an AUC-ROC of 0.92 with sensitivity of 92% and specificity of 91%. (4) Stryker Solar Model had an AUC-ROC of 0.86 with sensitivity of 80% and specificity of 96%. (5) Zimmer Bigliani-Flatow Model had an AUC-ROC of 1.0 with sensitivity of 100% and specificity of 100%.

Yongyu Jiang et al.[19] have investigated the performance of deep learning algorithms that examined the practicality in shoulder motion pattern recognition using sEMG signals from shoulder and upper limb muscles. In the research, the parameter impacts such as motion speed, individual variability, EMG recording device, and the amount of EMG datasets were examined. In the CNN Model the accuracy in motion pattern recognition was 97.57% for normal speed motions and for fast speed motions it was 97.07%. In the cross subjects CNN model the accuracy in motion pattern recognition was 79.64%. The accuracy in motion pattern recognition obtained was 88.93% for normal speed motion and it was 80.87% for mixed speed in the cross-device CNN model.

Gregor Urban et al.[20] have evaluated the use of deep learning for classifying shoulder implants in X-ray images and compared it with other classifiers. Out of seven deep learning architectures tested, the best accuracy of 80.4% was achieved with NASNet. It also observed that to obtain the good results, pretraining the CNNs ImageNet was important, and fine-tuning the entire CNN model on the X-ray data set was better than only fine-tuning the top hidden layers.

Paul Kulyk et al.[21] have proposed a deep learning-based method to automatically decide the articular marginal plane (AMP); the method was without segmentation. The dataset used for the study was taken from Institutes for Forensic Medicine of the Universities of Switzerland. In a 4-fold cross-validation the result to estimate mean error in articular marginal plane (AMP) center was 1.30 ± 0.65 mm and the angular error obtained was 4.68 ± 2.84 in the normal vector.

Steven Walczak et al.[22] present an ANN Model that was helpful in resource distribution and recognizing patients at risk of postoperative harmful effects. The ANNs model predicts that need of transfusion is 75% of the patients, the specificity is 80%, and the sensitivity is 67%. For the study 1.6 million surgical cases from the NSQIP-PUF database were used over a 2-year period.

Elham Taghizadeh et al.[23] present a method to automatically measure the level of degeneration of rotator cuff (RC) muscles using convolutional neural network (CNN) that was helpful for the diagnosis of preoperative planning in total shoulder arthroplasty. The method was able to provide a quick and reliable measurement of RC muscle atrophy and fatty infiltration from formal shoulder CT scans. The result was calculated in terms of satisfactory accuracy and reliability; the accuracy of CNN-derived segmentations was R2=0.61 which was compared to human raters, that is, R2=0.87.

Youngjune Kim et al.[24] present a method based on the deep learning algorithm that can eliminate significant rotator cuff tears. Based on the input dataset used from Philips Healthcare the result shows that approximately 30% of clinically suspected rotator cuff tears in patients accurately ruled out using this method. The sensitivity, negative predictive value (NPV), and negative likelihood ratio (LR−) obtained in the result were 97.3%, 96.6%, and 0.06, respectively.

Anirudh K. Gowd et al.[25] present a paper to improve the prediction of postoperative complications after total shoulder arthroplasty (TSA) than comorbidity indices using machine learning approaches. The database used for research was taken from American College of Surgeons–National Surgical Quality Improvement Program. In the random forest classifier method the accuracy and the AUC are 95.4% and 95.6%, respectively, and in logistic regression the accuracy and the AUC are 71.0% and 77%, respectively.

Yunpeng Liu et al.[26] present a joint convolutional neural network model that can segment MRI images of patients' shoulders and accurately find glenoid and humeral heads. This model helps the orthopedic surgeons in early diagnosis and shoulder arthroplasty. The dataset from Harvard Medical School/Massachusetts General Hospital used for the study includes 50 different groups of MRI images. The result of the first network uses the Mask R-CNN segmentation model in which the accuracy of Dice Coefficient was 0.91 ± 0.02, positive predicted value (PPV) was 0.95 ± 0.01, and sensitivity for glenoid and humeral head reaches 0.94 ± 0.02 respectively, and the second network uses the probability maps of voxel in which the accuracy of dice coefficient was 0.88 ± 0.01, positive predicted value (PPV) was 0.91 ± 0.02, and sensitivity 0.90 ± 0.02 respectively.

Seok Won Chung et al.[27] present paper for proximal humerus fractures detection and classification using deep learning algorithms, plain anteroposterior shoulder radio-graphs are used as input. For 4-part fracture the CNN accurately classified proximal humerus with an AUC of 0.98 for greater tuberosity fractures, 0.94 for surgical neck fractures, 0.90 for 3-part fractures, and 0.94 for 4-part fractures. The mean sensitivity/specificity in the

CNN model were 0.99/0.97, 0.97/0.94, 0.90/0.85, 0.88/0.83, and 0.93/0.85 for normal versus all, greater tuberosity, surgical neck, 3-part, and 4-part fractures, respectively.

D.H. Kim et al.[28] present the concept of transfer learning from CNNs in fracture detection on plain radiographs. The result is obtained in terms of the parameters of AUC 0.954, sensitivity and specificity values of 0.9 and 0.88, respectively. This study shows improvement in workflow productivity, minimizes the risk of error, and prevents patient's harm by reducing diagnostic delays.

Mariano E. Menendez, et al.[29] present a natural language approach using machine learning to understand patients' experience in the form of sentiment analysis; this paper studied and focused on the experience of patient after total shoulder arthroplasty (TSA), their associated factors, and their relationship with traditional methods of patient satisfaction and with perioperative outcomes. In the study 71% of patients provided at least 1 comment, overall 32% of the comments were negative and positive comments were 62%, the remaining 6% comments were mixed.

Murali Poduval, et al.[30] survey a paper for the acceptance of artificial intelligence into orthopedic practice, as these technologies are integrated into the mainstream orthopedics. This study elaborates about the importance of basics of artificial intelligence and what work was completed till date in the related area. In conclusion it presents a perspective that artificial intelligence plays a very important role in orthopedic surgery.

Anne P. Ehlers et al.[31] present a paper to study risk prediction and healthcare utilization before surgery using the machine learning approach. In the study database of patients undergoing elective surgery with greater than one comorbidity was used; it was taken from Marketscan Commercial Claims and Encounters. The supervised Naïve Bayes algorithm was used to predict risk of adverse events or death within 90 days of surgery, and the performance of the model compared with the Charlson's comorbidity index.

Dustin R. et al.[32] present a random forest machine learning model to predict which patients had a length of stay of 1 day or less who went through Total Shoulder Arthroplasty based on the medical comorbidities and demographic factors. The important correlated variables that decide the short or long stay of a patient in a hospital after surgery were identified using multivariable logistic regression. The input dataset for the study was taken from American College of Surgeons National Surgical Quality Improvement Program questionnaire. Table 9.1 details the performance of the existing machine learning and deep learning techniques.

TABLE 9.1   Performance of Existing Machine Learning and Deep Learning Techniques.

Author and year	Parameters	Techniques	Dataset input	Performance
Paul H. Yi et al.[18]	Total shoulder arthroplasty	Deep convolutional neural networks (DCNN)	Publically available Image repositories with native shoulders, reverse TSA (RTSA)implants	The performance of five different models are AUC in the range 0.86–1.0 with sensitivity 80–100% and specificity 91–100%.
Yongyu Jiang et al.[19]	Shoulder muscle activation pattern recognition	Convolutional neural network (CNN)	Model MP-36, Biopac Inc, and Delsys EMG work were used to collect EMG signals.	Accuracy is 97.57% for normal speed motions and 97.07% for fast speed motions. The accuracy of the cross subjects CNN model is 79.64%.
Paul Kulyk et al.[21]	Total shoulder arthroplasty	Deep learning	Institutes for Forensic Medicine of the Universities of Switzerland	Mean error for the center of the AMP of 1.30 ± 0.65 mm and a mean angular error of 4.68 ± 2.84
Steven Walczak et al.[22]	Total shoulder arthroplasty	Artificial neural network	Over 1.6 million surgical cases over 2 years from the NSQIP-PUF database	ANNs can predict >75% of the patients who will require transfusion specificity: 80% and sensitivity 67%
Elham Taghizadeh et al.[23]	Total shoulder arthroplasty	Convolutional neural network (CNN)	Dataset consisted of 103 shoulder CT scans from 95 different patients	Good estimates of muscle atrophy (R2 = 0.87), fatty infiltration (R2 = 0.91), and overall muscle degeneration (R2 = 0.91)
Youngjune Kim et al.[24]	Total shoulder arthroplasty	Convolutional neural network (CNN)	8263 patients dataset from Philips Healthcare	Sensitivity, NPV, and LR were 97.3%, 96.6%, and 0.06, respectively
Anirudh K. Gowd, et al.[25]	Total shoulder arthroplasty	Supervised machine learning	American College of Surgeons—National Surgical Quality Improvement Program database	Accuracy and the AUC is 95.4% and 95.6%, respectively in the random forest classifier and 71.0% and 77%, respectively in logistic regression

TABLE 9.1 *(Continued)*

Author and year	Parameters	Techniques	Dataset input	Performance
Yunpeng Liu et al.[26]	Total shoulder arthroplasty	MaskR-CNN segmentation model	50 groups of patients are from Harvard Medical School/ Massachusetts General Hospital	The accuracy of Dice Coefficient, positive predicted value (PPV), and sensitivity for glenoid and humeral head reaches 0.91 $\pm$ 0.02, 0.95 $\pm$ 0.01, 0.94 $\pm$ 0.02, and 0.88 $\pm$ 0.01, 0.91 $\pm$ 0.02, 0.90 $\pm$ 0.02 respectively
Seok Won Chung et al.[27]	Proximal humerus fractures	Deep convolutional neural network (CNN)	1891 plain shoulder AP radiographs from Konkuk University Medical Center and other hospitals	CNN showed promising results with 65–86% top-1 accuracy, 0.90–0.98 AUC, 0.88/0.83–0.97/0.94 sensitivity/specificity, for classifying fracture type.
D.H. Kim et al.[28]	Wrist radiographs	Deep convolutional neural network (CNN)	Anonymized lateral wrist radiographs from the Royal Devon and Exeter Hospital	AUC: 95.4% sensitivity and specificity values of 90% and 88%, respectively.

9.4 CONCLUSION

This paper presents a comprehensive review of the prediction of Shoulder Arthroplasty by using the machine learning and deep learning algorithms. In this review and study, the various machine learning and deep learning-based approaches are briefly introduced which are used for the prediction of Shoulder Arthroplasty. The observation of the survey paper is that in different scenarios different algorithm approaches are used and accordingly performance varied, but dataset and feature selection is very significant to get better predictions. We found that the accuracy and performance can be improved by using different machine learning and deep learning algorithms such as Deep Convolution Neural Network, Artificial Neural Network, and Supervised Machine Learning and in the future, we can also work on more parameters which helps to get better performance than the existing technique.

KEYWORDS

- **accuracy**
- **sensitivity**
- **specificity**
- **shoulder arthroplasty**

REFERENCES

1. Rugg, C. M.; Coughlan, M. J. M. J. M. J.; Lansdown, D. A. Reverse Total Shoulder Arthroplasty: Biomechanics and Indications. *Curr. Rev. Musculoskel. Med.* **2019**. DOI: 10.1007/s12178-019-09586-y.
2. Lin, D. J.; Wong, T. T.; Kazam, J. K. Shoulder Arthroplasty, from Indications to Complications: What the Radiologist Needs to Know. *Radiographics* **2016**. DOI: https://doi.org/1 0.1148/rg.2016150055.
3. Lung, B. E.; Kanjiya, S.; Bisogno, M.; Komatsu, D. E.; Wang, E. D. Preoperative Indications for Total Shoulder Arthroplasty Predict Adverse Postoperative Complications. *JES Open Access.* **2019**. DOI: https://doi.org/10.1016/j.jses.2019.03.003.
4. Rodríguez, J. A.; Entezari, V.; Iannotti, J. P.; Ricchetti, E. T. Preoperative Planning for Reverse Shoulder Replacement: The Surgical Benefits and Their Clinical Translation. *Ann. Joint* **2019**. DOI: 10.21037/aoj.2018.12.09.

5. Raiss, P.; Walch, G.; Wittmanna, T.; Athwal, G. S. Is Preoperative Planning Effective for Intraoperative Glenoid Implant Size and Type Selection During Anatomic and Reverse Shoulder Arthroplasty? *J. Shoulder Elb. Surg.* **2020**. DOI: https://doi.org/10.1016/j.jse.2020.01.098.

6. Khazzam, M.; Reyes, B.; Phelan, A.; Gates, S. Subscapularis Integrity, Function and EMG/Nerve Conduction Study Findings Following Reverse Total Shoulder Arthroplasty. *JSES Int.* **2020**. DOI: https://doi.org/10.1016/j.jseint.2020.02.015

7. Cabitza, F.; Locoro, A.; Banfi, G. Machine Learning in Orthopedics: A Literature Review. *Front. Bioeng. Biotech.* **2018**. DOI: 10.3389/fbioe.2018.00075.

8. Ramkumar, P. N.; Haeberle, H. S.; Bloomfield, M. R.; Schaffer, J. L.; Kamath, A. F.; Patterson, B. M.; Krebs, V. E. Artificial Intelligence and Arthroplasty at a Single Institution:Real-World Applications of Machine Learning to Big Data, Value-Based Care, Mobile Health, and Remote Patient Monitoring. *J. Arthroplast.* **2019**. DOI: https://doi.org/10.1016/j.arth.2019.06.018.

9. Roche, R. S.; Flurin, P.H.; Wright, T.; Zuckerman, J.; Routman, H. Comparison of the Accuracy Associated with Three Different Machine-Learning Models to Predict Outcomes After Anatomic Total Shoulder Arthroplasty and Reverse Total Shoulder Arthroplasty. *Orthop. Proc.* **2020,** *102-B* (SUPP_1).

10. Ker, J.; Wang, L.; Rao, J.; Lim, T. Deep Learning Applications in Medical Image Analysis Special Section on Soft Computing Techniques for Image Analysis in the Medical Industry Current Trends, Challenges and Solutions. *IEEE Access* **2017**. DOI: 10.1109/ACCESS.2017.2788044.

11. Shim, E.; Kim, J. Y.; Yoon, J. P.; Ki, S. -Y.; Lho, T.; Kim, Y.; Chung, S. W. Automated Rotator Cuff Tear Classification Using 3D Convolutional Neural Network. *Sci. Rep.* **2020**. DOI: https://doi.org/10.1038/s41598-020-72357-0.

12. Zhou, Z.; Zhao, G.; Kijowski, R.; Liu, F. Deep Convolutional Neural Network for Segmentation of Knee Joint Anatomy. *Magn. Reson. Med.* **2018**. DOI: 10.1002/mrm.27229.

13. Kumar, V.; Roche, C.; Overman, S.; Simovitch, R.; Flurin, P. -H.; Wright, T.; Zuckerman, J.; Routman, H.; Teredesai, A. Using Machine Learning to Predict Clinical Outcomes After Shoulder Arthroplasty with a Minimal Feature Set. *J. Shoulder Elb. Surg.* **2020**. DOI: 10.1016/j.jse.2020.07.042

14. Polce, E. M.; Kunze, K. N.; Fu, M.; Garrigues, G. E.; Forsythe, B.; Nicholson, G. P.; Cole, B. J.; Verma, N. N. Development of Supervised Machine Learning Algorithms for Prediction of Satisfaction at Two Years Following Total Shoulder Arthroplasty. *J. Shoulder Elb. Surg.* **2020**. DOI: https://doi.org/10.1016/j.jse.2020.09.007.

15. O'Donnell, E. A.; Fu, M. C.; White, A. E.; Taylor, S. A.; Dines, J. S.; Dines, D. M.; Warren, R. F.; Gulotta, L. V. The Effect of Patient Characteristics and Comorbidities on the Rate of Revision Rotator Cuff Repair. *J. Arthrosc. Realt. Surg.* **2020,** *36* (9), 2380–2388. DOI: https://doi.org/10.1016/j.arthro.2020.05.022.

16. Lindsey, R.; Daluiski, A.; Chopra, S.; Lachapelle, A.; Mozer, M.; Sicular, S.; et al. Deep Neural Network Improves Fracture Detection by Clinicians. *Proc. Natl. Acad. Sci.* **2018b** *115*, 11591–11596. DOI: https://doi.org/10. 1073/pnas.1806905115.

17. Olczak, J.; Fahlberg, N.; Maki, A.; Razavian, A. S.; Jilert, A.; Stark, A.; et al. Artificial Intelligence for Analyzing Orthopedic Trauma Radiographs. *Acta Orthop.* **2017**. DOI: 10.1080/17453674.2017.1344459.

18. Yi, P. H.; Kim, T. K.; Wei, J.; Li, X.; Hager, G. D.; Sair, H. I.; Fritz, J. Automated Detection and Classification of Shoulder Arthroplasty Models Using Deep Learning.

J. Int. Skelet. Soc. A J. Radiol. Pathol. Orthop. **2020**. DOI: https://doi.org/10.1007/s00256-020-03463-3.

19. Jiang, Y.; Chen, C.; Zhang, X.; Chen, C.; Zhou, Y.; Ni, G.; Muh, S.; Lemos, S. Shoulder Muscle Activation Pattern Recognition Based on sEMG and Machine Learning Algorithms. *Comput. Method. Progr. Biomed.* **2020**. DOI: https://doi.org/10.1016/j.cmpb.2020.105721.

20. Urban, G.; Porhemmat, S.; Stark, M.; Feeley, B.; Okada, K.; Baldi, P. Classifying Shoulder Implants in X-Ray Images Using Deep Learning. *Comput. Struct. Biotech. J.* **2020**, *18*, 967–972. DOI: 10.1016/j.csbj.2020.04.005.

21. Kulyk, P.; Vlachopoulos, L.; Fürnstah, P.; Zheng, G. Fully Automatic Planning of Total Shoulder Arthroplasty Without Segmentation: A Deep Learning Based Approach. *Comput. Method. Clin. Appl. Musculoskel. Imaging* **2019**, 11404. DOI: https://doi.org/10.1007/978-3-030-11166-3_3.

22. Walczak, S.; Velanovich, V. Prediction of Perioperative Transfusions Using an Artificial Neural Network. *PLoS ONE* **2020**, *15* (2), e0229450. DOI: https://doi.org/10.1371/journal.pone.0229450.

23. Taghizadeh, E.; Truffer, O.; Becce, F.; Eminian, S.; Gidoin, S.; Terrier, A.; Farron, A.; Büchler, P. Deep Learning for the Rapid Automatic Quantification and Characterization of Rotator Cuff Muscle Degeneration from Shoulder CT Datasets. *Eur. Radiol.* **2020**. DOI: https://doi.org/10.1007/s00330-020-07070-7.

24. Kim, Y.; Choi, D.; Lee, K. J.; Kang, Y.; Ahn, J. M.; Lee, E.; Lee, J. W.; Kang, H. S. Ruling Out Rotator Cuff Tear in Shoulder Radiograph Series Using Deep Learning: Redefining the Role of Conventional Radiograph. *Eur. Radiol.* **2019**. DOI: https://doi.org/10.1007/s00330-019-06639-1.

25. Gowd, A. K.; Agarwalla, A.; Amin, N. H.; Romeo, A. A.; Nicholson, G. P.; Verma, N. N.; Liu, J. N. Construct Validation of Machine Learning in the Prediction of Short-Term Postoperative Complications Following Total Shoulder Arthroplasty. *J. Shoulder Elb.* **2019**, *28* (12), E410–E421. DOI: https://doi.org/10.1016/j.jse.2019.05.017.

26. Liu, Y.; Wang, R.; Jin, R.; Sun, D.; Xu, H.; Dong, C. Shoulder Joint Image Segmentation Based on Joint Convolutional Neural Networks. In *RICAI 2019: International Conference on Robotics, Intelligent Control and Artificial Intelligence*, Sept, 2019; pp 236–241. DOI: https://doi.org/10.1145/3366194.3366235.

27. Chung, S. W.; Han, S. S.; Lee, J. W.; Oh, K. -S.; Kim, N. R.; Yoon, J. P.; Kim, J. Y.; Moon, S. H.; Kwon, J.; Lee, H. -J.; Noh, Y. -M.; Kim, Y. Automated Detection and Classification of the Proximal Humerus Fracture by Using Deep Learning Algorithm. *Acta Orthoped.* **2018**. DOI: https://doi.org/10.1080/17453674.2018.1453714

28. Kim, D. H.; MacKinnon, T. Artificial Intelligence in Fracture Detection: Transfer Learning from Deep Convolutional Neural Networks. *Clin. Radiol.* **2018**, *73* (5), 439–445. DOI: https://doi.org/10.1016/j.crad.2017.11.0150009-9260.

29. Menendez, M. E.; Shaker, J.; Lawler, S. M.; Ring, D.; Jawa, A. Negative Patient-Experience Comments After Total Shoulder Arthroplasty. *J. Bone Joint Surg.* **2019**. DOI: http://dx.doi.org/10.2106/JBJS.18.00695

30. Poduval, M.; Ghose, A.; Manchanda, S.; Bagaria, V.; Sinha, A. Artificial Intelligence and Machine Learning: A New Disruptive Force in Orthopaedics. *Indian J. Orthop.* **2020**, *54*, 109–122. DOI: 10.1007/s43465-019-00023-3.

31. Ehlers, A. P.; Roy, S. B.; Khor, S.; Mandagani, P.; Maria, M.; Alfonso-Cristancho, R.; Flum, D. R. Improved Risk Prediction Following Surgery Using Machine Learning

Algorithms. *J. Electron. Health Data Health Method.* **2017**. DOI: https://doi.org/ 10.13063/2327-9214.1278.

32. Biron, D. R.; Sinha, I.; Kleiner, J. E.; Aluthge, D. P.; Goodman, A. D.; Sarkar, I. N.; Cohen, E.; Daniels, A. H. A Novel Machine Learning Model Developed to Assist in Patient Selection for Outpatient Total Shoulder Arthroplasty. *J. Am. Acad. Orthop. Surg.* **2019**. DOI: 10.5435/JAAOS-D-19-00395.

33. Qiu, R.; Jia, Y.; Wang, F.; Divakarmurthy, P.; Vinod, S.; Sabir, B.; Hadzikadic, M. Predictive Modeling of the Total Joint Replacement Surgery Risk: A Deep Learning Based Approach with Claims Data. *AMIA Joint Summits Trans. Sci. Proc.* **2019**, 562–571.

CHAPTER 10

Role of Computer-Based Intelligence for Prognosticating Social Wellbeing and Identifying Frailty and Drawbacks

SANDEEP GUPTA[1], NITIN TYAGI[2], MANJULA JAIN[3], SHEKHAR SINGH[1], and KRISHAN KUMAR SARASWAT[1]

[1]Department of Computer Science and Engineering, JIMS Engineering Management Technical Campus, Noida, Uttar Pradesh, India

[2]Department of Electronics and Communication Engineering, JIMS Engineering Management Technical Campus, Noida, Uttar Pradesh, India

[3]Department of Management, Teerthanker Mahaveer University, Moradabad, Uttar Pradesh, India

ABSTRACT

This chapter gives an early assessment of computer-based intelligence (CBI) against nCOVID-19. The fundamental territories where CBI can add to the battle against nCOVID-19 are examined. It is presumed that CBI does not prove to be significant against nCOVID-19. Its utilization is obstructed by an absence of information, and by an excess of information. Conquering these limitations will demand a cautious equalization between information security and general wellbeing, and thorough man–computer-based intelligence (CBI) collaboration. It is implausible that all the mentioned problems would be taken care of in general so as to be of greater aid during the current pandemic. Meanwhile, broad social occasions of indicative information on

Computational Intelligence in Analytics and Information Systems, Volume 1: Data Science and AI, Selected Papers from CIAIS-2021. Hardeo Kumar Thakur, Manpreet Kaur, Parneeta Dhaliwal, Rajeev Kumar Arya, and Joan Lu (Eds.)

the one who is irresistible will be fundamental to spare lives, learn CBI, and breaking point monetary harms.

10.1 INTRODUCTION

The *nCOVID-19* widespread disaster represents various difficulties to the Computer-Based Intelligence (CBI) community. These are across these constraints "Would CBI aid in following and anticipating the disease?", "Would CBI be able to aid in the analysis and forecasts?", "Would it be able to be utilized in the quest for medicines, what's more, an antibody?", and "Would it be able to be utilized for enculturation?" This chapter is an endeavor to give an early survey of how Computer-Based Intelligence (CBI) has till now been rendered in such a manner, further to consider impediments, imperatives, and entanglements. These incorporate a need of information, to an extreme (loud and anomaly) information, and developing pressure between information security concerns and general wellbeing goals.

To begin with, let us examine the genuine and expected employment of CBI in the battle against *nCOVID-19*.

10.2 PURSUING AND PROGNOSIS

CBI can, on a basic level, be utilized to follow and foresee how the nCOVID-19 illness will unfurl after some duration and space. Truth be told, a CBI-based portrayal of wellbeing chart, at Boston Children's Emergency clinic (United States of America), resonated one of the initial cautions on December 30, 2019, nearly half an hour sooner than a researcher at the Program for Monitoring Emerging Diseases (PMED) giving an alarm. Furthermore, pursuing and prognosis of how nCOVID-19 will unfurl, be that as it may, CBI till now has been found to be extremely invaluable. This is because of various causes. The primary one is that CBI needs information on nCOVID-19 to prepare. A case of how this should be possible is the situation of the 2015 Zika-infection, whose growth was anticipated post factum utilizing a powerful neural system.[1] As nCOVID-19 is not quite the same as Zika, or other diseases, and on the grounds that there are at the hour of composing still not adequate information to assemble CBI portrayals that can pursue and gauge its growth. A large portion of the developing number of distributions giving an account of utilizing CBI for symptomatic and prescient reasons so far will in general utilize little, perhaps one-sided, and for the most part Chinese-based examples, further not being critically assessed.

Various promising activities, in any case, have been begun to assemble and disseminate information, including existing information, fresh information, and to prepare novel CBI portrayals. These incorporate W.H.O. Universal investigation on novel Coronavirus Malady information set, which additionally connects to other comparative activities. The first of which is publically accessible information of the Global Initiative on Sharing All Influenza Data. Among different activities, maybe, the most aggressive is the joint activity between Semantic Researcher, the Allen Institute for Artificial Intelligence, Microsoft, Facebook, and others, to make straight-forwardly accessible the nCOVID-19 public investigation information that contains around 44,000 academic articles for information mining.

Kaggle, an information science rivalry stage, has issued an information rivalry dependent on this information, an nCOVID-19 Public investigation information set challenge. Also, adding to the requirement for increasing (open) information, Elsevier made it freely accessible in its nCOVID Information Center beginning phase and companion checked investigation on nCOVID-19 and approximately 20,000 related articles on ScienceDirect, just as the full articles for information mining. Essentially, The Lens has allowed access to every one of its information on licenses in what it calls the Human nCOVID-19 Innovation Landscape Patent and Research Works Open Datasets to help the quest for new and remodeled medicine. What's more,[2] it has distributed the principal open nCOVID-19 Twitter information set.

Another motivation behind why CBI has till now not been much helpful in pursuing and prognosis the growth of the sickness. It is not just an absence of chronicled preparing information yet in addition because of issues with utilizing "huge information," for example, gathered from online life. The entanglements of enormous information and CBI with regards to irresistible ailments were shown in the scandalous disappointment of Google Flu Trends. In Ref. 3 it is eluded to as "large information hubris and calculation elements." For example, as the contamination keeps on spreading, the internet-based life traffic around it amasses, so the measure of commotion collects which must be sifted through before important patterns can be recognized. By and large, also this is likewise awful news for CBI gauging portrayals in different fields, including financial aspects and money, since for any forecast calculation that depends on past conduct, a worldwide exception occasion with its mass of fresh and extraordinary information, for example, nCOVID-19, can be portrayed as[4] does as "the kryptonite of present day Artificial insight." Subsequently, he reasons that over the close future "numerous businesses will be pulling the people once more into the gauging seat that was included through them by the portrayals."

Moreover, researchers should manage the spate of logical papers and new information being created, and move across. In excess of 500 logical articles on the pandemic currently show up every day. This embryonic data over-burden is, in any case, where information diagnostic apparatuses can assume a significant job. A case of an activity in such a manner is the nCOVID-19 Evidence Navigator, which gives computer-engendered proof guides of logical distributions on the pandemic, every day refreshed from PubMed.[5]

Because of an absence of information, uproarious internet-based life and anomaly information, large information hubris also computational methods elements, CBI estimates of the growth of nCOVID-19 are still not extremely precise or dependable. Consequently, until this point, a large number of portrayals utilized for following and anticipating do not utilize CBI techniques. Rather, most predictors favor setting up pandemic logical portrayals, supposed SIR portrayals.[6] For instance, the Robert Koch Institution located in Berlin utilizes the pandemic logical SIR portrayal that considers regulation measures by administrations, for example, lockdowns, isolates, and social separating remedies. This portrayal was enforced in China to outline that control can be fruitful in decreasing the growth to more slowly than the exponential rate.[7]

To follow nCOVID-19's growth continuously, an authentic industry of information "dashboard" production, for the representation of the malady, has developed. The primary, and much of the time utilized, is the John's Hopkins' Center for Systems Science and Engineering (CSSE).[8] The information gathered and made accessible via this dashboard is provided on a GitHub vault, at *https://www.githu b.com/CSSEGISandData/COVID-19.*

MIT Technology Review has put forth a positioning of these trackings and anticipating dashboards to encourage the creation of information dashboards of the pandemic, Tableau has made a nCOVID-19 Data Hub associating with a nCOVID-19 Starter Workbook.[9] that gives a Python script to delineate how one could remove information from the New York Times' nCOVID-19 information set and make information representations of the movement of the disease. The development of many dashboards and representations of nCOVID-19 has anyway additionally prompted calls for dependable percep-tion of nCOVID-19 information.[10]

10.3 IDENTIFICATION AND PREDICTION

Notwithstanding possibly following and foreseeing the growth of nCOVID-19, CBI can likewise be utilized in the determination and prediction of the sickness. Actually, this is maybe where the vast majority of the main surge of CBI activities concentrated on. Quick and exact analysis of nCOVID-19 can spare lives, restrict the growth of the ailment, and create information on which to prepare CBI portrayals. There is developing exertion to prepare CBI portrayals to analyze nCOVID-19 utilizing chest radiography pictures. According to the survey of CBI applications for nCOVID-19 by Ref. 10 contends that CBI may be as precise as people, can spare radiologists' duration, and play out a conclusion quicker and less expensive than with calibrated tests for nCOVID-19. Both X-beams and processed tomography sweeps may be utilized. Agent commitments in such a manner incorporate.[11,12] The last created nCOVID-Net, a profound convolutional neural system (see for example Ref. 13), which can analyze nCOVID-19 from chest radiography pictures. This is prepared on open store information from around 13,000 patients with different lung anomalies, encompassing nCOVID-19. In any case, as the writers demonstrate, it is "in no way, shape or form a feasible arrangement," and they approach mainstream researchers to create it further, specifically to "improve affectability."

Provided that not every individual determined to have nCOVID-19 will require escalated care, to have the option to figure who will be influenced all the much seriously may help in focusing on help and arranging clinical asset distribution and used[14] utilized Machine Learning to build up a prediction expectation calculation to foresee the causality probability of an individual which is contaminated, utilizing information by (just) 29 cases at Tongji Hospital in Wuhan, China. Furthermore, Ref. 15 provided a CBI which may foresee about 80% exactness that individuals influenced within nCOVID-19 can proceed to create intense respiratory pain disorder. The example which was utilized to prepare their CBI framework is, in any case, little (just 53 cases) and limited only to two Chinese clinics.

Generally the capability of CBI is concluded isn't yet continued into training, in spite of the fact that this is accounted for that various Chinese clinics have sent "simulated intelligence helped" radiology advances. Radiologists somewhere else have communicated their anxiety where isn't sufficient information accessible to prepare CBI models, that a large portion of the accessible nCOVID-19 pictures originate from Chinese emergency clinics and can experience the ill effects of choice inclination, further that utilizing CT-output and X-beams can sully hardware and unflur the malady further. To be sure, the utilization of CT examinations in European clinics has dipped following the pandemic spread, maybe mirroring this worry.[16] It is most likely right as Ref. 17 finishes up, "Nobody this spring will be providing a novel coronavirus finding by an CBI specialist." It additionally appears that relatively less exertion is on utilizing CBI for early analytic reasons, as an example, in recognizing whether somebody is not tainted earlier than it appears in X-beams or CT examines, or on discovering information steered recognition which have low defilement chance.

10.4 THERAPY AND IMMUNIZATIONS

A third zone in which CBI may conceivably produce a commitment in the battle against nCOVID-19 is in distinguishing potential medicines and immunizations. Indeed, even some time before the nCOVID-19 flare-up CBI was commended due to its capability to add to fresh medication revelation, see for example.[18,19] On account of nCOVID-19, various labs and servers have just demonstrated which are enlisting CBI to look for medicines to and an immunization for nCOVID-19. The expectation is that CBI may quicken both the procedures of finding new medications just as for re-reasoning present medications. Various specialists have just announced finding medicines for re-reasoning. These incorporate reports[20] about because of utilizing Machine Learning to distinguish that a current medication, atazanavir, might be reasoned to cure nCOVID-19, and, Ref. 21 who recognized Baricitinib, which was utilized to cure rheumatoid joint inflammation and myelofibrosis, as one of the possible medical care of nCOVID-19.

It isn't possible that these medicines (specifically an immunization) would be accessible sooner rather than later, in any event to be very useful at the time of the present pandemic. The explanation is given as the clinical and logical examines, experimentation, as well as management which should be implemented prior to these medications will be endorsed, when they have been recognized and examined, will require some serious energy—as indicated by gauges as long as year and a half for an antibody.[21] See Ref. 22 for a clarification of the procedure that a possible enemy of nCOVID-19 medication should experience.

10.5 SOCIAL CONTROLS

A fourth job for CBI in battling the nCOVID-19 pandemic encompasses public restriction. Computer-based intelligence has been contended as important to deal with the widespread epidemic by utilizing warm imaging to filter open places for individuals possibly tainted, and by implementing social separation and lockdown methods.[23] For instance as depicted by[24] "At air terminals and railway stations throughout China, IR cameras are utilized to examine swarms for elevated temperatures. Which are here and there utilized using a profile acknowledgment framework that may point to the person having an elevated temperature and whether the individual in question is put on a careful cover." It is accounted for that the given cameras may filter 200 people for every moment and will perceive the ones whose internal heat level surpasses 37.3°.[25] Temperature-based imaging has, in any case, been censured as being lacking to distinguish from a separation a high temperature in individuals those having spectacles (since checking the inward tear conduit provides the exact solid sign) and in light of the fact that it cannot recognize whether an individual's temperature is attacked in view of nCOVID-19 or another explanation.[26]

In any case, as[24] alarming reports, "This framework is additionally being utilized to guarantee residents comply with self-isolate orders. As indicated by reports, people who spurned the request and ventured out from the house will receive a call from the specialists, probably in the wake of being followed using the profile acknowledgment framework." This sort of utilization is not constrained to China. A United States of America PC based on vision startup is as of now offering "social removing recognition" programming, which utilizes camera pictures to identify when social separating standards are penetrated, afterward it would convey an admonition.[27] At the hour of composing, most exceptional economies have been thinking about and additionally testing different contacts following applications and related apparatuses to give public restriction, for example the conversation.[28]

CBI devices, for example, computer vision and machines are definitely not capable enough to prognosticate due to lack of archived data. Along these lines, we are almost certain above the present moment to see this kind of CBI being utilized and utilized in addition for public restrictions. Related innovations, for example, cell phones having CBI-fueled applications or wearable devices that collect area, use, and wellbeing information of their proprietors, are additionally bound to be utilized. As indicated by[29] such applications may "empower patients to get continuous holding up time data by their clinical suppliers, to furnish individuals within counsel and changes according to their ailment without them visiting a medical clinic face to face, and to tell people of potential disease hotspots progressively so those regions may be kept away from."

Helpful as these may be, the dread is that if the episode is finished, that disintegration of information protection could not be moved backward and that legislatures could keep on utilizing their elevated capacity to study their populaces and utilize the information got in the battle with nCOVID-19 to different purposes. As Ref. 30 cautions "In any event, when contaminations from nCOVID are reduced to null, a few information hungry administrations would contend they expected to store the biostatistics reconnaissance frameworks set up on the grounds that they dread a second influx of nCOVID, or in light of the fact that there is another Ebola strain developing evolving in focal Africa, or on the grounds that you get the thought."

10.6 CONCLUSION

Taking everything into account, CBI can possibly be an apparatus within the battle against nCOVID-19 and comparative widespread epidemic. In any case, with the aforementioned fast output of the present scenario, one needs to agree with Ref. 29 that "computer based intelligence" frameworks are still at a fundamental stage, and it will require some investment before the aftereffects of such "CBI measures are noticeable." In one of the principal studies of CBI portrayals utilized with nCOVID-19 concurs, presuming that "not many of the evaluated [CBI] frameworks have operational development at this stage"[10]

Obviously, information is integral to whether CBI can be a compelling instrument for upcoming pestilences and widespread epidemics. The apprehension is that general wellbeing concerns could best information protection concerns.

Strategic can happen; within administrations proceeding with the remarkable observation of their residents afterward the widespread epidemic is finished. Along these lines, worries about the disintegration of information security are supported.

Given the general wellbeing danger from the widespread epidemic, the European GDPR permits individual information assortment and investigation, until this has a reasonable and explicit general wellbeing point.[31] Adaptability to accumulate and examine enormous information quickly is fundamental in fighting the widespread epidemic, regardless of whether it might necessitate that the specialists gather more close to home information than numerous individuals could feel good with. In this manner, it is critical that the specialists take specific consideration in their treatment of such information and their legitimizations and interchanges to the general population on the loose.

The threat looming upon the individuals would no longer have faith in administration, that may, as Ref. 31 called attention to, "make individuals less inclined to follow general wellbeing guidance or on the other hand suggestions and bound to have less fortunate wellbeing results."

At long last, despite the fact that CBI's utilization has till now been fairly constrained, the widespread epidemic and the arrangement reactions to it might quicken the computerization of the all financial transactions, which includes the tilt toward more noteworthy robotization of human work, the reinforcing of creation exercises, and developing business sector predominance with a couple of enormous computerized stage firms. Accordingly, the advancements in CBI innovation that might be a result of the current emergency, might expect the public to gain quicker ground to set down proper systems for the administration of CBI.

KEYWORDS

- **CBI**
- **nCOVID-19**
- **scrutiny**
- **information analysis**
- **general wellbeing**

REFERENCES

1. Akhtar, M.; Kraemer, M.; Gardner, L. A Dynamic Neural Network Model for Predicting Risk of Zika in Real Time. *BMC Med.* **2019**. DOI: https://doi.org/10.1186/s12916-019-1389-3

2. Chen, J.; Wu, L.; Zhang, J.; Zhang, L.; Gong, D.; Zhao, Y.; Hu, S.; Wang, Y.; Hu, X.; Zheng, B.; Zhang, K.; Wu, H.; Dong, Z.; Xu, Y.; Zhu, Y.; Chen, X.; Yu, L.; Yu, H. Deep Learning-Based Model for Detecting 2019 Novel Coronavirus Pneumonia on High-Resolution Computed Tomography: A Prospective Study, 2020b. MedRxiv: https://doi.org/10.1101/2020.02.25.20021568

3. Lazer, D.; Kennedy, R.; King, G.; Vespignani, A. The Parable of Google Flu: Traps in Big Data Analysi's. *Science* **2014**, *343* (6176), 1203–1205.

4. Rowan, I. What Happens to AI When the World Stops (COVID-19)? *Medium Towards Data Sci.* **2020**.

5. Grunewald, E.; Antons, D.; Salge, T. *COVID-19 Evidence Navigator*; Institute for Technology and Innovation Management, RWTH Aachen University: Aachen, 2020.

6. Song, P.; Wang, L.; Zhou, Y.; He, J.; Zhu, B.; Wang, F.; Tang, L.; Eisenberg, M. An Epidemiological Forecast Model and Software Assessing Interventions on COVID-19 Epidemic in China, 2020. MedRxiv: https://doi.org/10.1101/2020.02.29.20029421

7. Maier, B.; Brockmann, D. Effective Containment Explains Sub-Exponential Growth in Confirmed Cases of Recent COVID-19 Outbreak in Mainland China, 2020. MedRxiv: https://doi.org/10.1101/2020.02.18.20024414

8. Dong, E.; Dua, H.; Gardner, L. An Interactive Web-Based Dashboard to Track COVID-19 in Real Time. *Lancet Infect. Dis.* **2020**. DOI: https://doi.org/10.1016/S1473-3099(20)30120-1

9. Sarkar, T.; Analyze, N. Y. Times Covid-19 Dataset. *Medium Towards Data Sci.* **2020**.

10. Makulec, A. Ten Considerations Before You Create Another Chart About COVID-19. *Medium Towards Data Sci.* **2020**.

11. Chen, E.; Lerman, K.; Ferrara, E. COVID-19: The First Public Coronavirus Twitter Dataset, 2020a. ArXiv: https://arxiv.org/abs/2003.07372v1.

12. Wang, L.; Wong, A. COVID-Net: A Tailored Deep Convolutional Neural Network Design for Detection of COVID-19 Cases from Chest Radiography Images, 2020. ArXiv: https://arxiv.org/abs/2003.09871.

13. Rawat, W.; Wang, Z. Deep Convolutional Neural Networks for Image Classification: A Comprehensive Review. *Neural Comput.* **2017**, *29*, 2352–2449

14. Yan, L.; Zhang, H. -T., Xiao, Y.; Wang, M.; Sun, C.; Liang, J.; Li, S.; Zhang, M.; Guo, Y.; Xiao, Y.; Tang, X.; Cao, H.; Tan, X.; Huang, N.; Luo, A.; Cao, B. J.; Xu, Z. H., Yuan, Y. Prediction of Criticality in Patients with Severe Covid-19 Infection Using Three Clinical Features: A Machine Learning-Based Prognostic Model with Clinical Data in Wuhan, 2020. MedRxiv: https://doi.org/10.1101/2020.02.27.20028027

15. Jiang, X.; Coffee, M.; Bari, A.; Wang, J.; Jiang, X.; Huang, J.; Shi, J.; Dai, J.; Cai, J.; Zhang, T.; Wu, Z.; He, G.; Huang, Y. Towards an Artificial Intelligence Framework for Data-Driven Prediction of Coronavirus Clinical Severity. *Comput. Mater. Contin.* **2020**, *63* (1), 537–551.

16. Ross, C.; Robbins, R. Debate Flares Over Using AI to Detect Covid-19 in Lung Scans. *Stat* **2020**.

17. Coldeway, D. AI and Big Data Won't Work Miracles in the Fight Against Coronavirus. *Techcrunch* **2020**.

18. Fleming, N. Computer-Calculated Compounds: Researchers Are Deploying Artificial Intelligence to Discover Drugs. *Nature* **2018**, *557*, S55–S57.

19. Smith, S. 6 Things We Learned About Artificial Intelligence in Drug Discovery from 330 Scientists. *BenchSci Blog.* **2018**.

20. Beck, B.; Shin, B.; Choi, Y.; Park, S.; Kang, K. Predicting Commercially Available Antiviral Drugs that May Act on the Novel Coronavirus (2019-nCoV), Wuhan, China Through a Drugtarget Interaction Deep Learning Model, 2020. BioRxiv: https://doi.org/10.1101/2020.01.31.929547

21. Stebbing, J.; Phelan, A.; Griffin, I.; Tucker, C.; Oechsle, O.; Smith, D.; Richardson, P. COVID-19: Combining Antiviral and Anti-Inflammatory Treatment's. *Lancet* **2020**, *20*, 400–401

22. Vanderslott, S.; Pollard, A.; Thomas, T. Coronavirus Vaccine: Here Are the Steps It Will Need to Go Through During Development. *Conversation* **2020**.
23. Rivas, A. Drones and Artificial Intelligence to Enforce Social Isolation During COVID-19 Outbreak. *Medium Towards Data Sci.* **2020**.
24. Chun, A. In a Time of Coronavirus, China's Investment in AI is Paying Off in a Big Way. South *China Morning Post* **2020**.
25. Dickson, B. Why AI Might Be the Most Effective Weapon We Have to Fight COVID-19. *Next Web* **2020**.
26. Carroll, J. Coronavirus Outbreak: Can Machine Vision and Imaging Play a Part? *Vis. Syst. Des.* **2020**.
27. Maslan, C. Social Distancing Detection for COVID-19. *Medium* **2020**.
28. Gershgorn, D. We Mapped How the Coronavirus Is Driving New Surveillance Programs Around the World. *Medium* **2020**. https://onezero.medium.com/the-pandemic-is-a-trojan-horse-for-surveillance-programs-around-the-world-887fa6f12ec9
29. Petropoulos, G. Artificial Intelligence in the Fight Against COVID-19. *Bruegel* **2020**.
30. Harari, Y. The World After Coronavirus. *Financial Times* **2020**.
31. Ienca, M.; Vayena, E. On the Responsible Use of Digital Data to Tackle the COVID-19 Pandemic. *Nat. Med.* **2020**. DOI: https://doi.org/10.1038/s41591-020-0832-5.

CHAPTER 11

Health Informatics Support for Occurrence Administration Using Artificial Intelligence and Deep Learning: COVID-19 Pandemic Response

AKSHAT JAIN[1], RITU PAL[2], and JAGDISH CHANDRA PATNI[1]

[1]School of Computer Science, University of Petroleum & Energy Studies, Dehradun, Uttarakhand, India

[2]Department of CSE, Dev Bhoomi Institute of Technology, Dehradun, Uttarakhand, India

ABSTRACT

The outbreaks of COVID-19 epidemic have caused worldwide health concerns since December 2019. As concluded in the studies, around 30% of patients have the critical illness and have the challenging conditions to recover. It was also concluded in the research that 62% is the mortality rate of the patients who were having the critical conditions. It now becomes very challenging and difficult to identify the patients from the infectious crowd. Now it becomes urgent to deal with this challenging situation based on the clinical data by using Artificial Intelligence, Machine Learning, and decision support systems. Our study toward the possible solution to deal with this kind of pandemic is based on the clinical data using machine learning that helps us in early diagnosis and treatment of critically ill patients without failure that definitely reduces the mortality rate.

Computational Intelligence in Analytics and Information Systems, Volume 1: Data Science and AI, Selected Papers from CIAIS-2021. Hardeo Kumar Thakur, Manpreet Kaur, Parneeta Dhaliwal, Rajeev Kumar Arya, and Joan Lu (Eds.)

11.1 INTRODUCTION

Severe acute respiratory syndrome coronavirus 2 (SARS-CoV-2) keeps on spreading universally. Around the world, more than 200,000 instances of coronavirus ailment 2019 and in excess of thousands of losses (now it is close to one million) have been accounted for. It has a very high mortality rate as compared to others like occasional flu, and other similar varieties that are accounted for. WHO speaks about the idea that the mortality rate would be 3.4% while some of the countries reported less than 1% of mortality rate.[1]

Only a few cases were reported early in February 2020, those were having the travel history of China and just in a few weeks it went up exponentially due to the contact with the other people. Starting from December 2019 COVID-19 spread all around the world with several critical conditions reported from various patients. A serious instance of novel coronavirus was initially reported in the month of February 2020. Within 14 days, numerous different instances of coronavirus in the encompassing zone were analyzed, including a considerable number of fundamentally sick patients. First based on the number of cases and of the propelled phase of the malady, it was estimated that the infection had been flowing inside the populace since December 2019.[2]

It is found that this coronavirus spreads by droplets and through direct contact of infected persons with others. It is not primarily an airborne infection. Figure 11.1 deals with the coronavirus structure. In this manner, guaranteeing routine bead hindrance safety measures, natural cleanliness, and generally speaking, sound disease anticipation practice is shown. To guarantee insignificant danger of disease while rewarding patients with this disease, WHO suggests the utilization of individual defensive hardware which includes respirator masks, PPE kits, gloves, face shields, goggles, etc. to protect ourselves. In any case, airborne safety measures were not utilized in day-by-day scheduled care of patients with general respiratory ailment.[1]

11.2 LITERATURE REVIEW

Starting from December 2019 COVID-19 spread all around the world with several critical conditions reported from various patients. During February 2020, several patients in Italy were tested positive for another coronavirus, extremely intense respiratory condition coronavirus 2, that resulted in the infection of novel coronavirus disease later known as COVID-19. Having the background marked by unusual pneumonia that is primarily not known and thereafter it goes into danger soon. The various cases were treated and answered by different agencies of various countries. Within 24 h, newly revealed positive cases expanded to more than 36. This circumstance was viewed as a genuine advancement in these new positive cases: the patient was strong and youthful; in less than 24 h, more than 36 extra cases were distinguished, without connections to understanding patients or treated as new positive cases as of now in the nation; it was unrealistic to relate to assurance the wellspring of transmission to quiet 1 at that point; and, in light of the fact that tolerant 1 was in the ICU and there were at that point more than 36 cases by day 2, that shows the rapid spread of the virus.[3]

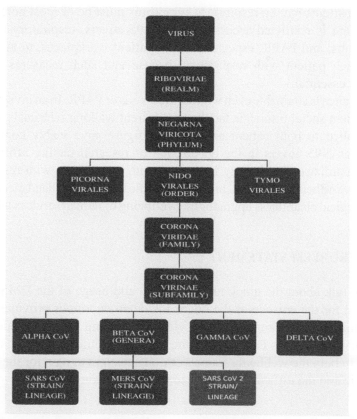

FIGURE 11.1 Coronavirus structure.

The acknowledgment that this outbreak likely happened by means of community spread recommended that a huge quantity of positive cases of coronavirus present in the area be marked. This expectation demonstrated right in the next few days. In view of the presumption that optional transmission was at that point happening, and even with regulation estimates that wellbeing specialists were setting up, it was accepted that numerous new instances of COVID-19 would happen, conceivably in the mass of people. In this manner, expecting a 5% ICU confirmation rate, it would not be possible to admit in the ICU to distribute all fundamentally sick patients to a most critically required ICU. The choice was to associate patients with 15 people on call center emergency clinics, picked in light of the fact that they either had mastery in irresistible ailment.[3]

The far-reaching utilization of suggested hindrance precautionary measures (e.g., covers, gloves, outfits, and eyewear) being adopted by all affected patients having respiratory symptoms must be of most noteworthy need. There is restricted accessibility of N95 covers, respiratory confinement rooms, and PAPR, especially in outpatient workplaces, to attainably assess each patient with respiratory disease and such measures are not routinely essential.[1]

Assurance is attainable even without N95 veils or PAPR. In an investigation of outpatient social insurance faculty in different walking rehearsals, clinical veils applied to both patient and parental figure gave viably comparable security as N95 covers in the occurrence of research facility affirmed flu among guardians who directly interacted with the patients with respiratory problems.[6] Adherence to CDC proof-based rules for covers, hand cleanliness, and ecological cleanliness upgrades the wellbeing of human services laborers.[1]

11.3   PROBLEM STATEMENT

Here we talk about the quick turn of events and usage of the DMS design important for the episode of the board inside an enormous provincial open scholastic wellbeing community in view of existing and newly deployed cases of COVID-19. Focused on the particular informatics devices we worked to help the wellbeing framework's endeavors to plan for the present pandemic and the difficulties related to this undertaking.[4]

11.3.1   EFFECTS OF HYPERTENSION

This announcement has been trailed by comparable proclamations from various social orders proposing patients to proceed with their present hypertensive drug routine. During March 2020 various research agencies of

United States of America reported that the coronavirus enters into the next stage of infection that causes various critical problems and recommended various stages of treatments for them.[5]

There is inadequate clinical or logical proof to decide how to suitably oversee hypertension in the setting of COVID-19. Accordingly, this gives a chance to the exploration network to all the more likely diagram the renin–angiotensin framework shown in Figure 11.2, while clinical information is collected to decide whether there is a connection between the utilization of ACEIs, ARBs, or both and COVID-19 mortality and grimness. Until increasingly significant information is accessible to direct dynamics one way or another, doctors ought to be accessible to tune in to patients' interests and give consoling exhortations about antihypertensive prescriptions in the period of the COVID-19 pandemic.[5] Figure 11.1 deals with the renin–angiotensin aldosterone system.

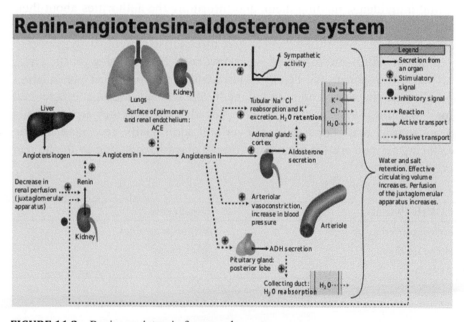

FIGURE 11.2   Renin–angiotensin framework.

11.3.2   CLINICAL CHARACTERISTICS

As per the published articles and research on the hospitalized patients collected from Wuhan, China, it was suggested that the average age was in

50's of those who were highly infected; 25% patients had the critical conditions and 10% patients required the ventilator. The spread of this pandemic was lesser in the younger population and children. As per the studies from clinical data around 85% of patients suffered from fever, dry cough was in nearly 80%, and laziness was in around 10–45%. Some other symptoms were also reported from clinical data such as headache, throat infection, stomach pain, and diarrhea.[6]

11.4   MANAGING A PANDEMIC

11.4.1   SCREENING PROCEDURES

The primary requirements for the wellbeing framework were the advancement of a fast and successful multimodal coronavirus screening process by calling individuals, mailing them, and informing the authorities about their health. These directions can be effectively gotten to by call focuses and triage attendants, permitting them to give direction to patients with respect to prerequisites for home confinement, proper areas to get testing for the virus, and when to report to the health department. So as to restrict presentation and alleviate the weight on physical medicinal services areas, computerized email warnings were sent to patients preceding their center arrangements demonstrating that people having fever and additionally new hack call the wellbeing framework for legitimate triage before introducing to the human services facility.[4]

COVID-19 triage	Urgent care
Patient concerns	Visitors screenings
Home isolation	Work excuse
Ambulance	

Template example recorded in various health bulletin

11.4.2   REPORTS AND ANALYSIS

Observing COVID-19 patient volume and dispersion over the wellbeing framework, COVID-19 test outcomes, emergency unit ventilator use and accessibility, and the effect of the flare-up on day by day walking visits. The correct side of the center board shows the quantity of ventilated patients; patients marked as ventilated and nonventilated that evolve research in this challenging area and extend testing limits, persistent confinement methodology, and a geographic cohort of patients and to screen adherence to understanding screening forms. Being able to screen the developing current condition of the wellbeing framework was a key tool for managing a pandemic.[4]

11.4.3   CONTAINMENT MEASURES

One of the key systems to control any pandemic and decrease the passing rates is early conclusion and early treatment of individual cases and COVID-19 is no special case. Individual case following and contact examination permits the social insurance framework to screen the patient through the continuum of care beginning from screening, enrolment, hazard appraisal, testing, treatment, and treatment result. The local administration and health department identified the containment zones and established strong measures in these zones by quarantine of the people in several clusters and the same was applied throughout all the cities and towns to slow down the growth and transmission of this novel coronavirus. Subsequently, the government should put in several measures by keeping people in self-isolation or home quarantine in the cases of light symptoms and get people admitted in hospitals in the severe cases and monitored and treated regularly.[9]

11.4.4   REAL-TIME CASE TRACKING AND INVESTIGATION

Since high hazard bunches with the distinct condition and family contacts are defenceless for COVID-19, contact examination permitting to relate family unit contact cases to affirmed COVID-19 cases gives a special way to deal with screen singular cases as well as networks generally inclined to getting the infection. The module can be utilized in any human services office, national and state fringes, air terminals, and effort/network setting. The module uses the WHO rules for COVID-19 screening and referral conventions and sets up chance appraisal calculations utilized in different nations.[9] Figure 11.3 deals with tracking systems with real-time data and Figure 11.4 deals with the growth of COVID-19.

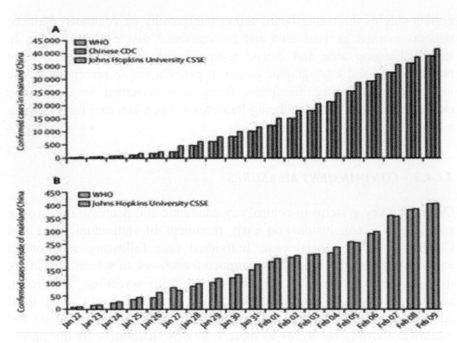

FIGURE 11.3   Tracking dashboard for COVID-19.

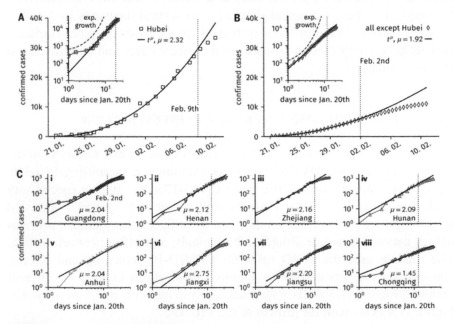

FIGURE 11.4   Growth of COVID-19

11.4.5 USE OF AI AND DEEP LEARNING

At present, continuous endeavors have been made to create novel analytic methodologies utilizing AI calculations. For instance, AI-based screening of SARS-CoV-2 measure plans utilizing a CRISPR-based infection identification framework was exhibited with high affectability and speed. Neural system classifiers were produced for huge scope screening of COVID-19 patients dependent on their particular respiratory example. Also, a profound learning-based examination arrangement of thoracic CT pictures was developed for computerized identification and checking of COVID-19 patients after some time. The quick improvement of robotized analytic frameworks dependent on man-made reasoning and AI cannot just add to expanded symptomatic precision and speed; however, it will likewise secure human services laborers by diminishing their contacts with COVID-19 patients.[8]

A successful remedial methodology is critically expected to treat quickly developing COVID-19 patients around the world. As there is no powerful medication demonstrated to treat COVID-19 patients, it is basic to creating effective ways to deal with repurpose clinically-affirmed medications or structure new medications against SARS-CoV-2.[8] Figure 11.5 explains the Artificial Intelligence and deep learning model for COVID-19.

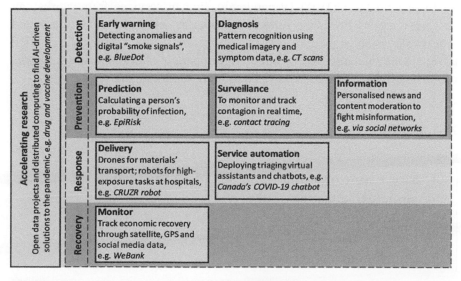

FIGURE 11.5 AI and deep learning model for COVID-19.

11.5   CONCLUSION

We depict a progression of upgrades intended to help the fast arrangement of new strategies, techniques, and conventions over a social insurance framework in light of the COVID-19 pandemic. Within the range of half a month, the size of the flare-up inside India turned out to be obvious to social insurance pioneers on neighborhood, state, and central levels.

As our own country confronted a developing number of known and suspected COVID-19 cases, just as an assortment of patient consideration and operational needs identified with the pandemic, we perceived the significance of the EHR and other innovation-based apparatuses as an empowering subordinate to quickened process plan and execution. The advancement of a multidisciplinary team including institutional pioneers, irresistible ailment and contamination counteraction pros, and innovation specialists is a basic initial phase intending to medical clinic explicit concerns and creating open and gainful correspondence.

An underlying needs-based evaluation was done of the present state to decide the essential operational procedures for the episode of the board, the current informatics structure to help these procedures, and the holes that should have been crossed over in an opportune manner. Doing so permitted us to conveniently suggest a decision support system to help COVID-19 episode of the board as nitty-gritty in this report.

Even with the COVID-19 pandemic, human services frameworks can best get ready by following rules and proposals set out by government and worldwide establishments. The electronic wellbeing record and related advances are fundamental and imperative apparatuses in supporting episodes of the board that ought to be utilized to their maximum capacity.

KEYWORDS

- **severe acute respiratory syndrome**
- **air-decontaminating respirator**
- **artificial Intelligence**
- **deep learning**
- **decision support system**

REFERENCES

1. Adams, J. G.; Walls, R. M. Supporting the Health Care Workforce During the COVID-19 Global Epidemic. *JAMA* **2020,** *323* (15), 1439–1440. DOI: 10.1001/jama.2020.3972.

2. Onder, G.; Rezza, G.; Brusaferro, S. Case-Fatality Rate and Characteristics of Patients Dying in Relation to COVID-19 in Italy. *JAMA* **2020,** *323* (18), 1775–1776. DOI: 10.1001/jama.2020.4683.

3. Grasselli, G.; Pesenti, A.; Cecconi, M. Critical Care Utilization for the COVID-19 Outbreak in Lombardy, Italy: Early Experience and Forecast During an Emergency Response. *JAMA* **2020,** *323* (16), 1545–1546. DOI: 10.1001/jama.2020.4031.

4. Reeves, J. J.; Hollandsworth, H. M.; Torriani, F. J.; Taplitz, R.; Abeles, S.; Tai-Seale, M.; Millen, M.; Clay, B. J.; Longhurst, C. A. Rapid Response to COVID-19: Health Informatics Support for Outbreak Management in an Academic Health System. *J. Am. Med. Inform. Assoc.* **2020,** *ocaa037*. DOI: https://doi.org/10.1093/jamia/ocaa037.

5. Patel, A. B.; Verma, A. COVID-19 and Angiotensin-Converting Enzyme Inhibitors and Angiotensin Receptor Blockers: What Is the Evidence? *JAMA* **2020,** *323* (18), 1769–1770. DOI: 10.1001/jama.2020.4812.

6. del Rio, C.; Malani, P. N. COVID-19—New Insights on a Rapidly Changing Epidemic. *JAMA* **2020,** *323* (14), 1339–1340. DOI: 10.1001/jama.2020.3072.

7. Wu, G.; Yang, P.; Woodruff, H.; Rao, X.; Guiot, J.; Frix, A. -N.; Moutschen, M.; Louis, R.; Li, J.; Li, J.; Yan, C.; Du, D.; Zhao, S.; Ding, Y.; Liu, B.; Sun, W.; Albarello, F.; D'Abramo, A.; Schininà, V.; Lambin, P. Development of a Clinical Decision Support System for Severity Risk Prediction and Triage of COVID-19 Patients at Hospital Admission: an International Multicenter Study, 2020. DOI: 10.1101/2020.05.01.20053413.

8. Alimadadi, A.; Aryal, S.; Manandhar, I.; Munroe, P. B.; Joe, B.; Cheng, X. Artificial Intelligence and Machine Learning to Fight COVID-19. *Physiol Genomics.* **2020,** *52* (4), 200–202. DOI: 10.1152/physiolgenomics.00029.2020.

9. https://gocovid-19.org/

10. Surendra, K.S.; Anunay, G.; Ashutosh, B.; et al. Aetiology, Outcomes & Predictors of Mortality in Acute Respiratory Distress Syndrome from a Tertiary Care Centre in North India. *Indian J. Med. Res.* **2016,** *143*, 782–792.

11. Johns Hopkins University Center for Systems and Science Engineering. Coronavirus COVID-19 Global Cases. https://coronavirus.jhu.edu/map.html (accessed Mar 18, 2020)

CHAPTER 12

Machine Learning Approach for Prediction Analysis of COVID-19

VAISHALI GARG, KHUSHBOO TRIPATHI, and DEEPTHI SEHRAWAT

Department of Computer Science, Amity University, Gurugram, India

ABSTRACT

This scary outbreak severe acute respiratory syndrome – Coronavirus (SARS-CoV-2) also known as COVID-2019 has put the entire lifeline into danger. The whole world is trying to find the best ways to fight against this pandemic in terms of finance, life, infrastructure, and many other resources. The researchers are focusing on their expertise to develop some mathematical formulas to analyze the severity of this pandemic and finding the best way out of it. Due to the high level of complexity and uncertainty of data, several models have shown low accuracy and it varies from nation to nation. So, this paper presents the prediction analysis of the COVID-19 outbreak cases.

12.1 INTRODUCTION

As in today's date, the total number of COVID-19 cases have crossed 55.6 million and the mortality rate is also increasing. This gradual increase in mortality rate is an alarming situation for the entire world. Transmission is being categorized into different modes according to their spread and time. Every country is finding its best possible solutions to overcome this virus.[1]

Computational Intelligence in Analytics and Information Systems, Volume 1: Data Science and AI, Selected Papers from CIAIS-2021. Hardeo Kumar Thakur, Manpreet Kaur, Parneeta Dhaliwal, Rajeev Kumar Arya, and Joan Lu (Eds.)

Many of the countries have adopted different methodologies, such as staying at home, wearing masks, travel restrictions, frequently washing of hands, and in addition to it, common places are sanitized to minimize the outbreak of this disease. Lockdown was imposed in most of the countries to stop unnecessary movements of the people. Up to some extent, this lockdown was helpful, but again the countries have come to the previous positions when the lockdown was restrained.[2] This virus has affected the economy of the entire world. In some places, there occurred shortage of food supplies and people started dying of hunger. The prime minister of the country gave the slogan of social distancing which proved to be helpful somehow. But the number of corona cases are increasing day by day. The person who is found infected is kept in isolation for at least 15 days and given the required treatment according to the severity of the infection in his or her body. Most of the people recovered after 15 days, but many people died because of ignorance and thus severity increased which led to low oxygen level, followed by death. In the initial stages, in India, the confirmed cases were of people who returned from overseas through local transmission, but gradually, this transmission increased. People above the age of 60 and below the age of 10 are more prone to this infection, so more precautions were taken for those people. Till date, no drug or vaccine is available for this virus. Many big paramedical companies have come up with the vaccine trials but could not make up. Due to lack of medical resources and less tests, this pandemic has increased.[3] Thousands of people are tested positive for this disease, it is quite difficult to check each and every person who shows the symptom. Moreover, people did not come forward for the test as there was a fear of isolation which led to sudden increase in the number. Apart from medical techniques and procedures, artificial intelligence and machine learning have come up with certain approaches and methods which can help in predicting and analyzing the rise in the number.[4] However, a large amount of dataset is required for classification and prediction in machine learning algorithms.

12.2   LITERATURE REVIEW AND BACKGROUND STUDY

On December 31, 2019, the People's Republic of China health authority reported a sudden ample number of cases of pneumonia of unknown etiology in Wuhan city of Central China. China reported these sudden cases to WHO. Although the cases were reported since December 8, 2019, but on January

7, this virus was originally given the name 2019-nCov by WHO, which was identified from the throat sample of a patient.[5] Later on, this pathogen was named as SARS-CoV-2 by the research group. Till the end of January, nearly 8K cases were reported in China and 82 cases in 18 different countries. After this, the WHO declared this as a public health emergency of international concern. According to China's report, the mortality rate was very less, nearly about 2–3% in February and 0.2% outside of China. But this rate kept on increasing gradually. So, basically, this review is about currently understanding the situation of this pandemic and getting the possible outcomes to come out of this pandemic as soon as possible.[1]

The following Table 12.1 describes the certain research and reviews done by different research groups. They have tried to figure out certain methods and algorithms which can help in predicting and analyzing the COVID-19 cases. The research groups have used machine learning algorithms like support vector machine, regression to predict the COVID-19 cases. Many of them have given their future plans for higher accuracy of the results.

12.2.1   LITERATURE GAP

The major issue emerging from the literature review comes out to be that different types of epidemic diseases have urged more innovative research on different diseases, viruses, and their effects on different people. More innovation must be done in certain fields such as cooperation of people with the government and biological hazard response. Another key issue which comes out in the machine learning approach is the maintenance of huge data which is very difficult to manage.

12.3   DATASETS AND ML TECHNIQUES

The dataset is being taken from the official website of Johns Hopkins University and WHO. The data consists of daily cases reported. In this paper, the data are in CSV format which include three tables of confirmed, recovered, and death cases of COVID-19. CSV data are also available in the Github data repository. Different strategies of machine learning are performed using python library in Jupyter Notebook to predict and analyze the number of COVID-19 cases. This prediction analysis will help in making the further determinations based on transmission growth, such as security check at

Computational Intelligence in Analytics and Information Systems, Vol. 1

TABLE 12.1   Literature Survey.

Author (s)	Title of papers	Contribution	Method used	Future plan
Sina F. Ardabili Amir Mosavi Pedram Ghamisi Filip Ferdinand	COVID-19 Outbreak Prediction with Machine Learning	Various predictions have been given on COVID-19	Many prediction models like regression have been used	For higher accuracy, models should be created on individual countries
Samuel Lalmuanawma	Applications of machine learning and artificial intelligence for COVID-19 (SARS-CoV-2) pandemic	To review the role of ML and AI as a significant method in screening, forecasting for Sars COVID-19	A selective assessment of information on the research algorithms of ML article was executed on the data that are related to the application of machine learning on COVID-19.	To improve the and AI to help in the ongoing pandemic
Jamal Hussain Lalrinfila Chhakchhuak				
Milind Yadav Murukessan Perumal Dr. M Srinivas	Analysis on novel coronavirus (COVID-19) using machine learning methods	Prediction of spread of corona virus across many regions have been calculated	Different prediction methods have been used to predict the no of cases, deaths	Through predictions warnings are to be created for non-infectious persons to save them from this virus
Ahmad Alimadadi Sachin Aryal Ishan Manandhar	Artificial intelligence and machine learning to fight COVID-19	Provides us with the dataflow diagram of applications of ML and AI in COVID-19	Various hypothesis have been reviewed to provide with best Approach for screening	Machine learning analysis of genetic variants from COVID-19 patients can be performed

airports, sanitation plans, supply of daily essential items, expanding the lockdown phase.

12.3.1 REGRESSION ANALYSIS

Regression analysis is a machine learning technique in which we estimate the relationships among one dependent and one or more than one independent variable. It can be represented as an equation of straight line which can be shown as:

$$Y = dZ + m, \qquad (12.1)$$

where
    Y – Dependent variable
    Z – Independent (explanatory) variable
    d – Intercept
    m – Slope

12.3.2 SUPPORT VECTOR MACHINE

It is a very important machine learning algorithm that plots a line which divides the data into different categories. In this ML algorithm, we calculate the vector to optimize the line. Here, data are plotted with a clear gap as wide as possible. With linear classification, it also performs nonlinear classification. This algo works well with a clear margin among datasets, and is effective in high-dimensional spaces. But it becomes difficult when the data are huge as training the data takes some time.

12.3.3 SIR MODEL

SIR is a simple model that considers a group of people that belongs to one of the following states:

1. **Susceptible (S).** The person has not contracted the disease, but there are chances that he or she may be infected due to transmission of the virus from the infected person.
2. **Infected (I).** This person is suffering from the disease.
3. **Recovered/Deceased (R).** Either the person has developed immunity against the disease or the person has deceased.

Figure 12.1 shows the SIR Model. This model has many states and can be implemented using differential equations in mathematics.

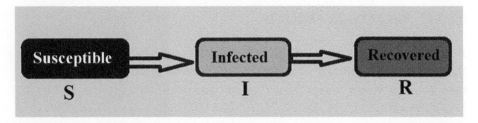

FIGURE 12.1   SIR model.

12.4   METHODOLOGY AND IMPLEMENTATIONS

As mentioned above, we need to analyze the data of COVID-19 using machine learning. Various models can be used to show the predictions. These models show accuracy accordingly. Every model is different on its own and uses a specific approach. Figure 12.2 shows the methodology in processing the data. This figure shows how the data are processed. First of all, the patient's data are collected, then the relevant data are extracted out of that data. Various methodologies, algorithms are used over the data then the relevant output is obtained.

12.4.1   DATA COLLECTION

As WHO declared Coronavirus pandemic as an international concern, all the hospitals and research groups were given open access to the data of the patients. The data were collected and filtered from the repository of Kaggle that includes the data of the patients who have shown the symptoms of this virus or other viruses.

12.4.2   PREPROCESSING

Preprocessing is a very essential step in machine learning. The data may contain some unnecessary information that needs to be filtered. There may be duplicate information present in the data set. Various steps are followed in this process. Data cleaning is the most important step in this process.

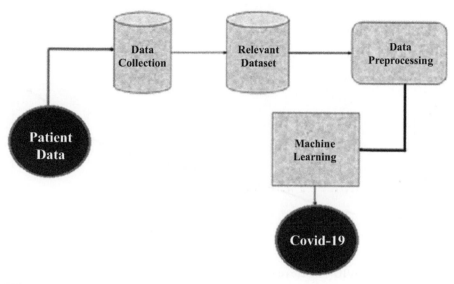

FIGURE 12.2   Methodology of COVID-19.

12.5   RESULTS AND DISCUSSION

COVID-19 has now become a very hot topic in discussion as it is affecting the entire world. All the countries of the world are badly affected because of this virus. Every tenth person has some new symptoms. It has become very difficult to get control over this life-taking virus. There is an urgent need to analyze the data and use the results out of this pandemic as soon as possible. Figure 12.3 shows the number of new cases daily vs number of days. It is clearly visible from the graph that the number of COVID-19 cases kept on increasing day by day. This figure shows the overall increasing figures from the dataset taken.

Figure 12.4 shows the count on the basis of gender. This clearly shows males are more affected than the females.

Figure 12.5 represents the output of the SIR model in which population vs time is shown. This figure tells the number of people who are susceptible, infected, and recovered from COVID-19.

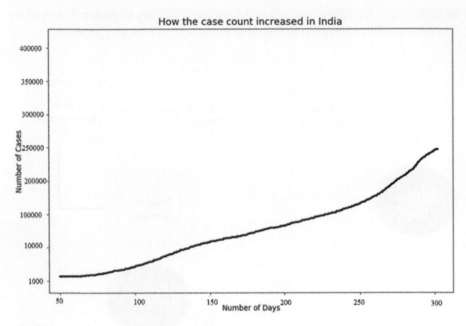

FIGURE 12.3   COVID-19 increasing figures.

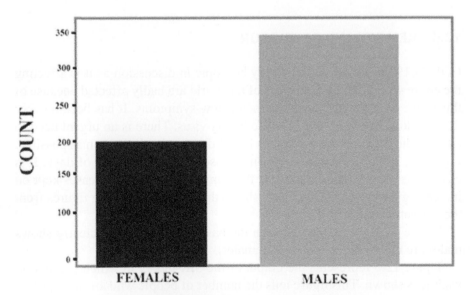

FIGURE 12.4   Counts on the basis of gender.

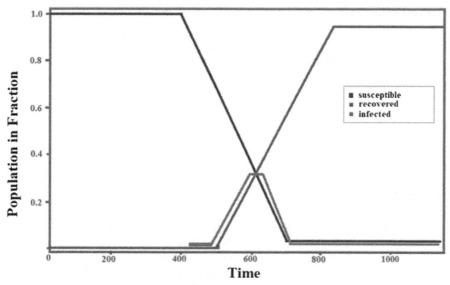

FIGURE 12.5   The output of SIR model.

12.6   CONCLUSION AND FUTURE SCOPE

In this review of this machine learning approach for prediction analysis of COVID-19, the results show the upward going curve of the number of cases. The whole world is under the control of this pandemic, and without any vaccine or medicine, it is quite difficult to come out of this situation.[9,10] Already, a number of people have lost their lives in this pandemic. Adaptive measures are being taken by the government. One way as perceived in China, the number of COVID-19 cases can be minimized by keeping sensitive people away from infected people which includes senior citizens and infants especially.[8] The future scope of machine learning is very bright as it is an emerging technology. Many predictions have been made using machine learning algorithms which somehow are proven correct. Many people have been diagnosed using artificial intelligence along with machine learning algorithms. The future of machine learning is very bright as in the growing world. Many further predictions, analysis can be done using machine learning algorithms. In the case of COVID-19 also, many more algorithms can be used for further analysis and predictions as per the use.

KEYWORDS

- **machine learning**
- **COVID-19**
- **SIR Model**
- **SVM**

REFERENCES

1. Liang, W.; Yao, J.; Chen, A. et al. Early Triage of Critically Ill COVID-19 Patients Using Deep Learning. *Nat. Commun.* **2020,** *11*, 3543.
2. Handay, A. M. U. D.; Rabani, S. T.; Khan, Q. R. Machine Learning Based Approaches for Detecting COVID-19 Using Clinical Text Data. *Int. J. Inf. Tecnol.* 2020, *12*, 731–739.
3. Li, Q.; Guan, X.; Wu, P. Early Transmission Dynamics in Wuhan, China, of Novel Coronavirus-Infected Pneumonia, 2020.
4. WHO. WHO Statement Regarding Cluster of Pneumonia Cases in Wuhan, China, 2020.
5. WHO. Novel Coronavirus (2019-nCoV). Situations Report 21; World Health Organization: Geneva, Switzerland, 2020.
6. Lu, R.; Zhao, X.; Li, J.; Niu, P.; Yang, B.; Wu, H. Genomic Characterization and Epidemiology of 2019 Novel Coronavirus: Implications for Virus Origins and Receptor Binding. *Lancet.* 2020.
7. Zhou, P.; Yang, X. L.; Wang, X. G.; Hu, B.; Zhang, L.; Zhang, W. A Pneumonia Outbreak Associated with a New Coronavirus of Probable Bat Origin. *Nature,* **2020.**
8. Watkins, J. Preventing a Covid-19 Pandemic, 2020.
9. Dashraath, P.; Jeslyn, W. J. L.; Karen, L. M. X.; Min, L. L.; Sarah, L.; Biswas, A.; Lin, S. L.; Coronavirus Disease 2019 (COVID-19) Pandemic and Pregnancy. *Am. J. Obstetr. Gynecol.* 2020.
10. Ciotti, M.; Ciccozzi, M.; Terrinoni A.; Jiang, W. C.; Wang, C. B.; Bernardini, S. The COVID-19 Pandemic. *Crit. Rev. Clin. Lab. Sci.* **2020,** *57* (6), 365–388.

CHAPTER 13

Assessment of Generalized Anxiety Disorder and Mood Disorder in Undergraduate Students During the Coronavirus Disease (COVID-19) Pandemic

DEVESH KUMAR UPADHYAY, SUBRAJEET MOHAPATRA, and NIRAJ KUMAR SINGH

Department of Computer Science and Engineering, Birla Institute of Technology, Mesra, Ranchi, India

ABSTRACT

The Coronavirus pandemic is the biggest outbreak of this century and has caused a great impact on the physical, emotional, behavioral, psychological, and social health of the human being. The undergraduate students are known to be the most active group of the society and are experiencing very high psychological pressure on their mental health. The research paper presents the results which are based on the survey carried out for the assessment of mood disorder and generalized anxiety disorder (GAD) among undergraduate students in India during the period of outbreak, using machine learning algorithms. In this study, we have compared the results of the classifiers and identified the best among them. It has been found successful in the correct identification of mood disorder and generalized anxiety disorder among undergraduate students. Here in this paper, we are focusing on the behavioral

Computational Intelligence in Analytics and Information Systems, Volume 1: Data Science and AI, Selected Papers from CIAIS-2021. Hardeo Kumar Thakur, Manpreet Kaur, Parneeta Dhaliwal, Rajeev Kumar Arya, and Joan Lu (Eds.)

aspects for the automatic detection of mood disorders and anxiety disorder in an early stage of illness, and for this purpose, the behavioral characteristics are fed as an input to K-Nearest Neighbors Algorithm (KNN), support vector machine (SVM), radial basis neural network (RBFN), Naïve Bayesian Classifier (NBC) and Multilayer Perceptron (MLP) classifier as an input, for the assessment of mood disorders among students. In our experiment, it was observed that SVM performed better with an accuracy of 93.91% as compared with RBFN with 90.43%.

13.1   INTRODUCTION

The COVID-19 outbreak was first reported in Wuhan in Hubei province of China on 17th November 2019, and it has been continuously spreading all over the world.[1] The first COVID-19 case in India was reported on 30th January 2020.[2] The COVID-19 outbreak was declared as pandemic by the World Health Organization (WHO) and released emergency guidelines for the whole world.[3]

Due to rapid spreading of coronavirus, all the organizations including educational institutes were closed and lockdown was implemented in India as well as almost all over the world.[4] The lockdown and closure of all the organizations created an environment of uncertainty among the people. The feelings of uncertainty about life have caused depression, anxiety, stress, fear, frustration, panic, and sleep disorder in human beings.[5] In the recent researches, it has been found that the corona pandemic has direct and indirect social and psychological impacts, which are affecting mental health of a human being and might be in recent future as well.[6] Social distancing, wearing masks, isolation strategy, and patient quarantine has been found to be very effective strategies in controlling transmission of a coronavirus.[7]

According to the studies, in India, normally, 10–12% of the people are affected by mental illness either due to depression, anxiety, stress or any other cause.[8] Now, it can be assumed that the psychological issues could have increased many times as compared with normal circumstances. It can be easily assumed that the psychological impacts of coronavirus outbreak are much more in sectors, such as education, information technology (IT), tour and travel, manufacturing, textiles, and other fields.

The undergraduate students are popularly known for their social life and the students are feeling bored, depressed, and distressed because of the uncertainty of opening of their institutes, classes, and examination as well. The final year students are more depressed and worried about their placements, jobs, and joining. In spite of the hard work by teachers, the optimum result in terms of the students' performance is not up to the mark. The contributing factors behind poor performance of students can be enumerated as absence of internet, smartphones, laptops, or due to their poor economic condition.[9,10]

A number of researches and surveys had been carried out for detecting the prevalence of depression, anxiety, and stress among students. Ebert et al.[11] in their study, analyzed the presence of mental illness among undergraduate students and tried to screen out the students at risk of suicide or self-harm, which may help them to recover prior to an accident.

Satyanarayan et al.,[12] in their research paper, used deep learning methods for the categorization of sleep. However, this approach was limited to binary classification of sleep and did not present any idea to deal with sleep disorder and mental illness.

In 2015, Rao et al.[7] carried out research in which they studied the presence of depression, anxiety, and stress among the industrial workers of Bangalore.

In another research, logistic regression was used by Pant et al.[13] to test the relationship between variables, such as age, leaves, and number of years served in an organization to depict the prevalence of depression and anxiety, but this approach was limited to some extent and was not able to predict accurately.

The undergraduate students are known for their active and social life and they are vulnerable to psychological illness. Hence, studying the impact of coronavirus outbreak on the mental health of undergraduate students is needed. The main objective of our study is to assess the level of mood disorder and generalized anxiety disorder among the students by using the machine learning algorithms[14] during the lockdown. In this study, we are considering depression from mood disorders and anxiety disorders. For this purpose, a dataset of 115 people was fed into the classifiers for assessing and predicting the results.

13.2 METHODOLOGY

The main objective of this research is the assessment of depression and anxiety. To satisfy this even handed, the necessary information was gathered with the assistance of questionnaire-based surveys. The proposed method is shown in Figure 13.1.

The set of questions in a questionnaire was based upon behavioral characteristics of anxiety and depression. The collection of sample data involved individuals responding to the questionnaire online in google form.

The data obtained were analyzed under the guidance of medical professionals and then was fed into the algorithms which involved data shuffling as a preprocessing step. The data shuffling step was performed to exempt the monotony of data. After data shuffling, the sample data were divided into two parts, training data and testing data. The model evaluation was done by cross-validation technique as a final step.

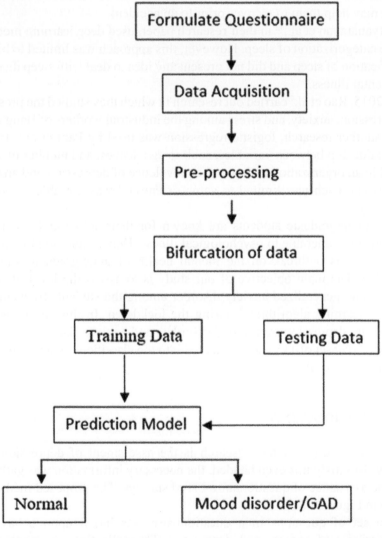

FIGURE 13.1   Proposed methodology.

In our research, we have used five different machine learning classifiers and they are MLP, FBFN, NBC, KNN, and SVM. The performances of all these five classifiers were recorded in terms of accuracy, specificity, and sensitivity.

a. Questionnaires and Characteristics Discussion

The mood disorder and anxiety disorder are the two important mental health disorders in which individuals experience symptoms, such as anger, anxiety, stress, lack of interest in daily work, and many more. The set of questions in a questionnaire were framed with the help of medical professional, based on the various behavioral characteristics of mood disorder and generalized anxiety disorder, such as depressed mood, anger, insomnia, anxiety. These questions are designed in such a way that it can cover all the characteristics of mood disorder and GAD. The questions in a questionnaire are based upon the Hamilton anxiety and depression scale and Hospital anxiety and depression scale (HADS).[15,16] A set of 14 questions were framed into a questionnaire considering seven behavioral characteristics of depression and seven behavioral characteristics of GAD.

b. Data Acquisition

The data collection was done by the web-based survey conducted on the undergraduate students of India, studying different streams in distinct educational organizations all over the nation; independent of their gender, religion, and background in the form of questionnaire. The web-based survey questionnaire was distributed between 10th May 2020 and 30th June 2020. The questionnaire was in the form of google forms that was spread randomly via Facebook, WhatsApp, Instagram, and an e-mail. A total of 115 participants who took part in our survey, and out of that 40 are females and 75 males. The sample collected 115 people, out of those, 60 individuals were normal and 55 were suffering from either mood disorder and GAD. The age group considered for this survey varies from 12 years to 30 years. The research was carried out under the guidance of medical professionals of RINPAS, Ranchi. The participants who took part in our survey are associated with both technical as well as nontechnical streams.

c. Data Preprocessing

In the preprocessing phase, the collected data were processed and cleaned by converting all the responses into the numeric case. Data shuffling was done for removing any biases. In machine learning, the entire dataset can be classified into two parts, that is, training data and testing data. The shuffling of data is done for removing the bias patterns from the dataset, before training is performed. Another advantage of data shuffling is that the neural network model will become more generalized.

Classification: The accurate detection of anxiety and depression is more important by using behavioral characteristics. It could be the aided advantage for both patients and the doctors, and for this purpose, the classification algorithms are used.[17] In this research, we have used five different classifiers and the results of these five classifiers were compared in terms of accuracy, specificity, and sensitivity.

1. **K-Nearest Neighbor (KNN):** The KNN is one of the most popular machine learning algorithms used for regression and classification problems. The KNN algorithm collects information and classifies recent information based on the closest measure. The collected information is then allotted to the class of the nearest neighbor. As KNN is easy to execute with better accuracy, it is often used to classify the future information.[18]

2. **Support Vector Machine (SVM):** The SVM classifier is one of the commonly used machine learning algorithms and it works for both regression and classification problems. The SVM classifier is mainly used in most of the classification problems because it has exceptional classification ability. The SVM divides the space into two separate classes of the hyperplane. SVM divides the hyperplane in such a way that the distance between two classes is wide.[19]

3. **Multilayer Perceptron (MLP):** The multilayer perceptron is a neural network model in which the signals are transmitted from input layer to output layer. It is unidirectional in nature and this unique feature does not allow output neurons to affect other neurons.[20] The architecture of MLP consists of three layers, namely, input layer, output layer, and hidden layer. The nonlinear activation function is the significance of MLP and any nonlinear function can be implemented with exception. The input layer's job is to relay the signals to the higher layer. The hidden layer contains activation function along

with weighted bias. There may be more than one hidden layer in the network. The hidden layer transmits the signal to the higher layer or output layer.

4. **Radial Basis Neural Network (RBFN):** The Radial basis neural network has two layered networks and each hidden layer consists of a radial activation function. The input layer of RBFN is nonlinear and the output layer is linear in nature. The signal received at the output layer is the weighted sum of the input signal from the hidden layer.[21] The main objective of this network is, through the application of radial kernels, such as Gaussian functions, to predict the target output. The RBFN learning is achieved by cost updating, which is the mean square error of the input layer to output layer mapping.

5. **Naïve Bayesian Classifier (NBC):** The naïve Bayesian classification algorithm is based on Bayes theorem and it is used for two class and multiple class classification problems. The NBC is one of the powerful machine learning classifiers which updates weights based on conditional probability. The NBC algorithm depends upon the naïve assumptions, where the input variables are independent.[22]

13.3 VALIDATION

In machine learning technique, when the classifiers are trained for any input dataset, it may or may not achieve accuracy for other datasets and for just avoiding this problem, the concept of cross-checking called validation was introduced.[23] The validation technique is not going to help us in increasing the accuracy level of any classifiers. It simply makes it more robust and generalized. The classifier processes each dataset in this method and has been run for K-times to measure precision for each subsequent run.

13.4 PERFORMANCE ANALYSIS

The performance analysis process is done by using machine learning algorithms to analyze the efficiency of the classifiers. The performance analysis is performed by using confusion matrix for the calculation of accuracy, sensitivity, specificity, error rate, precision, F1-measure, and kappa. Table 13.1 showing confusion matrix for performance assessment.

TABLE 13.1 Confusion Matrix for Performance Assessment.

Classifier Output	Psychiatrist Opinion	
	Positive (Mood disorder and anxiety disorder)	Negative (Normal)
Positive (Mood disorder / Anxiety)	TP (True-Positive): Correctly identified	FP (False-Positive): Correctly rejected
Negative (Normal)	FN (False-Negative): Incorrectly rejected.	TN (True-Negative): Incorrectly identified

The confusion matrices for performance assessment are governed by their respective formulas and are explained below:

$$Accuracy = \frac{TP + TN}{TP + FP + TN + FN} x\ 100$$

$$Specificity = \frac{TN}{TN + FP} x\ 100$$

$$Sensitivity = \frac{TP}{TP + FN} x\ 100$$

Error Rate = 1 – Accuracy.

$$Precision = \frac{TP}{TP + FP}$$

$$F1\ Measure = 2\ x \frac{\left(Precision\ x\ Sensitivity \right)}{\left(Precision + Sensitivity \right)}$$

13.5 RESULTS

The complete research study was carried out on a core i7 computer with 16 GB of ram. The operating system used was Windows 10 pro and the code was done using python. In this study, an automated system was developed for the assessment of mood disorder and GAD among undergraduate students. For this purpose, we have used the behavioral characteristics discussed above. A dataset of 115 people was taken in which 60 individuals were normal and 55 were suffering from either Mood disorder or GAD. For this process, the collected dataset was divided into training and testing data. The confusion matrix was used for performance assessment and the calculation of accuracy, specificity, and sensitivity.

To achieve the above objective, a system was designed and developed with the help of five different machine learning classifiers to predict the depression and anxiety among undergraduate students. The predicted result was obtained by following the steps explained in above flowchart shown in Figure 13.1. In the first step, the questionnaires were framed according to the behavioral characteristics of mood disorder and GAD and then the question-naires were distributed by various media. Responses of individuals were recorded under the guidance of medical professionals; this is explained in Section 13.2 (A). In Section 13.2 (B), the preprocessing of data is explained. In the next step, K-Fold validation was performed for fivefolds for all the classifiers KNN, SVM, RBFN, MLP, and Naïve bayes classifier. Table 13.2 displays the confusion matrix of all the five classifiers generated after five-fold cross-validation. In Table 13.2, a represents the presence of depression or anxiety among students, whereas b represents normal students.

TABLE 13.2 Confusion Matrix of Classifiers.

Classifier	Classified as	a	b
KNN	a	48	7
	b	9	51
NBC	a	40	15
	b	14	46
MLP	a	46	9
	b	13	47
RBFN	a	49	6
	b	5	55
SVM	a	51	4
	b	3	57

N.B.- a:Mood disorder/GAD present, b: Mood disorder/GAD absent

Table 13.3 displays the accuracy level of all the classifiers and from that we can find that SVM performed better with accuracy level of 93.91% and followed by RBFN with accuracy level of 90.43%. It is very clear from Table 13.3 and Figure13.2 that the SVM classifier performed better than the other four classifiers in each and every respect.

The computation time of any classifier is one of the important measures as it shows the time taken by the classifier to complete the classification process. Table 13.4 presents the computation time for all the classifiers. Here from Table 13.4 and Figure 13.3, it is very clear that SVM is taking minimum time as compared with others.

TABLE 13.3 Performance of Classifiers.

Classifiers	Accuracy	Sensitivity	Specificity	Error Rate	Precision	F1 Score
KNN	86.08	87.27	85	13.91	84.21	85.71
NBC	74.78	72.72	76.67	25.22	74.07	73.39
MLP	80.87	83.64	78.34	19.13	77.96	80.7
RBFN	90.43	89.09	91.66	9.57	90.74	89.5
SVM	93.91	92.73	95	6.09	94.45	93.58

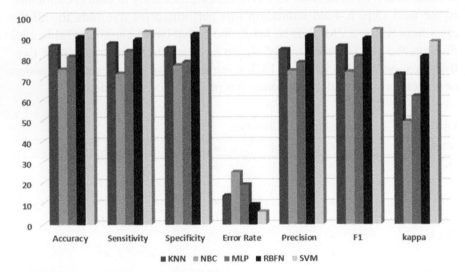

FIGURE 13.2 Performance of classifiers.

TABLE 13.4 Computation Time of Classifiers.

Classifiers	Time
KNN	1.32
NBC	1.14
MLP	3.57
RBFN	4.31
SVM	0.85

13.6 CONCLUSION

The mood disorder and generalized anxiety disorder are the emerging psychological disorders in the coronavirus outbreak. Depression, anxiety, and stress can challenge the vitality of students of any educational institute both mentally and physically. Hence, it is very alarming situation for not only students, it is for a human being. The announcement of lockdown and COVID-19 outbreak are building an atmosphere of fear, stress, and uncertainty of life as the people are forced to stay at home and these things are creating mood disorder and generalized anxiety disorder among undergraduate students. This study is based on the behavioral characteristics mood disorder and GAD. The proposed method is comparatively inexpensive and very simple as compared with other methods of detection. In this study, our objective was to formulate an algorithm, which can be used for the assessment of mood disorder and GAD with better accuracy, specificity, sensitivity, and also consume less time to do so. It was found from above results that the SVM is performed better with accuracy level of 93.91% as compared with others. Moreover, the system can be extended with further modifications. Our methodology can be standardized and it will definitely help the physician and others to diagnose the mood disorder and generalized anxiety disorder.

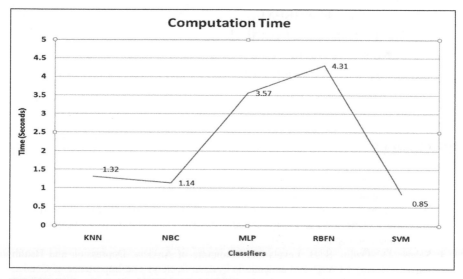

FIGURE 13.3   Computation time of classifiers.

ACKNOWLEDGMENTS

All the authors would like to thank all the participants who filled the questionnaire and became part of this survey. The authors acknowledge the

Department of Science and Technology, Govt. of India for financial support vide reference No. DST/CSRI/2017/400 under Cognitive Science Research Initiative to carry out this work. The authors wish to thank Dr. Varun S. Mehta, Associate Professor at Central Institute of Psychiatry, and Madhu Gupta, Research Scholar, Ranchi Institute of Neuropsychiatry and Allied Sciences, Ranchi for their guidance and support, which led to successful completion of this research.

KEYWORDS

- **mood disorders**
- **generalized anxiety disorder**
- **machine learning**
- **classifier**
- **support vector machine (SVM)**
- **K-nearest neighbor (KNN)**
- **Naïve Bayesian Classifier (NBC)**
- **radial basis neural network (RBFN)**
- **multilayer perceptron (MLP)**

REFERENCES

1. https://www.livescience.com/first-case-coronavirus-found.html.
2. https://covidindia.org/open-data/
3. World Health Organization. Rolling Updates on Coronavirus Disease (COVID-19). 2020. https://www.who.int/emergencies/diseases/novelcoronavirus-2019/events-as-they-happen (accessed on May 5, 2020).
4. Selçuk, Ö.; Özdin, Ş. B. Levels and Predictors of Anxiety, Depression and Health Anxiety During COVID-19 Pandemic in Turkish Society: The Importance of Gender. *Int. J. Social Psych.* **2020,** *8.* DOI: 10.1177/0020764020927051.
5. Holmes, E. A.; O'Connor, R. C.; Christensen, H.; Silver, R. C.; Everall, I.; Ford, T.; John, A.; Kabir, T.; King, K.; Madan, I.; Michie, S.; Przybylski, A. K; Shafran, R.; Sweeney, A.; Worthman, C. M.; Yardley, L.; Cowan, K.; Cope, C.; Hotopf, M.; Bullmore, E.; Multidisciplinary Research Priorities for the COVID-19 Pandemic: A Call for Action for Mental Health Science. *Lancet Psych.* **2020,** *7,* 547–560.
6. Aqeel, M.; Shuja, K. H.; Abbas, J.; Rehna, T.; Ziapour, A. The Influence of Illness Perception, Anxiety and Depression Disorders on Students Mental Health during

COVID-19 Outbreak in Pakistan: A Web-Based Cross-Sectional Survey. *BMC Public Health, Preprint* **2020.** DOI:10.21203/rs.3.rs-30128/v1.

7. Rao and Ramesh, N. Depression, Anxiety and Stress Levels in Industrial Workers: A Pilot Study in Bangalore, India. *Ind. Psych. J* **2015,** *24* (1), 23–28.

8. Vajpai, S. K. Identification of Factors Responsible for Early Onset of Dementia Among IT Sector Workers in India: A Survey Approach. *Int. J. Emerg. Technol. Innov. Res.* **2020,** *7* (6), 373–381.

9. Cao, W.; Fang, Z.; Hou, G.; Han, M.; Xu, X.; Dong, J. et al. The Psychological Impact of the COVID-19 Epidemic on College Students in China. *Psych. Res.* https://doi.org/10.1016/j. psychres.2020.112934.

10. Agha, E. Learning Rebooted: Online Education During Covid-19 Lockdown Puts Spotlight on India's Digital Divide, 2020. https://www.news18.com/news/india/learningrebooted-online-education-during-covid-19-lockdown-puts-spotlight-on-indias-digital-divide-2563265.html.

11. Ebert, D. D.; Buntrock, C.; Mortier, P.; Auerbach, R.; Weisel, K. K.; Kessler, R. C.; Cuijpers, P.; Green, J. G.; Kiekens. G.; Nock, M. K.; Demyttenaere, K.; Bruffaerts, R. Prediction of Major Depressive Disorder Onset in College Students. *Depress Anxiety* **2019,** *36* (4), 294–304. doi: 10.1002/da.22867. Epub 2018 Dec 6. PMID: 30521136.

12. Sathyanarayana, A. et al. Sleep Quality Prediction from Wearable Data Using Deep Learning. *JMIR mHealth and uHealth* **2015,** 4 (4), e125. DOI: 10.2196/mhealth.6562

13. Pant, Introduction to Logistic Regression. https://towardsdatascience.com/introduction-to-logistic-regression -66248243c148. 2019.

14. Michie, D.; Spiegelhalter, D. J.; Taylor, C. C. Machine Learning. *Neural Statistical Classification* **1994,** *13,* 1–298.

15. Evans, M. Diagnosis of Depression in Elderly Patients. *Adv. Psychiatr. Treat.* **2000,** *6* (1), 49–56.

16. Herrmann, N.; Mittmann, N.; Silver, I. L. et al. A Validation Study of the Geriatric Depression Scale Short Form. *Int. J. Geriatr. Psych.* **1996,** *11* (5), 457–460.

17. Imandoust, B.; Bolandraftar, M. Application of k-Nearest Neighbor (KNN) Approach for Predicting Economic Events: Theoretical Background. *Int. J. Eng. Res. App.* **2013,** 605–610.

18. Jabbar, M.; Deekshatulu, B.; Chandra, P. Classification of Heart Disease Using k-Nearest Neighbor and Genetic Algorithm. *Procedia Technol.* **2013,** *10,* 85–94.

19. Mohapatra, S. Development of Impulse Noise Detection Schemes for Selective filtering, Master's thesis, National Institute of Technology Rourkela, 2008.

20. Patrikar, A. M. Approximating Gaussian Mixture Model or Radial Basis Function Network with Multilayer Perceptron. *IEEE Trans. Neural Netw. Learn Syst.* **2013,** *24* (7), 1161–1166. DOI: 10.1109/TNNLS.2013.2249086.

21. Martinez-Arroyo, M.; Sucar, L. E. Learning an Optimal Naive Bayes Classifier. *18th Int. Conf. Pattern Recognition (ICPR'06) IEEE* **2006,** *3,* 1236–1239.

22. Friedman, N.; Goldszmidt, M. Bayesian Network Classifiers. *Machine Learn.* **1997,** *29* (2–3), 131–163.

23. Krishni. K-Fold Cross Validation, Dec 16, 2018. https://medium.com/datadriveninvestor/k-fold-cross-validation-6b8518070833.

CHAPTER 14

Evaluation of Deep Learning Models for Medical Tools Classification

SHWETA BALI and S. S. TYAGI

Department of Computer Science and Engineering,
Faculty of Engineering & Technology, Manav Rachna International
Institute of Research & Studies, Faridabad, India

ABSTRACT

Pandemic has engulfed society on a global scale so there is an urgent need to integrate artificial intelligence with the medical domain. To reduce the chances of infection and preparation time for different clinical activities, an automated system is proposed to assist the nurses in the process of classification of different medical tools. Deep learning models have superseded traditional machine learning models in different domains. These models use convolutional neural networks (CNNs) as the backbone and work on the assumption that large datasets are required to achieve high classification accuracies for solving different problems. In the medical domain, the datasets are either not available or have limited size, so the deep learning transfer learning-based models have emerged and shown good results to solve different kinds of the problems. In transfer, learning techniques CNNs-based pretrained models are used to transfer the learned knowledge to the problem at hand. The main assumption of such pretrained models is that the earlier layers of these networks are capable of detecting low different features, such as edges, shapes, contours of the objects, and the later layers are used to extract category-specific features of the problem dataset

Computational Intelligence in Analytics and Information Systems, Volume 1: Data Science and AI, Selected Papers from CIAIS-2021. Hardeo Kumar Thakur, Manpreet Kaur, Parneeta Dhaliwal, Rajeev Kumar Arya, and Joan Lu (Eds.)

by retraining the network. There are different types of CNN-architectures available such as VGG16, InceptionV3, Xception, Resnet50 which have been trained on 1000 categories of the ImageNet dataset. There exist two methodologies to customize a pretrained model. In the first approach, the pretrained models are used as feature extractors where there is no need to retrain the entire model, the CNN can extract generic features which serve as a good estimate of the image representations and classification part of the pretrained model is trained to work on specific classes. In this paper, two classifiers namely a fully connected feedforward network and global average pooling network are used. In the second approach, unfreeze the frozen model of the first approach and combine it with the newly added classifier and last layers of the base model. This is called fine-tuning. In the paper, four models are compared for classifying medical tools and experiments showed that different models gave good performance, but inceptionV3-Global average pooling model provided optimal performance. The computerized classification using transfer learning pretrained models has proved to be useful in the medical tools classification.

14.1   INTRODUCTION

Artificial intelligence (AI) has fostered the development of automated applications across different domains at a very rapid pace. This scope of integration covers applications ranging from laboratories to high-end diagnostics. By bringing AI and medicine closer, the clinicians can benefit from the computational power of technology to simplify tedious tasks and achieve assistance in making decisions. Deep learning-based models involve a sequence of nonlinear processing layers with the capacity to find high-level features from large datasets. The large number of benchmarked datasets and graphical processing units (GPUs) have contributed to the incredible success of deep learning architectures. Deep learning has made a lot of progress in recent years in solving large numbers of complex problems in various domains.[1] Deep learning architectures learn the representations in the large datasets by using the backpropagation algorithm and updating the parameters of the network in each epoch of the training.[2] Conventional machine learning techniques extracted features as per the domain expert's knowledge to convert data into feature vectors from which the classifier classifies the patterns. On the other hand, deep learning techniques extract features automatically for the process of classification. In image classification, the images are classified into a set of predefined classes. A significant amount of research in the medical field to solve the image classification has been performed on different types of images such as ultrasound images, tuberculosis radiograph, cervical histopathological images, and pulmonary images. Wireless sensor networks can be used as an effective method to collect data.[4] The deep learning architectures are used for the segmentation of nonrigid surgical instruments by taking advantage of multiscale feature extraction.[5] In one of the research, the authors combined statistical learning and geometry for detecting, segmenting, and 3D pose estimation for surgical tools.[6] The main challenge is the unavailability of medical datasets which is the main requirement of deep learning models to reach achievable targets. In real-world applications, the distribution of the training and test data is different and in case the data are not available in one domain then transfer learning techniques are used to transfer the knowledge to the other domain.[7] From the literature, it is found that there are three main methods that can be used for classification: training convolutional neural network (CNN) from scratch, using pretrained models for extracting the bottleneck features, and integrating unsupervised pretrained models with fine-tuning techniques. Another successful method is transfer learning. Two specific problems, detection of thoracoabdominal lymph nodes and classification of interstitial lung disease were solved.[8] Transfer learning techniques generate more generalized models and exhibit better performance than basic CNN models. Significant research has been done in transfer learning but its application for the medical tools remains limited. In this paper, we addressed the problem of classifying medical tools into four categories by creating a subset of images belonging to different tools from the ImageNet dataset. ImageNet is a large database created for use in object recognition containing more than 14 million images with bounding boxes.[9] Since the newly created dataset is small, pretrained models are used for classification. Scalpel and thermometer do not belong to 1000 classes on which pretrained models are trained and are also taken as part of the dataset. In Section 14.2, related literature is presented. Section 14.3 presents two architectures based on transfer learning techniques that are used to classify medical tools present in the images. Section 14.4 explores the datasets, methodology adopted, experimental results, and analysis of different network architectures used in the present work. Section 14.5 summarizes the findings. Section 14.7 highlights future work.

14.2 RELATED LITERATURE

In this section, the literature and the related work is discussed for different medical domain applications for classifying different types of the images.

The authors solved the problem of the absence of the labeled data and performed a feature extraction process with the help of deep learning models using VGGNet-16 and ResNet-50 for classification in ImageCLEF2015 and ImageCLEF2016 datasets. The overfitting problem was solved with data augmentation. The system comprises of various deep CNNs that have different depths and a voting system. The results in terms of accuracy were 76.87% in ImageCLEF2015 and 87.37% in ImageCLEF201 as compared the previous baselines of 60.91% and 85.38% in ImageCLEF2015 and ImageCLEF2016, respectively. As the future scope, they mentioned the use of more powerful CNNs such as ResNet-152 and multiple Kernel learning for better fusion.[10] The authors discussed the problem of classification of the surgical tools and combined two networks to create an ensemble to solve the problem of multilabel classification in laparoscopic videos.[11] The authors presented three techniques to use the pretrained CNNs for detecting tuberculosis from radiographs. The first method consists of three CNN-based architectures for feature extraction and support vector machine (SVM) for classification. In the second method, three CNN-based architectures are used to extract the features from subregions and later combined to yield a global descriptor that is fed to SVM for training. The best SVMs are used to create ensemble of the classifiers. They outlined the use of other datasets for chest radiographs, such as JSTR Digital Image database.[12] Ensemble transfer learning to classify cervical histopathological images. They experimented using different transfer learning models such as Xception, VGG-16, Resnet-50, InceptionV3 for classification, and a weighted-voting-based ensemble learning technique was introduced to boost the results.[13] Pretrained models such as InceptionV3 transfer learning model to classify pulmonary images to extract the features and the vectors are further fed to different models namely logistic model, Softmax model, and SVM model.[14] Data augmentation and fine-tuning techniques are employed for boosting the performance. AlexNet network architecture was used for classifying different types of tooth from dental cone-beam CT slices. The regions of interests were used to extract single teeth from CT slices. Images are rotated and intensity transformations are applied to reduce overfitting.[15] Deep learning systems were used for classifying four types of liver lesions from a small set of training examples using transfer learning and fine-tuning techniques.[16] Residual network architecture to classify 21 tools used in the videos of the cataract surgery named cataracts challenge dataset.[17] Each image is assigned more than one label and the dataset is highly imbalanced. They experimented that fine tuning the network produced better results than Resnet being used as feature extractor. The AUC score is 0.957 on the test set. In Ref. 18, the authors identified different datasets and analyzed them. They also made a comparison study on the complete pipeline from feature extraction till classification. The detectors were also compared. Technique to detect the surgical instruments using ensemble-based learning was proposed to reduce the computational requirements in retinal microsurgery and laparoscopic image sequences. They estimated 2D position orientation of the instruments in the image sequences. They also introduced the early stopping technique for the classification purpose.[19] Multilabel classification task was performed by addressing the class imbalance during the CNN training on M2CAI16 tool detection toolset.[20] They further highlighted the use of stratification, temporal smoothing for better prediction. The researchers worked toward developing a context-aware system to guide the surgical team and optimize the processes inside the operating room.[21] The CNN-based techniques are used to handle the imbalance in the data and improve classification performance.

14.3 NETWORK ARCHITECTURES

In this paper, two pretrained models VGG16 and InceptionV3 are used for classification of the medical tools.

14.3.1 VGG16 ARCHITECTURE

CNN-based architecture for image classification showed good performance on ImageNet dataset. Also, the results have proved that deeper networks improve classification accuracy. This architecture consists of 16 layers with 13 convolutional layers with 3×3 convolutional filters and max-pooling layers followed by three fully connected layers with 138 million parameters. The input to the network is an image of size 224×224 RGB image. After subtraction of mean average is subtracted from the image, it is passed to several convolutional layers. Convolutional layers use 3×3 filter kernel and stride = 1 and max-pooling layer that use 2×2 filter kernel and stride = 2. The architecture comprises two fully connected layers with 4096 nodes each followed by a SoftMax classifier. All hidden layers are supplied with ReLU activation to handle nonlinearity. Deeper VGG architectures are more prone to vanishing gradient problems and hence require more training and tuning of more parameters. As it has a large depth and a good number of fully connected nodes, it requires 533 MB of the memory. The network weights are also quite large.[22]

14.3.2   INCEPTIONV3 ARCHITECTURE

One of the major drawbacks of VGG-16 is the vast amount of the computation required the large number of parameters. A deep CNN architecture was proposed that produced outstanding results for image classification, object detection, and won the challenges in 2014.[23] GoogLeNet (Inception V1) has nine inception modules, and it consists of 22 layers with the increase in depth and width of their network. The architecture used 1×1 convolutions and rectified linear activations. The network consisted of global average pooling (GAP) added at the end of the last inception module and applied auxiliary classifiers. They applied the SoftMax function to outputs of two inception modules and then calculated auxiliary loss. To further improve the model, a new model Inception V2 came into existence in which 5×5 convolution was factored into two 3×3 convolution operations to improvise computational speed, they also factorized $n \times n$ convolutions to a grouping of $1 \times n$ and $n \times 1$ convolutions, filter banks in the module were made wider to remove representational bottleneck. Further a new architecture Inception V3 had RMSProp optimizer, batch normalization to auxiliary classifiers, factorized 7×7 convolutions, and added label smoothing as a regularizer.

14.4   PROCESS METHODOLOGY FOR MEDICAL TOOLS CLASSIFICATION

The methodology is subdivided into different steps. Data preprocessing is the initial step. The second step is to extract the bottleneck features from the pretrained model. The third step is to send the extracted feature vector to the classifier for the training. The classifier can be a fully connected network or GAP network. Finally, the model is evaluated on the validation set and then fine-tuned and later tested on the test data. The process is shown in Figure 14.1. Feature extraction is performed using the pretrained models and for classification there are two techniques either fully connected network or GAP classifier model are experimented.

14.4.1   PRETRAINED CNN AS FEATURE EXTRACTOR

The convolutional base of pretrained models is used for extracting the bottleneck features and fed to the classifier. Classifiers are added at the top of the network for classification solutions proposed by Chollet[24] with some modifications.

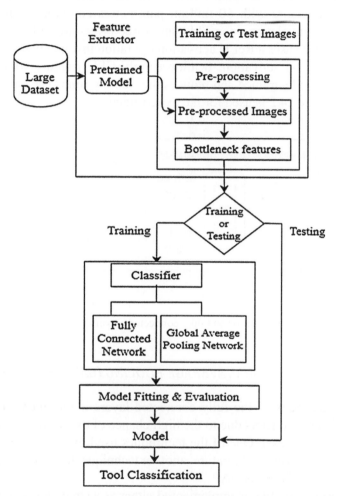

FIGURE 14.1 Process methodology for medical tools classification.

14.4.1.1 ADDING FULLY CONNECTED NETWORK AS CLASSIFIER

In this convolutional blocks are frozen, and fully connected layers are trained on the custom dataset. The weights of the convolutional blocks are not modified, whereas the weights of fully connected layers are trained and updated. The output feature maps from the last layer are first flattened into a vector and then they are mapped to a network of fully connected layers to the final output layer that has the same number of the nodes as the number of the classes and SoftMax activation function is used. AlexNet is a layered neural network architecture with 60 million parameters comprise of five layers that perform convolution operations, and three layers are fully connected.[22] This architecture uses a ReLU activation operation that handles nonlinearity replacing the tanh activation. It allows multi-GPU training which allows larger models to be trained and reduces the training time. The similar architecture in Figure 14.2 is used for the experiments.

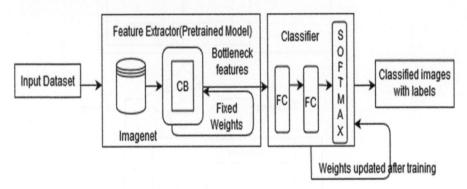

FIGURE 14.2   Feature extraction and fully connected classification network.

14.4.1.2   ADDING GLOBAL AVERAGE POOLING (GAP) AS CLASSIFIER

The main drawback of the fully connected layers is that there are a large number of the parameters due to the high chance of overfitting by the model on the training dataset. One of the techniques used by the researchers is to use the dropout layers. In literature, another technique that has been powerful to minimize overfitting is GAP.

This form of pooling is implemented either as a single layer at the top or near the top of the network. There is a dramatic reduction in the number of learnable parameters in the model and thus the requirement of computational resources is reduced, and it allows variable-sized input images. GAP makes the model more generalizable. The dimensions are reduced where a tensor with dimensions $h \times w \times d$ is reduced to a size of $1 \times 1 \times d$. This technique of GAP where the gap layers reduce $h \times w$ feature map to a single number by taking average of all hw values.[23] It reduces the data significantly and the resultant vector is fed to the final softmax activation function in the output layer which generates category-wise predicted probability. Due to no trainable parameters, it is faster to train the model. CNN that is equipped with the GAP layers can be used for both the classification and object detection. A similar technique is shown in Figure 14.3 in the experiments.

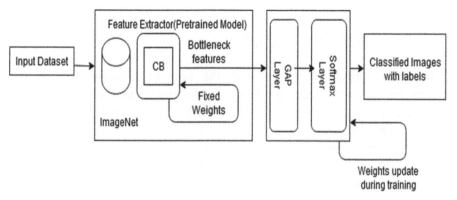

FIGURE 14.3   Feature extraction and global average pooling (GAP) classification network.

14.5   EXPERIMENTS ANALYSIS

In this section, Keras library with TensorFlow as the backend is used for experimentation. Architecture models for TensorFlow and pretrained weights were downloaded from the repositories. Experimentation is performed on Google Colab Tool with Tesla K80 GPU, pci bus id: 0000:00:04.0, compute capability: 3.7.

14.5.1   DATASET DESCRIPTION

The dataset is created as a subset of a benchmarked dataset named ImageNet.[26] The dataset comprises images of stethoscope, syringes, thermometer, and scalpels. A total of 464 images are in the training dataset,124 images in the validation dataset, and 152 images in the testing dataset. The images have different resolutions, so they need to be preprocessed to work on the pretrained models as per their architecture requirement. To work with pretrained models VGG-16 and Inception V3, the images were resized to be 224 × 224 for VGG-16 and 299 × 299 for Inception V3. These pretrained models are trained on 100 classes of ImageNet databases. The bottleneck features are extracted from the convolutional base of the pretrained models and fed to the classifier.

The classifier is trained on the features extracted for the custom dataset. Either the fully connected network or GAP network is used. Adam optimizer is used with a learning rate of 0.0001. Since the dataset is small, the model is trained for 15 epochs and batch size of 15. The model is evaluated on a validation dataset.

14.5.2   METRICS FOR EVALUATION

Different models are evaluated with the help of different performance metrics namely precision, recall, F1-score, accuracy specified in Table 14.1. In the medical tool classification process, positive means that the image contains one of the tools among scalpel, syringe, stethoscope, and thermometer. For example, for scalpel class, true positive (TP) means that the model predicted the image contains the scalpel and it is labelled as scalpel. False positive (FP) is defined as misclassification of the image without scalpel to label as image with scalpel. Negative means the tool which is searched is not present. False negative (FN) is defined as misclassification of the image with scalpel and is labeled as without scalpel. True negative (TN) means the image without scalpel is tested by the model and is correctly labeled as not scalpel.

TABLE 14.1   Metrics for Evaluation.

Metrics	Formulae
Accuracy	TP+TN/TP+TN+FP+FN
Precision	TP/TP+FP
Recall	TP/TP+FN
F1-score	2TP/2TP+FP+FN

14.5.3   MODEL PARAMETERS FOR EVALUATION

Table 14.2 lists the values of the different parameter values set for the models in the experiments. Four models are tested: Model-1 (VGG16 as feature extractor and fully connected classifier), Model-2 (VGG16 as feature extractor and GAP classifier), Model-3 (InceptionV3 as feature extractor and fully connected classifier), and Model-4 (InceptionV3 as feature extractor and GAP network).

TABLE 14.2   Different Model Parameters for Evaluation.

Feature extractor	VGG16/inceptionV3
Classifier	Fully connected network/global average network
Loss function	Cross-entropy
Activation function	ReLU
Optimization algorithm	Adam
Weights initialization	Random
Batch normalization	No
Learning rate	0.0001
Batch size	15
Epochs	15

14.5.4   RESULTS

Table 14.3 outlines the classification results for all the models in terms of accuracy.

TABLE 14.3   Classification Accuracy Results [in (%)].

Tool	Model-1	Model-2	Model-3	Model-4
Stethoscope	82	84	97	97
Scalpel	50	50	89	89
Thermometer	76	61	84	87
Syringe	70	61	92	87

It shows that Model-3 and Model-4 show good performance in classifying different tools. The accuracy for classifying syringes is better for the Model-3 whereas for all other tools the accuracy of Model-4 is greater. Table 14.4 depicts the classification results in terms of precision.

TABLE 14.4   Classification Precision Results [in (%)].

Tool	Model-1	Model-2	Model-3	Model-4
Stethoscope	76	63	90	93
Scalpel	66	54	87	87
Thermometer	62	72	94	89
Syringe	60	68	92	92

It is found that Model-4 depicts higher precision values for stethoscope, syringe, and scalpel. Table 14.5 shows the performance in terms of recall. It shows that Model-4 and Model-3 have comparable performance. Table 14.6 shows the F1-score for models and Model-4 and Model-3 are better than the other two models.

TABLE 14.5   Classification Recall Results [in (%)].

Tool	Model-1	Model-2	Model-3	Model-4
Stethoscope	82	84	97	97
Scalpel	50	50	89	89
Thermometer	76	61	89	87
Syringe	55	61	72	87

TABLE 14.6   Classification F1-Score Results [in (%)].

Tool	Model-1	Model-2	Model-3	Model-4
Stethoscope	78	72	94	95
Scalpel	57	52	88	88
Thermometer	68	66	89	88
Syringe	58	64	92	89

Figures 14.4 and 14.5 depicts accuracy score for training and validation datasets as well as loss on training and validation datasets with the number of epochs for different models. The validation loss fluctuates little but along with training loss in all the experiments. The validation loss and the training loss are close to each other in the case of model-4 in Figure 14.5. Model-4 shows the least amount of overfitting.

14.6   CONCLUSION

The objective of this paper is to find a model suitable for achieving highly accurate results on a small dataset of medical tools. The study covered different aspects of the CNN architecture as the backbone. We successfully found that the InceptionV3 architecture proved to be useful in the process of classifying different medical tools. A series of the experiments were conducted on the medical tools dataset. This study will help in the automation process that will help the doctors/nurses in the operating room. Some of the drawbacks of the research are listed as under:

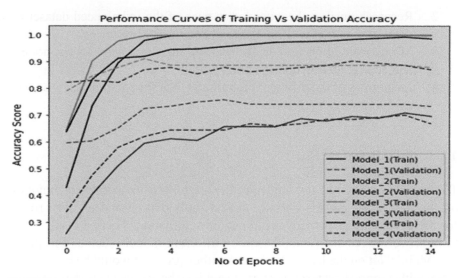

FIGURE 14.4 Accuracy curve results for different models used for medical tools classification.

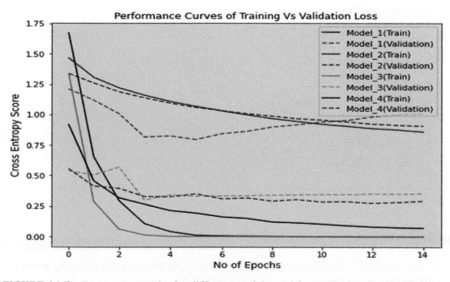

FIGURE 14.5 Loss curve results for different models used for medical tools classification.

1. All the experiments are carried on the image containing the single object. So, the model needs to check for occluded images, images with complex backgrounds.

2. Research needs to be extended in case of the imbalanced dataset as most of the other tools that are not considered are few.
3. More research on finding the optimal number of the layers, nodes, and activation function can be explored.
4. Ensembles of the different pretrained CNN for small datasets can be explored further.

14.7 FUTURE SCOPE

The experiments conducted confirmed the use of transfer learning techniques on the pretrained models on the medical tools dataset and allowed room for the development of many solutions for automation. There are still ways to improve the results by implementing different models such as Inception V4, MobileNet on the larger datasets. Another prospect would be blending a CNN with a long-short term memory, to achieve better results and efficiency.

KEYWORDS

- **deep learning**
- **transfer learning**
- **image classification**
- **artificial intelligence**
- **pretrained models**
- **medical tools**

REFERENCES

1. Schmidhuber, J. Deep learning in neural networks: An overview. *Neural Netw.* **2015**, *61*, 85–117.
2. Le Cun, Y.; Bengio, Y.; Hinton, G. Deep Learning. *Nature* **2015**, *521* (7553), 436–444.
3. Cheng, P. M.; Malhi, H. S. Transfer Learning with Convolutional Neural Networks for Classification of Abdominal Ultrasound Images. *J. Digital Imag.* **2017**, *30* (2), 234–243.
4. Dhand, G.; Tyagi, S. S. Data Aggregation Techniques in WSN: Survey. *Procedia Comput. Sci.* **2016**, *92*, 378–384.
5. Garcia-Peraza-Herrera, L. C.; Li, W.; Fidon, L.; Gruijthuijsen, C.; Devreker, A.; Attilakos, G., et al. Toolnet: Holistically-Nested Real-Time Segmentation of Robotic Surgical

Tools. In *2017 IEEE/RSJ International Conference on Intelligent Robots and Systems (IROS)*. IEEE, 2017 Sept; pp 5717–5722.

6. Hasan, M. K.; Calvet, L.; Rabbani, N.; Bartoli, A. Detection, Segmentation, and 3D Pose Estimation of Surgical Tools Using Convolutional Neural Networks and Algebraic Geometry. *Med. Image Analy.* **2021,** 101994.7.

7. Shin, H. C.; Roth, H. R.; Gao, M.; Lu, L.; Xu, Z.; Nogues, I., et al. Deep Convolutional Neural Networks for Computer-Aided Detection: CNN Architectures, Dataset Characteristics and Transfer Learning. *IEEE Trans. Med. Imag.* **2016,** *35* (5), 1285–1298.

8. Deng, J.; Dong, W.; Socher, R.; Li, L. J.; Li, K.; Fei-Fei, L. Imagenet: A Large-Scale Hierarchical Image Database. In *2009 IEEE Conference on Computer Vision and Pattern Recognition*; IEEE, **2009,** June; pp 248–255.

9. Yu, Y.; Lin, H.; Meng, J.; Wei, X.; Guo, H.; Zhao, Z. Deep Transfer Learning for Modality Classification of Medical Images. *Information* **2017,** *8* (3), 91.

10. Wang, S.; Raju, A.; Huang, J. Deep Learning Based Multi-Label Classification for Surgical Tool Presence Detection in Laparoscopic Videos. In *2017 IEEE 14th International Symposium on Biomedical Imaging (ISBI 2017)*; IEEE, **2017,** Apr; pp 620–623.

11. Lopes, U. K.; Valiati, J. F. 2017. Pre-Trained Convolutional Neural Networks as Feature Extractors for Tuberculosis Detection. *Comput. Biol. Med.* **2017,** *89,* 135–143.

12. Xue, D.; Zhou, X.; Li, C.; Yao, Y.; Rahaman, M.M.; Zhang, J.; Chen, H.; Zhang, J.; Qi, S.; Sun, H. An Application of Transfer Learning and Ensemble Learning Techniques for Cervical Histopathology Image Classification. *IEEE Access* **2020,** *8,* 104603–104618.

13. Wang, C.; Chen, D.; Hao, L.; Liu, X.; Zeng, Y.; Chen, J.; Zhang, G. Pulmonary Image Classification Based on Inception-v3 Transfer Learning Model. *IEEE Access* **2019,** *7,* 146533–146541.

14. Miki, Y.; Muramatsu, C.; Hayashi, T.; Zhou, X.; Hara, T.; Katsumata, A.; Fujita, H. Classification of Teeth in Cone-Beam CT Using Deep Convolutional Neural Network. *Comput. Biol. Med.* **2017,** *80,* 24–29.

15. Wang, W.; Iwamoto, Y.; Han, X.; Chen, Y. W.; Chen, Q.; Liang, D., et al. Classification of Focal Liver Lesions Using Deep Learning with Fine-Tuning. In *Proceedings of the 2018 International Conference on Digital Medicine and Image Processing*, **2018,** Nov; pp 56–60.

16. Prellberg, J.; Kramer, O. Multi-Label Classification of Surgical Tools with Convolutional Neural Networks. In *2018 International Joint Conference on Neural Networks (IJCNN)*, IEEE, **2018,** July; pp 1–8.

17. Bouget, D.; Allan, M.; Stoyanov, D.; Jannin, P. Vision-Based and Marker-Less Surgical Tool Detection and Tracking: A Review of the Literature. *Med. Image Analy.* **2017,** *35,* 633–654.

18. Sznitman, R.; Becker, C.; Fua, P. Fast Part-Based Classification for Instrument Detection in Minimally Invasive Surgery. In *International Conference on Medical Image Computing and Computer-Assisted Intervention*; Springer, Cham, **2014,** Sept; pp 692–699.

19. Sahu, M.; Mukhopadhyay, A.; Szengel, A.; Zachow, S. Addressing Multi-Label Imbalance Problem of Surgical Tool Detection Using CNN. *Int. J. Comput. Assisted Radiol. Surg.* **2017,** *12* (6), 1013–1020.

20. Alshirbaji, T. A.; Jalal, N. A.; Möller, K. Surgical Tool Classification in Laparoscopic Videos Using Convolutional Neural Network. *Curr. Directions Biomed. Eng.* **2018,** *4* (1), 407–410.

21. Simonyan, K.; Zisserman, A. Very Deep Convolutional Networks for Large-Scale Image Recognition. *arXiv preprint arXiv:1409.1556*, 2014.

22. Lin, M.; Chen, Q.; Yan, S. Network in Network. *arXiv preprint arXiv:1312.4400*, 2013.
23. Chollet, F. *Deep Learning with Python*, Vol. 361; Manning: New York, 2018.
24. Krizhevsky, A.; Sutskever, I.; Hinton, G. E. Imagenet Classification with Deep Convolutional Neural Networks. *Adv. Neural Inform. Process. Syst.* **2012,** *25*, 1097–1105.
25. Deng, A.; Berg, S.; Satheesh, H.; Su, A.; Khosla; Fei-Fei, L. ImageNet Large Scale Visual Recognition Competition, 2012 (ILSVRC2012). http://www.image-net.org/challenges/LSVRC/2012/.
26. Pan, S. J.; Yang, Q. A Survey on Transfer Learning IEEE Transactions on Knowledge and Data Engineering. **2010,** *22* (10), 1345, 1359.

CHAPTER 15

Cervical Cancer Diagnosis and Prediction: An Application of Machine Learning Techniques

MAMTA ARORA[1,2], SANJEEV DHAWAN[3], and KULVINDER SINGH[3]

[1]UIET, Kurukshetra University, Haryana, India

[2]Manav Rachna University, Haryana, India

[3]Department of CSE, UIET, Kurukshetra University, Haryana, India

ABSTRACT

Cancer of the cervix is cervical cancer that causes death in females. It is characterized as silent cancer as it does not disclose any pain or symptoms. It takes 10–15 years to develop; hence the timely prognosis and diagnosis of cervical cancer can save lives. The evidence shows that using machine learning (ML) techniques in this domain can result in better prediction accuracy. The most commonly used ML techniques in cancer prognosis and diagnosis include decision trees, random forest trees, artificial neural networks, and support vector machines. These techniques have been broadly applied in cervical cancer research for the advancement of predictive models, bringing about powerful and effective models. The present work paper aims to investigate the usage of ML techniques used in the modeling of cervical cancer prognosis.

Computational Intelligence in Analytics and Information Systems, Volume 1: Data Science and AI, Selected Papers from CIAIS-2021. Hardeo Kumar Thakur, Manpreet Kaur, Parneeta Dhaliwal, Rajeev Kumar Arya, and Joan Lu (Eds.)

15.1 INTRODUCTION

Cervical cancer is the fourth most leading cancer in females. The human papillomavirus (HPV) is the primary driver of this cervical cancer. This virus is present in everyone's body—the body's immune system relapses with time. But sometimes, this virus is not relapsed by the human immune system, thus causing damage to the cervix's cells. It usually takes two or three decades[3] to develop from normal to the precancerous stage (dysplasia). The dysplasia cells are not risky. These cells are known as cervical intraepithelial neoplasia (CIN), which is when in doubt of low quality, and they impact the outside of the cervical tissue. Most of these cells will backslide back to the ordinary. Over the long haul, a small extent of these cells will develop into a malignant growth.

The CIN was classified into two groups in 1994 by the Bethesda system. These groups are the low-grade squamous intraepithelial lesion and high-grade squamous intraepithelial lesion.[1]

As it will take more than a decade to come to an intrusive state, the occurrence and mortality identified with this malignant growth can be significantly diminished by early diagnosis and prediction. In recent years, there has been increasing interest in the application of machine learning (ML) in the medical domain. Owing to this reason, the use of ML-based classifier systems is gaining immense importance nowadays. Many researchers applied different ML methods to diagnose cervical cancer at an earlier stage before showing the symptoms. Table 15.1 shows the cervical cancer statistics. It can be clearly interpreted from the table that the patient's survival rate can exponentially fall from 91% to 17% if not diagnosed early.

TABLE 15.1 Cervical Cancer Statistics (World Health Organization n.d.).

Stage	Five-year survival rate (%)
Invasive cervical cancer	91
Spread to surroundings	57
Spread to a distant part of the body	17

Thus by the application of ML in the medical domain, early detection can be achieved. However, the prediction of a disease outcome with accuracy is the most challenging and exciting task for physicians.

The paper is organized into five sections. Section 15.2 throws light on cervical cancer screening taxonomy. The most commonly used ML and artificial neural network approaches used in cervical cancer prediction are described in Section 15.3. The survey of the ML algorithms in cervical cancer prognosis using image data and numerical data as input is covered in Section 15.4. Section 15.5 presents the conclusion of the entire work.

15.2 CERVICAL CANCER SCREENING

There are several methods that are employed for the screening of cervical cancer. All these cervical screening methods are majorly classified into two categories: (1) cellular-based and (2) tissue-based. The cellular-based approach is time-consuming as it requires collecting the specimen and later getting it analyzed by experts. On the other hand, in tissue-based practice, no specimen collection is needed. The experts' analysis can be directly obtained by visual examination.

15.3 MACHINE LEARNING TECHNIQUES

ML is a subset of artificial intelligence. It has a set of algorithms that work on data and make predictions by analyzing the data's relationship pattern. The set of learning algorithms is divided into two categories, namely supervised and unsupervised learning. Supervised learning uses the data labeled with correct output, which is used as feedback to the system for learning progression. On the other hand, unsupervised learning works with the unlabeled data. It derives the relationship among data by clustering them based on their similar features. There are many ML techniques available that are applied to the clinical data for prediction. A list of learning methods includes (1) multilayer perceptron (MLP), (2) decision trees (DTs), (3) random forest trees (RFTs), and (4) support vector machine (SVM). Based on the review, the commonly used techniques for the prediction of cervical cancer are presented in the following subsection.

15.3.1 MULTILAYER PERCEPTRON (MLP)

A MLP is a feed-forward neural network consisting of an input layer, an output layer, and at least one hidden layer, as shown in Figure 15.1. MLP is the fully connected network where each node is connected with every other node with a specific weight wij. The hidden layers perform various computations in between the input and output layers.[4]

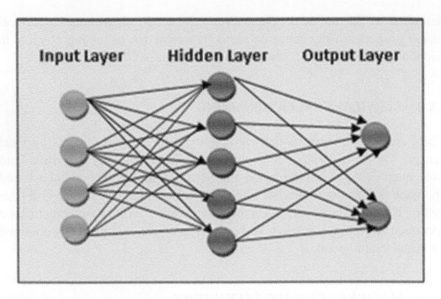

FIGURE 15.1   Illustration of MLP.

15.3.2   DECISION TREES

DTs are important algorithms of predictive modeling that use a tree-like structure. It has a root node, internal nodes, and leaf nodes. The root and internal nodes correspond to the input variable, whereas the leaf nodes correspond to the decision outcomes. The edge selected for traversal is based on the attribute value. DTs are one of the earliest and most widely used models for classification purposes. Based on the tree-like structure, it is very easy to interpret and quick to learn. Figure 15.2 represents an illustration of the DT. The variables X, Y, and Z are the feature set, denoted by a circle, and the target classes A and B are represented by a square.

15.3.3   RANDOM FOREST TREE

RFT is most widely used as a supervised ML technique in cervical cancer prediction. This strategy can be utilized for both classification and regression. The distinguishing feature of RFT is that it can work with an enormous dataset and choose the correct variable to get the expected output. In this technique, multiple trees are generated, and each tree gives a "vote" for the target class. In the case of the classification problem, the forest selects a tree that has a maximum vote for the class, and the regression average of a different tree is computed.

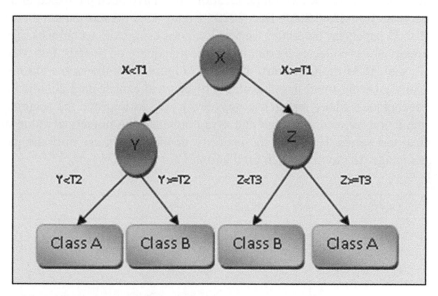

FIGURE 15.2   Illustration of decision tree.

15.3.4   *SUPPORT VECTOR MACHINE*

Like RFTs, the SVM can handle both the classification and regression problems. But mostly, it is used for classification problems. The main aim of SVM is to find the hyperplane that segregates data points into two classes. Initially, all data points are plotted into *n*-dimensional space, where *n* represents a number of features in the dataset. Then the hyperplane is plotted. The hyperplane with the maximum margin is used for a more reliable classification. Figure 15.3 illustrates the use of SVM in the application of cancerous and noncancerous cervix cells based on the shape and area. The distinguished hyperplane can be considered as a choice limit between the two classes. The choice limit can likewise have misclassification.

15.4   SURVEY OF MACHINE LEARNING APPLICATION IN THE PROGNOSIS OF CERVICAL CANCER

According to the survey, the rapid increase in published papers in the last decade is based on ML techniques for cervical cancer prediction. Even though it is beyond the realm of imagination to expect to get a total inclusion of the writing, we accept the papers published in the pub, IEEE, and ACM digital libraries. We focused on publications that have been published in the last 5 years from (Jan. 2015–Dec. 2020). Figure 15.4 depicts the number of published papers in predicting cervical cancer using ML techniques. The information was collected by running the search query on Scopus, Pub Med, IEEE, and ACM digital library databases. Figure 15.4 shows the chronologically growing trend in publications of cervical cancer prediction using ML techniques. Many research groups are trying to improve the accuracy of prediction by using the sign and symptoms and the numerical value of clinical test series. However, the majority of the studies use only the pap smear image data to make their predictions.

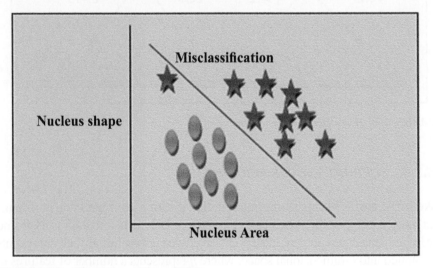

FIGURE 15.3   Illustration of linear SVM.

In the following, we will present the publications that make the prediction of cervical cancer by taking input to the model (1) image data and (2) numerical clinical values.

15.4.1   *DIAGNOSIS OF CERVICAL CANCER USING IMAGE DATA*

Prognosis of cervical cancer using image data uses a model that takes the cervix cell image as an input and gives cancerous and noncancerous cells as an output. The first step is image preprocessing and segmentation.

Preprocessing deals with making the poor quality image better by scaling intensity values. It prepares the image for the next steps. Segmentation deals with removing the background and emphasizing the objects that come under the region of interest. The preprocessed and segmented images are then passed to the next step, where the essential features of cervix cells are extracted. The commonly extracted features include nucleus and cytoplasm, shape, nucleus to cytoplasm ratio, local minima, local maxima, eccentricity, cell diameter, etc.

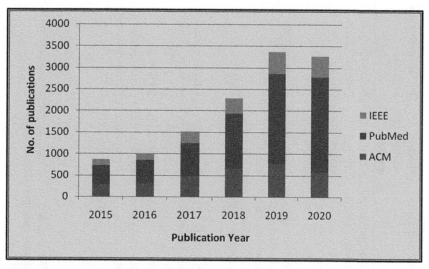

FIGURE 15.4 Publication of machine learning in cancer for the last 5 years.

The extracted features are then fed to the model for classification. The commonly used ML algorithms for classification are SVM, RFTs, DTs, and MLP. These algorithms work on feature datasets and further classify into normal and abnormal findings. Table 15.2 summarizes the publications that work on the above-described model. The table's major attributes include data source, preprocessing image technique, ML technique, the accuracy obtained, and various essential features. Out of the listed publications in Table 15.2, we selected a recent and very interesting study that works on pap smear images for cervical cancer prediction. The majority of the work in this area is carried out on a single cell image, but in reality, an image consists of multiple overlapped cells with many stains. The authors Mithlesh et al. in publication[6] emphasized working with the multiple and overlapped cells. The pap smear images were in JPEG format and collected from Jaipur pathology labs. The

TABLE 15.2 ML Methods Used in Cervical Cancer Prognosis Using Image Data.

References	Data source	Image preprocessing technique	ML technique	Single/ multiple cell images	2-Class/multiclass problem	Accuracy	Important features
Arya et al.[6]	Jaipur Pathology Lab	Gaussian Kernel filter	Support vector machine (SVM)	Cervical cytology images with multiple nucleus	3-class Problem (Normal, CIN1, CIN2/3)	96%	Number of nucleus in image, major axis, minor axis, aspect ratio, and eccentricity
Su et al.[7]	Department of Pathology and Lab, Cancer Center and Research Institute, Tampa, USA	Image enhancement and denoising (adaptive threshold segmentation	Two level cascade classifier (first level classifier: C4.5, second level classifier : LR)	Liquid-based cytology image	2-class problem	95.64%	20 Morphological and 8-texture feature
P. Guo et al.[11]	National Library of Medicine	Fusion-based epithelium	SVM/LDA classifier with leave-one-image out	Full color digitized histology image	4-class problem (Normal, CIN1, CIN2, CIN3 grades)	88.5%	Nucleus ratio
Ashok et al.[12]	Rajah Muthiah Medical College and Hospital, Annamali University	Gray level co-occurrence matrix (GLCM), local binary pattern (LBP) and Tamura method	Random forest tree	Single cell pap smear image	2-class problem (normal/abnormal cell)	81.71%	Texture features
Marinakis et al.[13]	Herlev New Dataset, Herlev University Hospital	Genetic algorithm	Weighted k-nearest neighbor	Single cell pep smear image	2-class problem 7-class problem	97.39% 97.39%	Nucleus area, cytoplasm area, etc.

TABLE 15.2 *(Continued)*

References	Data source	Image preprocessing technique	ML technique	Single/multiple cell images	2-Class/multiclass problem	Accuracy	Important features
Genctav et al.[14]	Department of Pathology, Hacteppe University	Unsupervised approach binary classifier (automatic thresholding)	Hierarchical clustering	Single cell pap smear image	Hierarchical clustering	—	Nucleus area, longest diameter, shortest diameter, elongation, roundness, maxima, minima, etc.
Kashyap et al.[15]	National Cancer Institute (NCI)	GLCM (gray level co-occurrence Matrix1) and principle component analysis (PCA)	Multiclass SVM: polynomial support vector machine	Single cell pap smear images	Detection and grade classification	95%	Geometric (area, eccentricity, N/C ratio) and 17 texture features (autocorrelation, contrast, dissimilarity, entropy, etc.)

obtained images are preprocessed by scaling the intensity value obtained by converting the RGB image to a grayscale image. The Gaussian Kernel filter is then applied to remove the noise, followed by a dilation operation where the pixels were added at the boundary to make the nucleus boundary rounded. In the feature extraction phase, six features of the nucleus were extracted, including a number of the nucleus, area, compactness of nucleus, major axis, minor axis, and aspect ratio. The images are then classified into three classes such as normal, CIN1, or CIN2+(CIN 2 or higher) using an SVM. It gives an accuracy of 96%.

In publication,[7] Su et al. proposed a two-level cascade classifier for classifying the images into two classes (normal and abnormal cells). They worked on 20,000 liquid-based cytology images. The data were collected from the Department of Pathology and Lab, Cancer and Research Institute, Tampa, USA. Images are enhanced and segmented using adaptive threshold segmentation. The number of extracted features is 28 in which 20 are morphological, and eight are textual features. In the two-level cascade classifier, the first level classifier is C4.5, which classifies the cells into four classes lymphocytes, epithelial cells, neutrophils, and garbage. Then second level classifier LR is applied to epithelial cells that further group the cells into normal epithelial and anomalous epithelial cells. The performance is evaluated with an accuracy of 95.64%.

15.4.2 DIAGNOSIS OF CERVICAL CANCER USING NUMERICAL DATA

In this section, we explained the publications that work on numerical clinical values. Table 15.3 summarizes a few recent publications in this domain. The attributes of the table include data source, ML technique, type of data, number of patient records, and number of features used and accuracy.

In the study,[8] the authors have presented a comparative analysis of 15 ML algorithms to diagnose cervical cancer. They have used the pap smear benchmark database prepared by Herlev University Hospital. They applied 15 algorithms on two datasets: old and new datasets with 500 and 917 single cell pap smear images. Among the 15 ML algorithms, ensemble of nested dichotomies outperformed both the dataset with an accuracy of 77.38% for the first dataset and 78.28% for the second dataset. On the other hand, this study also shows that Naive Bayes is the least performer with a predictive accuracy of 50% and 60% for the first and second sets, respectively. The MCPS dataset is obtained from their previous work,[17] which deals with

TABLE 15.3 Machine Learning Methods Used in Cervical Cancer Prognosis Using Numerical Data.

Publication	Data source	ML technique	Data type	No. of patients/ records	No. Of features used	2-Class/ multiclass problem	Accuracy	Important features
Sarwar et al.[8]	Herlev University Hospital	Ensemble of nested dichotomies	Pap smear numerical values	917	20	2-class problem	77.38%	Nucleus area, Cytoplasm area, etc.
Hemlatha and Usha Rani[9]	Herlev dataset	Multiclass perceptron	Modified cervical pap smear dataset	917	4	2-class problem	92.03%	Size of nucleus, gray level of cytoplasm and nucleus, etc.
Vidya[10]	NCBI (National Center for Bio-Technology Information)	RFT with k-means	Biopsy numerical value, gene	100	61	2-class problem (normal or abnormal cervix)	96.77%	Biopsy test numerical value
Bountris et al.[16]	Medical School of Athens' University	Ensemble of weighted random forest	Clinical data, numerical medical test value	740	35	2-class problem (CIN2 or CIN2+)	91.8%	Medical test results (Pap test, HPV, DNA test, flow cytometry, p. 16), age, gender, first visit date
Sowjanya Latha et al.[17]	Mitra et al.	J48	Boolean clinical data	203	21	4-class problem (Stage I/stage II/ Stage III/Stage IV)	93.03%	vulva: healthy, vulva: lesioned, Vagina: healthy, Vagina: spread to upper part, etc.
M. Arora et al.[18-20]	Kaggle	CNN	Cervigram images	1498		3 class problem		Images

the segmentation of cervical images. They applied the fuzzy edge detection method on the pap smear old dataset (Herlev University Hospital), which originally consisted of 917 images that are further described using 20 features. The algorithm with the less mean squared error is considered to be the best amongst others. The study shows that RBF has the highest classification accuracy with 100% but with a higher mean squared error value of 1. RBF cannot be used for classification as its classification will be more error-prone. But MLP gives an accuracy of 92.03% with a small mean squared error value of 0.0616. The work reveals that MLP outperforms the other three networks.

The published work in Ref. 10 is different from the above-stated work as they have used the biopsy test data instead of pap smear data for the prediction of cervical cancer. The authors applied a robust data mining algorithm on biopsy numerical data to classify the data into normal or cancer cervix. The data collected from National Center for Biotechnology Information consist of 500 records and 61 biopsy features, including gene identifiers. They have used a sample of 100 records for training and testing purposes. On the selected sample, CART, RFT, and RFT with K-means learning algorithm were applied for classifying the data into the normal and cancerous cervix. The study reveals that the proposed hybrid algorithm RFT with k-means outperformed among CART and RFT with the accuracy of 96.77% on NCBI biopsy data for predicting cervical cancer.

15.5   CONCLUSION

This review discussed the taxonomy of cervical cancer screening and commonly used ML techniques in prognosis of cervical cancer. The usage of ML algorithms in cancer prognosis is depicted in the form of a chart that shows the rapidly increasing demand of ML in healthcare. Most of the proposed studies last year used supervised ML techniques, including DT, RFT, CART, etc. The models used for the prediction of cervical cancer are classified in two major categories on the basis of input fed to the model. One type of models takes input as test screening image like single-cell pap smear image, multiple and overlapped cell image, biopsy image, and other that uses clinical numerical values like area of nucleus and cytoplasm, radius of nucleus, ratio of cytoplasm to nucleus, etc. In the future, we are planning to review models that use both image and clinical data together as an input to the model for prognosis of cervical cancer.

KEYWORDS

- cervical cancer
- machine learning
- cervical cancer screening

REFERENCES

1. Frankel, K.; Kulkarni, Y. Formal Proposal to Combine the Papanicolaou Numerical System with Bethesda Terminology for Reporting Cervical/Vaginal Cytologic Diagnoses. *Diagn. Cytopathol.* **1994,** *10* (4), 395–396.
2. Statistics. https://www.cancer.net/cancer-types/cervical-cancer/statistics (accessed 26 Oct 2017).
3. Jusman, Y.; Ng, S. C.; Osman, N. A. Intelligent Screening System for Cervical Cancer. *Sci World J* **2014,** *2014,* 1–15.
4. Rani, K. U. Analysis of Heart Diseases Using Neural Network Approach. *IJDKP* **2011,** *1* (5), 1–8.
5. Kourou, K.; Exarchos, T. P.; Exarchos, K. P.; Karamouzis, M. V.; Fotiadis, D. I. Machine Learning Applications in Cancer Prognosis and Prediction. *Comput. Struct.Biotechnol.* **2015,** *13,* 8–17.
6. Arya, M.; Mittal, N.; Singh, G. Cervical Cancer Detection Using Segmentation on Pap smear Images. In *Proceedings of the International Conference on Informatics and Analytics*; ACM: Pondicherry, India, 2016.
7. Su, J.; Xu, X.; He, Y.; Song, J. Automatic Detection of Cervical Cancer Cells by a Two-Level Cascade Classification System. *Analyt. Cell.Pathol.* **2016,** *2016,* 1–12.
8. Sarwar, A.; Ali, M.; Ali, M.; Sharma, V. Performance Evaluation of Machine Learning Techniques for Screening of Cervical Cancer. In *2nd International Conference on Computing for Sustainable Global Development (INDIACom)*, 2015.
9. Hemalatha, K.; Rani, K. U. An Optimal Neural Network Classifier for Cervical Pap Smear Data. In *7th International Advance Computing Conference (IACC)*; Hyderabad, India, 2017.
10. Vidya, R.; Nasira, G. Prediction of Cervical Cancer using Hybrid Induction Technique: A Solution for Human Hereditary Disease Patterns. *Indian J. Sci. Technol.* **2016,** *9* (30), 1–10.
11. Guo, P.; Banerjee, K.; Stanley, R. J. Nuclei-Based Features for Uterine Cervical Cancer Histology Image Analysis With Fusion-Based Classification. *IEEE J. Biomed. Health Inform.* **2015,** *20* (6), 2168–2194.
12. Ashok, B.; Anu, S.; Nair, H.; Puviarasan, N.; Aruna, P. Robust Diagnosing Technique for Cervical Cancer Using Random Forest Classifier. *Int. J. Adv. Res. Comput. Sci. Softw. Eng.* **2016,** *6* (11), 153–159.
13. Marinakis, Y.; Dounias, G.; Jantzen, J. Pap Smear Diagnosis Using a Hybrid Intelligent Scheme Focusing on Genetic Algorithm. *Comput. Biol. Med.* **2009,** *38* (1), 69–78.

14. Gençtava, A.; Aksoya, S.; Önderb, S. Unsupervised Segmentation and Classification of Cervical Cell Images. *Pattern Recognition* **2012,** *45,* 4151–4168.

15. Kashyap, D.; Somani, A.; Shekhar, J.; Bhan, A.; Dutta, M. K.; Burget, R.; Riha, K. Cervical Cancer Detection and Classification Using Independent Level Sets And Multi SVMs. In *39th International Conference on Telecommunications and Signal Processing (TSP)*; IEEE: Vienna, Austria, June, 2016.

16. Bountris, P.; Haritou, M.; Pouliakis, A.; Karakitsos, P.; Koutsouris, D. A Decision Support System Based on an Ensemble of Random Forests for Improving the Management of Women with Abnormal Findings at Cervical Cancer Screening. In *37th Annual International Conference of the IEEE Engineering in Medicine and Biology Society (EMBC)*; IEEE, 2015.

17. Latha, D. S.; Lakshmi, P.; Fathima, S. Staging Prediction in Cervical Cancer Patients-A Machine Learning Approach. *Int. J. Innov. Res. Pract.* **2014,** *2* (2), 14–23.

18. Arora, M.; Dhawan, S.; Singh, K. Exploring Deep Convolution Neural Networks with Transfer Learning for Transformation Zone Type Prediction in Cervical Cancer. In *Advances in Intelligent Systems and Computing*; Springer Nature: Singapore, 2019; pp 1127–1183.

19. Arora, M.; Dhawan, S.; Singh, K. Data Driven Prognosis of Cervical Cancer Using Class Balancing and Machine Learning Techniques. EAI Endorsed Transactions on Energy Web: Online First, 2020.

20. Arora, M.; Dhawan, S.; Singh, K. Deep Neural Network for Transformation Zone Classification. In *2018 First International Conference on Secure Cyber Computing and Communication (ICSCCC)*, 15–17 Dec 2018; IEEE: Jalandhar, India, 2019; pp 213–216.

CHAPTER 16

The Working Analysis on Machine Learning Algorithms to Predict Diabetes and Breast Cancer

SRIKANTH BETHU[1], VEMPATI KRISHNA[2], BODA SINDHUJA[1], DAMARLA LAKSHMI ROHITA[3], and P. GOPALA KRISHNA[4]

[1]Department of Computer Science and Engineering, GRIET, Hyderabad, Telangana, India

[2]Department of Computer Science and Engineering, TKR College of Engineering & Technology, Hyderabad, Telangana, India

[3]Department of Computer Science and Engineering, ACE Engineering College, Hyderabad, Telangana, India

[4]Department of Information Technology, GRIET, Hyderabad, Telangana, India

ABSTRACT

Discerning frameworks are the structures that can foresee some result subject to some model or attestation. Diabetes disease affirmation is that the system by which a patient's confirmation is performed reliant on responses dissected, which may cause excitement while imagining sullying sway. For instance, fever itself could be an indication of the different disorders that do not tell the human what the ailment is. Since the outcomes or end change from one master to a substitute, there is a fundamental to help a therapeutic pro, which

Computational Intelligence in Analytics and Information Systems, Volume 1: Data Science and AI, Selected Papers from CIAIS-2021. Hardeo Kumar Thakur, Manpreet Kaur, Parneeta Dhaliwal, Rajeev Kumar Arya, and Joan Lu (Eds.)
© 2024 Apple Academic Press, Inc. Co-published with CRC Press (Taylor & Francis)

will have relative supposition vehemently responses and scatters. It may finish by breaking down the data made by remedial information or helpful records. As per Breast Cancer Research, breast hazardous improvement is the sickness most evident in female individuals of the world. As shown by the clinical specialists, perceiving this unsafe advancement in its beginning period helps in sparing lives. The site cancer.net offers individualized partners for more than 120 sorts of dangerous progress and related innate issues. For the portrayal of risky chest improvement through progression, AI strategy is fantastically cherished. In this system, a versatile get-together AI calculation by considering among different methods is proposed for the completion of chest peril. A report was utilizing the Wisconsin Breast Cancer database used here. Along these lines, applying the AI calculations to imagine diabetes ought to finish. Computer-based intelligence calculations have been proposed for the early figure of sickness with higher exactness to spare human life and to reduce the treatment cost. The motivation behind this structure is to look at and clarify how ANN works and decide to break faith checks together, offer a superior reaction, then see breast risky advancement, notwithstanding how the segments lessened. This procedure shows that the neural system is also persuading for human urgent information assessment, and we can do preconfirmation with no astounding medicinal learning.

16.1 INTRODUCTION

The most noteworthy screening test for chest-threatening development is the mammogram. A mammogram is an X-light emission chest. It can recognize dangerous chest development up to 2 years before you or your PCP can feel the tumor. The data given to the made model are the mammographic[1] results as the model is set up by the past patient's data of mammographic results itself. Here, by using this model, we can decrease the patient keeping things under control time in the line for the expert.

As demonstrated by an assessment appropriated in the *Asia-Pacific Journal of Clinical Oncology*, harmful chest development was found as high as 41 for every 100,000 women in Delhi, trailed by Chennai 37.9, Bangalore 34.4, and Thiruvananthapuram District 33.7 in 2017. As demonstrated by this assessment number of occasions of breast, dangerous development will end up being twofold 17,97,900 by 2020. America has a high perseverance pace of around 90% while India has quite recently 66.1% of continuance rate.

Inherent diabetes happens in humans because of the natural flaws of insulin release, cystic fibrosis-related diabetes,[2] and large fragments of glucocorticoids and brief steroid diabetes. As a result, concerning the human, our bodies glitch as indicated by producing insulin and require the person between an impersonation of supplement insulin and raise an insulin siphon.[3] This class was once recently shown to have as much permanency as "Insulin-Dependent Diabetes Mellitus."

The second classification of DM is perceived to be specific "Type II DM"[4] along these lines a result as respects insulin encounter, a circumstance of any cells are ineffectual of agreement with endeavor insulin properly, incidentally combined all in all with an outright insulin deficiency. At last, "gestational diabetes" happen when considered ladies without a before.

The prior finding of diabetes, the danger of the intricacies can be evaded. Diabetic patients endure different infections, and it influences different pieces of various organs. Subsequently, successful measures must be taken to anticipate the sickness in the most punctual and control. To spread regard for chest-threatening development to all of the Indians, this errand accepts a minor activity. Data are so astounding; we can set up a machine with the goal that it understands the past data and use it for the investigation of fast approaching patients. Setting up a computer looks like applying appropriate models on the data to get the results accurately. Since model presentations change in regards to data. Here, we endeavored three such models and attempted to find the best fit for our data.

From the ongoing examinations, individuals who as of now have diabetes-related medical issues are probably going to have more terrible results on the off chance that they contract COVID-19[5] than individuals with diabetes who are in any case solid, whichever sort of diabetes they have. Individuals with diabetes do confront a higher possibility of encountering genuine inconveniences from COVID-19. All in all individuals with diabetes are bound to encounter serious indications and entanglements when tainted with an infection.

The Centers for Disease Control and Prevention[5] says that the danger of becoming truly sick from COVID-19 is low for a great many people. Notwithstanding, it is very important to realize that individuals being treated for bosom malignant growth may have a higher danger of serious disease on the off chance that they get COVID-19. Some breast cancer medications including chemotherapy, directed treatments, immunotherapy, and radiation can debilitate the safe framework and perhaps mess up the lung. Individuals who have debilitated insusceptible frameworks or lung issues have a lot higher danger of inconveniences on the off chance that they become contaminated with this infection. Individuals with bosom malignancy[6] that has metastasized to the lungs likewise can have lung issues that may deteriorate in the event that they create COVID-19.

So it is very necessary to identify many accurate methods to identify diseases at early stages. Artificial neural networks (ANNs)[7] and decision trees[7] have been used in threatening development acknowledgment and end for around 20 years. Today, AI methods are being used in a full extent of employments going from perceiving and requesting tumors by means of X-bar and CRT pictures[8] to the request for malignancies from proteomic and genomic and the looks at. As demonstrated by the latest PubMed estimations, more than 1500 papers have circulated regarding the matter of AI and illness. Nevertheless, by a long shot, the more significant part of these papers is stressed over using AI procedures to perceive, orchestrate, distinguish, or perceive tumors and various malignancies.

Computer-based intelligence, like estimations, is used to analyze and interpret data. Rather than opinions, be that as it may, AI strategies can use the Boolean method of reasoning—AND, OR, NOT, by and substantial possibility—IF, THEN, ELSE, prohibitive probabilities—the probability of X given Y, and capricious improvement frameworks to exhibit data or portray structures. These latest techniques truly take after the philosophies individuals ordinarily use to learn and describe. Artificial intelligence[9] still draws strongly from bits of knowledge and probability.

In machine learning, plenty of models are given, it is needed upon the understudy to find the model or discover the social affairs. It is somewhat intentionally taking after the methodology by which most graduate under-studies learn. Solo learning computations consolidate such systems as self-dealing with segment maps—SOMs,[10] dynamic gatherings, and K-means clustering figuring.[11] These approaches make bundles from unrefined, unlabeled, or unclassified data. These gatherings were used later to make request plans or classifiers.

16.2   RELATED WORK

In this chapter, we have given detailed information on the methods and algorithms that are recently used to produce accurate results. The survey information was gathered from journals and articles.

Local Energy-based Shape Histogram Feature Extraction Technique for Breast Cancer Diagnosis

Wajid and Hussain[26] proposed a novel neighborhood imperativeness-based shape histogram local energy-based shape histogram (LESH) as the rundown of abilities for affirmation of varieties from the standard in mammograms. It investigates the implications of this technique on mammogram datasets of the Mammographic Image Analysis Society and IN chest. In the evaluation, regions of interest were removed from the mammograms, their LESH features resolved, and they urged to enable vector to machine support vector machine (SVM) classifiers.[12]

Besides, the impact of picking a subset of LESH[27] incorporated on request execution was similarly viewed and benchmarked against a front-line wavelet-based segment extraction methodology. The proposed procedure achieved a higher portrayal accuracy of an extent of 99.00 ± 0.50, equally as an Az estimation of 0.9900 ± 0.0050 with different SVM parts, where the next piece performs with 100% precision for perceiving the inconsistencies.

Subsequently, the general limit of the proposed system was set up, in which it does not merely observe hurtful and agreeable cases for a variety from the standard yet likewise among different sorts of abnormalities. It is, as such, contemplated that LESH features are an incredible choice for isolating necessary clinical information from mammogram pictures with massive potential for application to 3D MRI pictures.

Hybrid Feature Selection Method based on Neural Networks and Cross-Validation for Liver Cancer with Microarray

Kim and Park[15] proposed a procedure that thinks of a rundown of capacities for exact infirmity assurance from a component (aptamer) show. Our strategy uses mechanized thinking of the neural framework and 10-cover cross-endorsements. It is checked by the p-estimation of the aptamer bunch response to instances of 80 liver sickness patients and 310 sound people. The proposed procedure is differentiated and the single course ANOVA system to the extent accuracy, number of features, and enrolling time to choose the rundown of capacities required to achieve a comparable precision. Information entered sports, all mentors had regarding factual detailing was who played, who scored, and who did not. This, all things considered, was the premise on which players in a specific game were assessed.

Foresee the Beginning of Diabetes Disease Using Artificial Neural Network—Pradhan and Kumar Sahu[19]

This speaks to 8.8% of the absolute ladies grown-up populace of the 18 years old or more in 2003 and this is almost a two overlap increment from 1995 (4.7%). Ladies of minority racial and ethnic gatherings have the most noteworthy predominance rates with two to multiple times the rates of the white populace. With the expanded development of minority populaces, the number of ladies in these gatherings who are analyzed will increase substantially in the coming years.

Diabetes is a metabolic issue where individuals experiencing it either have an absence of insulin or have a diminished capacity to use their insulin. Insulin is a hormone that is made by the pancreas and engages glucose to be changed over to centrality at the cell level. Diabetes that is uncontrolled, that is constantly peculiar proportions of blood glucose (> 200 mgL/dL), prompt downsized scale and full-scale vascular torment complexities, for example, visual insufficiency, lower farthest point departures, end plan renal infection, and coronary disease and stroke. Diabetes is found in roughly one of every 10 people, yet the odds increase to one of every five as the age group increases to 65 years old or more. Despite the fact that there is no settled solution for diabetes, in fact, the blood glucose level of diabetic patients can be constrained by entrenched medicines, legitimate sustenance, and customary exercise.

As of late, a few inquiries have been directed to order and demonstrate who is diabetic or not. Shanker utilized neural systems (NN)[3] to foresee the diabetic individual and furthermore demonstrated that neural systems got a superior exactness which was higher than different strategies like calculated relapse, include choice, choice tree, and so forth. This paper has investigated the plan of a novel ANN for information characterizations.

16.3 METHODOLOGY

16.3.1 PROPOSED METHOD AND USE OF MACHINE LEARNING

We proposed a social protection structure using beautiful clothing for practical prosperity checking. I had inside and out considered the heterogeneous architectures and achieved the best results for cost minimization on a tree and first route cases for different systems. Here we use utilized AI systems to perceive the dominating parts causing diabetes in individuals.

Factors that are accepted to be vital like age, BMI, high cholesterol, hyperthyroid, hypertension, age, and skin thickness are considered. Among these, the most important ones provoke diabetes.

Characteristics of each essential factor are found in diabetic and nondiabetic individuals, causing learning divulgence of significantly tremendous explanations behind diabetes overall. The entire enlightening file is also reliant upon request using four AI estimations, and an overall examination of the systems is in like manner grasped. A couple of sorts of research have to portray and show who is diabetic or not.

Neural networks were used to foresee the diabetic individual, and besides demonstrated that neural structures showed signs of improved accuracy, which was higher than various systems like determined backslide, feature assurance, decision tree, etc.

We have evaluated the ANN model for the endeavor of model portrayal in data. Human-made intelligence techniques are commonly used in foreseeing diabetes, and they get the best results. A decision tree is one of the notable AI procedures in the remedial field, which has grateful portrayal control. Self-assertive woods create various decision trees. A neural framework is a starting late surely understood AI technique, which has an unrivaled introduction from multiple perspectives.

Chest self-appraisal, BSE, and clinical chest evaluation, CBE, are used to screen for chest-threatening development. CBE has an affectability of 57.14% and an identity of 97.11%. Despite the way that it does not enable one to choose danger with affirmation, it is significant for recognizing suspicious chest wounds. PC-aided detection, CAD,[15] is a model affirmation programming that perceives doubtful varieties from the standard on pictures, checking them for the radiologist. PC helped configuration furthermore speaks to PC bolstered discovering, which suggests a structure that engravings definite or compromising photographs.

Mammography is the path toward using low essentialness X-bars to review the human chest. These test delayed consequences of various women were assembled and set away on a site as .csv archive. An examination was done on that data, and models were attempted to arrange noninfection genial and damaging unsafe stages.

Here we envision the scene using any of the portraying techniques, whose precision is more. Requests like K-nearest neighbor (KNN),[16] decision, trees, random forest, etc., can be handled and had gone by and large mulled over the heterogeneous systems and achieved the best results for cost minimization on the tree and essential path cases for different structures. For perceiving breast dangerous development, by and large, AI frameworks are used in CAD.

In this structure, we proposed an adaptable get-together throwing a polling form procedure for broken chest threatening development using the Wisconsin Breast Cancer Database.[17] The purpose of this work is to take a gander at and explain how ANN and determined computation give a predominant course of action when its work with bunch AI counts for diagnosing chest malady even if the components are decreased.

In this chapter, we used the Wisconsin Diagnosis Breast Cancer[18] dataset. The underlying advance is dimensionality decline, for which we use univariate feature decisions with 16 sections that select the best 16 portions from 32 attributes. By and by, what we get is a vector depiction as we procured in issue 1, which on a fundamental level surmises 569 models × 32 features. For item 2, we use an 80/20 split where 80% of data is used to set up a classifier, and 20% is used to test. Directly, we seek after a similar technique as we achieved for issue 1 we apply three classifiers, that is, linear SVM, nonlinear SVM with RBF part, and stratified k-infers cross-endorsement with four-cover, only for an estimation of $C = 0.001$ of variety.

16.4　ALGORITHM SELECTION AND IMPLEMENTATION

We displayed two earth-shattering instruments in current counts: regularization and outfits. As you will see, these frameworks "fix" some deadly flaws in increasingly settled techniques, which has to lead to their reputation. In this activity, we presented five very incredible AI counts for backsliding tasks. They each have a course of action accomplices, as well. As opposed to giving you a not inconsequential summary of computations, we will probably explain two or three fundamental thoughts (e.g., regularization, ensembling, customized feature decision) that will give you why a couple of estimations will all in all perform better than other individuals.

In applied AI,[18] solitary figurines should be swapped in and out dependent upon which performs best for the issue and the dataset. Along these lines, we will focus on impulse and sensible points of interest over math and speculation. To display the thought for a part of the impelled computations, we should start by discussing fundamental direct backslide. Direct backslide models are uncommonly typical, yet significantly blemished.

16.4.1　LINEAR REGRESSION AND REGULARIZATION IN MACHINE LEARNING[19]

Precise immediate backslide models fit a "straight line" (in truth, a hyperplane depending upon the number of features, anyway it is a comparable idea). They rarely perform well. We genuinely recommend skipping them for most AI issues. Their rule bit of space is that they are not hard to interpret and get it. In any case, our goal is not to consider the data and make an assessment report. We will probably shape a model that can make correct conjectures. In such a way, a bright, direct back slide encounters two huge imperfections: it is slanted to overfit with numerous data features. It can work just with critical exertion and express nondirect associations.

We ought to research how we can address the chief imperfection. We should take an unprecedented manual to depict why this happens: Let us say you have 100 observations in your planning dataset. Assume you in like manner have 100 features. If you fit a straight backslide model with those 100 features, you can marvelously "hold" the readiness set. Each coefficient would recall one discernment. This model would have perfect precision on the arrangement data anyway and perform inadequately on subtle data. It has not taught the authentic shrouded models; it has recently recalled the uproar in the arrangement data. Regularization is a framework used to deflect over-fitting by erroneously rebuffing model coefficients. It can cripple significant factors (by hosing them). It can moreover remove incorporates (by setting their ratios to 0). The "quality" of the discipline is tunable.

Backslide is a system for showing a target worth reliant on self-ruling markers. This method is generally used for envisioning and finding the conditions and intelligent outcomes associated between factors. Backslide techniques are typically dependent upon the amount of self-governing components and the sort of association between the free and ward elements. Clear immediate backslide is a backslide examination where the amount of free factors is one, and there is a direct association between the independent (x) and dependent (y) variables. Considering the given data centers, we endeavor to plot a route that models the centers the best. The track can be shown reliant on the straight condition exhibited as pursued.

16.4.2 DECISION TREE ALGORITHMS

Decision trees model data as a "tree" of different leveled branches, they make branches until they reach "leaves" that address desires. Tree ensembles, ensembles are AI systems for uniting desires from different separate models. There are several different methods for ensembling,[22] yet the two most ordinary are bagging, bagging[23] attempts to diminish the chance of overfitting[24] complex models. It plans innumerable "strong" understudies in parallel. A firm understudy is a model that is commonly unconstrained. Sacking by then joins all the strong understudies together to "smooth out" their desires.

Boosting[25] tries to improve the conscious flexibility of fundamental models. It readies a tremendous number of "fragile" understudies in the plan. A weak understudy is a constrained model (i.e., you could compel the most extreme significance of each decision tree). Each one in the program revolves around picking up from the slip-ups of the one going before it. Boosting then joins all the weak understudies into a single firm understudy. While pressing and raising are both gathering methods, they approach the issue from a backward orientation. Stowing uses complex base models and endeavors to "smooth out" their estimates while boosting uses direct base models and efforts to "help" their absolute multifaceted nature.

Ensembling is a general term, anyway when the base models are decision trees, they have unusual names: subjective woods and upheld trees.

16.4.3 MODEL TRAINING

To set up the data, it joins the going with advances like exploring the data, cleaning the data. Building new features again that is because better data beat different computations. In this activity, you will make sense of how to set up the entire exhibiting methodology to enlarge execution while safeguarding against overfitting. We will swap estimations in and out and usually find the best parameters for each one. We should start with a critical yet at this point and afterward ignore development: spending your data. Consider your data as an obliged resource.

If you value your model on similar data you used to set it up, your model could be overfitted, and you would not know! A model should settle on a choice on its ability to anticipate new, disguised data. As needs are, you should have separate planning and test subsets of your dataset.

Right when we talk about tuning models, we unequivocally mean tuning hyperparameters. There are two sorts of parameters in AI computations. The critical capability is that the model parameter can be picked up genuinely from the arrangement data, while hyperparameters cannot. Model parameters discovered characteristics that portray individual models, for example, backslide coefficients, for example, decision tree split zones. They can be picked up genuinely from the planning data. Hyperparameters express "progressively raised level" assistant settings for estimations, for example, the nature of the discipline used in regularized backslide, for example, the number of trees to consolidate into sporadic timberland. They were picked up before fitting the model since they cannot pick up from the data.

For all of your models, make desires on your test set. Find out execution estimations using those figures and the "ground truth" target variable from the test set. Finally, use these requests to help you with picking the triumphant model that has high performance, robustness, and consistency, in this chapter, we have discussed how the results are generated and given the comparison values.

16.5 RESULTS AND DISCUSSION

Pretaking is a data mining method that incorporates changing unrefined data into a legitimate arrangement. Genuine data are typically divided, clashing, and weak in explicit practices and inclined to contain various missteps. Data pretaking care of is a shown method for settling such issues. For pretaking care of, we have used the systematization method to preprocess the UCI dataset.[26] In the standardization system, the dataset is an everyday essential for a few AI estimators. In this chapter, we have made different data portrayal for data pretaking care off. At first, we counted the hurtful and sympathetic from all dataset and plot in graph position.

In the proposed work, we have made an original 16-component violin plot for assessment. By then, we draw a scatter plot (Figure 16.1) with noncovering centers. It gives an unrivaled depiction of the flow of characteristics. The outline we have made a relationship scatterplot between dataset features for all the more understanding.

In the proposed framework, we used machine figurines with ANN, KNN, SVM, and logistic regression for diabetes desire. The examinations are performed by considering the proposed strategy. Figure 16.1 gives the information of the arrangement of dataset features.

The affectability and disposition measures are enlisted. In the remedial zone, these two measures are required to test the structure execution in usable space. The affectability measure is obtained for positive events and the explicit rules for negative cases. Table 16.1 addresses different execution estimations of all plan counts decided on various criteria. From Table 16.1, it is dismembered that the ANN is exhibiting the most extreme precision. So the ANN AI classifier can anticipate the chances of diabetes with more precision when stood out from various classifiers. Better test exactness of 80.5% is obtained nearby other quantifiable execution parameters for the diabetes desire model. Figures 16.2 and 16.3 show the arrangement of cancer and diabetes dataset features using the discussed algorithms. The accuracy rate of each algorithm is listed in Table 16.1.

The decision tree, Figure 16.4 shows the tomahawks' parallel breaking points, while the $k = 1$ nearest neighbors fit close to the data centers. The pressing outfits were readied using ten base estimators with 0.8 subsampling of planning data and 0.8 subsampling of features. Figure 16.4 shows the relation between the algorithms. We can see the blending of decision points of confinement achieved by the stacking classifier. The figure in like manner shows that stacking achieves higher accuracy than solitary classifiers, and reliant on desires to assimilate data, it gives no signs of overfitting.

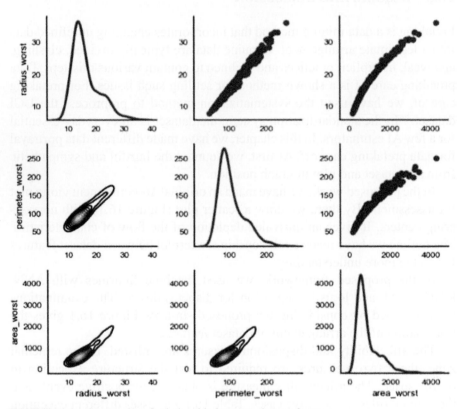

FIGURE 16.1   Scatterplot of relationship between dataset features.

TABLE 16.1   Classification of Algorithms and Their Accuracy.

Classification algorithm	Accuracy
Artificial neural network (ANN)	80.51948051948052
K-nearest neighbor (KNN)	77.92207792207793
Logistic regression	77.6563864812202
Support vector machine (SVM)	64.76785594302223

The AdaBoost estimation is portrayed in Figure 16.5. Each base understudy includes a decision tree with significance 1, along these lines describing the data reliant on a segment limit that fragments the space into two zones segregated by a straight decision surface that is parallel to one of the tomahawks. The figure similarly shows how the test accuracy improves with the size of the outfit and the desire to learn and adjust for getting ready and testing data.

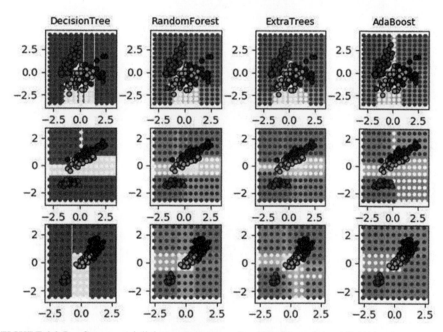

FIGURE 16.2   Cancer and diabetes accuracy using algorithms dataset features.

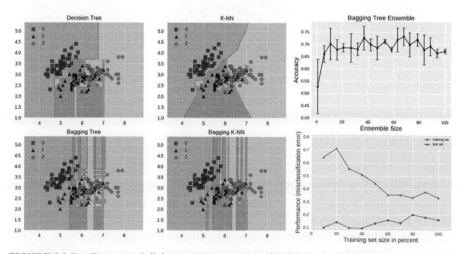

FIGURE 16.3   Cancer and diabetes accuracy using algorithms dataset features.

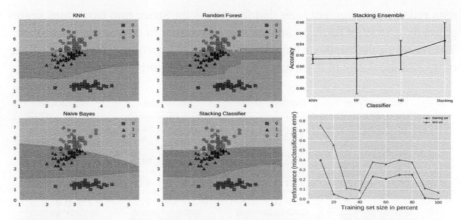

FIGURE 16.4   Relationship between KNN and random forest classifiers using dataset features.

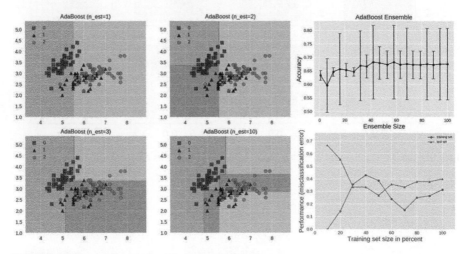

FIGURE 16.5   Adaboost classifier using dataset features.

16.6   CONCLUSION

Diabetes and cancer have been depicted as a heterogeneous disease containing a full scope of subtypes. The early investigation and expectation of a dangerous development type have transformed into a need in infection, as it can energize the following clinical organization of patients. Particular AI frameworks can be used for the assurance of dangerous chest development. All the above-mentioned machine learning estimations indicated predominant on the twofold gathering of chest illness, that is, choosing a benevolent tumor or risky tumor. In this manner, the accurate measures on the gathering issue were pleasing. In this, we separated chest danger data using three portrayal strategies KNN course of action, decision tree, and random forest to dissect ailment. Later we contemplated the results. The results exhibited that the random forest is the best classifier marker with the test dataset. Additionally, the limit of ML mechanical assemblies to understand the key features from complex datasets reveals their criticalness. Further examinations should be coordinated to improve the presentation of these game plan techniques by using more factors and choosing for a progressively expanded follow-up term. One of the limitations of this examination is the number of databases that were evaluated. At present, Embase and Web of Science were assessed. Undoubtedly, the point of convergence of this overview was clinical databases; therefore, logically specific databases, for instance, IEEE and Scopus, should be considered for new reviews. Future assessments should focus on the effect of AI on clinical outcomes and its impact.

The main advantage of defined proposed methods in this paper can produce different results using other AI Algorithms like K mean clustering, decision trees, ANN, etc. Particular datasets can be used with different frameworks for finding exactness and mix-up rates.

Considering the assessment of their findings, it is evident that the blend of multidimensional heterogeneous data together with the use of different techniques for feature assurance and portrayal can give promising contraptions to derivation in the threat territory.

The results of this examination may reinforce researchers and designers of AI-based structures and models under the vigilant gaze of patients with T2DM in picking systems, models, counts, and capable and perfect systems. It is suggested that ML, indisputable SVM and NB, computations are considered by fashioners and architects of models and structures. The present assessment, moreover, perceived the most noteworthy clinical variables used in the arrangement and headway of human-made awareness structures and models for the thought of patients with T2DM. This can give bits of information to picking key factors in T2DM, and data examination and system improvement using AI-based procedures.

The future enhancement can be implemented by redesigning the proposed work and stretched out for the disease's desire. Based on the availability of datasets, the proposed methods can also find the illness issues of COVID-19 disease.

KEYWORDS

- **breast cancer analysis**
- **diabetes analysis**
- **machine learning**

REFERENCES

1. Aberer, K.; Peng, Z.; Rundensteiner, E. Lecture Notes in Computer Science (Including Subseries Lecture Notes in Artificial Intelligence and Lecture Notes in Bioinformatics): Preface. *Lecture Notes in Computer Science (Including Subseries Lecture Notes in Artificial Intelligence and Lecture Notes in Bioinformatics)*, 2006.
2. Ambrose, J. Computerized Transverse Axial Scanning (Tomography): II. Clinical Application. *Br. J. Radiol.* **1973**. DOI: 10.1259/0007-1285-46-552-1023.
3. Amrane, M.; Oukid, S.; Gagaoua, I,; Ensari, T. Breast Cancer Classification Using Machine Learning. In *2018 Electric Electronics, Computer Science, Biomedical Engineerings' Meeting, EBBT 2018*. 2018. DOI: 10.1109/EBBT.2018.8391453.
4. Barrios-Rodiles, M.; Brown, K. R.; Ozdamar, B.; Bose, R.; Liu, Z.; Donovan, R. S.; Shinjo, F. et al. High-Throughput Mapping of a Dynamic Signaling Network in Mammalian Cells. *Science* **2005**. DOI: 10.1126/science.1105776.
5. Bloomgarden, Z. T. Diabetes and COVID-19. *J. Diab.* **2020**. DOI: 10.1111/1753-0407. 13027.
6. Chakrabarti, B. K., Chowdhury, R. R.; Chatterjee, T.; Mondal, N. R. M268 Epidemiology of Vulval Malignancy. *Int. J. Gynecol. Obstet.* **2012**. DOI: 10.1016/s0020-7292(12)61460-x.
7. Cui, Y. F.; Andersen, D. K. Diabetes and Pancreatic Cancer. *Endocrine-Related Cancer*. **2012**. DOI: 10.1530/ERC-12-0105.
8. De Camargo Cancela, M.; de Souza, L. B. L.; Martins, L. F. L.; Schilithz, A. C.; Souza, D.; Hanly, P.; Barchuk, A.; Soerjomataram, I.; Sharp, L.; Pearce, A. Disparities in Cancer Premature Mortality in Brazil: Predictions up to 2030 and Sustainable Development Goals. *J. Clin. Oncol.* **2020**. DOI: 10.1200/jco.2020.38.15_suppl.e13614.
9. DeSantis, C. E.; Ma, J.; Gaudet, M. M.; Newman, L. A.; Miller, K. D.; Sauer, A. G.; Jemal, A.; Siegel, R. L. Breast Cancer Statistics, 2019. *Cancer J. Clin.* **2019**. DOI: 10.3322/caac.21583.
10. Dunger, D. B.; Ahmed, M. L. Diabetes. In *Growth Disorders, Second Edition*. 2007. DOI: 10.7748/ns.31.19.64.s46.
11. Farrell, A.; Wang, G.; Rush, S. A.; Martin, J. A.; Belant, J. L.; Butler, A. B.; Godwin, D. Machine Learning of Large-Scale Spatial Distributions of Wild Turkeys with High-Dimensional Environmental Data. *Ecol. Evol.* **2019**. DOI: 10.1002/ece3.5177.
12. Gh, C. D.; Wkh, Y.; Qhexol, V.; Spectrometric Analysis; Li Bai, L. I.; Masukawa, N.; Yamaki, M. et al. H-ESI Probe User Guide. *ReVision* **2012**.
13. Goodfellow, I.; Bengio, Y.; Courville, A. *Adaptive Computation and Machine Learning. Adaptive Computation and Machine Learning Series*, 2016.

14. Jain, A. K. Data Clustering: 50 Years Beyond K-Means. *Pattern Recognition Lett.* **2010**. DOI: 10.1016/j.patrec.2009.09.011.
15. Kim, S.; Park, J. Hybrid Feature Selection Method Based on Neural Networks and Cross-Validation for Liver Cancer with Microarray. *IEEE Access.* **2018**. DOI: 10.1109/ACCESS.2018.2884896.
16. Kuncheva, L. I. Bagging and Boosting. In *Combining Pattern Classifiers.* 2004. DOI: 10.1002/0471660264.ch7.
17. Machine Learning. Programming Exercise 1: Linear Regression. *Machine Learning.* 2002. DOI: 10.1023/A:1012422931930.
18. Mellitus, D. Definition, Diagnosis and Classification of Diabetes Mellitus and Its Complications Part 1 : Diagnosis and Classification Of. *World Health.* 1999. DOI: 10.1002/(SICI)1096-9136(199807)15:7<539::AID-DIA668>3.0.CO;2-S.
19. Pradhan, M.; Sahu, R. K. Predict the Onset of Diabetes Disease Using Artificial Neural Network (ANN). *Int. J. Comput. Sci. Emerg. Technol.* **2011**.
20. Samson, S. L.; Garber, A. J. Type 2 Diabetes. In *Encyclopedia of Endocrine Diseases.* 2018. DOI: 10.1016/B978-0-12-801238-3.95795-7.
21. Silva, A. C.; Junior, P. E. F.; Carvalho, P. C. P.; Gattass, M. Diagnosis of Lung Nodule Using the Semivariogram Function. *Lecture Notes in Computer Science (Including Subseries Lecture Notes in Artificial Intelligence and Lecture Notes in Bioinformatics).* 2004. DOI: 10.1007/978-3-540-27868-9_25.
22. Srivastava, N.; Hinton, G.; Krizhevsky, A.; Sutskever, I.; Salakhutdinov, R. Dropout: Prevent NN from Overfitting. *J. Machine Learn. Res.* 2014.
23. Stolfo, S. J. KDD Cup 1999 Dataset. *UCI KDD Repository.* 1999. http://Kdd.Ics.Uci.Edu
24. Temurtas, H.; Yumusak, N.; Temurtas, F. A Comparative Study on Diabetes Disease Diagnosis Using Neural Networks. *Expert Syst. App.* 2009. DOI: 10.1016/j.eswa.2008.10.032.
25. Tu, Y. Machine Learning. In *EEG Signal Processing and Feature Extraction.* 2019. DOI: 10.1007/978-981-13-9113-2_15.
26. Wajid, S. K.; Hussain, A. Local Energy-Based Shape Histogram Feature Extraction Technique for Breast Cancer Diagnosis. *Expert Syst. App.* **2015**. DOI: 10.1016/j.eswa.2015.04.057.
27. Wajid, S. K.; Hussain, A.; Huang, K. Three-Dimensional Local Energy-Based Shape Histogram (3D-LESH): A Novel Feature Extraction Technique. *Expert Syst. App.* **2018**. DOI: 10.1016/j.eswa.2017.11.057.
28. Witten, I. H.; Frank, E.; Hall, M. A. *Data Mining: Practical Machine Learning Tools and Techniques (Google EBook). Complementary Literature None,* 2011.
29. Yaffe, M. J. Mammography. In *Medical Imaging: Principles and Practices.* 2012. DOI: 10.1201/b12939.

CHAPTER 17

An Ensemble of AdaBoost with Multilayer Perceptron for Heart Disease Prediction

SYED HEENA ANDRABI[1], MRINAL PANDEY[2], and RAM CHATTERJEE[2]

[1]*Department of Computer Science and Engineering,*
Islamic University of Science and Technology, J&K, India

[2]*Department of Computer Science and Technology,*
Manav Rachna University, Faridabad, India

ABSTRACT

In the present era, cardiovascular disease has become the main reason for mortality not only in developed countries but in low-income and middle-income countries also. The accurate diagnosis and proper treatment of heart disease at an early stage can reduce this death rate. This research paper proposes an ensemble technique AdaboostM1 using a multilayer perceptron as a base class. Three other classification techniques like bagging, boosting, and voting are also used for the validation and evaluation of the performance on the Statlog heart disease dataset. The results are compared and evaluated with the proposed ensemble technique using 10 cross-validation methods and the conclusion is drawn on the basis of their accuracy rate, precision, recall, specificity, and sensitivity. The experiment manifests that the proposed ensemble technique has outperformed other techniques by showing the highest prediction accuracy of 92.96%, precision of 94%, recall of 93%, along with the sensitivity rate of 92%, and specificity rate of 93.3%.

Computational Intelligence in Analytics and Information Systems, Volume 1: Data Science and AI, Selected Papers from CIAIS-2021. Hardeo Kumar Thakur, Manpreet Kaur, Parneeta Dhaliwal, Rajeev Kumar Arya, and Joan Lu (Eds.)

17.1 INTRODUCTION

Heart disease, also known as cardiovascular disease, refers to various conditions of the heart such as narrowed or blocked blood vessels which may lead to angina (chest pain), heart attack, or stroke. Cardiovascular disease includes other diseases of the heart like cerebrovascular, peripheral arterial, coronary, rheumatic, and congenital heart disease. There are numerous factors that lead to heart diseases, namely, smoking, alcohol, blood pressure, physical inactivity, blood sugar level, cholesterol, and technology. The World Health Organization has aimed to reduce the mortality rate due to heart diseases up to 25% by 2025 by considering and adopting these factors.[1]

As a substantial number of people suffer from heart disease across the globe, resulting in a large number of deaths every year, the diagnosis of heart disease, followed by its appropriate treatment can reduce the mortality rate. However, its prophecy beforehand becomes a challenging task due to its dependency on various factors. Hence, in diagnosis and decision-making systems, there is a need for computational intelligence which can assist the medical professionals.[2] So, researchers have been using different data mining techniques on health care data which can help medical professionals in the diagnosis of diseases.[3] Data mining is a process of analyzing and distinguishing the hidden knowledge from data by applying various machine learning algorithms.[4] In healthcare, medical data mining plays an efficient but complicated role in the diagnosis and treatment of diseases. According to the existing study, medical data mining is used in prophecy of diseases like cancer,[5] heart disease,[6] diabetes,[7] etc.

This research paper proposes an ensemble algorithm AdaboostM1 using MLP as a base classifier for heart disease prediction. The dataset used is the Statlog heart disease dataset taken from the University of California Irvine (UCI) repository. The results manifested from the proposed ensemble technique have proved to be more reliable in performance when compared to other techniques, like bagging, boosting, and voting.

The organization of this paper is as follows: In Section 17.2, the literature survey in the field of diagnosis of heart disease using various single and hybrid data mining, classification techniques have been covered. In Section 17.3, the Statlog dataset is analyzed followed by different data mining techniques. In Section 17.4, the results have been discussed. Finally, Section 17.5 summarizes the conclusions and future work.

17.2 LITERATURE SURVEY

For the prognosis of heart disease in patients, various machine learning techniques have been used. These techniques assist physicians to analyze and predict heart disease. Several single data mining techniques such as Naive Bayes, neural network, support vector machine (SVM), and linear regression have been used in diagnosis of heart disease whose results have concluded in different degrees of accuracy, specificity, and sensitivity. Presently, researchers have been focusing on the use of hybridization of data mining techniques for heart disease diagnosis and the results have proven to be more accurate than single data mining classifiers.[8] Some of the profound work in heart disease diagnosis has been cited below.

In study,[2] researchers proposed a decision support model for the identification of heart disease using the Cleveland dataset. The model used SVM for dividing the dataset into five classes, where the absence of disease is indicated by 0, and classes 1, 2, 3, and 4 indicate different kinds of heart disease. To increase the accuracy and speed of the model, authors have used a genetic algorithm to select only relevant features. Researchers in[9] have used four different data mining techniques such as an artificial neural network (ANN), decision tree, rule-based RIPPER, and SVM for the heart disease classification and prediction. The comparison has been made between these techniques based on accuracy, specificity, sensitivity, error rate, etc. The results concluded that SVM had the highest accuracy rate of 84.12% for correctly predicting cardiovascular diseases. In study,[10] an experiment on patient's heart disease data obtained from the UCI repository has been performed. The study used various classification techniques such as CART, decision tree, and ID3 for predicting the presence or absence of heart disease. The experiment showed that the CART classifier has the highest accuracy and lowest error rate. Study[11] presented a system for predicting the possibility of heart disease among patients. The system proposed in this study is based on supervised learning techniques, such as cascading neural network (CNN) and SVM both using the RBF kernel. The result of CNN was concluded to be better than SVM. In the experiment,[12] five classification techniques, namely, Bayes Net, J48, REPTREE, Naive Bayes, and simple cart have been used to predict heart disease and proposed a model that helps doctors to prognosticate the presence of cardiovascular disease. The experiment is performed by applying 10 cross-fold validation on the dataset and the confusion matrix obtained by applying validation implies the accuracy, sensitivity, and specificity of the classifiers. Researchers in the study[13] conducted an experiment on the heart disease dataset. The dataset included around 909 records with 13 attributes; however, among these attributes only a few were relevant for heart disease prediction so, in order to improve the accuracy of diagnosis of disease, the irrelevant attributes were removed using genetic algorithm; such that the final set of attributes got reduced to only 6. In this work, data mining techniques like Naïve Bayes, decision tree, and classification by clustering have been used and the result showed that decision tree has outperformed the other two techniques. Experiment[14] presented a novel ensemble based technique for heart disease prediction. The proposed system used bagging along with five other single classifiers such as linear regression, Naïve Bayes, quadratic discriminant analysis, instance-based learning, and SVM on five different heart disease datasets taken from the UCI repository. These techniques have been compared on various parameters such as accuracy, sensitivity, specificity, ANOVA, etc. The results proved that the proposed ensemble technique (BagMOOV) has outperformed other techniques. Study[15] has proposed a new technique for ensembles that is independent of instability. In this study, authors have used C4.5 as a base classifier with meta classifiers such as randomizing, boosting, and bagging. The experiment concluded that boosting outperformed bagging and randomizing. Authors in the study[16] used various data mining techniques to compare the accuracy, sensitivity, specificity, PPV, and NPV such as SVM, bagging, random subspace, and boosting on Statlog heart disease dataset. The results concluded that boosting has the highest accuracy of 83.22% followed by bagging with an accuracy of 81.85%. Study[17] explored various data mining approaches such as AdaBoostM1, bagging, IBK, Naïve Bayes, non-nested generalized examples, random forest, and RBF network for the prediction of heart disease. The dataset has been taken from long beach VA consisting of 200 samples, out of which only 40 samples were used for testing. Then, these test datasets were compared on the basis of accuracy, precision, recall, F measure, etc. The result concluded that the RBF network had the highest accuracy rate of 88.2% with the lowest error rate. In experiment,[18] heart disease dataset taken from the Hungarian Institute of Cardiology consists of 76 attributes out of which only 11 attributes were used. In this experiment, classification techniques such as J48, Naive Bayes, and bagging have been evaluated using 10-fold cross-validation and the results have been compared based on TP, FP, precision, time taken to build the classifier, and so on. The experiment concluded that Bagging has the highest accuracy of 85.03% and also the time taken by this classifier is 0.05 s.

17.3   PROPOSED METHODOLOGY

The methodology for this research work as given in Figure 17.1 starts with the collection of datasets followed by preprocessing, construction of ensemble model, and evaluation of the model and ends with the comparison of ensemble model.

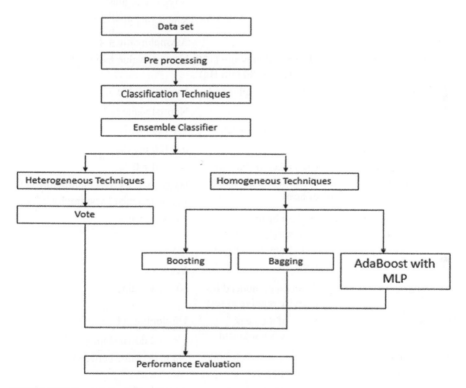

FIGURE 17.1   Methodology.

17.3.1   DATA COLLECTION

In this study, the Statlog heart dataset[19] is obtained from UCI repository. Table 17.1 gives the complete description of the dataset. It includes 270 instances with 14 attributes. The dataset consists of two classes that indicate the presence and absence of heart disease with corresponding descriptions.

TABLE 17.1 Dataset Description.

S.No	Attributes	Description	Value
1	Age	Age given in years	Numeric
2	Sex	Male or female	Male = 0
			Female = 1
3	Chest	Chest pain type	Typical angina =1
			A typical angina = 2
			Nonangina pain = 3
			Asymptomatic = 4
4	Resting blood pressure	Ideal blood pressure (120 mm Hg over 80 mm Hg)	Numeric value in mm HG
5	Serum cholesterol	HDL, LDL, triglycerides	Numeric value in mg/dL
			Normal value is 200 mg/dL
6	Fasting blood sugar	Blood glucose level	$1 \geq 120$ mg/dL
			$0 \leq 120$ mg/dL
7	Resting electro-cardiographic results	Uses ECG to show any abnormal functionality of heart	Normal = 0
			Having ST-T wave abnormality = 1 Left ventricular hypertrophy = 2
8	Maximum heart rate achieved	Highest heart rate, individual can have	Numeric value
9	Exercise-induced angina	Blood supply to heart is less	No = 0
			Yes = 1
10	Old peak	Depression induced by exercise relative to rest	Numeric value
11	Slope	Slope of the peak exercise ST segment	Un sloping = 1
			Flat = 2 down sloping = 3
12	Number of major vessels	The major vessels and veins of heart	Numeric value between 0 and 3
13	Thal	Thalassemia blood disorder	Normal = 3
			Fixed = 6
			reversible defect = 7
14	Class	Absence or presence	Absence = 0
			Presence = 1

17.3.2 DATA PREPROCESSING

Data preprocessing is defined as the process of refining or transforming the available data into an understandable form. Basically, in real world, data are considered as noisy, incomplete, or inconsistent.[20] So, various preprocessing techniques can be applied to the data to remove these anomalies in order to refine the raw data and make it available for future study.

17.3.3 ATTRIBUTE SELECTION

Attribute selection is also called feature selection. It is the process by which only the attributes relevant to the problem are selected from the given dataset. Attribute selection is done to enhance the accuracy of classification by simultaneously decreasing the dimensionality of the dataset.[21] In this paper, InfoGainAttributeEval is used on Statlog heart dataset such that the attributes like serum_cholestrol, resting_blood_pressure, and fasting_blood_sugar which are ranked zero by the filter are removed from the dataset, reducing attributes to 11 only.

17.3.4 RESAMPLING MODEL

Resampling confirms a filtering process that generates random subsamples of the given data. This method is performed by either replacing or without replacing the samples. In this method, the requisite is that the entire dataset must be stored in memory, and also the generated instances must be specified.[22]

17.3.5 CROSS-VALIDATION TECHNIQUE

It is the process of dividing the data into two sets that are the training set with the testing set. The training set trains replica and test set validate it. In this paper,[23] 10 cross-validation techniques have been used. The data are segmented into 10-sized folds or partitions and the training and testing cycle repeats 10 times. During each cycle, onefold is used for testing and the rest of the ninefold are used to train the model such that all the 10-fold are used for both training and testing.

17.3.6 DATA MINING TECHNIQUES

The following mining methods have been used in our stipulated work and their description is given below.

17.3.6.1   BAGGING

Bagging, which is the bootstrap aggregation,[23] is an ensemble data mining technique, used to enhance the result of base classifiers such as Naive Bayes, decision tree, SVM, IBK, etc. In bagging, the given dataset is divided into different bootstraps of the same size, where each bootstrap represents a classifier. It combines the result of all the classifiers where each of them is given the same weight to produce the final outcome. The sampling method used in bagging is either done by using all the instances or by discarding some using methods like disjoint partition (each instance is being used only once), small bags (may select instances repeatedly), no replication small bags (instances are selected independent of other without repetition), or disjoint bags (size of subsets is greater than original dataset).[24]

17.3.6.2   BOOSTING

It is the learning algorithm to boost the performance of weak classifiers by assigning weights to the instances.[25] Initially, the instances are assigned with equal weights, however, during each learning iteration, some new results are generated due to which the weights change. The examples that are properly classified are assigned lower weights and instances with incorrect classification are assigned a higher weight. In the next learning iteration, the incorrectly classified instances are selected in order to classify them accurately. This process continues till the classifier is completely constructed. Finally, the results are taken from all the classifiers by using a majority voting approach.

17.3.6.3   VOTING

This ensemble approach integrates the results from many classifiers.[26] It can take place either by using majority voting, considering the final decision if the vote is more than 50%, unanimous voting; when all classifiers have the same opinion about the final prediction or plurality voting where the majority of votes decide the final result. For this research purpose, ZeroR algorithm is used as the base classifier.

17.3.6.4 MULTILAYER PERCEPTRON

Multilayer perceptron is a supervised learning technique from ANN. It uses a feedforward backpropagation network to train the data. It is composed of an input layer, hidden layers, and an output layer.[27,28] In Figure 17.2, the working of multilayer perceptron is depicted. Initially, the network is fed with training data. Based on its internal classification, adjustments on output will be generated which will divide the training data into two classes. The output generated will be compared with the expected output, if there is any difference between the two it will indicate an error which will be updated and fed back to the network. The whole process will repeat till the termination condition gets satisfied.

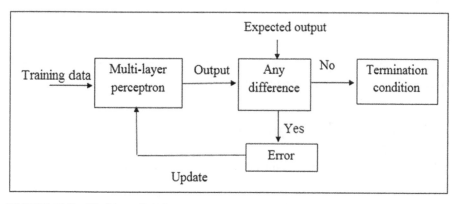

FIGURE 17.2   Working of MLP.

Following is a basic explanation of the multilayer perceptron algorithm.

1. Using the training data initializes the weights either to 0 or some random value.
2. Pick a learning rate between zero and one.
3. Repeat until the termination condition is satisfied.
4. For each training, instance compute activation output.
5. Learning rule: Error = output – expected output.
6. If there is no difference, that is, termination condition is satisfied; stop.
7. Otherwise update weights and continue in a loop.

17.3.7   ADABOOST WITH MLP ENSEMBLE CONSTRUCTION

The suggested ensemble technique is used to boost the performance of multi-layer perceptron using AdaBoostM1. Figure 17.3 displays the block diagram of the proposed methodology. It shows how AdaBoostM1 takes training data as input and applies a base classifier on it by repeatedly calling the base classifier on the training data until all the instances are correctly classified. Finally, it takes the voted average of all the base classifiers, resulting in a single boosted classifier.

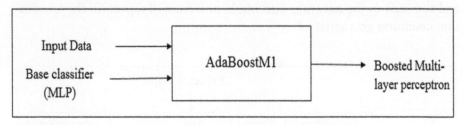

FIGURE 17.3   Block diagram of proposed methodology.

17.3.8   ADABOOST WITH MLP ALGORITHM

STEP 1: - Consider training dataset D with S samples, (x_1, y_1), to (x_s, y_s).

  X_s: Instances
  Y_s: Class [absent, present]

STEP 2: - Select AdaBoost M1 ensemble technique with multilayer perceptron as base classifier.

STEP 3: - Initially weights are not assigned to instances, so assume weights to be equal

$$w_i = \frac{1}{S} i = 1, 2, \text{ to } S$$

STEP 4: - Repeat for $t = 1$ to T

  T: total number of iterations

  a)   Train the MLP $C(x)$ on training data.
  b)   Compute error rate

$$e_t = \frac{1}{S} \sum_{i=1}^{T} I(y_i \neq C_t(x_i))$$

c) Calculate α, it specifies the measuring constant assigned to MLP C_t depending on training error.

$$\alpha_t = \frac{(1 - e_t)}{2}$$

d) Update weights.

$$w_i = \{w_i * (1 - \alpha_t), \text{if } y_i = C_t(x_i) w_i * (1 + \alpha_t), \text{if } y_i \neq C_t(x_i)$$

e) Normalize weight vector W, such that weights add up to 1.
f) Training data reweighted.

STEP 5: - Final output will be the weighted vote of all the classifiers.

$$C(x) = \text{sign}(\sum_{t=1}^{T} \alpha_t c_t(x))$$

17.4 MODEL EVALUATION AND COMPARISON

This paper is a replica that could help physicians to forecast the heart disease (if any). The experiment is carried out on the Statlog heart illness dataset having 14 attributes and 270 instances. For this experimental setup, InfoGain-AttrributeEval is used to remove irrelevant instances, reducing the instances to only 11, as mentioned. Various data mining classifiers such as multilayer perceptron, bagging, boosting, and voting were applied on the dataset using Weka toolkit. Then, finally the proposed algorithm: ADABOOST with MLP was tested on the same dataset to check the accuracy rate. The result of each of the classifiers was retrieved on 10 cross-validation and on average taken from the 10th fold of each fold. The results from each classifier were analyzed to determine the classifier with the highest accuracy in prognosticating heart disease. The classifiers were assessed on the source of their accurateness measures, including sensitivity, specificity, precision, recall, and finally, a confusion matrix was drawn.

The mathematical equation for accuracy,[29] precision,[30] recall,[31] specificity,[32] and sensitivity[33] are given in Eqs (17.1–17.5), respectively.

$$\text{Accuracy} = (TP + TN) / (TP + TN + FP + FN) \qquad (17.1)$$

$$\text{Precision} = TP / (TP + FP) \qquad (17.2)$$

$$\text{Recall=TP} / \text{(TP+FN)} \tag{17.3}$$

$$\text{Specificity} = \text{TN} / \text{(FP+TN)} \tag{17.4}$$

$$\text{Sensitivity} = \text{TP} / \text{(TP+FN)} \tag{17.5}$$

Here TP, TN, FP, and FN symbolize true positives, true negatives, false positives, and false negatives correspondingly.

Figure 17.4 represents the result of these classifiers in terms of accuracy percentage. Tables 17.2 and 17.3 display the contrast of ADABOOST with MLP and other classifiers.

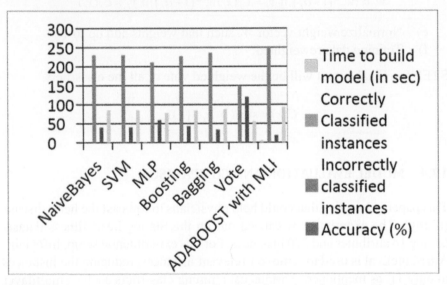

FIGURE 17.4   Comparisons of experimental statistics for various classifiers with the Adaboost (MLP).

TABLE 17.2   Contrast Between Accuracy Measures of Various Classifiers.

Classifier	TP	FP	Precision	Recall	Class
Boosting	0.880	0.208	0.841	0.880	Absence
	0.792	0.120	0.841	0.792	Presence
Bagging	0.887	0.142	0.887	0.887	Absence
	0.858	0.113	0.858	0.858	Presence
Vote	0.953	0.133	0.899	0.953	Absence
	0.867	0.047	0.937	0.867	Presence
ADABOOST with MLP	0.933	0.075	0.940	0.933	Absence
	0.925	0.067	0.917	0.9251	Presence

TABLE 17.3 Comparison Between Accuracy Measures of Various Classifiers.

Classifier	TP	FP	Precision	Recall	Class
NaiveBayes	0.887	0.192	0.853	0.887	Absence
	0.808	0.113	0.851	0.808	Presence
SVM	0.880	0.183	0.857	0.880	Absence
	0.817	0.120	0.845	0.817	Presence
MLP	0.780	0.217	0.818	0.780	Absence
	0.783	0.220	0.740	0.781	Presence
ADABOOST with MLP	0.933	0.075	0.940	0.933	Absence
	0.925	0.067	0.917	0.9251	Presence

A confusion matrix shows the performance of classifiers. In this study, as a binary classification problem has been used, the instances are classified into either an absence or presence of the class. Tables 17.4 and Table 17.5 depict the actual count of examples that are accurately and incorrectly classified by the classifier to predict the robustness of the model.

TABLE 17.4 Confusion Matrix.

Classifier	Class	Absence	Presence
Boosting	Absence	132	25
	Presence	18	95
Bagging	Absence	133	17
	Presence	17	103
Vote	Absence	143	16
	Presence	7	104
ADABOOST with MLP	Absence	140	9
	Presence	10	111

TABLE 17.5 Confusion Matrix.

Classifier	Class	Absence	Presence
NaiveBayes	Absence	133	17
	Presence	23	97
SVM	Absence	132	18
	Presence	22	98
MLP	Absence	117	26
	Presence	33	94
ADABOOST with MLP	Absence	140	9
	Presence	10	111

17.5   CONCLUSION AND FUTURE WORK

Among the noncongenital diseases, cardiovascular illness is considered as the main reason of death globally and the preceding research has shown how various machine learning algorithms can help in its proper diagnosis and correct treatment. Hence, the main purpose of this paper is to use various mining classification techniques for data such as multilayer perceptron, bagging, boosting, voting, MLP, SVM, Naïve Bayes, and proposed ensemble technique, that is, ADABOOST with MLP for heart disease prediction. The classification techniques were then applied on the dataset and were validated using 10 cross-fold techniques, and the results were finally compared based on accuracy, specificity, sensitivity, recall, and precision levels, respectively. The results concluded that ADABOOST with MLP has outperformed other classification techniques by having the highest accuracy rate of 92.96%. Since at present, only Statlog Heart disease dataset has been used, in later prospect the projected algorithm will be used on a variety of other heart disease datasets to evaluate and compare their accuracies in the comparative and contrasted manner in the context of its implementation. The main focus will be to automate the implementation and result analysis via a customized tool for the proposed algorithm.

KEYWORDS

- **ensemble techniques**
- **AdaboostM1**
- **bagging**
- **boosting**
- **multilayer perceptron**

REFERENCES

1. Yusuf, S.; Wood, D.; Ralston, J.; Reddy, K. S. The World Heart Federation's Vision for Worldwide Cardiovascular Disease Prevention. *Lancet* **2015,** *386* (9991), 399–402.
2. Bhatia, S.; Prakash, P.; Pillai, G. N. SVM Based Decision Support System for Heart Disease Classification with Integer-Coded Genetic Algorithm to Select Critical Features.

In *Proceedings of the World Congress on Engineering and Computer Science*, Oct 2008; pp 34–38.

3. Shouman, M.; Turner, T.; Stocker, R. Using Data Mining Techniques in Heart Disease Diagnosis and Treatment. In *2012 Japan-Egypt Conference on Electronics, Communications and Computers*; IEEE, Mar 2012; pp. 173–177.

4. Srinivas, K.; Rani, B. K.; Govrdhan, A. Applications of Data Mining Techniques in Healthcare and Prediction of Heart Attacks. *IJCSE* **2010,** *2* (02), 250–255.

5. Zolbanin, H. M.; Delen, D.; Zadeh, A. H. Predicting Overall Survivability in Comorbidity of Cancers: A Data Mining Approach. *Decision Support Syst.* **2015,** *74*, 150–161.

6. Palaniappan, S.; Awang, R. Intelligent Heart Disease Prediction System Using Data Mining Techniques. In *2008 IEEE/ACS International Conference on Computer Systems and Applications*; IEEE, Mar 2008; pp 108–115.

7. Iyer, A.; Jeyalatha, S.; Sumbaly, R. Diagnosis of Diabetes Using Classification Mining Techniques. *arXiv preprint arXiv:1502.03774*, 2015.

8. Zhang, L.; Zhou, W. D. Sparse Ensembles Using Weighted Combination Methods Based on Linear Programming. *Pattern Recogn.* **2011,** *44* (1), 97–106.

9. Kumari, M.; Godara, S. Comparative Study of Data Mining Classification Methods in Cardiovascular Disease Prediction, **2011,** *1*.

10. Chaurasia, V.; Pal, S. Early Prediction of Heart Diseases Using Data Mining Techniques. *Caribbean J. Sci. Technol.* **2013,** *1*, 208–217.

11. Chitra, R.; Seenivasagam, V. Heart Disease Prediction System Using Supervised Learning Classifier. *Bonfring Int. J. Softw. Eng. Soft Comput.* **2013,** *3* (1), 01–07.

12. Masethe, H. D.; Masethe, M. A. Prediction of Heart Disease Using Classification Algorithms. In *Proceedings of the World Congress on Engineering and Computer Science*, Vol. 2, Oct 2015; pp 22–24.

13. Anbarasi, M.; Anupriya, E.; Iyengar, N. C. S. N. Enhanced Prediction of Heart Disease with Feature Subset Selection Using Genetic Algorithm. *Int. J. Eng. Sci. Technol.* **2010,** *2* (10), 5370–5376.

14. Bhatia, S.; Prakash, P.; Pillai, G. N. SVM Based Decision Support System for Heart Disease Classification with Integer-Coded Genetic Algorithm to Select Critical Features. In *Proceedings of the World Congress on Engineering and Computer Science*, Oct 2008; pp 34–38.

15. Dietterich, T. G. An Experimental Comparison of Three Methods for Constructing Ensembles of Decision Trees: Bagging, Boosting, and Randomization. *Machine Learn.* **2000,** *40* (2), 139–157.

16. Subha, V.; Revathi, M.; Murugan, D. Comparative Analysis of Support Vector Machine Ensembles for Heart Disease Prediction. *Int. J. Comput. Sci. Commun. Netw.* **2015,** *5* (6), 386–390.

17. Aydin, S.; Ahanpanjeh, M.; Mohabbatiyan, S. Comparison and Evaluation of Data Mining Techniques in the Diagnosis of Heart Disease. *IJCSA* **2016,** *6* (1), 1–15.

18. Chaurasia, V.; Pal, S. Data Mining Approach to Detect Heart Diseases. *IJACSIT* **2014,** *2*, 56–66.

19. *UCI Repository*. UCI Repository, n.d. http://archive.ics.uci.edu/ml/datasets.html/statlog/Heart (accessed Jan 10, 2021).

20. García, S.; Luengo, J.; Herrera, F. *Data Preprocessing in Data Mining*, Vol. 72, Springer International Publishing: Cham, Switzerland, 2015.

21. Dash, M.; Liu, H. Consistency-Based Search in Feature Selection. *Artif. Intell.* **2003,** *151* (1–2), 155–176.

22. Xu, G.; Zong, Y.; Yang, Z. *Applied Data Mining*; CRC Press, 2013.

23. Kohavi, R. A Study of Cross-Validation and Bootstrap for Accuracy Estimation and Model Selection. *Ijcai* **1995,** *14* (2), 1137–1145.

24. Efron, B.; Tibshirani, R. J. *An Introduction to the Bootstrap*; CRC Press, 1994.

25. Machová, K.; Barcak, F.; Bednár, P. A Bagging Method Using Decision Trees in the Role of Base Classifiers. *Acta Polytechnica Hungarica* **2006,** *3* (2), 121–132.

26. Freund, Y.; Schapire, R. E. Experiments with a New Boosting Algorithm. *Icml* **1996,** *96,* 148–156.

27. Salih, A. H. S. M.; Abraham, A. Computational Intelligence Data Analysis for Decision Support and Health Care Monitoring System. *J. Netw. Innov. Comput.* **2015,** *3* (2015), 088–104.

28. Karaduzovic-Hadziabdica, K.; Kökerb, R. Diagnosis of Heart Disease Using a Committee Machine Neural Network. *Proc. 9th Int. Conf. Appl. Inform* **2015,** *1,* 2014, 351–360.

29. Fayyad, U.; Piatetsky-Shapiro, G.; Smyth, P. From Data Mining to Knowledge Discovery in Databases. *AI Magaz.* **1996,** *17* (3), 37–37.

30. Delen, D.; Walker, G.; Kadam, A. Predicting Breast Cancer Survivability: A Comparison of Three Data Mining Methods. *Artif. Intell. Med.* **2005,** *34* (2), 113–127.

31. Ghumbre, S.; Patil, C.; Ghatol, A. Heart Disease Diagnosis Using Support Vector Machine. In *International Conference on Computer Science and Information Technology (ICCSIT') Pattaya,* Dec 2011.

32. Sharma, D.; Yadav, U. B.; Sharma, P. The Concept of Sensitivity and Specificity in Relation to Two Types of Errors and Its Application in Medical Research. *J. Reliab. Statist. Studies* **2009,** 53–58.

33. Grzymala-Busse, J. W.; Marepally, S. R. Sensitivity and Specificity for Mining Data with Increased Incompleteness. In *International Conference on Artificial Intelligence and Soft Computing.* Springer, Berlin, Heidelberg, 2010; pp 355–362.

34. Ghoniem, R. M. A Novel Bio-Inspired Deep Learning Approach for Liver Cancer Diagnosis. *Information* **2020,** *11* (2), 80.

35. Abdar, M.; Książek, W.; Acharya, U. R.; Tan, R. S.; Makarenkov, V.; Pławiak, P. A New Machine Learning Technique for an Accurate Diagnosis of Coronary Artery Disease. *Comput. Methods Programs Biomed.* **2019,** *179,* 104992.

36. Tjahjadi, H.; Ramli, K. Noninvasive Blood Pressure Classification Based on Photoplethysmography Using K-Nearest Neighbors Algorithm: A Feasibility Study. *Information* **2020,** *11* (2), 93.

PART III
Techniques for Natural Language Processing

PART III

CHAPTER 18

An Empirical Study of Text Summarization Techniques Using Extractive Approaches

SUMITA GUPTA[1] and MOHIT GAMBHIR[2]

[1]*Amity School of Engineering and Technology, Amity University, Noida, Uttar Pradesh, India*

[2]*Director, Innovation Cell, Ministry of Education, Government of India, India*

ABSTRACT

It becomes very crucial to manage and analyze the relevant data among clusters of non-useful and redundant data available online. It is very hectic to skim through this kind of data for distilled and appropriate information. This chapter describes the solution to the same with the method of automatic text summarization. It is the procedure where a brief gist of the text document which contains all the salient information and essence of content is created. A text summarizer extracts relevant information that intends to meet the standards of human-produced summary but comparatively in much less time. The only goal of automatic text summarizer is to produce such concise text that fits the human proximity of summarization. It hence reduces the hard work and can help in areas, such as business analysis, market review, paper reviews, writing minutes. This is a natural language processing problem and can be solved by various approaches. Here, the focus is on discussing

Computational Intelligence in Analytics and Information Systems, Volume 1: Data Science and AI, Selected Papers from CIAIS-2021. Hardeo Kumar Thakur, Manpreet Kaur, Parneeta Dhaliwal, Rajeev Kumar Arya, and Joan Lu (Eds.)

and comparing the implementation of various extractive techniques for text summarization in detail.

18.1   INTRODUCTION

In the fast-paced world, no one has the time to go through the data to find out the useful text. It is simply a waste of both effort and time to read the whole text. Constructing these texts in short summaries using automatic text summarization is the best solution one can opt for. This reduces both chaos and time and helps in effective work. Humans generally rephrase, break or join sentences to frame a summary keeping in mind to keep only important points. An Automatic summarizer[6] intends to meet the same quality but might not be as abstract as one wants it to be. There are two methods available: An abstractive approach and an extractive approach.

An extractive summarization approach[7] is where a summary contains exact sentences from the original text selected by an algorithm on numerous factors, such as number of words, length of the sentence, title, proximity. Here scoring of sentences is done using various techniques and the highest score sentence is most likely to come in summary according to the maximum size of summary provided. The approach generally includes methods, such as clustering-k-means and degree centrality, frequency count approach, term frequency-inverse document frequency method (Tf-Idf), graph-based approaches, LexRank, and latent semantic analysis (LSA). These methods are part of supervised learning. Other supervised learning methods include machine learning implementations, such as support vector machine, Naive Bayes. A drawback to this approach is that if a sentence is too long, it is likely to get incorporated in summary because of which some other vital sentences may get discarded. This chapter focuses on Extractive approach implementation and comparison among them.

Another approach is abstractive text summarization.[5] Abstractive summaries are one where the original text is summarized to more of human understandable and semantic form, where sentences are rephrased and not just directly copied. The summary generated via this approach is different from the original document. The sentences that are generated are like man-made—short and precise. Intense training is required to train the model where the sentences present in the document are paraphrased so that it does not change the meaning of the document. This approach is a bit complex and can be implemented using deep learning methods.

The chapter is categorized as follows: In Section 18.2, the study of various research papers based on text summarization techniques has been done. An overlook to all the methodologies used and their algorithmic design has been done. Further in Section 18.3, an implementation study of these methods has been explained with snapshots. Later, in Section 18.4, a comparative analysis has been carried out of all the methodologies distinguished on various factors from the information collected. Section 18.5 finally concludes the chapter with the result of empirical study and future goals.

18.2 RELATED WORK

This section focuses on various methodologies proposed for text summarization.[2] L.A Bewoor et al.[17] gives a descriptive analysis about extractive approaches including term frequency,[4] Graph-based, clustering and latent semantic approach and abstractive[5] ones, including semantic, information and neural network approach have been mentioned. The LSA method is best described which helps to find semantically similar words from a matrix of sentences, hence helping to avoid synonyms and redundancy between sentences.

Utsav Gupta et al.[8] gives the solution to text summarization by clustering approach. The methods discussed in this chapter are K-means[16] and degree centrality.[2,11] Result summary was compared with the human-produced summary using the criteria of number of common sentences.

Prabhudas et al.[18] depicts details about text features and its representation that how the text is vectorized into sparse matrices and their sentence similarity is found out on the basis of cosine similarity of sentences. It introduces Graph-based approach – LexRank[9] and semantic-based LSA method[4,7] that how each sentence acts like vertex to graph and semantic similarity is found between them. This chapter also gives a brief representation and method for Rouge score evaluation.

Chin-Yew Lin et al.[12] gave the tool, which we used to compare the methods, that is, ROUGE score. ROUGE stands for Recall-Oriented Understudy for Gisting Evaluation. It includes measures to determine the quality of a summary (system generated) by comparing it to other (ideal) summaries created by humans. The author has defined four measures, namely, ROUGE-S, ROUGE-W, ROUGE-L, and ROUGE-N that are based on different criteria to compare the machine and human-made summaries.

18.3 METHODOLOGIES

18.3.1 TERM FREQUENCY—INVERSE DOCUMENT FREQUENCY METHOD (TF-IDF)

It is a statistical approach[7,14] through which we can generate the summary which contains the sentences which have high importance. This method forms the base of every other method as it includes the basic steps of extractive approach as shown in Figure 18.1.

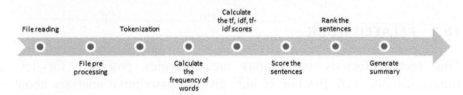

FIGURE 18.1   Flowchart describing Tf-Idf approach.

As described in Figure 18.1, the file is considered as an input from the user, to which the preprocessing is applied. In preprocessing, removal of stop words, white spaces, etc. occur. The next step is tokenization, where first sentences are separated and then words. The next step is to calculate the Tf-Idf scores, which is used to score and rank the sentences. Later, the summary is generated with the sentences having the maximum score. The only disadvantage with this method is that if the length of the sentence is long then it can be added in the summary even if it is not important.

This method has two components- Tf and Idf score. Tf score (tf) refers to the count of a term, that is, how many times the term appeared in a document. It can be calculated as shown in (18.1):

$$t_f = \frac{\text{Frequency count of a term in the document}}{\text{Total number of terms in the document}} \qquad (18.1)$$

idf score (Idf) refers to the importance of a term in a document. In calculation of Tf, every term is considered as important and hence even the less important words like "is," "this" get unnecessary weightage, just because they occur frequently in the text. Thus, we need to weight down the frequent terms while scaling up the rare ones. The idf score (Idf) of any term t is computed as shown in equation (18.2):

$$\text{Id}_f = \frac{\text{Total number of documents}}{\text{number of document where term appears}} \qquad (18.2)$$

Tf-Idf score (p) refers to the product of Tf, Idf scores as shown in equation (18.3). It helps in scoring the sentences. It can be calculated as:

$$p = t_f * Id_f \tag{18.3}$$

Illustrative Example: Let's consider an example in order to understand the working of Tf-Idf method. An input text is considered as shown below:

"Data mining is defined as a process used to extract usable data from a large set of raw data. It implies analyzing data patterns in large batches of data using one or more software. Data mining has applications in multiple fields, like science and research. Data mining is also defined as knowledge discovery in databases, the process of discovering usable patterns in large volumes of data."

Preprocessing of input text computes the frequency count (FC) of each term as shown in Table 18.1.

TABLE 18.1 Frequency Count for Input Text.

Term	FC	Term	FC	Term	FC	Term	FC
Data	8	Usable	2	Software	1	Knowledge	1
Mining	3	Large	3	Application	1	Discovery	1
Defined	2	Set	1	Multiple	1	Database	1
Process	2	Raw	1	Field	1	Discovering	1
Used	1	Implies	1	Science	1	Volume	1
Extract	1	analyzing	1	Research	1	Pattern	2

Table 18.1 depicts the values obtained after calculation of Tf, idf, Tf-idf scores using Eqs. (18.1), (18.2), (18.3), respectively. The Tf-idf score will help to deduce scoring of sentences and then include the highest ranked ones in the summary.

18.3.2 LATENT SEMANTIC ANALYSIS (LSA)

LSA,[17] a part of unsupervised learning, is an algebraic method which extracts hidden semantic structure of the words and the sentences. It has three major steps.

Input matrix creation: The input document is converted into a matrix, referred to as document term matrix where each cell is filled by Tf-idf values that represent the importance of the words in sentences. Higher the value, the more importance it has in the sentence and is more semantically related, though it might be less important in the document.

Singular value decomposition (SVD): SVD is an algebraic method which models the relationship among the words and the sentences. The idea behind this is that the document matrix can be represented as a vector. SVD is performed on the document term matrix, it helps in removing the noise and helps in increasing the accuracy.

Illustrative Example 1: Let's consider an example to understand the working of LSA method.

Let A [m x n] matrix where all the entries are real and m>n. A can be written as:

$$A = U\Sigma V^T \tag{18.4}$$

where U is left singular vector ($m*r$ orthogonal matrix), Σ is singular values ($r*r$ diagonal matrix), V^T is right singular vectors ($n*r$ orthogonal matrix).

Let's assume, A as the input matrix where the rows define the user's ratings and the columns define whether the user likes the movie or not, the user rates 1 if he likes it and 0 if he does not.

$$A = [\,1\ 0\ 1\ 0\ 0\ 1\ 0\ 1\,]$$

Thus, the matrix can be defined as the product of three matrices according to (18.4). The calculation of U, Σ and V are as follows:

$$U_{mxr} = \frac{1}{\sigma_1} Av_1 \frac{1}{\sigma_2} Av_2 \frac{NS(A^T)}{|NS(A^T)|} \tag{18.5}$$

Here, A is the input matrix, v_n is the eigenvectors and σ n are the singular values, $NS(A^T)$ refers to calculating the null space of A^T.

$$\Sigma = [\sigma_1\ 0\ 0\ \sigma_2\ 00] \tag{18.6}$$

[Note: To make a matrix similar to the input matrix A, so after placing the σ_n values, fill in the blank spaces with 0.]

Here, $\sigma_n = \sqrt{\lambda_n}$, where λ are the eigenvalues.

$$V^T = [v_1 v_2] \tag{18.7}$$

Here, v_n are the eigenvectors.

First, compute the eigenvalues and eigenvectors. Eigenvalues $\lambda 1$ and $\lambda 2$ comes out to be $\lambda 1 = \lambda 2 = 2$,

The eigenvectors are [10] and [01]

Thus, the singular values are as: $\sigma_n = \sigma_n = \sqrt{2}$ (*as* $\sigma_n = \sqrt{\lambda_n}$)

The value of $\sum$ as per (18.6) is:

$$\sum = \left[\sqrt{2}\,0000\,\sqrt{2}\,00 \right] \tag{18.6a}$$

And,

$$U = \frac{1}{\sqrt{2}} \left[1010010110 - 10010 - 1 \right] \tag{18.5a}$$

$$V = \left[1\ 0\ 0\ 1 \right] \tag{18.7a}$$

Thus, the input matrix can be represented as the multiplication of the above three matrices.

Sentence selection: The final step where sentences are selected using a cross-method coverage concept method, where highest weighted edges are used to generate summary.

18.3.3 CLUSTERING

Clustering[16] is the activity of clubbing together a number of sentences in a way that the sentences of the same cluster are more alike compared with sentences in other clusters. A similarity matrix is there to describe the relationship strength between two data objects. Clustering is mainly used for exploratory data mining.

18.3.3.1 K-MEANS CLUSTERING

The k means is a part of centroid-based clustering.[8,16] An iterative approach where the text is divided into smaller groups or partitions to make it as similar as possible. The process of clustering is illustrated as:

1. Let k be a set of n data points: $x = \{x_1, x_2, \ldots\ldots, x_N\}$.
2. Let S be the set of "k" clusters, $S = \{s_1, s_2 \ldots s_n\}$. Initialize centroids by shuffling the dataset and then randomly selecting k points as centroids without any replacement. Let C be set of centroids, $C = \{c1, c2\}$
3. Compute the sum of squared distance between data points and centroids and thus assigning data points to closest cluster. Less number of variations means that clusters are more homogeneous. Take the average of all data points in a cluster to find the new centroid. The objective function is as shown in (18.8):

$$J = \sum_{i=1}^{m} \sum_{k=1}^{K} w_{ik} \| x^i - \mu_k \|^2 \tag{18.8}$$

Here, $w_{ik} = 1$ for data point xi if it is in cluster k; $w_{ik} = 0$. Also, $\mu_k = $ centroid of xi cluster.

4. Repeat the third step until no change of centroid occurs.

Illustrative Example: Consider the input text given in example 1, after the term frequency table is created (as shown in Table 18.1), K-means clustering is applied considering two clusters. The output is shown in Table 18.2.

TABLE 18.2 Clustering of Sentences for Example 1.

Sentences	Cluster no.
Data mining is defined as a process used to extract usable data from a large set of any raw data	0
It implies analyzing data patterns in large batches of data using One or more software	0
Data mining has applications in multiple fields, like science and research	1
Data mining, is also defined as knowledge discovery in databases, the process of discovering Usable patterns in large volumes of data	0

Table 18.2 describes the clusters which are produced. After the creation of the clusters, rank the sentences and generate the summary. Here, Tf-Idf approach helps to find frequency, the sentence with highest frequency signifies the theme of the content and one with lowest are considered as outliers. Hence, the important sentences are then combined to form a summary.

18.3.3.2 DEGREE CENTRALITY

Degree centrality[2] is a statistical approach that identifies the nodes that reach most of the nodes directly. This measure captures local importance of a node, where each sentence is represented as a vector. Cosine similarity between the edges is calculated.

Centrality score of a sentence at position i is denoted as Ci, scaled between 0 and 1. Then, this measure is linearly combined with the measure capturing position importance discussed earlier to get the final score from a sentence as follows:

$$R_i = W_c \times C_I + W_p \times P_i. \tag{18.9}$$

Here, the weights are (centrality score) and Wp (position score). The sentences are then ranked according to the final scores. Figure 18.2 describes the algorithm for degree centrality.

Algorithm: **Degree Centrality**

Input: Text file of 2-3 pages.

Output: Summary retaining 30% of the original text

Step 1: Tokenize the sentences and do the pre-processing

Step 2: Compute the degree of each sentence and pick the node with higher degree

Step 3: Find the similarity between the sentences

Step 4: Compute the similarity matrix.

Step 5: Rank the sentences

Step 6: Generate summary

FIGURE 18.2   Algorithmic approach for degree centrality method.

18.4   RESULT ANALYSIS

For result analysis, approximately, 100 text files of different genres—data security, networking, politics, cloud, sports, etc. are considered as dataset for comparing the different approaches as discussed above. A comparison between these approaches is displayed in Table 18.3 based on the different criteria, such as advantages, disadvantages, cohesion, and relevancy. For experimental analysis, Precision, Recall, and F-measure parameters are calculated on basis of Rouge-1 evaluation. In Figure 18.3, a bar graph is showing for comparing the above-discussed methods based on precision, recall, and f-measure.

18.5   CONCLUSION

In this chapter, there was successful implementation and comparison of different approaches. There was deep study of approaches considering the

TABLE 18.3　Comparison Study of various Extractive Text Summarization Methods.

Method	TF-IDF	Degree Centrality	K-means Clustering	LSA
Description	Preprocess the text and rank the sentences based on word frequency count	Treats each sentence as a vector and computes the cosine similarity between the sentences	Select random sentences as centroid and based on closest distance make clusters	The input text is converted to a document term matrix, as vectors so as to find a semantic relationship between them
Advantages	Base for every extractive approach	Remove similar sentences and be efficient in identifying the nodes that humans consider important	Outliers or less important sentences are removed Gives full generative semantics	SVD helps in removing noise, increasing accuracy. It Captures salient combination patterns
Limitations	Long, non-important sentences would be part of the summary as they have high frequency weightage	Threshold value should be apt as it can lead to loss of important sentences.	Data points are "hard assigned" to a cluster, that is, either they are in cluster or not.	Very sensitive to a stop list and Lemmatization and cannot handle dynamic document collection.
Relevancy^	Yes	Yes	No	No
Cohesion*	Yes	Yes	No	No

*Cohesion refers to how much the sentences are conceptually related to each other

^Relevancy means how much of the summary is relevant and, how much it makes sense

pros and cons of methodologies. Many papers reviewed and explained methods but less of them showed implementation and hardly a few came up with concept of rouge score or comparative analysis. This chapter effectively gave result to search for best approach by putting reference human summary against machine produced summary. The system produced summary was made to retain 30% of the original text. According to references and formulas used, ROUGE-1 turns out to be sufficient for single document summaries. Other Rouge types work effectively for multidocument summaries. Hence, from the bar chart results, we can conclude that for our data, the best method turns out to be degree centrality under ROUGE-1 evaluation as it is both high in precision and f-score.

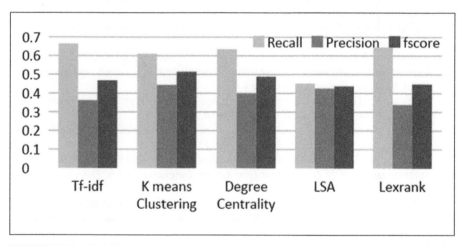

FIGURE 18.3   Recall, precision, F-score values for various extractive methods on dataset.

KEYWORDS

- **extractive text summarization**
- **Lex-rank**
- **term frequency-inverse document frequency**
- **latent semantic analysis**
- **rouge score**
- **clustering**

REFERENCES

1. Barzilay, R.; Elhadad, M. Using Lexical Chains for Text Summarization. *Adv. Automat. Text Summarization* **1999**, 111–1121.
2. Bhole, P.; Agrawal, A. J. Single Document Text Summarization Using Clustering Approach Implementing for News Article. *IJETT*, **2014**, *15* (7).
3. Gaikwad, D. K.; Mahender, C. N. A Review Paper on Text Summarization. *Int. J. Adv. Res. Comput. Commun. Eng.* **2016**, *5* (3), 154–160.
4. Katiyar, S.; Borgohain, S. K. A Novel Approach Towards Automatic Text Summarization Using Lexical Chain. *Int. J. Recent Innov. Trends Comput. Commun.*, ISSN-2321–8169. **2015**, 3 (8), 5115–5121.
5. Modi, S.; Oza, R. Review on Abstractive Text Summarization Techniques (ATST) for Single and Multi Documents. In *2018 International Conference on Computing, Power and Communication Technologies (GUCON)*; IEEE, Sept 28, 2018; pp 1173–1176.
6. Singla, S.; Duhan, N.; Kalkal, U. A Novel Approach for Document Ranking in Digital Libraries Using Extractive Summarization. *Int. J. Comput. App.* **2013**, *74* (18), 25–31.
7. Andhale, N.; Bewoor, L. A. An Overview of Text Summarization Techniques. In *2016 International Conference on Computing Communication Control and Automation (ICCUBEA)*; IEEE, Aug 12, 2016; pp 1–7.
8. Agrawal, A.; Gupta U. Extraction Based Approach for Text Summarization Using K-Means Clustering. *Int. J. Sci. Res. Pub.* **2014**, *4* (11), 1–4.
9. Erkan, G.; Radev, D. R. Lexrank: Graph-Based Lexical Centrality as Salience in Text Summarization. *J. Artif. Intell. Res.* **2004**, 22, 457–479.
10. Verma, P.; Pal, S.; Om, H. A Comparative Analysis on Hindi and English Extractive Text Summarization. *ACM Trans. Asian Low-Resour. Language Inform. Process. (TALLIP)* **2019**, *18* (3), 1–39.
11. Gutiérrez Hinojosa, S. J.; Calvo, H.; Moreno-Armendáriz, M. A. Central Embeddings for Extractive Summarization Based on Similarity. *Computación y Sistemas*. **2019**, *23* (3).
12. Lin, C. Y.; Och, F. J. Automatic Evaluation of Machine Translation Quality Using Longest Common Subsequence and Skip-Bigram Statistics. In *Proceedings of the 42nd Annual Meeting on Association for Computational Linguistics*; Association for Computational Linguistics, Jul 21, 2004; p 605.
13. Moratanch, N.; Chitrakala S. A Survey on Extractive Text Summarization. In *2017 International Conference on Computer, Communication and Signal Processing (ICCCSP)*; IEEE, Jan 10, 2017; pp 1–6.
14. Madhuri, J. N.; Kumar, R. G. Extractive Text Summarization Using Sentence Ranking. In *2019 International Conference on Data Science and Communication (IconDSC)*; IEEE, Mar 1, 2019; pp 1–3.
15. Dalal, V.; Malik L. A Survey of Extractive and Abstractive Text Summarization Techniques. In *2013 6th International Conference on Emerging Trends in Engineering and Technology*; IEEE, Dec 16, 2013; pp 109–110.
16. Singh, S.; Gill, N. A. Analysis and Study of K-Means Clustering Algorithm. *Int. J. Eng. Res. Technol.* **2013**, *2*, 2546–2551.
17. Nagwani, N. K.; Verma, S. A Frequent Term and Semantic Similarity Based Single Document Text Summarization Algorithm. *Int. J. Comput. App.* **2011**, *17* (2), 36–40.

18. Janjanam, P.; Reddy, C. H. Text Summarization: An Essential Study. *Second International Conference on Computational Intelligence in Data Science (ICCIDS-2019)*, 2019.
19. Munot, N.; Govilkar, S. S. Comparative Study of Text Summarization Methods. *Int. J. Comput. App.* **2014,** *102* (12).

APPENDIX

The appendix shows the practical evaluation of the above extractive approaches, a fragment of sample input paper is considered (given in Figure 18.4). Tf-Idf method computes the Tf-Idf score (as shown in Figure 18.5) for ranking the sentences. K-means algorithm forms the clusters (as shown in Figure 18.6) for generating the summary. And, degree centrality method forms a similarity matrix in order to compute the similarity between sentences. The centrality score and weights of sentences give the final scores in order to do ranking sentences and finally the sentences having higher rank are considered in the summary (as shown in Figure 18.7).

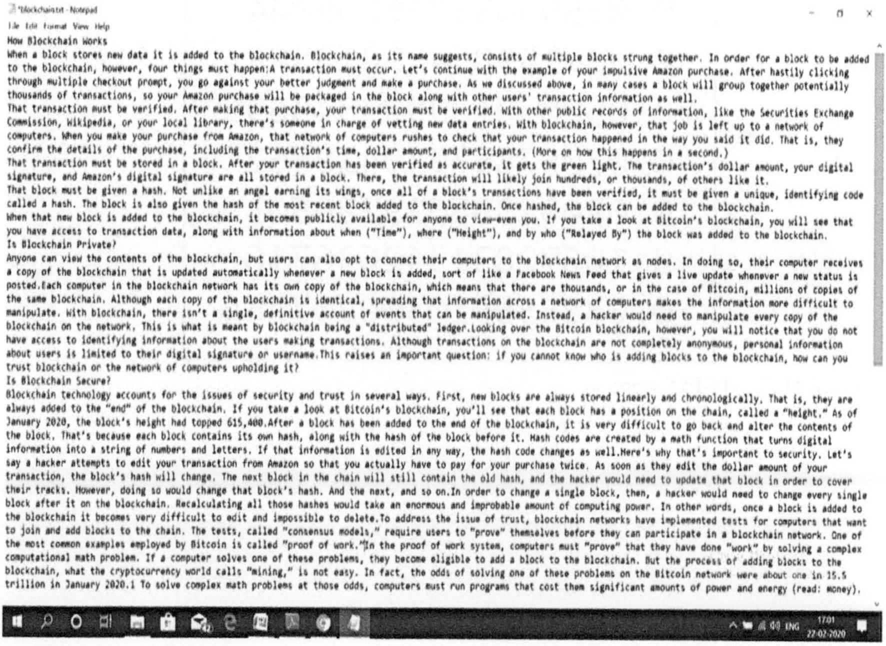
*blockchain.txt - Notepad
File Edit Format View Help
How Blockchain Works
When a block stores new data it is added to the blockchain. Blockchain, as its name suggests, consists of multiple blocks strung together. In order for a block to be added to the blockchain, however, four things must happen:A transaction must occur. Let's continue with the example of your impulsive Amazon purchase. After hastily clicking through multiple checkout prompt, you go against your better judgment and make a purchase. As we discussed above, in many cases a block will group together potentially thousands of transactions, so your Amazon purchase will be packaged in the block along with other users' transaction information as well.
That transaction must be verified. After making that purchase, your transaction must be verified. With other public records of information, like the Securities Exchange Commission, Wikipedia, or your local library, there's someone in charge of vetting new data entries. With blockchain, however, that job is left up to a network of computers. When you make your purchase from Amazon, that network of computers rushes to check that your transaction happened in the way you said it did. That is, they confirm the details of the purchase, including the transaction's time, dollar amount, and participants. (More on how this happens in a second.)
That transaction must be stored in a block. After your transaction has been verified as accurate, it gets the green light. The transaction's dollar amount, your digital signature, and Amazon's digital signature are all stored in a block. There, the transaction will likely join hundreds, or thousands, of others like it.
That block must be given a hash. Not unlike an angel earning its wings, once all of a block's transactions have been verified, it must be given a unique, identifying code called a hash. The block is also given the hash of the most recent block added to the blockchain. Once hashed, the block can be added to the blockchain.
When that new block is added to the blockchain, it becomes publicly available for anyone to view-even you. If you take a look at Bitcoin's blockchain, you will see that you have access to transaction data, along with information about when ("Time"), where ("Height"), and by who ("Relayed By") the block was added to the blockchain.
Is Blockchain Private?
Anyone can view the contents of the blockchain, but users can also opt to connect their computers to the blockchain network as nodes. In doing so, their computer receives a copy of the blockchain that is updated automatically whenever a new block is added, sort of like a Facebook News Feed that gives a live update whenever a new status is posted.Each computer in the blockchain network has its own copy of the blockchain, which means that there are thousands, or in the case of Bitcoin, millions of copies of the same blockchain. Although each copy of the blockchain is identical, spreading that information across a network of computers makes the information more difficult to manipulate. With blockchain, there isn't a single, definitive account of events that can be manipulated. Instead, a hacker would need to manipulate every copy of the blockchain on the network. This is what is meant by blockchain being a "distributed" ledger.Looking over the Bitcoin blockchain, however, you will notice that you do not have access to identifying information about the users making transactions. Although transactions on the blockchain are not completely anonymous, personal information about users is limited to their digital signature or username.This raises an important question: if you cannot know who is adding blocks to the blockchain, how can you trust blockchain or the network of computers upholding it?
Is Blockchain Secure?
Blockchain technology accounts for the issues of security and trust in several ways. First, new blocks are always stored linearly and chronologically. That is, they are always added to the "end" of the blockchain. If you take a look at Bitcoin's blockchain, you'll see that each block has a position on the chain, called a "height." As of January 2020, the block's height had topped 615,400.After a block has been added to the end of the blockchain, it is very difficult to go back and alter the contents of the block. That's because each block contains its own hash, along with the hash of the block before it. Hash codes are created by a math function that turns digital information into a string of numbers and letters. If that information is edited in any way, the hash code changes as well.Here's why that's important to security. Let's say a hacker attempts to edit your transaction from Amazon so that you actually have to pay for your purchase twice. As soon as they edit the dollar amount of your transaction, the block's hash will change. The next block in the chain will still contain the old hash, and the hacker would need to update that block in order to cover their tracks. However, doing so would change that block's hash. And the next, and so on.In order to change a single block, then, a hacker would need to change every single block after it on the blockchain. Recalculating all those hashes would take an enormous and improbable amount of computing power. In other words, once a block is added to the blockchain it becomes very difficult to edit and impossible to delete.To address the issue of trust, blockchain networks have implemented tests for computers that want to join and add blocks to the chain. The tests, called "consensus models," require users to "prove" themselves before they can participate in a blockchain network. One of the most common examples employed by Bitcoin is called "proof of work."In the proof of work system, computers must "prove" that they have done "work" by solving a complex computational math problem. If a computer solves one of these problems, they become eligible to add a block to the blockchain. But the process of adding blocks to the blockchain, what the cryptocurrency world calls "mining," is not easy. In fact, the odds of solving one of these problems on the Bitcoin network were about one in 15.5 trillion in January 2020.1 To solve complex math problems at those odds, computers must run programs that cost them significant amounts of power and energy (read: money).

FIGURE 18.4 Sample.

```
0.0
0.040081315799918017
0.063292128565668016
0.056009114391760044
0.056842020566630829
0.053701178923204533
0.044846412129194366
0.049860497792262951
0.098166242312288203
0.066655344904031669
0.070499259067454188
0.045018323955926166
0.055966813567658444
0.097159854178135588
0.060830489997343695
0.070578579404186662
0.080983956297865033
0.106728313426367166
0.038555310300207264
```

FIGURE 18.5   Tf-Id f score.

	Sentence	Cluster no.
How Blockchain Works When a block stores new d...		3
Blockchain, as its name suggests, consists of...		4
In order for a block to be added to the block...		0
Let's continue with the example of your impul...		4
After hastily clicking through multiple check...		2
As we discussed above, in many cases a block ...		0
That transaction must be verified		0
After making that purchase, your transaction ...		0
With other public records of information, lik...		4
With blockchain, however, that job is left up...		4
When you make your purchase from Amazon, that...		0
That is, they confirm the details of the purc...		4
(More on how this happens in a second		1
) That transaction must be stored in a block		0
After your transaction has been verified as a...		4

FIGURE 18.6   Sentences belonging to different clusters.

Summarize Text:
How Blockchain Works When a block stores new data it is added to the blockchain.In order for a block to be added to the blockchain, however, four things must happen: A transaction must occur.Each computer in the blockchain network has its own copy of the blockchain, which means that there are thousands, or in the case of Bitcoin, millions of copies of the same blockchain.This is what is meant by the Bitcoin network and blockchain being "decentralized."Blockchain vs. Bitcoin The goal of blockchain is to allow digital information to be recorded and distributed, but not edited.If you take a look at Bitcoin's blockchain, you will see that you have access to transaction data, along with information about when ("Time"), where ("Height"), and by who ("Relayed By") the block was added to the blockchain.The block is also given the hash of the most recent block added to the blockchain. In other words, once a block is added to the blockchain it becomes very difficult to edit and impossible to delete.Anyone can view the contents of the blockchain, but users can also opt to connect their computers to the blockchain network as nodes.This raises an important question: if you cannot know who is adding blocks to the blockchain, how can you trust blockchain or the network of computers upholding it?Once hashed, the block can be added to the blockchain.When that new block is added to the blockchain, it becomes publicly available for anyone to view-even you.That block must be given a hash.Is Blockchain Secure?Is Blockchain Private?After a block has been added to the end of the blockchain, it is very difficult to go back and alter the contents of the block.As we discussed above, the completed transaction is publicly recorded and stored as a block on the blockchain, at which point it becomes unalterable.Although each copy of the blockchain is identical, spreading that information across a network of computers makes the information more difficult to manipulate.That's because each block contains its own hash, along with the hash of the block before it.As we discussed above, in many cases a block will group together potentially thousands of transactions, so your Amazon purchase will be packaged in the block along with other users' transaction information as well.If a hacker wanted to coordinate an attack on the blockchain, they would need to control more than 50% of all computing power on the blockchain so as to be able to overwhelm all other participants in the network.This is where the blockchain comes in.Looking over the Bitcoin blockchain, however, you will notice that you do not have access to identifying information about the users making transactions.

FIGURE 18.7   Summary produced by degree centrality approach.

CHAPTER 19

Design and Comparative Analysis of Inverted Indexing of Text Documents

GUNJAN CHANDWANI, SARIKA NARENDER, and MEENA CHAUDHARY

Department of Computer Science & Technology, Manav Rachna University, Faridabad, India

ABSTRACT

The economic feasibility of maintaining large databases of documents has created a tremendous demand for robust ways to access and manipulate the information these documents contain. Documents are indexed by their content or by metadata attached to the document. In this chapter, we have proposed a new document indexing algorithm and its comparative analysis with the traditional indexing algorithm approach.

19.1 INTRODUCTION OR THE NEED OF DOCUMENT INDEXING

The purpose of a database is to store data through which one can retrieve information which is relevant to a given query. Depending on the nature of the data to be accessed (fielded, full text, or image) different techniques must be used for creating indexes, formulating queries, and retrieving records.

19.1.1 DOCUMENT INDEXING

Indexing is the process of tagging or associating information with a document file so that it can be used for search and retrieval purposes. The index data

Computational Intelligence in Analytics and Information Systems, Volume 1: Data Science and AI, Selected Papers from CIAIS-2021. Hardeo Kumar Thakur, Manpreet Kaur, Parneeta Dhaliwal, Rajeev Kumar Arya, and Joan Lu (Eds.)

are put away or coordinated into an information base or record the board framework for easy accessibility of the document.

19.1.1.1   *NEED OF DOCUMENT INDEXING*

Indexing can sound discretionary since the title and substance of a report make a satisfactory showing of depicting it.

- *Fast document access:* Data indexing measures helps to find any document simpler than a keyword search.
- *Time efficiency:* The time will be saved, while searching for documents.
- *Efficient document management and organization:* Metadata groups each document with similar ones based on the keywords used and hence makes it easier to organize large volumes of documents based on specific categorizations.

19.1.1.2   *TYPES OF DOCUMENT INDEXING*

Full-text indexing: allows for documents search using any keyword/text contained within the document, including full phrases/passages.

- Field-based indexing: It provides tagging documents with metadata, or information about the data itself.
- The transformed file is the procedure which was generally embraced for full-text ordering of huge printed assortments,[9] and is upheld by numerous DBMSs for putting away and dealing with organized, unstructured information just as semi-organized information.

Figure 19.1 shows an automatic indexing process of structured data.

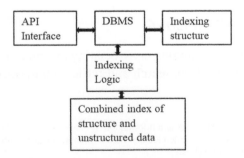

FIGURE 19.1   Index process.

19.2   LITERATURE REVIEW

Author	Title	Method
David Doermann[11]	Semantic and Conceptual indexing using Wikipedia	The technique finds information from the document or main topics by linking concepts of document with existing knowledge base. The authors utilized Wikipedia for extracting important terms and keywords, indexing records and using semantic associatedness to recover important attributes. The graphs of each term are combined together to produce a diagram called directed acyclic graph for a document. The cosine calculation on vectors is weighted by TF-IDF scoring, key phrases and watchword extraction strategy.
Gupta R.K., et al.[3]	Document indexing by hashing approach	The process requires preprocessing which converts the document into feature vectors possessing the important features. Terms are arranged in descending order of their frequency. Similarly, one hash number is also assigned to each document which is further used for probing the records. The term Ids of words in query is used as a key for hash function. The set retrieved from the intersection of terms Ids and terms in document set are chosen as appropriate documents.
Norbert Fuhr, et al.[18]	Probabilistic approach for document indexing	The approach is adopted for IR systems in real applications and is proved to be superior to other indexing approaches. Terms in documents are assigned weights based on their relevancy information. Relevancy is estimated on the basis of user feedback
Shufeng Hao, et al.[4]	Latent semantic indexing (LSI)	This is a variation variety of the vector recovery strategy or SVD,[12] that misuses conditions or "semantic similarity" among terms. It is believed that there exists a couple of fundamental or "latent" structure in the sample of word use all through reports, and can be resolved statistically.[10] LSI has been utilized in huge form of learning tasks, which includes search and retrieval, classification and filtering[4]
Tekli J., et al.[6]	Semantic indexing	The semantic data (inside the articles being ordered) improves the nature of data recovery. Semantic indexes in which objects are indexed by the concepts that has the terms used to represent them. It utilizes a bunch of semantic connections among the list terms, dictated by methods for thesauri, for example, the Medical Subject Headings.[28] Classification frameworks, for example, Library of Congress or Dewey Decimal, center around various leveled connections. The principal connections utilized are: • Equivalence – equivalent word terms • Hierarchical – more extensive and smaller terms • Associative – all the more inexactly related terms

19.3   PROPOSED METHODOLOGY

This chapter proposes an algorithm for creation of an inverted index for a text file whose flowchart has been shown in Figure 19.2. In this algorithm, we identify an index table and then we identify columns to associate for an index. We preprocess the textual data by removing punctuation marks and stop words and create tokens of unstructured text data and then we build an inverted index by generating B tree structure on associated columns.

19.4   IMPLEMENTATION RESULT OF INVERTED INDEX OF A TEXT FILE

The first step is the creation of a text document. In the second step, we count the number of textual lines in that file whose pseudocode is shown in Figure 19.3. We remove the punctuation marks and stop words from each line in the text file by stemming process (pseudo code shown in Figure 19.4). After removal of stop words, we create tokens (pseudo code shown in Figure 19.5). Finally, these tokens are organized in a b tree structure to create an inverted index (pseudocode shown in Figure 19.6).

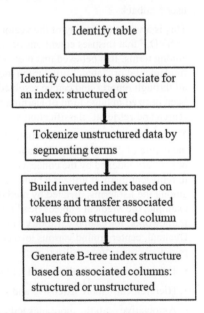

FIGURE 19.2   Proposed inverted index creation process.

```
Open the text file in read mode
Move the pointer to 0 position or to the start of text file
        Initialize line=1
for each word in text file do
        Check if word is a newline character

do

        line=line+1
        print line
```

FIGURE 19.3   Count number of lines.

```
Initialize punc=!@*&()^&#$%{}[]:"?><
for each word in text file do
        check if word is a punc character
do

        replacepunc with " "
```

FIGURE 19.4   Remove punctuation.

```
for each word in file
do
        find tokens
        remove stop words from tokens such as-,
        if, they, was, etc
Print tokens.
```

FIGURE 19.5   Tokenization.

```
for each word in line do
        for each word in tokens

do
        append word in B tree
```

FIGURE 19.6   Inverted index of text file.

19.5   EXPERIMENTAL RESULTS AND COMPARISON ANALYSIS

The information retrieval system based on conventional inverted index file works by removing the stop words and punctuation marks from the document, and if the word is already present, then the reference of the document is added to the index, otherwise, a new entry is created. To show the comparative analysis of traditional index and proposed inverted index algorithm, the user is asked to select the text documents set which include topic "60th independence anniversary." The words "patriotism," "independence" and other query words were used for searching both in conventional inverted index and the proposed inverted index. The program calculates the time taken to compare the efficiency of two kinds of indexes. The experimental results are given in Table 19.1 and histogram of search time is shown in Figure 19.7.

TABLE 19.1　The Two Inverted Index Approach Time Comparison.

	Conventional inverted index			Proposed inverted index		
No of documents	10	15	20	10	15	20
Independence	3.98	12.81	36.45	3.91	8.45	20
Patriotism	3.84	9.78	15.32	3.07	7.13	14.21
Republic	3.4	5.3	15.36	2.32	6.84	12.59

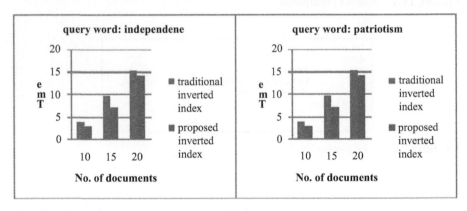

FIGURE 19.7　Time comparison of the two inverted indexes.

19.6　CONCLUSION

Indexing is the most efficient means of faster retrieval of documents. Conceptual or the semantic indexing is the utmost important indexing as it considers the underlying structure of data. In this paper, the proposed inverted index is created which is more efficient than traditional inverted files by creating tokens of the keywords which are stored in B tree data structures which makes searching more efficient. The future work is to apply inverted indexing over a cluster of documents rather than applying indexing over a single document.

KEYWORDS

- **document retrieval**
- **inverted indexing**
- **piFCM**
- **Bhattacharya distance**

REFERENCES

1. Lopez-Otero, P.; Parapar, J.; Barreiro, A. Efficient Query-by-Example Spoken Document Retrieval Combining Phone Multigram Representation and Dynamic Time Warping. *Inform. Process. Manage.* **2019**, *56* (1), 43–60.
2. Rad, H. Z.; Tiun, S.; Saad, S. Lexical Scoring System of Lexical Chain for Quranic Document Retrieval. *J. Lang. Stud* **2018**, *18* (2).
3. Gupta, R. K.; Patel, D.; Bramhe, A. A Hash-Based Approach for Document Retrieval by Utilizing Term Features. In *Computational Intelligence in Data Mining*, 2019; pp 617–627.
4. Hao, S.; Shi, C.; Niu, Z.; Cao, L. Concept Coupling Learning for Improving Concept Lattice-Based Document Retrieval. *Eng. App. Artif. Intell.* **2018**, *69*, 65–75.
5. Biswas, S.; Ganguly, A.; Shah, R.; Thankachan, S. V. Ranked Document Retrieval for Multiple Patterns. *Theor. Comput. Sci.* **2018**.
6. Tekli, J.; Chbeir, R.; Traina, A. J.; Traina, Jr, C. SemIndex+: A Semantic Indexing Scheme for Structured, Unstructured, and Partly Structured Data. *Knowledge-Based Syst.* **2019**, *164*, 378–403.
7. Hao, S.; Shi, C.; Niu, Z.; Cao, L. Modeling Positive and Negative Feedback for Improving Document Retrieval. *Expert Syst. App.* **2019**, *120*, 253–261.
8. Madaan, R.; Sharma, A. K.; Dixit, A.; Bhatia, P. Indexing of Semantic Web for Efficient Question Answering System. In *Software Engineering*, 2019; pp 51–61.
9. Chevalier, M.; El Malki, M.; Kopliku, A.; Teste, O.; Tournier, R. Implementation of Multidimensional Databases with Document-Oriented NoSQL. *Big Data Analytics and Knowledge Discovery* **2016**, 379–390.
10. Martinho, B.; Yasmina Santos, M. An Architecture for Data Warehousing in Big Data Environments. *Res. Pract. Issues Enterprise Inform. Syst.* **2016**, *268*, 237–250.
11. Doermann, D. The Indexing and Retrieval of Document Images: A Survey. *Comput. Vision Image Understanding* **1998**, *70* (3), 287–298.
12. Mothe, J.; Chrisment, C.; Dousset, B.; Alaux, J. DocCube: Multi-Dimensional Visualisation and Exploration of Large Document Sets. *J. Am. Soc. Inform. Sci. Technol.* **2003**, *54* (7), 650–659.

13. Thammasut, D.; Sornil, O. A Graph-Based Information Retrieval System. In *Proceedings of International Symposium on Communications and Information Technologies*, 2006; pp 743–748.

14. Jarke, M.; Koch, J. Query Optimization in Database Systems. *ACM Comput. Surveys* **1984**, *16*, *2*, 111–152.

15. Yang, Y.; Chute, C. G. An Example-Based Mapping Method for Text Categorization and Retrieval. *ACM Trans. Inform. Syst.* **1994**, *12* (3), 252–277.

16. Horng, J. T.; Yeh, C. C. Applying Genetic Algorithms to Query Optimization in Document Retrieval. *Inform. Process. Manage.* **2000**, *36* (5), 737–759.

17. González, S. M.; Berbel, T. D. R. Considering Unstructured Data for OLAP: A Feasibility Study Using a Systematic Review. *Revista de Sistemas de Informacao* **2014**, *14*, 14.

18. Fuhr, N.; Buckleya, C. Probabilistic Learning Approach for Document Indexing. *ACM Trans. Inform. Syst.* **1991**, *9* (3), 223–224.

CHAPTER 20

Acoustic Musical Instrument Recognition

USHA MITTAL, POOJA RANA, DILPREET SINGH, and
PRIYANKA CHAWLA

Department of Computer Science Engineering,
Lovely Professional University, Phagwara, Punjab, India

ABSTRACT

Music production industry is one of the most fast-growing industries out there and there are more and more people now-a-days getting into music production. The cost of production that goes into is very high and, even if cost is not an issue, most of the audio recorded through equipment has some form of noise in it. Although today there are several techniques that are available to remove the noise from the audio, it's costly and doesn't ensure that it will completely remove the noise from the audio. And that's where deep neural networks come in. For example, convolution neural network is great at working with noisy data and they can also be used in musical instrument classification or for classifying human voice from rest of the musical instruments. So, by the use of deep neural networks, one can separate a single sound wave from the all the rest of the sound waves or noise. And, once the sound wave has been identified, it is quite easy to separate it from the rest of the sound waves using some common mathematical function. The prime objective of this paper is to explain the approaches of identification of instrument recognition using machine learning and compare which approach gives the best results.

Computational Intelligence in Analytics and Information Systems, Volume 1: Data Science and AI, Selected Papers from CIAIS-2021. Hardeo Kumar Thakur, Manpreet Kaur, Parneeta Dhaliwal, Rajeev Kumar Arya, and Joan Lu (Eds.)

20.1   INTRODUCTION

Although it is possible to classify musical instruments using machine learning algorithms such as SVM or K-NN, these algorithms have their limit. For instance, they are weak against noisy data, but deep neural networks fare quite well against such problems. There are several different types of deep neural networks that are available that can be used to handle different domains of problems. But mainly these models can be divided into three basic categories called generative architectures, discriminative architectures, and hybrid deep learning architectures. For example, a deep belief network is just a restricted Boltzmann machines (RBM) and can be used to solve problems such as how to handle non-convex objective functions and local minima when using a multilayer perceptron. Then there's convolutional neural network (CNN), which are great at classifying images, and recurrent neural networks (RNN) used for dealing with problems related to the time domain. Other than that, there are autoencoders capable of learning coding patterns. And, lastly, there is a combination of reinforcement learning with neural networks, which is made possible by hybridizing dynamic programming and supervised learning. In a sense, deep neural networks are a part of machine learning in which neural network is used to generate a hypothesis for a given problem.

Acoustic is the physics to help understanding and manipulating waves to produce sound. It gives us insights on how to produce, control, transmit, and receive sound waves. According to acoustics, sound waves are just vibrations produced by a vibrating molecule and since these are produced by vibrating molecules, they require some form of medium to travel, that is, if there is no way to transfer those vibration, they will eventually die out. So, in a way these can be thought of as energy. Since they are a form of energy, they can be recorded over time. Also, it is possible to superimpose a set of waves traveling in the same medium at the same time, which makes sense since it was established that sound waves are energy and when energy is added to energy to increases. And, it is also possible to get the original waves back since the wave has not been changed, so the information about the wave is still present but in a different form. Although there are a lot more that goes into determining the original waves, this paper won't talk about that because it is not relevant information to what need to be accomplish. There are only two things that needed to be kept in mind to distinguish different sound waves. First being that a complex wave can be traced back to a much simpler wave and second it is possible to get the original wave from a superimposed wave.

Since music is nothing but a combination of various forms of waves, it is also possible to get those individual waves but first it needs to recognize which wave belongs to which source (i.e., instrument). That's where machine learning comes in. In using machine learning, it is possible to recognize patterns in a wave. For example, it is possible to distinguish a cat from a dog using CNN's, similarly distinguishing different types of waves using CNN should be possible or another solution would be to use an RNN, since a sound wave is recorded over time domain and RNN's work great at recognizing the patterns along the time domain. But the only downside is that it requires a large amount of data. So, given that enough data is available to work with, it is possible to train our models to recognize patterns in the sound waves and distinguish different instruments from each other.

20.1.1 CNN OVERVIEW

A convolutional neural network is a class of deep neural networks, mostly used for image recognition. It is a multilayer abstraction algorithm that is used to abstract high-level characteristics of an image. Not only that, CNN's are quite good at handling noisy data and are fast compared to RNNs. Some commonly known CNN architectures are AlexNet, VGG, RestNets, Inception, and Xception, etc. A CNN was inspired from the structure of a human eye and it's based on how our eyes send signals to our brain.

A convolutional neural network consists of an input layer, output layer, and multiple hidden layers. And, these hidden layers usually consist of convolutional layers that convolve the input matrix and some dense layers. A CNN can be divided into two parts: feature extraction and classification, as shown in Figure 20.1. The feature extraction part usually contains a combination of convolutional and pooling layers and classification is made up of fully connected artificial neural networks (ANN).

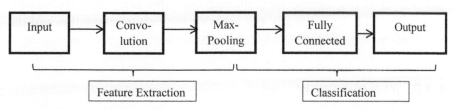

FIGURE 20.1   CNN architecture.

Source: Adapted from https://medium.com/techiepedia/binary-image-classifier-cnn-using-tensorflow-a3f5d 6746697.

20.1.1.1   CONVOLUTION

A convolution layer convolves an input and passes it to the next layer. The convolution process is performed using something called a feature map. And feature maps are specially designed matrices responsible for extracting special feature from an image or input, reducing the size of our input in the process. This process is important because if convolution is not performed on an image, the trainable parameters of out model would make it harder to train our model.

20.1.1.2   POOLING

Pooling layers are usually included to streamline the computations and make our model run faster. Pooling layers reduce the dimensionality of our data by merging the cluster of output from the last or the layer before the current layer into a single neuron. There are several different types of pooling available to us, such as local pooling, which combines small clusters (2 x 2) and global pooling that combines all the neurons from the convolutional layer. Other than that, there's max pooling, which takes the maximum value from each cluster, and average pooling for taking average of all the neurons from the layer before the current one.

20.1.1.3   FULLY CONNECTED

Fully connected layers or the dense layer connect every neuron from a layer to every neuron in the next layer. But for an input to be processed in the dense layers, the shape of our input matrix needs to be changed to one-dimensional array.

20.1.1.4   FLATTEN

Flatten layer is responsible for flattening our input array into one-dimensional array. This layer usually sits between the Feature extraction and the classification part of a CNN.

20.1.2   RNN OVERVIEW

A recurrent neural network (or RNN) is a class of deep neural networks, which are exceptionally good at handling sequence of data. Figure 20.2

shows a standard feed-forward recurrent neural network. The only thing that makes recurrent neural network different from other deep neural networks is that RNNs have memory, that is, they are able to save the date in the current state (time step) and send it to the next state. This is what makes an RNN able to handle a sequence of data or data that has a time domain attached to it, making them the perfect choice to be used while classifying musical instruments since music is a set of sound signals recorded over time. Some commonly known RNN architectures are LSTM, GRU, IndRNN, DNC, and NTM.

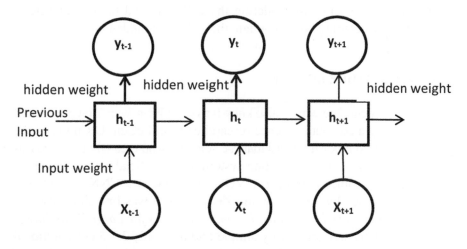

FIGURE 20.2   Recurrent neural network.

Source: This photo by unknown author is licensed under CC BY-SA.

20.1.2.1   LSTM OVERVIEW

Long short-term memory is a recurrent neural network that has a feedback connection. A LSTM is made up of a cell, input gate, output gate, and a forget gate. What makes a LSTM different from a regular RNN is its ability to forget and add parts of previously stored memory.

20.1.2.1.1   Cell

A LSTM cell remembers the data overtime and the gates are used to control the flow of information in and out of the cell.

20.1.2.1.2   Forget Gate

The forget gate is used to reset (or forget the results of the previous state or time step) the cell state to a default state avoiding indefinite growth of cell data. Not only that it is also able to decide which information should be discarded and which should be allowed to enter the cell.

20.1.2.1.3   Input and Output Gate

Input gate is responsible for updating the cell state and the output gate is responsible for deciding how to update the values of hidden units.

20.2   LITERATURE REVIEW

Convolutional neural networks, also known as ConvNets, were first introduced in the 1980s by a computer science researcher Yann LeCun. LeCun used the work of Kunihiko Fukushima, a Japanese scientist who created the noncognition, a very simple image recognition system using artificial neural networks.

The visual geometry group (or VGG) network is a CNN architecture that was developed by Simonyan and Zisserman. It was first showcased in their 2014 paper, *Very Deep Convolutional Networks for Large Scale Image Recognition*. This network is very simple and uses only 3 × 3 convolutional layers. Its characteristics are the stacked convolutional layer one on top of the other in the increasing depth of a neural network.

Recurrent neural networks were created by taking motivation from David Rumelhart's work in 1986. Hopfield networks—a special kind of RNN— were first discovered in 1982 by John Hopfield.

Long short-term memory (or LSTM) networks were created by Hochreiter and Schmidhuber in 1997 and were quite popular due to their applications in many problems regarding a wide variety of domains. It was created to solve the problem of vanishing gradient but at first the LSTM didn't have the forget gate and was introduced later on that allowed to reset its own state in 1999.

20.3   DATASET

For this paper, I am going to use a data containing several instruments. It is very difficult to come across music data because the quantity of such data is very small. But I am going use a dataset called PCMIR. As there are not many examples present in the data, I am to take a single audio file and randomly cut 1 s of data and treat it as a single sample and by maintaining a probability distribution, I can control that I do not get the same file more than once allowing me to create a well-balanced set of samples.

20.3.1 DATA PREPARATION

Once the dataset has been downloaded from Kaggle, it will be divided in separate folders with folder name being the name of the instrument it uses. However, the data files will be in mp3 format, which isa compressed form of an audio file. Therefore, the format needs to be changed from mp3 to wav. In this case, a freely available software for ubuntu was used which will allow to change the format of the files. And by using two libraries called "os" and "librosa," it is possible to load our data into the python file to work on it.

20.3.2 DATA PRE-PROCESSING

The first thing is to remove the noise from our audio data. In Figure 20.4 on the left, there is an audio signal that has noise at the end and start of the signal, which is not particularly useful. So, the noise can be removed by creating a mask that checks for the signal below a certain threshold, but doing so will also lead to loss of some important information. Instead of just creating a mask, a better alternative is to create an envelope of the wave, then drop the parts of our signal fall below a particular threshold. Once the envelope has been applied, the wave format will be similar to Figure 20.3.

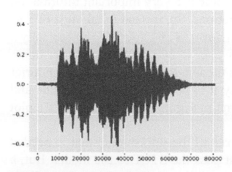 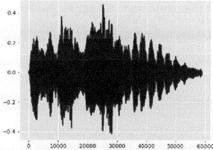

FIGURE 20.3 Audio signal.

Now that the noise has been removed for the waves, it is possible to train our model; but this would not yet give the kind of result expected of the model, because right now it only knows one thing about this wave that the amplitude of the wave over time and it would quite difficult train our model on just the amplitude and time. So, next let us try to get more information out of this wave and that can be done using a fast Fourier transform (FFT) and once FFT has been calculated, the wave will look something like as shown in Figure 20.4.

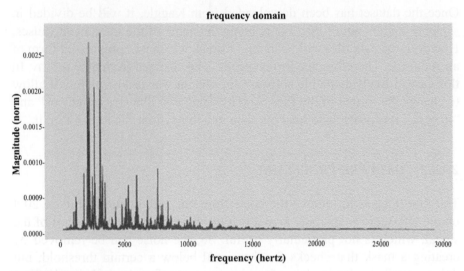

FIGURE 20.4   FFT.

Now, FFTs have the magnitude of the wave and the frequency of the wave but in doing so, our data lost one import information that is time and since our model is dealing with waves, time is a very important information for the model to yield some good predictions. So, instead of taking a FFT of the wave, apply short-term Fourier transform (STFT). A STFT is basically a Fourier transform applied in a part of wave, so by applying a Fourier transform on 1 s of the wave and then move the window by 1 s and apply Fourier transform on the next second, that way it is possible to get magnitude and frequency with respect to the time domain. Figure 20.6 shows a STFT plot of the wave.

Now, this looks promising and it has all the information that is needed to train the model. It is possible to just pass the STFT to the model. But, a human ear has a limit up to which it can interpret data and since music is always under that range, it doesn't really make sense to actually include those higher frequencies to the sample data, so instead it is a better way to just compute the Filter Banks by applying triangular filters (in such a way that these filter are less discriminative toward higher frequencies) on the mel scale to the power spectrum that was obtained previously.

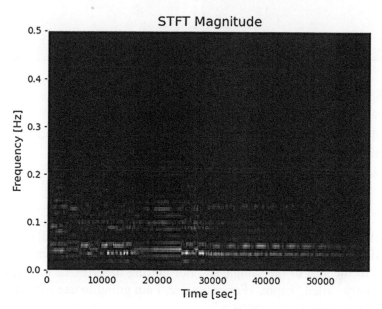

FIGURE 20.5   STFT.

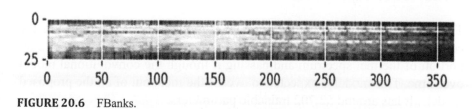

FIGURE 20.6   FBanks.

However, the calculated FBanks, shown in Figure 20.6, can be problematic in some machine learning algorithm, but luckily, there is a solution for that problem. And the answer is to calculate the mel-frequency cepstral coefficients (MFCCs) by applying a discrete cosine transform (DTC) on the previously calculated FBanks and then perform mean normalization to get an even better spectrum.

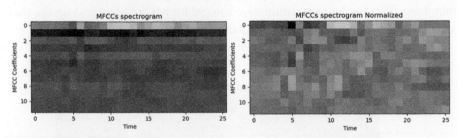

FIGURE 20.7   MFCCs.

And, finally, this spectrogram can be used to train the model to lean different types of musical instrument.

20.4   PROPOSED MODEL

For building the models, I am going to use TensorFlow 2.0 and all the models will train for 10 epochs and batch size of 32. It will also have a validation set of 20% of the size of the sample set. For getting the MFCC, I am going to use a library called "kapre." For optimizer, I am going to use adam and loss will be "categorical_crossentropy."

20.4.1   PROPOSED MODEL 1

This model is a one-dimensional convolution model, which wraps the convolutional layer into a time-distributed layer because it is taking a small portion of the mel spectrum and passing it though the convolutional model over time. This model is expected to overfit the most out of all the proposed models. It has around 52,702 trainable parameters.

20.4.2   PROPOSED MODEL 2

This model uses the common approach used for image classification and is quite similar to the VGG model and has four convolutional layers. This model has 135,222 trainable parameters.

```
Layer (type)                     Output Shape           Param #
=================================================================
stft_input (InputLayer)          [(None, 16000, 1)]     0
stft (STFT)                      (None, 100, 257, 1)    0
magnitude (Magnitude)            (None, 100, 257, 1)    0
apply_filterbank (ApplyFilte     (None, 100, 128, 1)    0
magnitude_to_decibel (Magnit     (None, 100, 128, 1)    0
batch_norm (LayerNormalizati     (None, 100, 128, 1)    256
td_conv_1d_tanh (TimeDistrib     (None, 100, 125, 8)    40
max_pool_2d_1 (MaxPooling2D)     (None, 50, 62, 8)      0
td_conv_1d_relu_1 (TimeDistr     (None, 50, 59, 16)     528
max_pool_2d_2 (MaxPooling2D)     (None, 25, 29, 16)     0
td_conv_1d_relu_2 (TimeDistr     (None, 25, 26, 32)     2080
max_pool_2d_3 (MaxPooling2D)     (None, 12, 13, 32)     0
td_conv_1d_relu_3 (TimeDistr     (None, 12, 10, 64)     8256
td_conv_1d_relu_4 (TimeDistr     (None, 12, 7, 128)     32896
global_max_pooling_2d (Globa     (None, 128)            0
dropout (Dropout)                (None, 128)            0
dense (Dense)                    (None, 64)             8256
softmax (Dense)                  (None, 6)              390
=================================================================
Total params: 52,702
Trainable params: 52,702
Non-trainable params: 0
```

FIGURE 20.8   Architecture 1.

```
Layer (type)                     Output Shape           Param #
=================================================================
stft_1_input (InputLayer)        [(None, 16000, 1)]     0
stft_1 (STFT)                    (None, 100, 257, 1)    0
magnitude_1 (Magnitude)          (None, 100, 257, 1)    0
apply_filterbank_1 (ApplyFil     (None, 100, 128, 1)    0
magnitude_to_decibel_1 (Magn     (None, 100, 128, 1)    0
batch_norm (LayerNormalizati     (None, 100, 128, 1)    256
conv2d_tanh (Conv2D)             (None, 100, 128, 8)    400
max_pool_2d_1 (MaxPooling2D)     (None, 50, 64, 8)      0
conv2d_relu_1 (Conv2D)           (None, 50, 64, 16)     3216
max_pool_2d_2 (MaxPooling2D)     (None, 25, 32, 16)     0
conv2d_relu_2 (Conv2D)           (None, 25, 32, 16)     2320
max_pool_2d_3 (MaxPooling2D)     (None, 13, 16, 16)     0
conv2d_relu_3 (Conv2D)           (None, 13, 16, 32)     4640
max_pool_2d_4 (MaxPooling2D)     (None, 7, 8, 32)       0
conv2d_relu_4 (Conv2D)           (None, 7, 8, 32)       9248
flatten (Flatten)                (None, 1792)           0
dropout (Dropout)                (None, 1792)           0
dense (Dense)                    (None, 64)             114752
softmax (Dense)                  (None, 6)              390
=================================================================
Total params: 135,222
Trainable params: 135,222
Non-trainable params: 0
```

FIGURE 20.9   Architecture 2.

20.4.3   PROPOSED MODEL 3

This is a RNN-based model and uses a bidirectional LSTM and before going into the LSTM layer, the input passes through a time-distributed dense layer, which extracts some import feature and after going through the LSTM layer, those features are concatenated with output of the LSTM. This model is expected to work the best and has around 95,110 trainable parameters.

```
Layer (type)                    Output Shape          Param #     Connected to
===================================================================================
stft_2_input (InputLayer)       [(None, 16000, 1)]    0

stft_2 (STFT)                   (None, 100, 257, 1)   0           stft_2_input[0][0]

magnitude_2 (Magnitude)         (None, 100, 257, 1)   0           stft_2[0][0]

apply_filterbank_2 (ApplyFilter (None, 100, 128, 1)   0           magnitude_2[0][0]

magnitude_to_decibel_2 (Magnitu (None, 100, 128, 1)   0           apply_filterbank_2[0][0]

batch_norm (LayerNormalization) (None, 100, 128, 1)   256         magnitude_to_decibel_2[0][0]

reshape (TimeDistributed)       (None, 100, 128)      0           batch_norm[0][0]

td_dense_tanh (TimeDistributed) (None, 100, 64)       8256        reshape[0][0]

bidirectional_lstm (Bidirection (None, 100, 64)       24832       td_dense_tanh[0][0]

skip_connection (Concatenate)   (None, 100, 128)      0           td_dense_tanh[0][0]
                                                                  bidirectional_lstm[0][0]

dense_1_relu (Dense)            (None, 100, 64)       8256        skip_connection[0][0]

max_pool_1d (MaxPooling1D)      (None, 50, 64)        0           dense_1_relu[0][0]

dense_2_relu (Dense)            (None, 50, 32)        2080        max_pool_1d[0][0]

flatten (Flatten)               (None, 1600)          0           dense_2_relu[0][0]

dropout (Dropout)               (None, 1600)          0           flatten[0][0]

dense_3_relu (Dense)            (None, 32)            51232       dropout[0][0]

softmax (Dense)                 (None, 6)             198         dense_3_relu[0][0]
===================================================================================
Total params: 95,110
Trainable params: 95,110
Non-trainable params: 0
```

FIGURE 20.10   Architecture 3.

20.5   RESULTS

All the models were trained using NVIDIA GTX 1050Ti 4 GB graphic card, Intel Core i7 Processor, 16 GB RAM, and built using "TensorFlow." All the models were trained on six classes for 10 epochs. Although all the models performed well, as expected, the mode 3 (bidirectional LSTM) gave better results as compared to the other two models. But, the one-dimensional convolutional model wrapped in time-distributed layers performed unexpectedly better than the two-dimensional convolutional neural network. In terms of speed, the two-dimensional convolutional model was faster than the one-dimensional convolutional model. However, both in terms of accuracy and speed, LSTM performed exceptionally well and it is most probably due to adding a dense layer before the LSTM layer and later combining their results to get more features, as LSTM cuts the data in half. The result of the training is shown in Tables 20.1 and 20.2.

TABLE 20.1 Comparison of Models Based upon Training, Validation, and Testing Accuracy.

Model	Training accuracy	Validation accuracy	Testing accuracy
Model 1	0.9863248	0.988127	0.9866
Model 2	0.984427	0.980413	0.9805
Model 3	0.991932	0.989746	0.9896

TABLE 20.2 Comparison of Models Based upon Training, Validation, and Testing Loss.

Model	Training loss	Validation loss	Testing loss
Model 1	0.054431	0.049981	0.0524
Model 2	0.067537	0.082865	0.0816
Model 3	0.03978	0.043771	0.0448

20.6 CONCLUSION

This paper explains the proper procedure to process the audio data to give it to a machine learning model to train and three different architectures that can be used for this kind of problem. In my opinion, for classifying audio data, RNN is the better choice, but the 2D CNN would also work. Although it is not recommended to use the 1D CNN for audio classification as it might overfit as the number of classes increase, in this case, there were only six classes, so it turned out quite well. And these models were trained and tested on audio files that only contain a single instrument, which could work in situations such as studio's where the sounds are isolated; but; in case of working in an environment where it is required to classify multiple set of sound waves, a much more better and robust architecture might be needed. However, these architecture should have no problem classifying a single sound wave that it has been trained on. Other than that, the audio input needs to be streamlined to a fixed rate for it to be useful in real-life situations.

KEYWORDS

- convolutional neural networks (CNN)
- recurrent neural networks (RNN)
- long short-term memory (LSTM)
- musical instruments
- mel-frequency cepstral coefficients (MFCC)
- fast Fourier transform (FFT)
- short-term Fourier transform (STFT)

REFERENCES

1. Mousavi, S. M. H.; Surya Prasath, V. B. Persian Classical Music Instrument Recognition (PCMIR) Using a Novel Persian Music Database. In *2019 9th International Conference on Computer and Knowledge Engineering (ICCKE)*; IEEE, 2019.
2. Choi, K.; Joo, D.; Kim, J. On-GPU Audio Preprocessing Layers for a Quick Implementation of Deep Neural Network Models with Keras. Book: Machine Learning for Music Discovery Workshop at 34th International Conference on Machine Learning.
3. Mittal, U.; Chawla, P. Acoustic Sound Based Emergency Vehicle Detection Using Convolution Neural Network.
4. Yun, M.; Bi, J. Deep Learning For Musical Instrument Recognition, Department of Electrical and Computer Engineering University of Rocheester.
5. Solanki, A.; Pandey, S. Music Instrument Recognition Using Deep Convolutional Neural Networks.
6. Haidar-Ahmad, L. Music and Instrument Classification using Deep Learning Technics. Department of Computer Science, Stanford University.
7. Cohen, R.; Ruinskiy, D.; Zickfeld, J.; IJzerman, H.; Lavner, Y. Baby Cry Detection: Deep Learning and Classical Approaches. *Stud. Comput. Intell.* **2020,** *867,* 171–196. https://doi.org/10.1007/978-3-030- 31764-5_7
8. Engineering, C. Acoustic Scene Classification using Time-Frequency Representations as Texture Images Shamsiah Abidin, 2019.
9. Tang, B.; Li, Y.; Li, X.; Xu, L.; Yan, Y.; Yang, Q. Deep CNN Framework for Environmental Sound Classification using Weighting Filters. In *Proceedings of 2019 IEEE International Conference on Mechatronics and Automation, ICMA,* 2019; pp 2297–2302. https://doi.org/10.1109/ICMA.2019.8816567
10. Hicham, B.; Ahmed, A.; Mohammed, M. Vehicle Type Classification Using Convolutional Neural Network. *Colloquium in Information Science and Technology, CIST,* 2018 October, *3,* 313–316. https://doi.org/10.1109/CIST.2018.8596500
11. Chauhan, M. S.; Singh, A.; Khemka, M.; Prateek, A.; Sen, R. Embedded CNN Based Vehicle Classification and Counting in Non-Laned Road Traffic. ArXiv, 2019.

12. Zhang, X.; Chen, Y.; Liu, M.; Huang, C. Acoustic Traffic Event Detection in Long Tunnels Using Fast Binary Spectral Features. *Circ. Syst. Signal Process.* **2020,** *39* (6), 2994–3006. https://doi.org/10.1007/s00034-019-01294-9

13. Impedovo, D.; Balducci, F.; Dentamaro, V.; Pirlo, G. Vehicular Traffic Congestion Classification by Visual Features and Deep Learning Approaches: A Comparison. *Sensors (Switzerland)* 2019, *19* (23). https://doi.org/10.3390/s19235213

14. Marchegiani, L.; Newman, P. Listening for Sirens: Locating and Classifying Acoustic Alarms in City Scenes. *ArXiv,* 2018.

15. Han, Y.; Jiang, T.; Ma, Y.; Xu, C. Pretraining Convolutional Neural Networks for Image-Based Vehicle Classification. *Adv. Multimedia* **2018.** https://doi.org/10.1155/2018/ 3138278

16. Mandel, M.; Salamon, J.; Ellis, D. P. W. Proceedings of the Detection and Classification of Acoustic Scenes and Events 2019 Workshop (DCASE), 2019.

17. Kang, B.; Choo, H. A Deep-Learning-Based Emergency Alert System. *ICT Express* **2016,** *2* (2), 67–70. https://doi.org/10.1016/j.icte.2016.05.001

18. Salamon, J.; Bello, J. P. Deep Convolutional Neural Networks and Data Augmentation for Environmental Sound Classification. *IEEE Signal Processing Lett.* **2017,** *24* (3), 279–283. https://doi.org/10.1109/LSP.2017.2657381

19. Abdoli, S.; Cardinal, P.; Lameiras Koerich, A. End-to-End Environmental Sound Classification Using a 1D Convolutional Neural Network. *Expert Syst. App.* **2019,** *136,* 252–263. https://doi.org/10.1016/j.eswa.2019.06.040

20. Nanni, L.; Costa, Y. M. G.; Aguiar, R. L.; Mangolin, R. B.; Brahnam, S.; Jr, C. N. S. Ensemble of Convolutional Neural Networks to Improve Animal Audio Classification, 2020.

21. Kahl, S.; Hussein, H.; Fabian, E.; Schloßhauer, J.; Thangaraju, E.; Kowerko, D.; Eibl, M. Acoustic Event Classification Using Convolutional Neural Networks. *Lecture Notes in Informatics (LNI), Proceedings - Series of the Gesellschaft Fur Informatik (GI)* **2017,** *275,* 2177–2188. https://doi.org/10.18420/in2017_217

22. Bianco, M. J.; Gerstoft, P.; Traer, J.; Ozanich, E.; Roch, M. A.; Gannot, S. et al. Machine Learning in Acoustics: Theory and Applications. ArXiv **2019,** 3590. https://doi.org/ 10.1121/1.5133944

23. Su, Y.; Zhang, K.; Wang, J.; Madani, K. Environment Sound Classification Using a Two-Stream CNN Based on Decision-Level Fusion. *Sensors (Switzerland)* **2019,** *19* (7), 1–15. https://doi.org/10.3390/s19071733

24. Boddapati, V.; Petef, A.; Rasmusson, J.; Lundberg, L. Classifying Environmental Sounds Using Image Recognition Networks. *Procedia Comput. Sci.* **2017,** *112,* 2048–2056. https://doi.org/10.1016/j.procs.2017.08.250

25. Han, Y.; Lee, K. Acoustic Scene Classification Using Convolutional Neural Network and Multiple-Width Frequency-Delta Data Augmentation **2016,** *14* (8), 1–11. http://arxiv.org/ abs/1607.0238

CHAPTER 21

Classification of Accented Voice Using RNN and GAN

ARCHIT PRASHANT PATIL, PARIKANSH AHLUWALIA,
SIDDHARTH YADAV, and PREETI KAUR

Computer Science and Engineering Department, Netaji Subhas University of Technology (formerly NSIT), Delhi, India

ABSTRACT

Accent conversion (AC), the process of transforming the accent of one speaker as if they had the accent of another speaker, has been cited as a prospective solution for challenges faced in language learning and voice-based technologies. The focus of this paper is to be able to shift speech from non-native to the native accent after the recognition and detection of the "foreign" accents. The main aim of this paper is the accurate classification of a given speech clip into a native or a non-native accent. We propose a methodology to perform the task of accent conversion by the usage of multiple methods: neural style transfer applied to audio fragments and recurrent neural networks with training labels as the native accent. We apply the accent classifier upon the results generated by all the methods, and present the comparative results.

21.1 INTRODUCTION

Technology has flourished, leading to a number of new state-of-the-art systems such as commercial speech recognition and machine translation

Computational Intelligence in Analytics and Information Systems, Volume 1: Data Science and AI, Selected Papers from CIAIS-2021. Hardeo Kumar Thakur, Manpreet Kaur, Parneeta Dhaliwal, Rajeev Kumar Arya, and Joan Lu (Eds.)

improvements. Nonetheless, it can be argued that not all potential users and uses have achieved these advantages to the same degree. Taking an example, most commercial systems such as Google Translate, Siri, Alexa have increased in the number of languages available, but when considering the robustness of these systems across languages, it is often apparent that the systems work much better with languages that have more speakers across the globe such as English or Spanish. In some instances, such as newer products, the native language of a customer may not be available yet, which may encourage them to relegate to English. Accent translation can be extended to expand the number of available accents of text-to-speech language systems with prominent accents such as English or Spanish.

The goal of this paper is to shift speech from non-native to the native accent after the recognition and detection of the "foreign" accents. Practically, the native accent should be equivalent to a voice message sent through WhatsApp by a foreign colleague. The main challenge with Foreign Accent Classification is to segment the speech message into accent-related signals and quality of voice.[13] Along with voice metamorphosing, frame matching, and phonological synthesis, many approaches are suggested. These approaches may reduce non-native proclamation accent, but they have limitations. Voice metamorphosing often produces voices that make it feel like a "third" speaker, one that is dissimilar from both speakers. Frame-pairing methodologies can metabolize speech that emulates the voice of the non-native speaker, but the syntheses possess certain aspects of the voice quality of the native speaker; this is because the native speaker's excitation information is used to synthesize speech. Ultimately, articulatory processing requires advanced tools to capture articulation information so that they are not realistic for applications in the real world.[1]

Like the transformation of tone, accent translation is committed to transforming a reference speaker's language to sound like a target sound. Nevertheless, in addition to speaking exactly like the intended voice, accent transformation is focused specifically on morphing the tone of the speech message. Accent translation faces another problem in relation to sound conversion as the source speaker's audio and target speaker cannot be forced-aligned solely because the target speaker's voice quality and dialect will remain. This implies that accent transformation may entail more advanced methods of alignment than normal frame-by-frame synchronization, which can help conserve the correct speaker detail while removing the other undesirable information.

To deal with this issue, we propose a model based on their phonological content that fits origin and target frames. We derive phonetic data from that of the posterior gram by using developments in auditory and acoustic modeling. The first step is to train a speaker-independent acoustic system on natural speech which is used to measure the posterior-gram for each origin and target speech frame. Instead, to fit origin and target images, we use the symmetric Kullback-Leibler (KL) separation in the posterior-gram domain. The consequence is a set of aligned source-target frames focused on their phonetic pronunciation and similarity. In the final step of our approach, we utilize the frame pairs to train a Gaussian Mixture Model (GMM) modeling the joint distribution of origin and goal Mel-Cepstral Coefficients (MCEPs), then projecting source MCEPs into target MCEPs using the total probability approximation of spectral variable trajectories given the reference speaker's global variance.

The major benefits of the proposed model are that first, it removes the need for the native reference speech to import vibrational information, which avoids the facets of the voice quality of the native speaker from leakage through the generated speech. Second, our approach did not necessarily need the indigenous speaker's data for the purpose of training. Therefore, during research we have always had the freedom to choose any source voices. Third, through a sequence preserving sequence generating model, our system has demonstrated state-of-the-art efficiency and generates better sound quality.

21.2 LITERATURE REVIEW

21.2.1 SPOKEN LANGUAGE TECHNOLOGY FOR EDUCATION

Over the decades, as language engineering has evolved and started to display its value, many researchers have been constantly testing its limits by innovating a variety of systems to tackle the issue of pronunciation. Such programs include methods such as CAPT, which aim to teach pronunciation by means of clear instruction and new, gamified techniques, which are then used to coerce non-native speakers into a much more effective practice of pronunciation.[2] These systems generally use some form of automatic speech recognition (ASR) to record a presenter and compare the recordings (typically) to a gold standard for native speakers.

To recognize the relationship between language education and spoken language technology, Neri et al.[1] presented a complete overview of the two sectors. In this paper, it is shown that in addition to the classroom, the conclusions of linguistics/language pedagogy seem to be linked to technology. Partially, the reason, they claim, is that there are no "simple guidelines" on how acquisition work in second languages should be adapted and that many CAPT programs do not fulfill appropriate pedagogical needs. For example, some of the CAPT systems, including Pronunciation[2] and the Tell me More sequence,[2] are critical for using feedback systems that provide users with feedback in waveforms or spectrograms that cannot be understood easily without experience.

While authors in Ref. 1 make sound recommendations to develop CAPT systems, designing pronunciation systems can be challenging for most research groups. Instead, some tried to adapt existing infrastructure and construct a small architecture around it. For example, the authors in reference[2] experimented with using artificial voices in a pronunciation training tool for corrective suggestions. They use the Android text-to-speech (TTS) program of Google as an input for Spanish students of English B1 and B2 and focus on the six pairs of most challenging vowels. However, due to the fact that the study had to be limited to single words and only six pairs of vowels, more experiments are required to truly understand whether these students can make their training more generalized or not.

21.2.2   VOICE CONVERSION

A variety of attempts have been made to model voice conversion systems using different techniques. In the field of speech technology, earlier systems of voice conversion used Mel-frequency cepstrum (MFCC) and Gaussian Mixture Models (GMM) for conversion and later progressed to use more advanced features.

The variant of GMM voice conversion proposed by the authors in reference[3] has become the standard setup. We argue that, while standard GMMs perform relatively well in voice transformation, it also contributes to a degradation in voice quality.

In the case of instantly converting voice, i-vectors consist of GMM-trained speaker super-vectors and low-size features representing features of an individual speaker are presented in reference.[4] This is measured per utterance and then averaged in an i-vector. An i-vector represents a single speaker, in this case. This allows the i-vectors of a source speaker to be approximated to the i-vectors of a target speaker by creating a map using a neural network and Gaussian mixture model.

21.2.3 ACCENT CONVERSION

Due to the special nature of accent conversion, fewer papers and programs are available as reference as compared to voice conversion. In addition, most recent articles on accent conversion have all been published by the same team of researchers at the Texas A&M University.

Nevertheless, prior to such research, studies like[5] and[6] analyzed various features to observe their relationship with the apparent voice accent. They control spectral characteristics, intonation patterns, and length in[5] to observe their association with British, Australian, and American accents. Through an ABX perception test, 75% of the synthesized utterances were identified as having native accent and the potential for segmental accent conversion was emphasized. The correlation between intelligibility and morphing of various segment and sub-segmental features, such as pitch, rhythm, and segments of English TTS, built for "accented" Japanese, is explored in Ref. 6.

21.3 APPROACH AND EXPERIMENTS

21.3.1 ACCENT CLASSIFIER

In this section, we propose a method to classify any given accented voice input into two broad categories: native and non-native. For the purpose of this study, we define Indian accent as "native" and any other foreign accent as "non-native." It gives us a baseline to distinguish two types of accent for the study. The task of voice accent transfer requires a speech input in a native accent to a speech output of another accent, namely, non-native accent as shown in Figures 21.1 and 21.2.

21.3.2 DATASET

For the purpose of this research, we decided to use a dataset, available openly on the Kaggle platform. The dataset contains 2140 speech samples, each from a different talker reading exactly the same passage. Talkers come from 177 countries and have 214 different native languages. Each talker is speaking in English. This dataset was collected by many individuals under the supervision of Steven H. Weinberger. The most up-to-date version of the archive is hosted by George Mason University. We concluded that a 30-s sample would be too large for it to be efficiently used in any classifying technique. Also, the classification algorithm could certainly not gain the nuances of any accent in long samples of voice input. The samples needed to be trimmed down for the above-mentioned two reasons. Each 30-s voice sample was divided into 10 subsamples, each of a duration of 3-s. This was done using a Python language library, pyDub.

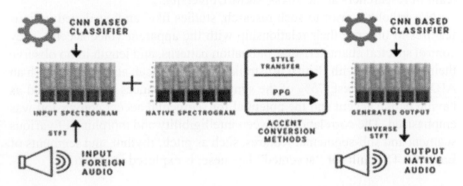

FIGURE 21.1 Overview of the complete Voice Accent Conversion procedure using two proposed methods: Style Transfer and PPG.

FIGURE 21.2 Each generated 3-s audio sample is converted into a spectrogram for input to CNN.

21.3.3 METHODOLOGY

Here, we apply a transformation process on each 3-s audio sample.[11] Each sample undergoes Fast Fourier Transform process. This generates a spectrogram of the audio sample. The spectrogram is then input to the Convolutional Neural Network or CNN for the classification task.

21.3.3.1 SPECTROGRAMS

"A spectrogram is a visual representation of the spectrum of frequencies of a signal as it varies with time. Spectrograms are basically two-dimensional graphs, with a third dimension represented by colors."

21.3.3.2 CONVOLUTIONAL NEURAL NETWORK FOR IMAGE CLASSIFICATION

The convolution neural network works on the basis of the fundamental neural networks. CNN algorithms have two primary components: convolution and sampling on convolution layers and max pooling layers.

- **Convolution Process:** From the previous layer, each neuron receives a rectangular n × n section. The rectangular section is known as the receptive field.
- **Sampling Process:** A pooling layer can follow after each convolutional layer. The sampling cycle therefore takes place between the convolution layer and the pooling layer. In our research work, we use a CNN for classifying spectrogram images into native or non-native accented voice spectrogram. We use the 22,000 spectrogram images as the training and test data for the convolutional neural network. 90% of the samples are used for training, while 10% of the data samples are reserved for testing the classification accuracy of the CNN.

In our technique we generate a non-native speaker PPG in the first step using a speaker-independent acoustic framework conditioned on a massive corpus of indigenous expression. Then we create a sequence-preserving speech generator/synthesization, which produces another sequence, capturing the non-native speaker's voice quality. That synthesizer accepts a faux-native speaker PPG series as the information and generates the same sequence of mel-spectrograms as the output. Finally, a neurological vocoder, "WaveGlow," is being trained to transform the mel-spectro into an unprocessed or raw, speech signal. During the test, we provide the synthesizer, an input, from an indigenous expression with a PPG series. The resultant performance contains the speech characteristics of the native speaker and the voice quality of those in the non-native speaker. Figure 21.3 displays the proposed model.

21.3.3.3 SETUP

We used the corpus of "Librispeech" to effectively train and prepare the acoustic model, comprising 860 hours for indigenous English content, mostly from the continent of America. The acoustic model has four hidden layers and a 5616 senones throughput layer. We conditioned the Phonetic Posteriorgram-to-Mel and "WaveGlow" models from the publicly accessible L2-ARCTIC corpus[14] on two quasi-native speakers, YKWK (indigenous Korean male speaker) and ZHAA (indigenous Arabic speaker). We used Audacity to eliminate ambient soundscapes noise on the initial "L2-ARCTIC" transcriptions. Two American voices, "BDL (M)" and "CLB (F)" from the "ARCTIC" corpus for the indigenous comparison speech, were used. The same collection of ~1100 sentences, approximately an hour and a half of speech, was recorded by each presenter in "L2-ARCTIC" and "ARCTIC." Only used up to the ~1000 phrases for template learning for each "L2-ARCTIC" speaker, the next 50 phrases for verification and the final 50 phrases for evaluation. At 15 KHz, the sound signals have been filtered. With an 8-ms shift and a 56-ms range, we used 75 filter banks to remove mel-spectrograms and produced accent transformation for "BDL-YKWK" and "CLB-ZHAA."

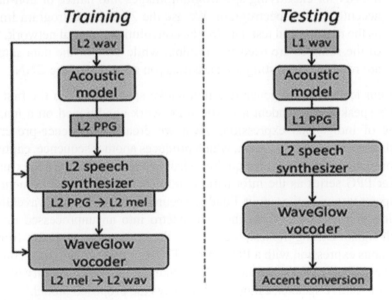

FIGURE 21.3   The architecture and the flow of the model proposed by us. L1: native, L2: non-native.

21.3.4   *METHODOLOGY*

Our system consists of three major components: a speech-independent acoustic mechanism (AM) that extracts PPGs, a non-native speaker speech synthesizer that transforms PPGs to mel-frequency-spectrograms, and a "WaveGlow vocoder" that produces real-time speech waveform.

21.3.4.1 ACOUSTIC SIMULATION AND REMOVAL OF PPG

We use a deep neural network with several concealed layers and the nonlinearity of the P-norm as the AM. We prepare the AM on an indigenous speaking corpus by reducing the boundary-entropy between inputs and senone markings acquired from a forcedaligner pretrained "GMM-HMM." Native speech learning is important because in an indigenous phonetic room the local and faux-native frames need to be balanced.

21.3.4.2 PPG-TO-MEL-SPECTROGRAM TRANSITION

We use a revised "Tacotron 2" design[12] to transform PPGs from non-native speakers into their respective mel-spectrograms. The existing "Tacotron 2" machine takes a one-hot character vector representation and transfers it to an LSTM encoder that transforms it into a secret representation that is then transferred to a LSTM decoder with a proximity-sensitive attention mechanism that determines the mel-spectrogram. The embedding character is passed across several convolution surfaces until being presented to the LSTM encoder to boost template efficiency. Before moving the projected mel-frequency-spectrogram (MFCC) to the attention and decoder Long-Short-Term-Memory to retrieve structural data, the decoder adds a PreNet (two fully integrated layers). It also adds a "PostNet" afterward the decoder to forecast spectral information and attach those to that of the raw estimation.

In this research, we substitute the character-embedding surface with a phonetic-posteriorgram-embedding system (PPG PreNet) that contains two hidden layers fully connected to the nonlinearity of ReLU. Compared to the "PreNet" in "Tacotron 2," this PPG-embedding network converts the initial big-dimensional input PPGs into lower bottleneck functionality. The above phase is the key to the integration of the framework. The transformation model "PPG-to-Mel" is shown in Figure 21.4.

21.3.4.3 MEL-FREQUENCY-SPECTROGRAM TO AUDIO

To transform the speech synthesizer output back into a voice waveform, we utilize the "WaveGlow vocoder." "WaveGlow" is a flow-based network capable of producing mel-spectrograms of high-quality expression (that can be compared to WaveNet[9]). It takes specimens from a null mean radial Gaussian with a similar number of dimensions as the expected output and moves those specimens across a sequence of layers that convert the simple distribution into one with the desired distribution. We utilize "WaveGlow" to simulate the propagation of audio recordings on a mel-spectrogram in the context of preparing a vocoder. Using a single neural net, WaveGlow can produce a real-time inference speed, while WaveNet takes more time to metabolize an expression due to its automatic-regression nature.

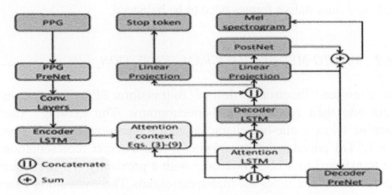

FIGURE 21.4   Phonetic-Posteriorgram to Mel transformation mechanism

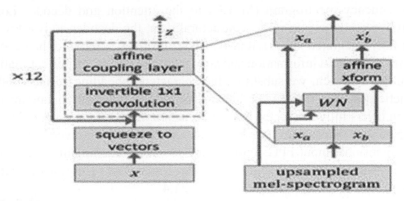

FIGURE 21.5   The WaveGlow model for the generation of audio-speech from MFCC spectrograms

21.3.4.4   ACCENT CONVERSION USING RECURRENT NEURAL NETWORKS

We used the recurrent neural network setup in machine translation, which is typically used as an encoder and decoder combination. Figure 21.6 displays the basic architecture. The spectrogram is sent to the first LSTM layer as an input. The output is then combined and transferred to the second layer of LSTM. In the last stage, the output of both layers is combined with the input and transferred to a fully connected layer.

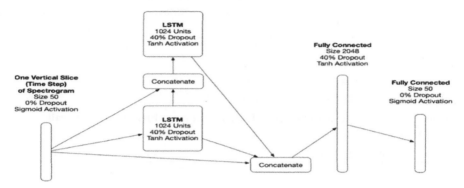

FIGURE 21.6 Architecture of the RNN model.

The two-layer recurring neural network configuration is used in language translation as the encoder and decoder layers. For similar configurations, we evaluated both GRU and LSTM versions. Figure 3.7 defines the two-layer LSTM model with two fully connected layers. One-time step is transferred to an LSTM layer first. The state of the first LSTM is connected to the input and then passed to the subsequent LSTM layer. The LSTM states and the input are then combined and passed into a fully connected layer. The prediction is finally produced by another completely connected layer with the output image height scale.

21.5 RESULTS

The CNN classifier was trained using 85% of the samples and validated on separate 15% of the samples generated. The classifier classifies into two categories: native and non-native. For the purpose of research, Indian accent is considered native while any other accent is considered non-native. The classifier attained an overall validation accuracy of 84% as shown in Table 21.1 and Table 21.2.

21.6 DISCUSSION AND CONCLUSION

The Verbal Language Processing culture tends to be the subject of prosodic language processing and synthesizing. The ability to analyze articulated

Computational Intelligence in Analytics and Information Systems, Vol. 1

prosody systematically is a transformational method in social-linguistic work that examines how language activities affect (and form) societies and cultures.

TABLE 21.1 Evaluation Metrics for CNN Model, with Train Set Consisting of eight ARCTIC Datasets (US, Canadian, Indian) and Test Set Consisting of four ARCTIC (Two US and Indian).

Accents	Accuracy	CE Loss		
Korean to US	86.14%	0.13		
Arabic to US	93.8%	0.08		
Indian to US	90.45%	0.05		
Model	Train Accuracy	Test Accuracy	Precision	Recall
8 CONV layers	89.9%	85.4%	91.6%	97.1%
10 CONV layers	89.4%	86.1%	94.2%	98.3%

TABLE 21.2 Confusion Matrix on the Test Set.

True labels ↓	Predicted labels	
	Non-native	Native
Non-native	2980	58
Native	52	1947

The proposed accent classification system attained an overall validation accuracy of 84%. In the future we will extend this work in the direction to generate the accent-transferred clips.

KEYWORDS

- **artificial neural networks**
- **speech conversion**
- **generative adversarial networks**

REFERENCES

1. Neri, A.; Cucchiarini, C.; Strik, H.; Boves, L. The Pedagogy-Technology Interface in Computer Assisted Pronunciation Training. Computer Assisted Language Learning. *Comput. Assist. Lang. Learn.* **2002,** *15* (5), 441–467. DOI: 10.1076/call.15.5.441.13473

2. Tejedor-Garćıa, C.; Escudero, D.; Gonzalez-Ferreras, C.; C´amara-Arenas, E.; Ćardenoso-Payo, V. Evaluating the Efficiency of Synthetic Voice for Providing Corrective Feedback in a Pronunciation Training Tool Based on Minimal Pairs. In *Proc. 7th ISCA Workshop on Speech and Language Technology in Education*, 2017; pp 25–29. DOI: 10.21437/SLaTE.2017-5

3. Toda, T.; Black, A. W.; Tokuda, K. Voice Conversion Based on Maximum Likelihood Estimation of Spectral Parameter Trajectory. *IEEE Trans. Audio Speech Lang. Process.* **2007,** *15* (8), 2222–2235. DOI: 10.1109/TASL.2007.907344.

4. Wu, J.; Wu, Z.; Xie, L. On the Use of I-Vectors And Average Voice Model For Voice Conversion Without Parallel Data. In Proc. Asia-Pacific Signal and Information Processing Association Annual Summit and Conference (APSIPA), 2016; pp 1–6.

5. Yan, Q.; Vaseghi, S.; Rentzos, D.; Ho, C.-H. Analysis by Synthesis of Acoustic Correlates of British, Australian and American Accents. In *Proc. IEEE International Conference on Acoustics, Speech, and Signal Processing (ICASSP)* 2004; pp 631–637. DOI: 10.1109/ICASSP.2004.1326066.

6. Huckvale, M.; Yanagisawa, K. Spoken Language Conversion with Accent Morphing. 6th ISCA Workshop on Speech Synthesis, 2007.

7. Felps, D.; Bortfeld, H.; Gutierrez-Osuna, R. Foreign Accent Conversion in Computer Assisted Pronunciation Training. *Speech Commun.* **2009,** *51* (10), 920–932. DOI: 10.1016/j.specom.2008.11.004

8. Aryal, S.; Gutierrez-Osuna, R. Can Voice Conversion be Used to Reduce Non-native Accents? In *Proc. IEEE International Conference on Acoustics, Speech and Signal Processing*, 2014; pp 7879–7883. DOI: 10.1109/ICASSP.2014.6855134

9. Oord, A.; Dieleman S.; Zen H. WaveNet: A Generative Model for Raw Audio, 2016; pp 1–15. https://arxiv.org/abs/1609.03499

10. Foote, D.; Yang, D.; Rohaninejad, M. Do Androids Dream of Electric Beats? 2016. audiostyletransfer.wordpress.com/

11. Arik, Sercan Ö. Arik, Chrzanowski, M.; Coates, A.; Diamos, G. et al. Deep Voice: Real-Time Neural Text-To-Speech. In *Proc. 34th International Conference on Machine Learning*, 2017; pp 195–204.

12. Wang, Y. et al. Tacotron: Towards End-to-End Speech Synthesis, 2017. https://arxiv.org/abs/1703.10135

13. Bearman, A.; Josund, K.; Fiore, G. Accent Conversion Using Artificial Neural Networks, 2018. http://web.stanford.edu/class/cs224s/reports/Amy_Bearman.pdf

14. Kominek, J.; Black, A. W. The CMU Arctic Speech Databases. ISCA Speech Synthesis Workshop **2004,** 2.

15. Gatys, A.; Ecker, S.; Bethge, M. Neural Algorithm of Artistic Style, 2015. https://arxiv.org/pdf/1508.06576

16. Munro, M.; Derwing, T. Foreign Accent, Comprehensibility, and Intelligibility in the Speech of Second Language Learners. *Lang. Learn.* **1995,** *45* (1), 73–97.

17. Mehri, S.; Kumar, K.; Gulrajani, I.; Kumar, R.; Sotelo, J.; Bengio, Y. Sample RNN: An Unconditional End-to-End Neural Audio Generation Model, 2017.

18. Wang, F. Voice Accent Transfer Using Recurrent Neural Networks on Spectrograms, 2018. http://web.stanford.edu/class/cs230s/reports/Henry_Wang.pdf

19. Ulyanov, D.; Lebedev, V.; Vedaldi, A.; Lempitsky, V. Texture Networks: Feed-Forward Synthesis of Textures and Stylized Images. In *Proceedings of the 33rd International Conference on International Conference on Machine Learning*, 2016; pp 1349–1357.

CHAPTER 22

Speech Emotion Recognition Using LSTM

SARIKA GAIND, SHUBHAM BUDHIRAJA, DEEPAK GAUBA, and
MANPREET KAUR

*Department of Computer Science & Engineering, Manav Rachna University,
Faridabad, Haryana, India*

ABSTRACT

Effective speech emotion recognition is very critical for improving the
experience of human–machine interaction to a great level. Therefore, this
field demands attention of researchers to develop new methods for creating
next-generation virtual chat assistants. Thus, the aim of this paper is to
propose a model by applying deep learning to analyze the emotional state
through speech and improve the performance of virtual personal assistants
such as Siri, Alexa. The analysis of voice samples is done on features such as
amplitude, frequency, and Mel-Frequency Cepstral Coefficients (MFCCs).
Speech signals from two datasets SAVEE and CREMA-D are extracted.
Datasets with six emotions happy, sad, fear, anger, disgust, and neutral are
used to get better insights on emotion analysis using the Recurrent Neural
Networks classifier. Working of an LSTM model is reviewed and an accuracy
of 92.3% is achieved with Binary Cross Entropy function as the loss function.

22.1 INTRODUCTION

Speech is a rich and effective way of transmitting information among one
another. Speech analysis can be of two types: linguistic and emotional. Virtual

Computational Intelligence in Analytics and Information Systems, Volume 1: Data Science and AI,
Selected Papers from CIAIS-2021. Hardeo Kumar Thakur, Manpreet Kaur, Parneeta Dhaliwal,
Rajeev Kumar Arya, and Joan Lu (Eds.)

Personal Assistants such as Siri and Alexa have attracted a remarkable amount of audience as a virtual helping hand to get things done quickly with ease. But still they lack the ability to analyze the emotional state and react according to that. This is why the need for emotion analysis arises. Through machine learning techniques, an effective model can be developed to predict emotions using the concept of Neural Networks. And for an effective model, the dataset has to have audio samples recorded at different frequencies corresponding to varying amplitude for better classification. This paper uses a combination of two datasets: SAVEE and CREMA-D. A brief analysis is done based on different features such as amplitude, frequency, and Mel-Frequency Cepstral Coefficients (MFCC). An effective LSTM model for speech emotion analysis is created using a deep learning algorithm called Recurrent Neural Networks (RNN),[1,4,8] which yields the highest accuracy of 92.3%.

Most of the researchers in this field of study have worked majorly on RNN and Convolutional Neural Networks (CNN). For instance, Kerkeni[1] used the RNN classifier to distinguish seven emotional states of audio samples found in the Berlin and Spanish datasets, Arti Rawat[4] performed RNN for emotion detection of speech samples using signals of human speech. However, Roopa[2] used a different model called Inception Net V3 Model for emotion recognition on the IEMOCAP dataset. Also, Wei Gong[3] used Deep Belief Networks and SVM for speech emotion classification.

22.1.1 EMOTION RECOGNITION

Emotion Recognition is the process of analyzing and predicting human emotions using video or audio signals or both. In our daily life, we go through many emotional states such as angry, happy, sad, fear, surprise, disgust, neutral. It is one of these emotions only that helps someone understand what a person must be going through. Such feelings or thoughts can be expressed in terms of both facial and vocal expressions.

22.1.2 NEURAL NETWORKS

There is no contradiction to the fact that machines have brains too. Neural networks in machine learning are a concept based on the neurons in a human brain. A neuron inside a human brain receives an input and based on that input, generates an output that is used by another neuron. The neural network simulates this behavior in learning about collected data and then predicting outcomes. In machine learning, neural networks are used to detect patterns that can be used to predict the outcome of inputs for unstructured data such as images, transcripts.

22.1.3 LSTM

Algorithm used is Long Short-Term Memory (LSTM). LSTM is an artificial recurrent neural network (RNN) architecture used in the field of deep learning. An LSTM has feedback connections. It can not only process single data points (such as images), but also entire sequences of data (such as speech or video). A common LSTM unit is composed of a cell, an input gate, an output gate, and a forget gate. The cell remembers values over arbitrary time intervals and the three gates regulate the flow of information into and out of the cell.

This paper is divided among different sections as follows: Section 22.3, to get better insights on the dataset used and how different attributes vary with different values. Section 22.4 describes the model functioning and performance, and at last, Section 22.5 includes the key learnings and scope of improvements.

22.2 LITERATURE REVIEW

Emotion recognition through speech samples has been one of the most renowned research topics in the past decade. Different researchers used different algorithms for their projects.[1] Kerkeni, Raoof, and Serrestou used the dataset InterISP; the MLR classifier was performed for better results with a feature combination of MS and MFCC and applied RNN on it with 78% of model accuracy.[2] Roopa S., Prabhakaran and Betty used the IEMOCAP dataset and approached it with a different algorithm called Inception Net V3 Model. This has evolved from GoogLeNet Architecture with some enhancements. They ended up with the model accuracy of 38%.[3] Gong, Wenlong, and Feng used the BUAA dataset and applied the DBN machine learning algorithm with 86% of remarkable accuracy scores.[4] Arti Rawat and K. Mishra performed RNN on the SAVEE dataset that achieved the model accuracy of 90%.[5] B. Ingale and D.S. Choudhary performed CNN on the CREMA-D dataset, which is a vast dataset of over 7000 audio samples and obtained 64% as the accuracy scores.[6] S. Lalitha, Bharath B., and S. Saketh used the SVM classifier for classifying seven different emotions. Audio samples were obtained from a Berlin database. Their model achieved the highest accuracy score of 81%.[7] S. Tripathi and his team used audio samples from the IEMOCAP dataset and developed two CNN models for speech features and transcripts separately. Predictions for speech features were 75% accurate while those of transcripts were 65% up to the mark.

22.3 EXPERIMENTAL SETUP

22.3.1 DATASET

On the route to develop an effective model to recognize the emotion of a particular speech segment, two existing datasets are combined and taken as base datasets. CREMA-D (Crowd Sourced Emotional Multimodal Actors Dataset), has 7422 original clips from 91 actors and SAVEE (Survey Audio-Visual Expressed Emotion) with 480 audio files. It is a very good combination to move forward with as they ensure that the model does not overfit.[11] Both the datasets include audio segments defining all six types of emotional states—happy, sad, angry, fear, disgust, and neutral.

22.3.2 FEATURE EXTRACTION AND DATA PREPROCESSING

The audio files in our dataset are classified among twelve different categories namely, male sad, male angry, male disgust, male fear, male happy, male neutral, female sad, female angry, female disgust, female fear, female happy, and female neutral. The purpose of feature extraction is to analyze and compare the voice signals falling under these 12 categories. Figure 22.2 shows that speech analysis for both the genders is equally important due to the difference between amplitude in their voice. Samples from both the datasets are analyzed based upon the frequency and amplitude as shown in Figure 22.1. For example, when the speaker is angry, the amplitude of his or her voice is too high while it is generally too low when he or she is sad or depressed. Figure 22.3 depicts comparison between male and female voices for varying emotional state is done using a spectrogram.

22.4 RESULTS AND DISCUSSION

22.4.1 MODEL DESCRIPTION

A function named *evaluate_model ()* is defined that takes the train and test dataset, fits a model on the training dataset, evaluates it on the test dataset, and returns an estimate of the model's performance. A single LSTM hidden

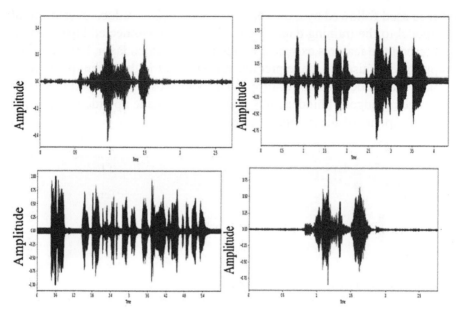

FIGURE 22.1 The change in amplitude of audio with time for emotional states: neutral, happy, angry, and sad respectively (left to right).

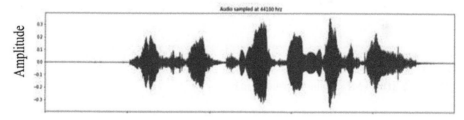

FIGURE 22.2(a) The change in amplitude of male audio.

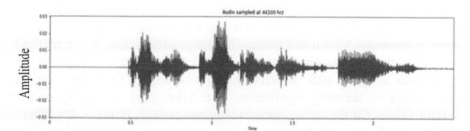

FIGURE 22.2(b) The change in amplitude of female audio.

FIGURE 22.2 Comparison between amplitude values of audio samples for emotional state- "angry."

layer is used followed by a dropout layer intended to reduce overfitting of the model to the training data. Then a dense fully connected layer is used to interpret the features extracted by the LSTM hidden layer, before a final output layer is used to make predictions. Dropout is the technique used to prevent the model from over-fitting. Dropout works by randomly setting the outgoing edges of hidden units (neurons that make up hidden layers) to 0 at each update of the training phase.

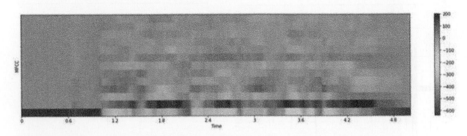

FIGURE 22.3(a)   MFCC plot for male audio.

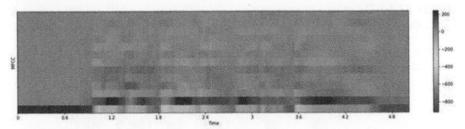

FIGURE 22.3(b)   MFCC plot for female audio.

The efficient Adam version of stochastic gradient descent was used for optimizing the network, and the binary cross entropy loss function. The Adam optimization algorithm is an extension to stochastic gradient descent that has recently seen broader adoption for deep learning applications in computer vision and natural language processing. It is a method that calculates the learning rate for each parameter that is shown by its developers to work well in practice and to compare favorably against other adaptive learning algorithms. The developers also propose the default values for the Adam optimizer parameters as Beta1 – 0.9, Beta2 – 0.999 and Epsilon – 10^{-8}.

22.4.2 EVALUATION METRIC

The model achieved the highest accuracy of 92.3% using varying layers and input parameters as shown in Table 22.1. The loss function used is Binary cross-entropy loss. It is also termed Sigmoid Cross-entropy Loss, and is a sigmoid activation plus a cross-entropy loss.

TABLE 22.1 Model Summary.

MODEL SUMMARY		
Layer(type)	**Output Shape**	**Parameters**
lstm_2(LSTM)	None, 200)	161600
dropout_2(Dropout)	None, 200)	0
dense_3(Dense)	None, 200	40200
dense_4(Dense)	None, 200	2613
	Total parameters:	204,413
	Trainable parameters:	204,413
	Non-trainable parameters:	0

Use of the dropout layer has prevented the models from over-fitting.

The loss computed for every neural network output vector component is not affected by other vector component values. That's why it is used for multi-label classification, where the insight of an element of a particular class does not influence the prediction for another class.

Since the dataset has multi-labels of emotions such as male_disgust, female_disgust, male_fear, female_fear, it fits the data in the best possible way and is further used for the prediction on testing dataset.

22.4.3 RESULTS

LSTM was applied on the CREMA-D and SAVEE datasets and it showed remarkable results with an emotion prediction accuracy of 92.31%.

So the proposed model is compared with the similar model used in[8] and found it better by a significant difference of 19% in the prediction accuracy as shown in Figure 22.4. Therefore, the model is tested on a recorded audio sample and the emotion prediction shows rather convincing results.

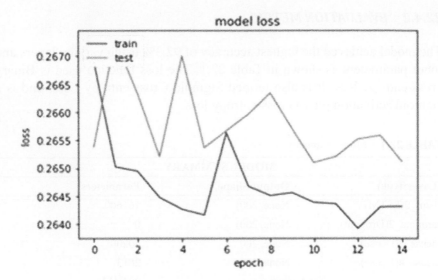

Test accuracy: 0.9230767488479614

FIGURE 22.4　The accuracy score of the proposed model.

22.5　CONCLUSION

The proposed model, after some polishing, was integrated with the virtual personal assistants to make the interaction more effective. Binary Cross Entropy loss function showed significantly good results with our multivariate dataset. Amplitude and frequency of male and female voices were analyzed by generating MFCC plots.

KEYWORDS

- **emotion recognition**
- **long short-term memory (LSTM)**
- **mel-frequency cepstral coefficients (MFCC)**
- **deep learning**
- **neural networks**

REFERENCES

1. Kerkeni, L.; Serrestou, Y.; Mbarki, M.; Raoof, K.; Mahjoub, M. A. Speech Emotion Recognition: Methods and Cases Study. *ICAART* Jan **2018,** *2,* 175–182.
2. Nithya Roopa, S.; Prabhakaran, M.; Betty, P, Speech Emotion Recognition Using Deep Learning. *IJRTE* **2018,** *7* (4S), pp.247–250.
3. Huang, C.; Gong, W.; Fu, W.; Feng, D. A Research of Speech Emotion Recognition Based on Deep Belief Network and SVM. *Math. Prob. Eng.* **2014,** 2014.
4. Rawat, A.; Mishra, P. K. Emotion Recognition Through Speech Using RNN, 2015.
5. Ingale, A. B.; Chaudhari, D. S. Speech Emotion Recognition. *IJSCE* **2012,** *2* (1), 235–238.
6. Lalitha, A. M.; Bhushan, B.; Saketh, S. Speech Emotion Recognition International Conference on Advances in Electronics. *Comput. Commun.* 2014.
7. Tripathi, S.; Kumar, A.; Ramesh, A.; Singh, C.; Yenigalla, P. Deep Learning Based Emotion Recognition System Using Speech Features and Transcriptions. arXiv preprint arXiv:1906.05**681,** 2019.
8. Wang, J.; Xue, M.; Culhane, R.; Diao, E.; Ding, J.; Tarokh, V. Speech Emotion Recognition with Dual-Sequence LSTM Architecture. In *ICASSP 2020–2020 IEEE International Conference on Acoustics, Speech and Signal Processing (ICASSP)*; IEEE, May 2020; pp 6474–6478.
9. Lim, W.; Jang, D.; Lee, T. Speech Emotion Recognition Using Convolutional & Recurrent Neural Networks, 2016.
10. Hochreiter, S.; Schmidhuber, J. Long Short-Term Memory. *Neural Comput.* **1997,** *9* (8), 1735–1780.
11. Ying, X. An Overview of Overfitting and Its Solutions. *J. Phys.* Feb **2019,** *1168,* (2), 022022.
12. El Ayadi, M.; Kamel, M. S.; Karray, F. Survey on Speech Emotion Recognition: Features, Classification Schemes, and Databases. *Pattern Recogn.* **2011,** *44* (3), 572–587.
13. Gadhe, R. P.; Shaikh Nilofer, R. A.; Waghmare, V. B.; Shrishrimal, P. P.; Deshmukh, R. R. Emotion Recognition from Speech: A Survey. *Int. J. Sci. Eng. Res.* **2015,** *6* (4), 632–635.

CHAPTER 23

Interpretation of the American Sign Language Using Convolutional Neural Networks

VIKAS THADA[1], UTPAL SHRIVASTAVA[2], and APRESH AGRAWAL[1]

[1]*Amity University Haryana, Haryana, India*

[2]*G L Bajaj Group of Institution, Uttar Pradesh, India*

ABSTRACT

Sign language is a language that helps people with hearing or speech impairments to interact with each other or with other community members through visual communication. Despite being one of the most understudied multimodal communication domain fields. In the field of deep learning, there are many ranging implication and applications which are based on neural networks for comprehension of sign language. With the average person lacking the knowledge and understanding of sign languages, it becomes difficult for them to interpret the signs, and even more difficult for the person signing to express himself effectively. In this research work, an attempt was made to develop a serverless, highly available, highly scalable, high-performance application using deep learning and AWS cloud services that would interpret signs in real-time and translate them for those who do not know the sign language. The sign language used is the American Sign Language. In this analysis, based on the ASL MNIST dataset from Kaggle Sign Language, a convolutional neural network was trained and 100% test

Computational Intelligence in Analytics and Information Systems, Volume 1: Data Science and AI, Selected Papers from CIAIS-2021. Hardeo Kumar Thakur, Manpreet Kaur, Parneeta Dhaliwal, Rajeev Kumar Arya, and Joan Lu (Eds.)

accuracy was achieved. The network model and network weights were recorded for the real-time scheme after network training was completed.

23.1 INTRODUCTION

Sign language is a language that helps people with hearing or speech impairments to interact with each other or with other community members through visual communication. Despite being one of the most understudied fields in the domain of multimodal communication, there are far ranging implications and applications that neural networks may have for sign language comprehension, in line with recent developments in the field of deep learning.

23.1.1 AMERICAN SIGN LANGUAGE

American Sign Language (ASL) has the same linguistic properties as of spoken languages including grammar for English, and is a comprehensive natural language. ASL is used for facial and hand movements. It is a language and is distinct from English. This language has all the basic characteristics of language, including its own rules for word formation, pronunciation, and order. For North Americans who are deaf and having hearing problems, it is the primary language. Sometimes, such languages are used even if there is no problem in hearing as per situation.[11] Using signs to spell out words is called Fingerspelling. Each sign corresponds to the letters in the words. The unique hand shape is used to represent an alphabet in the fingerspelled. One of the reasons that the fingerspelling alphabet plays such a vital role in sign language is because it is used by signers to spell out names of everything for which there is no sign. For proper names or to indicate the English word, fingerspelling is often used. Fingerspelling is also used by signers who sign in ASL, they use American Fingerspelled Alphabet (also called the American Manual Alphabet).

23.1.2 WHAT IS DEEP LEARNING?

Deep learning, often referred to as end to end learning, is a machine learning technique inspired by the structure of the human brain to achieve artificial intelligence that learns features and tasks directly from unstructured and unlabeled data through algorithms without the need for human supervision.

Data can be images, text, or sound. There are different datasets and methods to obtain these features and tasks. Based on this, researchers evaluate which datasets are appropriate and what other functionalities are available for the deep learning algorithms to achieve the desired results. Typically, deep learning involves a computing architecture called the deep neural network that performs classification and regression.

23.1.3 DEEP NEURAL NETWORKS

A deep neural network or DNN is a simplification of the human brain. Instead of producing that simulated "thinking" process of the brain, a DNN just crunches huge amounts of data, compares it with that stored in databases, and produces the best match, much like a human brain. Unlike the traditional machine learning algorithms, DNNs are far better at learning complex nonlinear mappings and produce more accurate output classification results. The term "deep" simply refers to the number of hidden layers stacked together in the neural network such that the leftmost layer will always be the input layer and the rightmost layer will always be the output layer. Traditionally, neural networks only consisted of two or three hidden layers, but the recent deep networks may have hundreds of them. Deeper networks learn nonlinear mappings better, but could also lead to overfitting. The dimensionality of the data, its quality, the frequency and number of clusters, the representation of the data as vectors or matrices, and the method used to compute the activation functions of the network are considered to be key ingredients in the different layers of the network. Figure 23.1 shows a general deep learning model.

The development of large DNNs has been used for a variety of applications, including vision, speech recognition, pattern recognition, natural language processing, image segmentation, statistical learning, signal processing, and prediction.

23.2 RELATED WORK

In image recognition and classification issues, convolutional neural networks (CNNs) have been extremely effective. In recent years, researchers have been successfully implemented for human gesture recognition. In proposed work based on deep CNNs for sign language recognition, with input-recognition not only having image pixels but is sensitive even more. With the use of contour sensing cameras and depth, the process is simpler for each sign language gesture by creating characteristic depth and motion profiles.[1]

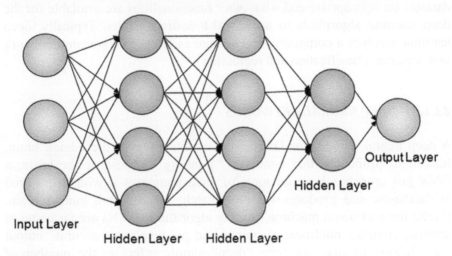

FIGURE 23.1　General deep learning model.

In the study of sign and gesture recognition, the two most common approaches used are vision-based and sensor-based. A low-cost marker-less hand gesture recognition device using the webcam for a vision-based approach was suggested.[15] This study used contours, Haar cascade and convexity defects to conduct hand detection, and stated that complex background impacted the detection accuracy negatively. Then, a stereo camera was adopted for hand gesture recognition.[14] Using Gaussian mixture mModel (GMM), this study achieved 98.6% accuracy for 10 Arabic numbers recognition by skin segmented technique. The technique effectively overcame the difficulties of handling occlusion between overlapping areas of hands and the face. In addition, Molchanov[15] used a 3D-based convolutional neural network (ConvNet) to combine the color camera, depth camera, and short-range radar for 10 dynamic gesture recognition. The analysis revealed the highest precision rate of 94.1% by using all features extracted from three cameras, while features extracted from the color camera delivered the lowest accuracy (60.1%).

23.2.1　PROPOSED CONCEPT

The primary objective of this project is to leverage the power of CNNs to train a deep learning model that can classify various hand gestures in

American Sign Language accurately by opting for the best optimizer through the evaluation of the performance of the various optimizers on the training dataset.

The other objective is to develop a cloud-based serverless web application that can act as an interface for people to classify the hand gestures in real time using this trained model.

The concept proposed is one of the basic supervised learning. The task is to identify every alphabet in ASL using deep CNN. The inputs are 28×28 fixed-scale images. These images are used to train a model using different algorithms (SGD, RMSprop, Adadelta, Adagrad, Adamax, Nadam, and FTRL) over 32,64, and 128 batch sizes. The model with the highest accuracy and the minimum loss is then selected to develop a cloud-based, serverless real-time ASL classifier using the OpenCV library and Amazon Web Services.

23.3 EXPERIMENTATION

23.3.1 EXPERIMENTATION ENVIRONMENT

The experiment is conducted on Google Colaboratory, which is a cloud-based, collaborative development environment by Google based on Jupyter Notebook and is free for public use. It provides free access to GPUs and runtime for the execution of Python code with most of the commonly used machine learning/data science libraries, such as PyTorch, Tensorflow, Keras, and OpenCV preinstalled. No configuration is required.

23.3.2 WORKING

First and foremost, we import all the required libraries to our Python environment and load the training and testing data (images) along with their labels. Then we preprocess our images using NumPy and Pandas, and Scikit-Learn. After the preprocessing is done, our data are ready to be fed to the sequential CNN model that we will create using built-in APIs of Keras. After the model is created, we compile it with one of the available optimizers in Keras and begin training our model. After the model is trained, we expose it to the testing data and validate the accuracy of the model and save the results, the visualizations (using Matplotlib and Seaborn), and the model. The process of compilation and training continues until we have used all the available optimizers. This is explained in (Figure 23.2).

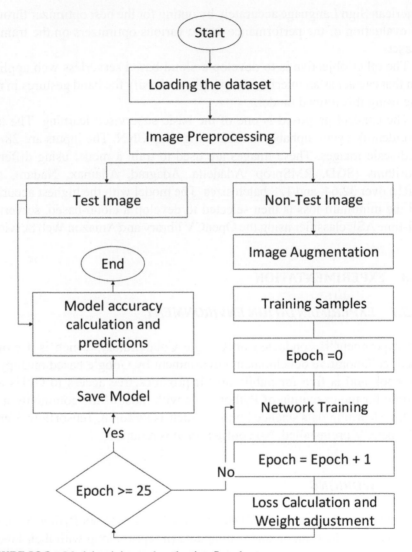

FIGURE 23.2   Model training and evaluation flowchart.

Once all the optimizers are used, we analyze their performance and choose the best optimizer for our dataset. Then we use the model we trained with the chosen optimizer and use it to develop a cloud-based serverless web application using Amazon Web Services serverless offerings—AWS Lambda, Amazon API Gateway, and Amazon Simple Storage Service (Amazon S3).

23.3.3 IMPLEMENTATION

The main objective of this research work was to develop a deep learning model that is capable of predicting the ASL alphabets with high accuracy. Since the data on which the model was to be trained were images, the CNN architecture was the best fit for the model.

Figure 23.3 shows the architectural design of the CNN model used in this research work. The model consists of multiple layers—Convolutional, Pooling (Max-Pooling), Normalization (Batch Normalization), Regularization (Dropout), Reshaping (Flatten), and Core (Fully Connected/Dense) layers. The kernels of size 3 × 3 × 75, 3 × 3 × 50, and 3 × 3 × 25 are used respectively in the convolutional layers, and the same padding is used so as to keep the size of the output layer the same as the input layer. The final layer uses an activation function called softmax, which is used to obtain probabilities of the input being in a specific class (classification).

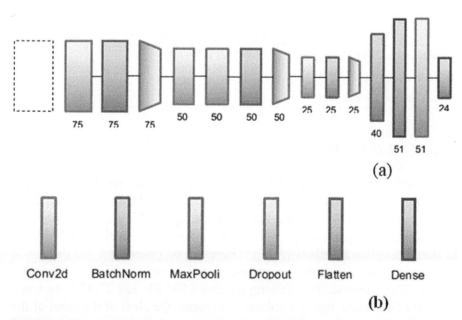

FIGURE 23.3 (a) Architecture of the model with different types of layers, (b) convention used to represent layers in CNN.

The detailed summary of the model is given in Table 23.1.

TABLE 23.1 Summary of the Architecture Model.

Layer (type)	Activation	Input shape	Output shape	Parameter #
Conv2D	ReLu	(None, 28, 28, 1)	(None, 28, 28, 75)	750
Batch normalization	–	(None, 28, 28, 75)	(None, 28, 28, 75)	300
MaxPooling2D	–	(None, 28, 28, 75)	(None, 14, 14, 75)	0
Conv2D	ReLu	(None, 14, 14, 75)	(None, 14, 14, 50)	33,800
Dropout	–	(None, 14, 14, 50)	(None, 14, 14, 50)	0
Batch normalization	–	(None, 14, 14, 50)	(None, 14, 14, 50)	200
MaxPooling2D	–	(None, 14, 14, 50)	(None, 7, 7, 50)	0
Conv2D	ReLu	(None, 7, 7, 50)	(None, 7, 7, 25)	11,275
Batch Normalization	–	(None, 7, 7, 25)	(None, 7, 7, 25)	100
MaxPooling2D	–	(None, 7, 7, 25)	(None, 4, 4, 25)	0
Flatten	–	(None, 4, 4, 25)	(None, 400)	0
Dense	ReLu	(None, 400)	(None, 512)	205,312
Dropout	–	(None, 512)	(None, 512)	0
Dense	Softmax	(None, 512)	(None, 24)	12,312

Total params: 264,049

Trainable params: 263,749

Non-trainable params: 300

23.3.3.1   THE DATASET

The American Sign Language (ASL) dataset used in the experiment has been taken from Kaggle and is called the Sign Language MNIST (Figures 23.4, 23.5). There are 27,455 images for the training and 7172 images available for testing, where each image is 28 × 28 in dimension. Each image belongs to the 25 English alphabets (A–Y). There are no cases for 9 = J or 25 = Z because of gesture motions. The dataset is available in the comma separated values (CSV) format. The training dataset CSV file has 27,455 rows and 785 columns, where the first column represents the class or the label of the image and the remaining 784 columns represent the pixel values between 0 and 255. The test dataset contains 7172 rows and follows the same paradigm as the training dataset.

The count of alphabets used for training and testing is given in Table 23.2.

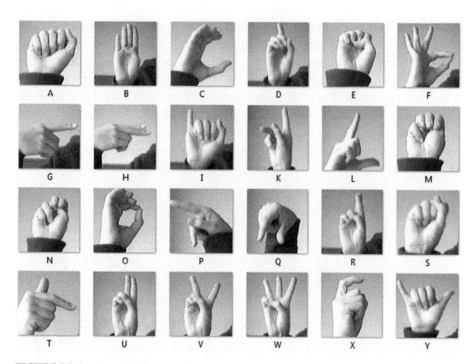

FIGURE 23.4   Cropped image montage panel of various users and backgrounds for American Sign Language letters.[2]

23.3.3.2   *TRAINING THE CLASSIFIER*

The first step toward training the CNN model is to import the necessary libraries mentioned above into the python environment (in this case, Google Colaboratory). The dataset is then loaded into two separate dataframes (training and testing data) using the Pandas library. The label columns are separated out from the dataframes thus formed, converted to one-hot encoding using the fit_transform method of LabelBinarizer class of the Scikit-Learn library, and stored separately for later use. The remaining data in the dataframes is then normalized and reshaped from one-dimension to three-dimensions as required by the input layer of the CNN model. To prevent overfitting, a technique called data augmentation is used and implemented through the ImageDataGenerator class of the Keras image data preprocessing utilities. After this, a sequential CNN is created using the Keras APIs and the training process is started. The process is carried out on the training data for each of the available optimizers in Keras, in batch sizes of 32, 64, and 128, for 25 epochs. Batch size indicates how many images will be loaded in each iteration while the epoch number indicates the cumulative time in which all images loaded for training into the neural network. Softmax activation is applied at the output layer to classify the images based on the probabilities. A logistic regression Softmax regression that normalizes an input value in a value vector which follows a distribution of probabilities. The sum probabilities are up to 1. After each iteration in the process, the model is validated against the testing data and the results of the performance of the optimizers are tabulated and visualized using the Matplotlib library.

FIGURE 23.5   Grayscale image montage panel when rescaled to 28 × 28 pixels with (0–255) pixel values.[2]

23.4   RESULTS

The CNN model trained on 27,455 ASL images gave the highest accuracy of 99.9308% with the RMSProp algorithm on a batch size of 64. The following tables and figures depict the comparison between the various optimizers on the performance factors, such as Validation Accuracy, Training Accuracy, Validation Loss, and Training Loss. From the graphs (Figures 23.6, 23.7), it can be inferred that the accuracy of the model increased and the loss decreased with the increase in the number of epochs.

TABLE 23.2 Count of Alphabets for Training and Testing.

Label	Alphabet	Number of training examples	Number of testing examples
0	A	1126	331
1	B	1010	432
2	C	1144	310
3	D	1196	245
4	E	957	498
5	F	1204	247
6	G	1090	348
7	H	1013	436
8	I	1162	288
9	J	0	0
10	K	1114	331
11	L	1241	209
12	M	1055	394
13	N	1151	291
14	O	1196	246
15	P	1088	347
16	Q	1279	164
17	R	1294	144
18	S	1199	246
19	T	1186	248
20	U	1161	266
21	V	1082	346
22	W	1225	206
23	X	1164	267
24	Y	1118	332
25	Z	0	0

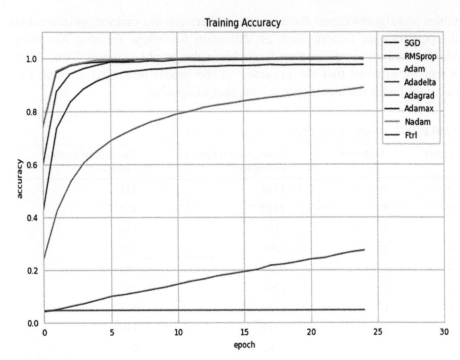

FIGURE 23.6   Training accuracy on a batch size 64.

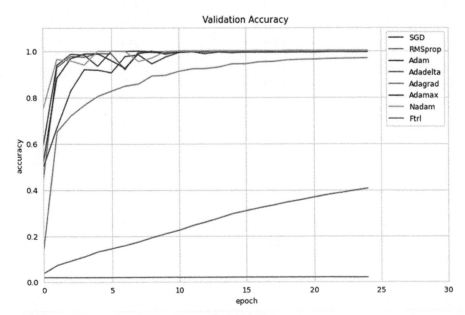

FIGURE 23.7   Validation accuracy on a batch size 64.

23.4.1 PERFORMANCE OF THE OPTIMIZERS ON A BATCH SIZE OF 64 (Table 23.3)

TABLE 23.3 Performance of the Optimizers on a Batch Size of 64.

Optimizer	Train_Accuracy	Validation_Accuracy	Train_Loss	Validation_Loss
Nadam	0.999344	1.000000	0.002717	0.000143
RMSprop	0.999308	1.000000	0.002412	0.000015
Adam	0.999381	0.999861	0.002081	0.001092
Adamax	0.995593	0.998048	0.019745	0.006997
SGD	0.974394	0.994702	0.087776	0.026453
Adagrad	0.887088	0.968349	0.359398	0.175644
Adadelta	0.274231	0.406999	2.433563	2.183427
Ftrl	0.047132	0.020078	3.178039	3.178113

23.5 CONCLUSION

The primary objective has been met successfully. The CNN model trained on 27,455 ASL images gave the highest training accuracy of 99.9308% and validation accuracy of 100% with the RMSProp algorithm on batch size 64. Although, the real-time system developed using this trained model did not work as expected because of the high amount of noise in the real-time image data captured through the web camera. The interference of upper body parts and the other objects made it difficult for the classifier to classify the images. The research work demonstrated how we can leverage the advancement in artificial intelligence to build an application for people, who communicate through signs, to speak with other people without the need of an interpreter (person) to translate their signs into words.

The real-time application can be improved to deliver more accurate results by:

a) Using a dataset that has less noise. The preprocessing could be done such that the background of the image can be made completely black (pixel value of 0). The area of the hand could be made completely white (pixel value of 255) so that the noise reduces and the neural network could learn to recognize the features more precisely.

b) Using hand detection techniques of computer vision to extract only the required part of the frame from the real-time video feed to perform classification and preprocess it as mentioned in (1). The extraction of the selective part of the frame ensures less interference of the unwanted objects with the accuracy of the prediction of the classifier.

Given the right training with a larger dataset, the application would be able to accurately recognize gestures in the complete ASL and translate them into actual words and will speak for the person itself. This application of interpretation of sign languages can be implemented practically into video chat applications to make it easier for deaf/mute people to socialize with other people.

ACKNOWLEDGMENTS

The authors would like to thank Google for quick and efficient results on selected keywords, Google colaboratory. Sincere thanks to mentors for guiding well and helping from design and development of deep learning CNN model.

KEYWORDS

- **sign language**
- **convolution network**
- **deep learning**
- **fingerspelling**

REFERENCES

1. Agarwal, A.; Thakur, M. Sign Language Recognition using Microsoft Kinect. In *IEEE International Conference on Contemporary Computing*, 2013.
2. https://www.kaggle.com/datamunge/sign-language-mnist/version/1 (accessed Oct 24, 2020).
3. https://pandas.pydata.org (accessed Oct 24, 2020).
4. Pedregosa, S. *Scikit-Learn: Machine Learning in Python*, 2nd ed.; JMLR Press, **2011**; pp 2825–2830.
5. Keras backends. https://keras.io (accessed Oct 26, 2020).
6. R Interface to Keras. https:// keras.rstudio.com (accessed Oct 26, 2020).
7. Why Use Keras? https://keras.io (accessed Oct 26 2020).

8. Van, R.; Drake, G. *Python 3 Reference Manual*, 2nd ed.; Scotts Valley: CA, 2009.
9. Vis, N. A Visual Grammar for Automatically Generating Publication-Ready CNN Architecture Visualizations. *arXiv:1902.04394v5 [cs.LG]*.
10. https://www.nidcd.nih.gov/health/american-sign-language (accessed Oct 21, 2020).
11. Mckinney. Data Structures for Statistical Computing in Python, McKinney. *Proc. 9th Python Sci. Conf.* **2010,** *445.*
12. Chollet, F. *Deep Learning Using Keras*. https://keras.io.
13. Haria, A.; Subramanian, A.; Kumar, A.; Poddar, S. Direct Hand Gesture Recognition for Human Computer Interaction. *Procedia Comput. Sci.* **2017,** *115,* 367–374.
14. Elmezain, M.; Al-hamadi, A. A Hidden Markov Model-Based Isolated and Meaningful Hand Gesture Recognition. *Int. J. Electr. Comput. Syst.* **2009,** *3* (3)**,** 156–163.
15. Molchanov, P.; Gupta, S.; Kim, K.; Pulli, K. Multi-Sensor System for Driver's Hand-Gesture Recognition. In *Proceedings 11th IEEE International Conference on Face Gesture Recognition*, **2009**; pp 1–8.

CHAPTER 24

Emotional Intelligence: An Approach to Analyze Stress Using Speech and Face Recognition

SHAMBHAVI MISHRA, SEERIPI NAGA SURYA, and SUMITA GUPTA

Amity School of Engineering and Technology, Amity University, Noida, Uttar Pradesh, India

ABSTRACT

For the completion of every work, stress evolves in students that ends up with anxiety, depression, disappointment, suicide, heart attack, stroke, etc. To overcome their stress, they need to have good emotional intelligence but at some point, due to lack of guidance, they do not know how to analyze the situations without taking stress. Students who lack emotional intelligence are not able to manage stress in their life. Evolution of human–computer interaction is helpful in many fields including the medical science field. This application can be used for emotion analysis among students. For conveying the emotion, verbal and nonverbal mode of communication can be used. Emotion recognition is the most researched area where verbal (like speech) and nonverbal (like body movements, facial expressions) parameters can be used as the input. The classification of emotions can be done by using machine learning and deep learning methods. This paper presents an extensive study of various methods which are utilized for emotion recognition using speech, body postures with facial expressions and other body movements. This paper covers the comparison study of existing technologies based on databases used in every research, how emotions are extracted, their advantages and limitations.

Computational Intelligence in Analytics and Information Systems, Volume 1: Data Science and AI, Selected Papers from CIAIS-2021. Hardeo Kumar Thakur, Manpreet Kaur, Parneeta Dhaliwal, Rajeev Kumar Arya, and Joan Lu (Eds.)

24.1   INTRODUCTION

Emotional Intelligence plays a very crucial and important role in the workplace environment. We work to a great extent in groups, not in confinement, for one task whether it can be office, school, college, or social gatherings, etc. Lack of emotional intelligence can prompt genuine medical issues like uncontrolled pressure raises blood pressure, stifles the immune system, increases the danger of heart failures and strokes, adds to barrenness, and rates up the maturing cycle.

24.1.1   EMOTIONAL INTELLIGENCE

Emotional intelligence (EQ) is the capacity of perceiving, controlling, communicating feelings, comprehending their result and to utilize that ability to manage our sentiment and activities, furthermore to deal with common interconnection completely and delicately. It is different from IQ because a person who thinks intellectually and makes rational interconnections with ease, are the ones with higher IQs. Those with high EQ can deal with their feelings as well as utilize their feelings to encourage their reasoning and comprehend the feelings of others.

24.1.2   RELATIONSHIP BETWEEN EMOTIONAL INTELLIGENCE AND STRESS MANAGEMENT

Emotional intelligence plays a very important role to manage stress. Various surveys were conducted to examine their relationship between emotional intelligence and stress management. A connection between emotional intelligence and stress management in a group of members, a quantitative investigation was done by Saras Ramesar.[1] The relationship and relapse results appear to demonstrate that stress management is a segment of emotional intelligence, while stress can be either an information or a surge of emotional intelligence or the scarcity in that department. Mayuran[2] explores the relationship between EQ and stress management in the school and Bank in Jaffna district. Studies were distributed to 14 schools and 17 banks. The stress management among teachers and bank staff was discovered to be moderate in this investigation and a moderate positive relationship was found among EQ and stress management of teachers. Emotional recognition and expression, understanding others' feelings, feelings of direct intellectual and enthusiastic control were distinguished as huge determinants of stress management of teachers and feeble positive relationships were found among EQ and stress management of bank staff. Ravi Kant's goal in his examination[3] was to investigate the degree of emotional intelligence of College's students and to discover the distinction between emotional intelligence based on gender, territory, level of course, and school of study. Consequences of this investigation uncovered that females are more emotionally intelligent than males. Comparing students based on their locality, provincial students were more emotionally intelligent than their metropolitan partners.

24.1.3 *MACHINE LEARNING AND DEEP LEARNING APPROACH IN EMOTION RECOGNITION*

With the recent advancement of machine learning and deep learning, stress management can be done efficiently, easily, and accurately. Because it is the need of the hour, where students need to manage their stress and emotions according to the situations they face in their life. Advancements in the technology lead to the development of emotion recognition system (ERS), where a software uses the method of emotion recognition to identify the correct emotions a person is facing at that point. Emotion recognition is a current area for research. In this literature review, for our research, we will be taking two modes, the direct mode to analyze the emotion includes voice which is the fastest way of communicating and expressing. And the indirect mode to analyze the emotion comprises body languages which include body postures, facial expressions, body movements, eye movements. It covers the researcher's contribution toward this research, different methodologies they adopted, and how accurate were their results and the advantages and limitations related to it. Using machine learning and deep learning algorithms, we can find out which technique can be best suited to recognize human emotions through voice and body languages.

24.2 RELATED WORK

Emotion Recognition System (ERS) is a framework used to recognize emotions by using different parameters. It consists of three basic components based on which other recognition systems are built. The three fundamental components of ERS are signal preprocessing, feature extraction, and classification as shown in Figure 24.1.

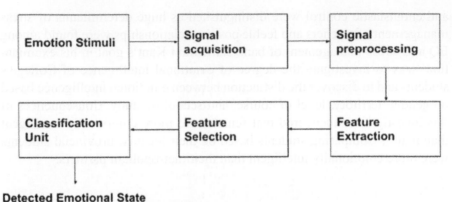

FIGURE 24.1   Block diagram of emotion recognition system.

As various researchers and authors have published their research, in which they proposed a more efficient and accurate working model of following emotion recognition systems like speech emotion recognition, facial emotion recognition, emotion recognition through body movements, multimodal emotion recognition, etc.

24.2.1   SPEECH EMOTION RECOGNITION SYSTEM (SER)

Han et al.[4] proposed to use DNNs to separate elevated level features from crude data and show that they are viable for SER. They first produced an emotion state likelihood dispersion for each fragment utilizing DNNs, from which utterance level features are developed and used to decide the expression level emotion state. Rather than DNN, these utterance level features were utilized to recently create a single hidden layer neural network called extreme learning machine (ELM) to direct utterance level feeling classification. ELM is a single hidden layer neural network which requires a lot more concealed units than normally required by the conventional neural networks (NNs) to accomplish impressive classification exactness. In ELM, the loads between the input layer and the hidden layer are haphazardly allocated and afterwards fixed. The loads between the hidden layer and the output layer can be scientifically decided through a straightforward summed up reverse activity of the hidden layer output matrices. They focused on emotional conditions, such as excitement, frustration, happiness, neutral and sadness. They performed their strategy on the IEMOCAP database. The proposed strategy beats SVM by 20% relative exactness improvement, indicating that the training time of ELMs is around multiple times quicker than that of SVM.

Rawat and Mishra[5] proposed an approach where they used a high-pass filter before feature extraction. Their purpose of using a high-pass filter was to reduce the noise and pass only high frequency while diminishing lower frequency. They also explained the detailed steps of feature extraction using MFCC. They used neural networks as a classifier to classify different sets of emotions, such as sad, anger, happy, neutral, disgust, from the database that they used in their study. The overall performance of the whole proposed model was good but execution time was a bit lengthy.

Noroozi et al.[6] proposed two processes where the first step was to recognize different emotions by different types of classifiers, such as K-NN, Random Forest, C4.5, Hoffding tree, LogitBoost, AdaBoost.M1, Bayesian Network, and Naïve Bayes, Bagging, SVM, Random Subspace, and in the second step, prediction of the next emotional reactions using the nonlinear autoregressive time series neural network method. The Polish database was utilized for demonstrating the emotional state. The boredom, fear, joy, and happiness feelings were picked. Eleven spectral features, to be specific, pitch, power, the initial four formants and their data transmissions and standard deviation, were separated. Using the above-mentioned algorithms, the researchers of this paper get to know the best average recognition rate of about 86.25% was obtained by Random Forest Algorithm, showing that quality speech is impor-tant enough for differentiating between types of emotional states. And for the second step using the neural networks, the speech signals containing the four emotions (boredom, fear, joy and happiness), which had similar lengths were connected. At that point, the time-arrangement was made, which consisted of the entire spans of boredom, fear and bliss signs, and two-fifths of the sadness signals. The time-arrangement was worked by tuning in to the pitch and power features of the linked signs. The unfinished pieces of the sadness signals were utilized as test samples. They found that the prediction rate was 60.30%.

Franti et al.[7] introduced deep convolutional neural network for emotion detection from voice. As input data, they used MFCC for CNN and PRAAT software for analysis of speech and preprocessing. Along with that, they used the Keras model-level library and tensorflow. CNN classified six classes of emotions, namely, happiness, sadness, disgust, anger, fear, surprise. The whole architecture was trained on Romanian Language samples. This imple-mentation was used for the hardware implementation of companion robots.

They pointed to the issue of emotion recognition to the subjectivity of feeling voice relationship in the event of human activity who just tune into the voice and have no other data for the circumstance and character of the speaker.

Nithya Roopa et al.[8] presents deep learning and image classification methods for recognizing and classifying emotions from the speech signals. They proposed an emotion recognition model by using transfer learning, CNN model, and Inception Net V3 model. Transfer learning is consolidated at whatever point there is any need to lessen calculation cost, accomplish exactness with less training. The IEMOCAP database is used in this chapter for training the model. The Inception model is utilized for programmed image classification and image labeling as indicated by the picture. By implementing, they achieved an accuracy of 35.95%, showing transfer learning, less dataset as the factors for less accuracy.

Kerkeni et al.[9] presents a relative investigation of Speech Emotion Recognition Systems that depends on various classifiers and various techniques for feature extraction, such as MFCC and Modulation spectral features. Various classifiers, such as Recurrent Neural Network, Multivariate Neural Network, and Support Vector Machine were used for classifying emotions and their performance was compared with each other. RNN gave 94% on Spanish database without speaker normalization (SN) and feature selection (FS). Also, for the Berline database, all the referenced classifiers accomplish an exactness of 83% when a speaker normalization (SN) and a feature selection (FS) are applied to the highlights. From such outcome, it was inferred that RNN frequently performs better with more data and it experiences the issue of long training time, while SVM and MLR models have a decent potential for reasonable use for restricted data. For better performance, fusion of classifiers and combining datasets is recommended. Also, the feature selection method's quality affects the rate of emotion recognition.

Jiang et al.[10] showed in their research that for the better execution of the SER system, feature extraction, feature unification and fusion network are some of the important processes. They proposed a hybrid deep neural design to draw out recognized features represented from heterogeneous acoustic features. So as to accomplish better execution, they utilize a four-layer deep neural network which goes about as a feature fusion system to catch the relationship between the coalesced features. After evaluating the proposed architecture by different classifiers, SVM gave an accuracy of 64%. The advantage of using heterogeneous unification module and fusion network module was to increase the performance of the work proposed. Further, this design can also deal with multimodal features for emotion recognition.

Huang et al.[11] utilized Deep Belief Network to prepare a five-layer deep network to remove speech emotion features. It fuses the speech emotion features of all the more continuous frames, to assemble a high-scope attributes and uses SVM classifier to classify the voice. In their process, the model has little complex nature and 7% higher final acknowledgement rate than conventional artificial extract and this technique can extricate emotional quality boundaries precisely, improving the recognition pace of emotional speech recognition. Yet, the time cost for preparing DBN's component extraction model was 136 hours. It was longer than the other feature extraction model. Bakhshi et al.[12] proposed a Conv-BiGRU network as an element extractor and indicator, to identify emotional states from speech signal data. Considering the qualities of the time and recurrence data in crude speech signals, they planned the Deep speech emotion recognition model. In this, Concordance Correlation Coefficient (CCC) presented by audio-video emotion challenges (AVECs) was utilized as comparison estimation instrument between the network forecast and highest quality level, procured from the explanation of a dimensional model of emotion. Here, the RECOLA database is utilized for the proposed model. The problem that occurs only here is the incomplete use of the database used. But the CCC prediction outperforms the other state-of-the-art end to end methods that shows its advantage in the proposed model.

Wadhwa et al.[13] proposed an SER system that utilizes features, such as MFCC, Mel spectrogram, Chroma, and librosa package. They used discrete classification emotions, such as anger, happiness, boredom. instead of dimensional representation. They also utilized five different datasets for their study: TESS, SAVEE, RAVDESS, CREMA-D, and Berlin. And they chose to analyze the acoustics features of speech, such as pitch, tone. The whole datasets were used to train machine learning algorithms, such as SVM, XGB, CNN 1 D (shallow), CNN 1D (deep), and CNN 2D. In between the process, they faced an overfitting problem, which denoted the need of larger dataset volume. They used dimensionality reduction methods to nullify this problem in their research too. They also gave one more technique to increase the dataset volume by augmentation method like time-shifting or speeding up/slowing down the audio. Kahail et al. and Kumar and Mahajan [14,15] showed what a speech emotion recognition system looks like and how it can execute. Basic components of an SER were explained in these papers and also pointed toward the importance of datasets and varieties of datasets. They also discussed the different types of machine learning and deep learning techniques along with their working and obtained results in the previous study. They also introduced different types of speech features, such as MFCC, LPCC, PLP, and RASTA

24.2.2   FACIAL EMOTION RECOGNITION SYSTEM (FER)

Mali et al.'s[16] main purpose was to show the importance of neural networks for the development of a smart system for facial image recognition classification. In their research, they used two databases, namely, BU-3DEE database and Grand Challenge database. They presented about facial motion phases also. They showed how facial detection methods provide a quick and hands-on approach for noninvasive detection. They come to the conclusion that in facial emotion recognition, deep learning can be the best approach that can be used for smooth human–computer communication and interaction. Paweł Tarnowski[17] carried out examinations for seven emotional states (neutral, joy, sadness, surprise, anger, fear, disgust). Features that were used in their paper, were the coefficients that describe the facial expressions. MLP neural network classifiers got better accuracy in this research. This paper showed the importance of real-life influenced features that can affect the accuracy rate and can also increase complexity.

Nithya Roopa[18] also aims to show emotional recognition through facial expression using a deep learning approach. For the whole purpose, they used the Inception Net V3 model for training and building emotion recognition framework that can be used in any application. Along with its tensorflow that is used for training the model is also used. Transfer learning is also used here. After implementation, they got an accuracy of 29% which shows the limitation of this research that transfer learning should be applied on a large dataset for each class of emotions which in return can give more accuracy. Ferreira et al.[19] also proposed a deep neural network design alongside a very much planned loss function for facial emotion recognition. That comprises three main components; facial parts components, representation components and classification components. The loss function is characterized in such a way to regularize the whole learning measure, so that the proposed model can naturally learn articulation explicit features. They applied their architecture on the datasets used and got outperforming results. It was also proposed that this architecture can also be applied with smaller datasets.

Tarnowski et al.[20] examined the emotion recognition system by using one parameter that is eye movement. They prepared their dataset by experimenting with 30 participants that were examined by showing them some video materials of 21 fragments of movies for evoking emotions in them.

During this process, the data of their eye movements were recorded. For this experiment, they used fixation, saccades like elements, specific to eye movements as features that are related to pupil diameter calculation. For the whole process of making their dataset, eye tribe optical eye tracker was used that has a built-in algorithm used to classify a sample of signals and informs whether it represents fixation or not and six fixations were discovered. It also measures the diameter of the pupil. In the whole process, SVM gave classification accuracy of 80%. They also pointed toward some limitations and facts that the components like luminance change the pupil diameter. It should be guaranteed that the lighting condition continues as before all through the cycle. The effect of luminance should likewise be remunerated by utilizing regression or principal component analysis (PCA).

24.2.3 EMOTION RECOGNITION THROUGH BODY MOVEMENTS

Santhoshkumar and Kalaiselvi Geetha[21] aimed to achieve emotion recognition through body movements. This study was motivated by the purpose of monitoring, where facial activities might not be appropriately examined but body movements (like hand, legs, center of the body) can help to recognize human emotion. For this purpose, they used a feed-forward deep convolutional neural network (FDCNN). This model shows deep convolutional features to remove saliency data at various scales. They also achieved 94% accuracy compared with other paper's used methodology. In another work, Santhoshkumar and Kalaiselvi Geetha[22] showed how they tried to achieve emotion recognition through body movements using FDCNN and BAIV features. They evaluated their proposed model on another dataset. One model shows deep convolutional features to separate saliency data at numerous scales. Also, another model concentrates BAIV features and gives input to the random forest classifier for emotion prediction. After that, both the models were evaluated to analyze machine learning and deep learning methods and got to know that FDCNN was the better model than BAIV features as input to random forest classifiers.

Behera et al.[23] in their study, associated facial expressions and upper body gestures to improve the smart system. They investigated the automatic identification of student's nonverbal conduct including hand over face signals, head and eye movements through facial appearances during learning. They created their dataset by examining the practices in-depth over the long haul in a classroom meeting of 40-min including perusing and critical thinking assessment varying simple, medium, and difficulty of levels. The activities in the meetings are partitioned into three classifications, for example, simple, medium, difficult. Also, they discovered that there is an increase in head and eye movements as time advances just as with the increase in the trouble level. When they examined using classifiers, they get to know that HoF gestures appeared more frequently during problem-solving exercises, that is, easy–23.79%, medium – 19.84%, difficult – 30.46% which compared with reading activity easy – 16.20%, medium – 20.06%, difficult – 20.18%. The proposed deep neural network gave a classification accuracy of 86.87%.

Masood and Alghamdi[24] built up a remote sensor model that records physiological and neural signs from the brain, heart, breath, and skin conductance of a human body inside a difficult atmosphere. The members went through a progression of intellectual difficulties that prompted mental pressure changing in seriousness. Initiated metal pressure was registered from the extricated highlights that were resolved utilizing power densities and strategic relapse procedures that were utilized on the physiological and the neural signs. A deep convolutional neural network (CNN) structure is utilized for preparing and approving the information datasets. According to them, the convention for their psychological tests was very much planned, yet, in future, more members must be locked in for the examinations. Additionally, genuine scenes of stress can be added to the research facility tests. Notwithstanding that firefighting circumstances can be additionally checked as firefighting goes through constant pressure.

Kilimci et al.[25] gathered information which can be of two classes' physical and behavioral data. In which the actual information contains estimations of the clients, such as pulses, rest quality, energy developments, and versatility boundaries. Neurophysical information contains keystroke designs like typing velocity and typing blunders. Client's passionate/mind-set statuses are additionally researched by taking every day questions. Their point was to show that there is an association between client's physical/neurophysical boundaries and temperament/passionate conditions. They did this emotional classification task by both machine learning and deep learning algorithms separately. Accuracy, precision, recall and F measures are utilized as assessment measurements in the tests. In the accuracy level of machine learning, decision trees performed best because of reliance on features on one another. In the accuracy level of deep learning algorithms, CNN shows characterization achievement. Further, the analysis' outcomes exhibit that the utilization of deep learning technique and the blend of both physical and neurophysical boundaries upgrade the order achievement of the framework to anticipate the sensitivity or emotional condition of the clients. Even though there are a few drawbacks in this process. CPU was utilized in the analyses on account of the little size of the dataset. The utilization of GPU can be considered as an alternative when the quantity of clients increments.

24.2.4 MULTIMODAL EMOTION RECOGNITION SYSTEM

Tripathi et al.[26] utilized multiple types of data given by IEMOCAP dataset, for effective emotion recognition detection using neural networks. Here they wanted to build a model that can capture emotional states from speech, face, and movements of the hand. They adopted ensemble-based architecture that comprises long short-term memory (LSTM), convolutional neural network, fully connected multilayer perceptron and compliment them utilizing procedures, such as Drop out, Versatile analyzers, for example, Adam, Pre-trained word-installing models, Consideration-based R-NN decoders.

After building the ensemble model, they get to know that speech emotion detection system gives 55.65%, text-based emotion detection system gives 64.78%, and Mo-cap data gives 51.11% accuracy. And combining all three models, the final accuracy obtained was 71.04% accuracy. This showed the effectiveness of neural networks in multimodal ERS. They suggested some future approaches, such as, they could utilize transfer learning from automatic speech recognition model and calibrate it for emotion identification. One such example is Frederik Calsius[27] who wanted to create a system that can help people to prepare for their job interviews, which gives importance to body language and facial expression. They wanted to create a system that can analyze and give feedback about the candidate. For posture recognition, they used CNN because of previously proven promising results on such examinations. And for facial recognition, their approach was to use Face-API that used depth-wise convolutions and densely connected blocks. The advantage of using such a method was for quicker calculation. The only disadvantage of such implementation was the lack of depth calculation because of lightweight devices such as mobile.

24.3 COMPARISON STUDY

In this section, a comparison study among papers used in the literature survey is given. Tables 24.1 and 24.2 demonstrate the performance of classifiers used to build emotion recognition systems using voice and body languages (facial expressions, body postures, and eye movements) on different datasets along with their advantages and limitations.

TABLE 24.1 Comparison Table of Speech Emotion Recognition-Based Papers.

S. No	Paper	Techniques	Database	Accuracy	Advantages	Limitations
1	Nithya Roopa et al.[8]	Transfer learning, inception net v3	IEMOCAP	35.6%	Took advantage of transfer learning and inception net	Less accuracy due to less dataset and transfer learning shows good performance on large dataset
2	Noroozi et al.[6]	K-NN, Randon Forest, C4.5, Hoffding tree, LogitBoost, AdaBoost.M1, Bayesian Network, Naïve Bayes, Bagging, SVM, Random Subspace, Neural network method	Polish database	86.25% in first process and 60.30% in second process	It shows next reaction prediction that cannot be seen in any papers so easily	No limitations just deep learning can also be used for its adopted architecture
3	Fu Wen long et al.[11]	Deep belief network, SVM	1200 sentences containing different types of emotions	Got 7% higher accuracy	Proposed architecture can extract emotion accurately and can improve the recognition rate	Training cost of DBN was high
4	Kerkeni et al.[9]	RNN, MLR, SVM	Spanish database, Berlin database	On Spanish dataset got 94% and on Berlin dataset got 83%	Compared with other researches and showed better results	Datasets can be merged and tested with other classifiers for better accuracy
5	Han et al.[4]	DNN, ELM, SVM	IEMOCAP	ELM got 20% more than SVM	Shows alternate of DNN, that is, ELM	No limitations shown
6	Jiang et al.[10]	K-NN, Logistic Regression, Random Forest, SVM	IEMOCAP	64% by SVM	Fusion network module is better for giving greater performance in work	No limitations, just gave suggestion for using the architecture for multimodal feature

TABLE 24.1 *(Continued)*

S. No	Paper	Techniques	Database	Accuracy	Advantages	Limitations
7	Voichita et al.[7]	CNN, PRAAT software	Romanian Language sample	71.33%	Mentioned ways to improve the accuracy	Combination of features required for better accuracy
8	Rawat et al.[5]	Neural network, High-pass filter	10 samples of five different emotions of five different people	High accuracy rate than previous study	Showing advantage of high-pass filter	Taking long time to execute and bigger datasets needed for better accuracy
9	Wadhwa Mohit et al.[13]	SVM, XGB, CNN 1D (shallow and deep), CNN 2D, dimensionality reduction	TESS, SAVEE, RAVDESS, CREMA-D, Berlin	Got accuracy greater than other previous methods	Showed how to reduce overfitting problem through dimensionality reduction	Should explore more acoustic features of sound data, add more data volume and discrete classification was used here.
10	Bakhshi et al.[12]	Deep conv-RNN, concordance correlation coefficients (CCC)	RECOLA dataset	Got greater accuracy than previous study	CCC prediction outperforms the results achieved by previous methods	Database was not fully complete

TABLE 24.2 Comparison Table of Body Languages (Face, Body Movements, Eye Movements) Based Papers

S.No	Paper	Techniques	Database	Accuracy	Advantages	Limitations
1	Nithya Roopa[18]	Deep learning, Inception Net v3, transfer learning	Kaggle's facial emotion recognition challenge dataset, Karlinska directed emotional faces datasets	35%	Showed advantage of transfer learning and inception net	Low accuracy due to transfer learning. Need for larger dataset
2	Santhoshkumar and Kalaiselvi Geetha[21]	FDCNN	dataset of 29 actors, GEMEP dataset of 10 actors	94%	FDCNN showed its significance by showing the better results	No limitations shown
3	Santhoshkumar and Kalaiselvi Geetha[22]	FDCNN, BAIV feature using Random forest	dataset of 15 varieties of emotions	FDCNN better than BAIV feature	FDCNN showed its significance by showing the better results	No limitations just comparison shown with other methods
4	Tarnowski et al.[20]	SVM, LDA, K-NN	Shown 21 movie fragments for invoking emotions and recorded those data	80% by SVM	The effect of luminance must also be compensated by using regression or component analysis	The factors like luminance in changes in the pupil diameter. It should be ensured that the lighting condition remain the same.
5	Behera et al.[23]	Deep learning technique	Conducted examination ranging difficulty level, and reactions were recorded	86.87%	They created their dataset by their own which is real dataset	No limitations shown. Just need to create more realistic dataset
6	Majkowski et al.[17]	K-NN, MLP neural network	KDEF database	MLP classifier got better accuracy	They used features that have been calculated for 3D face model	Classification can be affected by purposefully creating the dataset
7	Tripathi et al.[26]	LSTM, CNN, fully connected perceptron	IEMOCAP	71.04%	Their approach is to use multiple modes to analyze the emotion	They showed requirement of using transfer learning in their proposed architecture

TABLE 24.2 (Continued)

S.No	Paper	Techniques	Database	Accuracy	Advantages	Limitations
8	Punjabi et al.[16]	K-NN, MLP, SVM	BU-3DFE, Grand challenge datasets	Deep learning shows more accuracy which shows its importance	Showed importance of neural networks for facial emotion recognition system	No limitations shown as such
9	Ferreira et al.[19]	DNN with loss function	CK+ dataset, JAFEE dataset, SFEW dataset.	Got accuracy more than previously studied papers	Architecture proposed shown promising results	Shown requirement of using such architecture on smaller datasets
10	Masood and Alghamdi[24]	Deep convolutional neural network	Dataset created by creating stressful environment	DCNN showed its importance sue to its greater accuracy	Due to non- linear nature of dataset, deep CNN importance is shown for such purpose	Real examination of stress and firefighting situation can be added
11	Kilimci et al.[25]	FFNN, CNN, RNN, LSTM, SVM, decision tree, random forest, MNB, decision integration strategy	Stressful scenario created by taking keystroke error count of 15 people	Decision tree got 77.87% and CNN got 79.06%	It took the scenarios of student when they face anxiety under pressure through keystroke errors	Dataset was less, recommended to use large dataset

24.4   CONCLUSION

Emotion recognition is the most researched area where verbal like speech and nonverbal like body movements, facial expressions are used as the input. Development of machine learning and deep learning techniques contributed to this research. Various papers have shown the importance of these techniques on various datasets involving those emotions. This shows how accurately these techniques can be used to predict emotions and categorize the type of emotions evolving under a student. This chapter presents the variety of datasets used. The research pointed toward the dataset of being real rather than fake for better accuracy and real prediction results. And it also showed how the models can be further modified for better and accurate results according to the need of the research.

KEYWORDS

- **emotional intelligence**
- **speech emotion recognition**
- **facial emotion recognition**
- **multimodal emotion recognition system**
- **deep learning**
- **machine learning**

REFERENCES

1. Ramesar, P. K.; Oosthuizen, M. R. The Relationship Between Emotional Intelligence and Stress Management. *SA J. Ind. Psychol.* **2009**.
2. Mayuran, L. Impact of Emotional Intelligence on Stress Management: Study of Schools with Banks in Jaffna District. *Global J. Commerce Manage. Persp.* **2013**, *2* (6), 5.
3. Kant, R. Emotional Intelligence: A Study on University Students. *J. Educ. Learn. (EduLearn)* **2019**, *13*, 6.
4. Han, K.; Yu, D.; Tashev, I. Speech Emotion Recognition Using Deep Neural Network and Extreme Learning Machine. *Interspeech* **2014**, 5.
5. Rawat, A.; Mishra, P. Emotion Recognition through Speech Using Neural Network. *Int. J. Adv. Res. Comput. Sci. Softw. Eng.* **2015**, *5* (5), 7.

6. Noroozi, F.; Akrami, N.; Anbarjafari, G. Speech-Based Emotion Recognition and Next Prediction Reaction, 2017.

7. Franti, E.; Ispas, I.; Dragomir, V.; Dascalu, M.; Zoltan, E.; Stoica, I. Voice Based Emotion Recognition with Convolutional Neural Networks for Companion Robots. *Romanian J. Inform. Sci. Technol.* **2017**, *20* (3), 20.

8. Nithya Roopa, S.; Prabhakaran, M.; Betty, P. Speech Emotion Recognition Using Deep Learning. *IJRTE* **2018**, *7* (4S), 4.

9. Kerkeni, L.; Serrestou, Y.; Mbarki, M.; Raoof, K.; Ali Mahjoub, M.; Cleder, C. Automatic Speech Emotion Recognition Using Machine Learning, **2019**, 16.

10. Jiang, W.; Wang, Z.; Jin, J. S.; Han, X.; Li, C. Speech Emotion Recognition with Heterogeneous Feature Unification of Deep Neural Network, **2019**, 15.

11. Huang, C.; Gong, W.; Fu, W.; Feng, D. A Research of Speech Emotion Recognition Based on Deep Belief Network and SVM, 2014.

12. Bakhshi, A.; Wong, A. S.W.; Chalup, S. End-To-End Speech Emotion Recognition Based on Time and Frequency Information Using Deep Neural Networks. In *24th European Conference on Artificial Intelligence—ECAI 2020*, 2020; p 7.

13. Wadhwa, M.; Gupta, A.; Pandey, P. K. Speech Emotion Recognition (SER) Through Machine Learning. Analytics Insight, July 5, 2020. https://www.analyticsinsight.net/speech-emotion-recognition-ser-through-machine-learning/ (accessed Nov 3, 2020).

14. Khalil, R. A. et al. Speech Emotion Recognition Using Deep Learning Techniques: A Review, **2019**, 19.

15. Kumar, Y.; Mahajan, M. Machine Learning Based Speech Emotion Recognition System. *Int. J. Sci. Technol. Res.* **2019**, *8* (07), 9.

16. Punjabi, V. D.; Mali, H.; Birari, S.; Patil, R.; Patil, A.; Mahajan, S. Prediction of Human Facial Expression Using Deep Learning. *IRJET* **2019**, *06* (12), 6.

17. Tarnowski, P.; Kołodziej, M.; Majkowski, A.; Rak, R. J. Emotion Recognition Using Facial Expressions. *Int. Conf. Comput. Sci. ICCS 2017*, **2017**, 10.

18. Nithya Roopa, S. Emotion Recognition from Facial Expression using Deep Learning. *IJEAT* **2019**, *8* (6S), 5.

19. Ferreira, P. M.; Marques, F.; Cardoso, J. S.; Rebelo, A.Physiological Inspired Deep Neural Networks for Emotion Recognition, 2018; p 14.

20. Tarnowski, P.; Kołodziej, M.; Majkowski, A.; Rak, R. J. Eye-Tracking Analysis for Emotion Recognition. *Hindawi* **2020**, *2020*, 13.

21. Santhoshkumar, R.; Geetha, M. K. Deep Learning Approach: Emotion Recognition from Human Body Movements. *J. Mech. Continua Math. Sci.* 2019, *14*, 14.

22. Santhoshkumar, R.; Geetha, M. K. Deep Learning Approach for Emotion Recognition from Human Body Movements with Feedforward Deep Convolutional Neural Network. In *International Conference on Pervasive Computing Advances and Applications—PerCAA 2019*, 2019; p 8.

23. Behera, A.; Matthew, P.; Keidel, A.; Vangorp, P.; Fang, H.; Canning, S. Associating Facial Expressions and Upper-Body Gestures with Learning Tasks for Enhancing Intelligent Tutoring Systems. *Int. J. Artif. Intell. Educ.* **2020**, 35.

24. Masood, K.; Alghamdi, M. A. Modeling Mental Stress Using a Deep Learning Framework, 2019; p 9.

25. Kilimci, Z. H.; Güven, A.; Uysal, M.; Akyokus, S. Mood Detection from Physical and Neurophysical Data Using Deep Learning Models. *Hindawi* **2019**, *2019*, 16.

26. Tripathi, S.; Tripathi, S.; Beigi, H. Multi-Modal Emotion Recognition on IEMOCAP Dataset Using Deep Learning, 2018, 6.

27. Calsius, F. Using Machine Learning to Analyse Body Language and Facial Expressions. Medium, Aug 23, 2019. https://medium.com/jstack-eu/using-machine-learning-to-analyse-body-language-and-facial-expressions-a779172cc98. (accessed Nov 3, 2020).

CHAPTER 25

Proposed Integrated Framework for Emotion Recognition: A Futuristic Approach

RAMESH NARWAL and HIMANSHU AGGARWAL

Computer Science and Engineering Department, Punjabi University, Patiala, Punjab, India

ABSTRACT

Emotion recognition and detection (ERD) is the method that is used for the recognition and detection of human beings' emotions with the help of various data such as text, images, audio, and video. Using various machine and deep learning methods, we can fetch humans' emotions using various data types. These days, we can recognize and detect emotions because we did not have extensive data available earlier, technologies such as AI, deep learning, and powerful computing devices. Much research is currently going on human emotions because that is the only thing that is not available in the machine. Because since the dawn of new technology, researchers wanted to create a machine that is a replica of human beings. Scientists have had much success in building such a machine that can think and act like human beings, but they are not able to add emotions into machines up to now. In this research paper, we proposed an integrated framework for the detection of emotions. Earlier a lot of research work was going on emotion detection from various data

Computational Intelligence in Analytics and Information Systems, Volume 1: Data Science and AI, Selected Papers from CIAIS-2021. Hardeo Kumar Thakur, Manpreet Kaur, Parneeta Dhaliwal, Rajeev Kumar Arya, and Joan Lu (Eds.)

sources. However, no framework is thereby used; we can detect emotions from all data sources.

25.1 INTRODUCTION

Human emotion recognition and detection are current needs so that Artificial Intelligence (AI) systems can gauge and emulate reactions from various data sources such as text, image, audio, and video. These systems can help identify security-related threats, promotion of offers, and intention of a person. Recognizing and identifying emotions from the text, images, audio, and video is a straightforward task for the human eye. However, it is tough and challenging for machines that require many machine learning and deep learning data processing techniques. Recognition and detection of emotions by machine learning and deep learning require training and testing of algorithms on suitable dataset.

On social media platforms, we generate a lot of textual, audio, images, and video data containing rich information regarding their emotions and play an important role in emotion detection and recognition.

25.2 RELATED WORKS

In the traditional system, we have to define features that the machine can extract. However, in a deep learning system, they automatically learn feature representation and extraction from data. Using deep learning, researchers achieved much success in emotion recognition and human action recognition.[1] Mostly Long Short-Term Memory (LSTM) and Convolution Neural Networks (CNN) models of deep learning are used in emotion detection and recognition. As compared with tradition Recurrent Neural Network (RNN) model, LSTM that is a variation of RNN gives a better result in the analysis of emotions.[2]

For categorization of emotions in the video, the authors investigated the LSTM-RNN model-based encoding. LSTM-RNN can record emotions' evolutions for long-range video frames and can separate emotion clue frame from other frames.[3]

The authors[4] state that emotions' subjective concepts related to fuzzy boundaries and the disparity in perception and expression are the significant challenges in automated emotion recognition and detection. To measure and detect the user's emotion in live text streams, the authors proposed an online method. The authors developed a computational model for analyzing and tracking the user's emotion during online chatting.[5]

Various authors[6,7] combined around two datasets such as text-audio, audio-video to predict emotions and build automatic emotion recognition system. The authors proposed a novel deep learning approach to recognize and detect emotions such as angry, happy, and sad in textual dialogues.[8] They combined sentiment and semantic-based approaches to improve the accuracy of emotion recognition.

Emotion prediction systems also have various applicabilities in the stock market. A lot of research is also going on emotion-based stock prediction systems.[9] Various deep learning techniques such as Convolutional Neural Network (CNN), Recurrent Neural Networks (RNN), Deep Belief Network (DBN), Recursive Neural Networks (ReNN), and Auto Encoder (AE) are used for speech emotion recognition.[10]

Researchers even tried to decode emotion hidden in various language texts. For example, the authors[11] proposed a model to extract emotions from Arabic text using the CNN-LSTM deep learning model.

25.3 EMOTION CLASSIFICATIONS

Emotion recognition and detection systems are based on emotion models because they define emotion representation. According to models, emotion exists in different states that how they differentiate different types of emotions. There are many models available, but here we explain a few models that are easy to understand and implement.

25.3.1 EKMAN'S SIX BASIC EMOTIONS

Ekman researched different cultures and devised a list of emotions. He devised a list of primary emotions by describing a situation or showing facial expressions to people and noted emotions expressed by them. After researching, he found six basic emotions: anger, disrespect, fear, happiness, sadness, and surprise.[12] Figure 25.1 depicts Ekman's six basic emotions.

25.3.2 PLUTCHIK'S EIGHT BASIC EMOTIONS

Robert Plutchik created "Wheel of Emotions" that demonstrated how different emotions relate to or blend into each other and devised new emotions.

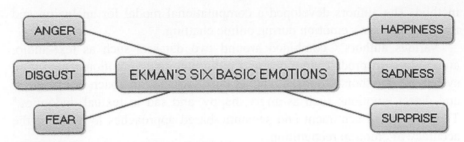

FIGURE 25.1   Ekman's six basic emotions.

Plutchik gave eight bipolar emotions: anger versus fear, trust versus disgust, joy versus sadness, and surprise versus anticipation. Plutchik devised more emotion types by using their different intensities.[13]

25.3.3   PROFILE OF MOOD STATES (POMS) SIX MOOD STATES

POMS (Profile of Mood States) is a psychological scale developed by McNair, Droppleman, and Lorr. It is used to measure six different mood swings dimensions over a time which includes anger or hostility, tension or anxiety, fatigue or inertia, vigor or activity, confusion or bewilderment, and depression or dejection.[14]

25.4   INTEGRATED FRAMEWORK FOR EMOTION RECOGNITION

Emotion recognition by a machine is one of the challenging fields and has many application areas. Various models recognize emotions from the text, audio, images, and video data and use them separately. According to author's knowledge currently, there is no model or framework by which we can process all of these data types and process them individually. So, in this paper, we propose an integrated framework by using we can accomplish this task. The proposed framework is given in Figure 25.2. The given models have various components that are explained below.

25.4.1   EMOTION RECOGNITION FROM TEXT DATA

Emotion recognition and detection are applications of Sentiment Analysis related to the extraction and analysis of emotions.[15] Various studies have been carried out in text analysis and mining due to the easy availability of text data. The core purpose of Sentiment Analysis is to analyze human languages written on social media or anywhere else by extracting ideas, thoughts, and opinions through the polarities positive, negative, and neutral. These are a subfield of emotion recognition related to the extraction of fine-grained emotions such as angry, sad, and happy.[16]

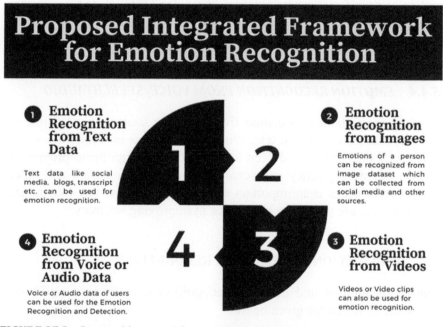

FIGURE 25.2 Proposed integrated framework for emotion recognition.

25.4.2 EMOTION RECOGNITION FROM IMAGES

In human–computer interaction, emotion recognition and detection from facial images are scorching research topics. The earlier approach worked only on nearly frontal and frontal view images. These days, emotion recognition can be done even from random and nonfrontal view images, but it is more complicated than the previous one but has more practical applications.[17]

Emotion recognition and detection based on static images are among the most complicated problems among the pattern recognition problems because of the ambiguous nature of facial expression and any possibilities of interpretations.[18]

25.4.3   *EMOTION RECOGNITION FROM VIDEOS*

The main aim of audio-video emotion recognition is to classify video into emotions. In Human–Machine Interaction Systems, automatic emotion recognition is an essential component. Recognizing and detection of human emotions by machines is a challenging problem. In human communication, emotions are a significant component. The author presents a system for the recognition of emotion using a facial expression from the video. Through video sequence, audio-video emotions can be captured. In this process, the face is divided into different action units. These units help to extract facial emotion features.[19]

25.4.4   *EMOTION RECOGNITION FROM VOICE/SPEECH/AUDIO*

All of us can fathom information from multiple sources or domains, for example, speech, visual, and text. With advancements in technologies such as Artificial Intelligence and deep learning, there is significant progress in speech recognition latency and accuracy. Emotion recognition and detection from the speech is an important aspect to build a machine-like human. However, there are still many challenges in improving accuracy.[20]

25.5   APPLICATIONS OF EMOTION RECOGNITION

Emotion recognition and detection recognition have various application areas some of which are given below.

25.5.1   *GAUGING CITIZENS' HAPPINESS*

In today's world, governments and organizations have started paying attention to their citizens' social well-being and happiness, measured by happiness index and societal well-being metrics. Using emotion detection, governments can gauge their citizens' happiness.[21]

25.5.2   *PERVASIVE COMPUTING*

Emotion detection is used for pervasive computing to serve individuals better. It can be done by checking anxiety through speech, text, image, and video to suggest help.

25.5.3 UNDERSTANDING CONSUMER

Emotion recognition can be used to detect sales and brand reputation by analyzing consumer's emotions regarding their product and services.

25.6 CONCLUSIONS AND FUTURE WORK

Research in emotion recognition is categorized into two main phases. Out of these two phases, one is language representation, and the other is classification. Contextual information extracted in language representation is essential because it forms the bedrock for the classification accuracy improvement.[22] For the extraction of contextual information from the text, there is a need for a robust technique. Transformer- based embedding shows a significant increase in contextual information extraction quality. However, it also has some limitations such as increased complexity, out of vocabulary, and in the method of overfitting in small networks.[23] Neuro-fuzzy networks and ensemble attention can reduce the limitation effects in transformers and improve classification accuracy. Before classification, fuzzy neural networks offer classification and comprehensibility of extracted features while attention networks give the best result in the extraction of relevant features.[24] Text-based emotion detection systems had not been well explored for life saving and real-life applications such as crime detection by identifying threatening sentences or words, depression detection etc.

The ambiguity in sentences interpretation by machine learning algorithms is one of the challenging problems when we do text-based emotion recognition due to lack of voice modulation and facial expressions. Our proposed model solves this problem because it can process any type of data.[8]

There are significantly fewer resources of emotion labeled for non-English languages. Researchers are encouraged to balance work done on emotion recognition and detection in different languages because other languages such as Hindi, French, Spanish etc. have rich resources.

Due to many applications in various areas such as military, entertainment, e-learning, marketing, medicine, and monitoring, there is a dire need of an automatic emotion recognition system that can process any data such as text, audio, speech, video, and images as proposed in this paper.

KEYWORDS

- **emotion**
- **recognition**
- **detection**
- **machine learning**
- **deep learning**

REFERENCES

1. Cai, L.; Liu, X.; Chen, F.; Xiang, M. Robust Human Action Recognition Based on Depth Motion Maps and Improved Convolutional Neural Network. *JEI* **2018**, *27* (5), 051218. DOI: 10.1117/1.JEI.27.5.051218.

2. Li, D.; Qian, J. Text Sentiment Analysis Based on Long Short-Term Memory. In *2016 First IEEE International Conference on Computer Communication and the Internet*, Oct, 2016; pp 471–475. DOI: 10.1109/CCI.2016.7778967.

3. Chao, L.; Tao, J.; Yang, M.; Li, Y.; Wen, Z. Long Short Term Memory Recurrent Neural Network Based Encoding Method for Emotion Recognition in Video. In *2016 IEEE International Conference on Acoustics, Speech and Signal Processing*, Mar, 2016; pp 2752–2756. DOI: 10.1109/ICASSP.2016.7472178.

4. Hasan, M.; Rundensteiner, E.; Agu, E. Automatic Emotion Detection in Text Streams by Analyzing Twitter Data. *Int. J. Data Sci. Anal.* **2019**, *7* (1), 35–51. DOI: 10.1007/s41060-018-0096-z.

5. Chen, C. -H.; Lee, W. -P.; Huang, J. -Y. Tracking and Recognizing Emotions in Short Text Messages from Online Chatting Services. *Inf. Process. Manag.* **2018**, *54* (6), 1325–1344. DOI: 10.1016/j.ipm.2018.05.008.

6. Cai, L.; Hu, Y.; Dong, J.; Zhou, S. Audio-Textual Emotion Recognition Based on Improved Neural Networks. *Math. Probl. Eng.* **2019**. https://www.hindawi.com/journals/mpe/2019/2593036/ (accessed Jan 15, 2021).

7. Noroozi, F.; Marjanovic, M.; Njegus, A.; Escalera, S.; Anbarjafari, G. Audio-Visual Emotion Recognition in Video Clips. *IEEE Trans. Affect. Comput.* **2019**, *10* (01), 60–75. DOI: 10.1109/TAFFC.2017.2713783.

8. Chatterjee, U. G.; Chinnakotla, M. K.; Srikanth, R.; Galley, M.; Agrawal, P. Understanding Emotions in Text Using Deep Learning and Big Data. *Comput. Human Behav.* **2019**, *93*, 309–317. DOI: 10.1016/j.chb.2018.12.029.

9. Chun, J. A.; Kim, Y.; Lee, S. Using Deep Learning to Develop a Stock Price Prediction Model Based on Individual Investor Emotions. *J. Behav. Finance* **2020**, *0* (0), 1–10. DOI: 10.1080/15427560.2020.1821686.

10. Khalil, A.; Jones, E.; Babar, M. I.; Jan, T.; Zafar, M. H.; Alhussain, T. Speech Emotion Recognition Using Deep Learning Techniques: A Review. *IEEE Access.* **2019**, *7*, 117327–117345. DOI: 10.1109/ACCESS.2019.2936124.

11. Abdullah, M.; Hadzikadicy, M.; Shaikhz, S. SEDAT: Sentiment and Emotion Detection in Arabic Text Using CNN-LSTM Deep Learning. In *2018 17th IEEE International Conference on Machine Learning and Applications*, Dec, 2018; pp 835–840. DOI: 10.1109/ICMLA.2018.00134.

12. Ekman, P. An Argument for Basic Emotions. *Cognit. Emot.* **1992,** *6* (3–4), 169–200. DOI: 10.1080/02699939208411068.

13. Plutchik, R. Chapter 1—A General Psychoevolutionary Theory of Emotion. In *Theories of Emotion*; Plutchik, R., Kellerman, H., Eds.; Academic Press, 1980; pp 3–33.

14. Norcross, C.; Guadagnoli, E.; Prochaska, J. O. Factor Structure of the Profile of Mood States (POMS): Two Partial Replications. *J. Clin. Psychol.* **1984,** *40* (5), 1270–1277. DOI: 10.1002/1097-4679(198409)40:5<1270::aid-jclp2270400526>3.0.co;2-7.

15. Rout, K.; Choo, K. -K. R.; Dash, A. K.; Bakshi, S.; Jena, S. K.; Williams, K. L. A Model for Sentiment and Emotion Analysis of Unstructured Social Media Text. *Electron. Commer. Res.* **2018,** *18* (1), 181–199. DOI: 10.1007/s10660-017-9257-8.

16. Acheampong, F. A.; Wenyu, C.; Nunoo-Mensah, H. Text-Based Emotion Detection: Advances, Challenges, and Opportunities. *Eng. Rep.* **2020,** *2* (7), e12189. DOI: https://doi.org/10.1002/eng2.12189.

17. Zheng, W.; Tang, H.; Lin, Z.; Huang, T. S. Emotion Recognition from Arbitrary View Facial Images. In *Computer Vision—ECCV 2010*, Berlin, Heidelberg, 2010; pp 490–503. DOI: 10.1007/978-3-642-15567-3_36.

18. Boubenna, H.; Lee, D. Image-Based Emotion Recognition Using Evolutionary Algorithms. *Biol. Inspir. Cognit. Archit.* **2018,** *24*, 70–76. DOI: 10.1016/j.bica.2018.04.008.

19. KalaiSelvi, R.; Kavitha, P.; Shunmuganathan, K. L. Automatic Emotion Recognition in Video. In *2014 International Conference on Green Computing Communication and Electrical Engineering*, Mar, 2014; pp 1–5, DOI: 10.1109/ICGCCEE.2014.6921398.

20. Singh, M.; Fang, Y. Emotion Recognition in Audio and Video Using Deep Neural Networks, Jun, 2020. arXiv: 2006.08129 [cs, eess]. [Online]. Available: http://arxiv.org/abs/2006.08129 (accessed Jan 14, 2021).

21. Yam, C. Y. Emotion Detection and Recognition from Text Using Deep Learning. In *CSE Developer Blog*, Nov 29, 2015. https://devblogs.microsoft.com/cse/2015/11/29/emotion-detection-and-recognition-from-text-using-deep-learning/ (accessed Jan 10, 2021).

22. Salido Ortega, G.; Rodríguez, L. -F.; Gutierrez-Garcia, J. O. Towards Emotion Recognition from Contextual Information Using Machine Learning. *J. Ambient. Intell. Human Comput.* **2020,** *11* (8), 3187–3207. DOI: 10.1007/s12652-019-01485-x.

23. Allouch, A. A.; Azoulay, R.; Ben-Izchak, E.; Zwilling, M.; Zachor, D. A. Automatic Detection of Insulting Sentences in Conversation. In *2018 IEEE International Conference on the Science of Electrical Engineering in Israel*, Dec, 2018; pp 1–4. DOI: 10.1109/ICSEE.2018.8646165.

24. Ahanin, Z.; Ismail, M. A. Feature Extraction Based on Fuzzy Clustering and Emoji Embeddings for Emotion Classification. *Int. J. Technol. Manag. Inf. Syst.* **2020,** *2* (1), Art. no. 1.

PART IV

Computational Intelligence in Smart Cities

CHAPTER 26

A Review on Machine Learning Techniques for Human Actions Recognition

DIANA NAGPALL[2] and RAJIV KUMAR[1]

[1]*Department of Computer Science and Engineering, Chandigarh University, Gharuan, Punjab, India*

[2]*Guru Nanak Dev Engineering College, Ludhiana, Punjab, India*

ABSTRACT

The recognition of human activities is a remarkable research bearing in the field of computer vision. Automatic recognition of human exercises, for example, HAR has now been developed as a cutting edge zone in human–computer relationship, mobile computing, and many more. Human activity recognition provides data on a client's conduct that permits computing frameworks to proactively help clients with their undertakings. Currently, we are using smartphone sensors to detect human activities such as accelerometer, gyroscope, barometer. In this paper, a brief understanding of human action recognition (HAR) has been provided, that is, sensor-based and vision-based HAR. The best in time techniques of machine learning such as decision trees, K-nearest neighbors have been reviewed for HAR. The results obtained by every technique and the sort of dataset they have utilized are being introduced. Also, deep learning neural network strategies have been depicted, for example, artificial neural network, recurrent neural network, and convolutional neural network, and the results obtained by these methods have also been introduced.

Computational Intelligence in Analytics and Information Systems, Volume 1: Data Science and AI, Selected Papers from CIAIS-2021. Hardeo Kumar Thakur, Manpreet Kaur, Parneeta Dhaliwal, Rajeev Kumar Arya, and Joan Lu (Eds.)

26.1   INTRODUCTION

Understanding human behavior has become one of the most dynamic study themes in computer vision. Human activity recognition is a difficult assignment that includes foreseeing the development of an individual dependent on sensor information. Recently, profound learning techniques, for example, convolutional neural networks, recurrent neural networks have demonstrated best in class results via naturally learning features from the raw sensor information.

There are four classes of human activities relying on the body parts that are associated with activity:

a)   Gesture: Gesture is body activity that represents a particular message. It is a development done with different body parts rather than verbal communication, for example, okay gesture and thumbs up gesture.

b)   Action: Action is a collection of physical movements such standing, sitting, walking, and running.

c)   Interaction: It is a set of actions executed by at most two actors in which at least one subject is a person and the other one can be a human or an object.

d)   Group Activities: These exercises are the blend of gestures, activities, and interactions. The quantity of subjects is at any rate more than two, for example, hurdle racing, playing football etc.[19]

Human activity recognition has increased significantly nowadays on account of its applications in different fields, for example, amusement, security and observation, wellbeing, and intelligent situations. Much work has already been accomplished on human activity recognition and specialists have even utilized a wide range of approaches. An examination proposed another scientific classification for sorting the exploration work led in this area of activity recognition and separating current writing into three subterritories: activity based, movement based, and cooperation based.[1]

26.2   LITERATURE SURVEY

26.2.1   SENSOR-BASED HUMAN ACTION RECOGNITION

Because of the low expense and progression in sensor technology, the vast majority of the exploration in this area has moved toward a sensor-based methodology. Various sensors are utilized to check the behavior of a human beings when they are performing daily life exercises in this technology.[2] In the wearable approach, notable measures of work have already been accomplished in this area utilizing wearable approach; however, the major problem with wearable sensor is that tag is not comfortable all the time.

From the previous years, scientists are concentrating on device-free methodology. In this technique, users are not asked to bring tags or any kind of device with them. Primary thought is to install sensors in the environment. For example, the sensors are installed at such places where the activities are carried out. Whenever any individual plays out any activity, the information will be caught through those sensors, which would then be able to be utilized for the recognition of various activities. This method is more efficient than the other two methodologies since it does not ask the person to bring any device when they are doing any activity. In any case, there are some challenges in this methodology as well. The major challenge is, for example, obstruction from nature. In the past few years, the sensors are getting faster, cheaper, and smaller which have multiple technologies in it. A study presents active and assistive learning (AAL) highlights the recent technologies and trends in AAL.[3]

Figure 26.1 depicts the general architecture of any Human Activity Recognition system. An instrument of feature extraction figures out any symbolic data extracted from some pictures or any kind of video outlines. At that point, labels are accordingly influenced by these removed highlights by a classifier. The procedure comprises numerous methods that guarantee the productive portrayal of activities.[19]

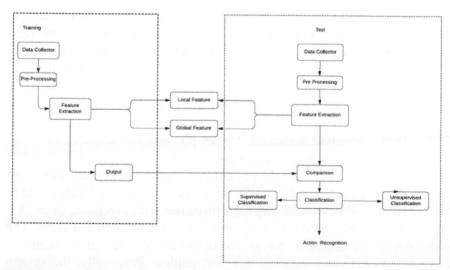

FIGURE 26.1 General architecture of the framework for HAR system.[24]

26.2.2   *VISION-BASED HUMAN ACTION RECOGNITION*

An optimal scheme of recognition of the human action system was suggested.[4] This hypothesis did a thorough investigation of best in class strategies for human activity recognition and proposed a progressive scientific categorization for classifying these techniques. They reviewed various methodologies, for example, uni-modal and multi-modal and as per the source channel each of these methodologies employs perceived human activities.

Vision-based action recognition of humans has pulled in numerous researchers because of its difficulties and heaps of assortment of uses. For instance, the applications may start from straightforward gesture recognition to convoluted behavior understanding in the surveillance framework. This prompts significant improvement in the methods identified with human movement representation and recognition. Another hypothesis underlines human movement representation. Also, it represents some recognition techniques alongside the preferences and drawbacks of these techniques.[5]

Deep, convolutional, and recurrent approaches have been used that beats the cutting edge strategies.[6] They have also provided guidelines for the researchers who want to apply deep learning in their problem solving. An investigation features the advances of the best in class activity recognition approach, essentially for the activity representation and classification techniques. This examination means to give a review of representation and classification strategies and look at them.[7]

A study provides high-quality and learning-based procedures for human activity recognition.[8,9] However, it concludes that studies based on high-quality techniques are not suitable for complex circumstances. Then again, learning-based procedures are more suitable. Preparing a robot that can estimate human pose and trajectory in the near future is another study[10] with the help of dynamic classifier selection architecture. A vision-based gait analysis approach was proposed which can be performed on a smartphone using cloud computing assistance.[11] They planned and actualized a lot of shrewd video surveillance frameworks in the parking environment.[12,13] This audit expects to present the key cutting edge in marker less movement capture investigated from PC vision which has probably a future effect in biomechanics, while considering the difficulties with precision, strength.[14] The framework was used for strange behaviors' recognition and alarm. The technologies introduced are foreground detection, feature extraction, movement behavioral categorization, and recognition. Practically, the system worked well and the identification result of strange behaviors was palatable. An algorithm in the field of deep machine learning, that is, YOLO (you only look once) was developed to reduce the burden of inspectors by automatically detecting crime scenes in video surveillance.[15]

Human activity recognition stays to be a significant issue in computer vision. This is the reason for some applications, for example, video observation, medicinal services, and human computer cooperation. In any case, challenges despite everything exist while confronting sensible views. The hypothesis proposes a reliable technique for activity location and recognition of certifiable observation video datasets.[16] Recently, deep CNNs are used to perceive the activity of humans along with an arrangement of pictures. This theory proposed a capsule neural network to achieve this.[17] To detect and recognize human walking and running motion even in darker surroundings in video streams, a line skeleton scalable model was developed.[18]

Another theory presented a detailed correlation of all the current datasets in this area.[19] A study explores machine learning techniques for the authentication of users by recording different activities, for example, walking, running, sitting, and standing.[20] They proposed a human recognition system by implementing 10 different machine learning algorithms on the HugaDB database. The samples were collected from 18 participants and the system gives 99% accuracy.

A study approves a two-camera open pose-based marker framework for gait investigation by thinking about three variables for exactness: video resolution, relative distance of the camera, and the direction of gait. The study infers that the expansion of camera distance and resolution of video assists with accomplishing the best performances.[21] Another theory assesses the machine learning methods dependent on recurrent neural networks to check fatigue dependent on various repetitive activities.[22]

26.2.3 *LEARNING METHODS FOR HUMAN ACTION RECOGNITION*

HAR is an area of study that has increased noteworthy consideration lately because of the inescapability of sensors, which are presently accessible in smartphones and wearable gadgets.

Activity recognition can be perceived as a classification issue, a typical sort of issue found in supervised learning.[23]

In an investigation, the activity recognition chain (ARC) was proposed[24] in which an arrangement of steps is followed so as to fabricate HAR frameworks as appeared in Figure 26.2. It shows the various advances associated with the ARC.

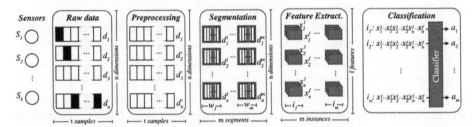

FIGURE 26.2   Steps involved in ARC.[25]

a) According to the execution mode, the framework can be disconnected or on the web. On account of an online framework, the framework can perform activity recognition progressively.

b) According to its speculation capacity, the framework can be client autonomous or client explicit. In client-free cases, the framework ought to have the option to perceive the activity in any event. It is helpful for the kind of clients who are utilizing the framework just for the first time.

c) In accordance with this sort of recognition, this framework can process nonstop floods of information or confined information. In that case, the counterbalance of every activity is recently known.

d) In accordance with the sort of exercises, the exercises could be occasional, irregular, or static.

e) In accordance with the framework model, it tends to be stateless or stateful. On account of stateful, the framework does not exclusively know about the sensor's information yet additionally considers a model of environment.[27]

26.3   MACHINE LEARNING TECHNIQUES

26.3.1   *CLASSIC MACHINE LEARNING TECHNIQUES*

A survey was conducted on the machine learning techniques first for the best in time techniques.[26] As shown in Table 26.1, an outline of decision trees and KNN is presented after conducting the survey.

TABLE 26.1   Outline of Decision Tree and KNN.

Method	Dataset	Model/variation	Accuracy
Iterative Dichotomise 3 Decision Tree (ID3 DT)[26,29]	Using smartphones (accelerometers)	Vector (POS, action)	73.72
		POS (decision tree for the classification of smartphone position)	79.56
		Action (classify activity-position independent)	88.32
K-Nearest Neighbor (KNN)[30]	Online activity recognition framework working at Android stages	KNN algorithm	-
		K-nearest neighbor (clustered)	92

26.3.2   NEURAL NETWORK METHODS

26.3.2.1   ARTIFICIAL NEURAL NETWORKS

In another theory, an information-securing module model has been created.[29] It collects the statistics of the affected person and perceives an abnormal reputation of the affected person's wellbeing with the aim that early remedy might be accessible.

For arm pose recognition,

- Information gadget: Accelerometer installed in smart watch.
- Preprocessing: Filtering, standardization, feature extraction.

Another dataset with various arrangements of accelerometer information and information from pulse sensors was utilized to recognize different exercises.

26.3.2.2   CONVOLUTIONAL NEURAL NETWORKS

In another hypothesis, Convolutional Neural Networks or CNNs are being suggested to group human exercises.[31] These models utilize crude data obtained from many inertial sensors.

They utilized a few blends of exercises, for example, walk, strolling balance, standing parity, and quality. They have likewise investigated sensors to demonstrate how movement signs can be adjusted to be taken care of into CNNs by utilizing diverse system models. Information gadgets utilized are inertial development unit sensors and triaxial sensors.[28]

TABLE 26.2　Summaries of ANN, CNN, and RNN.

Dataset used	Classification of activities	Implementation method	Accuracy
Self-made dataset[31]	Arm movement (forward, upwards, backwards, horizontal)	ANN	100%
Self-made dataset[31]	Sitting left and right lateral recumbent	ANN	99.96%
Different Dataset[26,31]	Standing, Walking (Forward, Backward), Running (Forward, Backward)	ANN	99.08%
Otago exercise dataset[32]	Walk, Walking Balance, Standing Balance, Strength	CNN	Mix of a few sensors produces better outcomes.

26.3.2.3 RECURRENT NEURAL NETWORKS

The theory presented a profound learning model that figures out how to group human exercises without utilizing any earlier information. The examination proposes a Long Short Term Memory (LSTM) RNN that is equipped for remembering things. LSTM was applied to three genuine keen home datasets. The proposed approach outflanks the current ones as far as exactness and execution.[33]

The information gadgets utilized are sensors that are empowered at different areas of the house.

26.4　CONCLUSION

To automatically comprehend and analyze the activities of any human is a fascinating, yet complicated, task. Also, real-life applications in uncontrolled conditions make it more demanding and fascinating. In this paper, an intensive investigation of different procedures has been completed, for example, the strategies that could be utilized in the field of human activity recognition. It incorporated various machine learning algorithms and also various neural network techniques. Various procedures had been applied on various datasets and most of them had changing perceptions that relied on the environmental conditions, kind of information utilized, for example, accelerometer information or online activity recognition framework or any other sensor information, sensor placement, and techniques for execution. It tends to be concluded from this examination that there is no single strategy that is suitable to perceive any activity. Different environmental conditions, position of sensors, and sort of information collected should be considered so as to select a specific method for a particular application. For instance, if information is being gathered by sensors various sensors should be put on by the individual; then the placement of the sensors is another problem. If classification methods are being used, for example, decision trees and the neural networks, over estimation can occur and in case of SVM, under estimation can occur if the data that is available is less trained. In this way, despite having various techniques, certain difficulties stay open and should be resolved.

KEYWORDS

- **human action recognition**
- **machine learning**
- **neural networks**

REFERENCES

1. Hussain, Z.; Sheng, M.; Zhang, W. E. Different Approaches for Human Activity Recognition: A Survey. *arXiv preprint arXiv:1906.05074,* 2019.
2. Wang, S.; Zhou, G. A Review on Radio Based Activity Recognition. *Digital Communications and Networks* **2015,** *1* (1), 20–29.
3. Manoj, T.; Thyagaraju, G. S. Active and Assisted Living: A Comprehensive Review of Enabling Technologies and Scenarios. *Int. J. Adv. Res. Comput. Sci.* **2018,** *9* (1).
4. Vrigkas, M.; Nikou, C.; Kakadiaris, I. A. A Review of Human Activity Recognition Methods. *Front. Robot. AI* **2015,** *2,* 28.
5. Kale, G. V.; Patil, V. H. A Study of Vision Based Human Motion Recognition and Analysis. *IJACI* **2016,** *7* (2), 75–92.
6. Hammerla, N. Y.; Halloran, S.; Plötz, T. Deep, Convolutional, and Recurrent Models for Human Activity Recognition Using Wearables. arXiv preprint arXiv:1604.08880, 2016.
7. Zhang, S.; Wei, Z.; Nie, J.; Huang, L.; Wang, S.; Li, Z. A Review on Human Activity Recognition Using Vision-Based Method. *J. Healthcare Eng.* 2017.
8. Sargano, A. B.; Angelov, P.; Habib, Z. A Comprehensive Review on Handcrafted and Learning-Based Action Representation Approaches for Human Activity Recognition. *Appl. Sci.* **2017,** *7* (1), 110.
9. Jiang, W.; Yin, Z. Human Activity Recognition Using Wearable Sensors by Deep Convolutional Neural Networks. In *Proceedings of the 23rd ACM International Conference on Multimedia,* Oct 2015; pp 1307–1310.

10. Perera, A. G.; Law, Y. W.; Al-Naji, A.; Chahl, J. Human Motion Analysis from UAV Video. *Int. J. Intell. Unmanned Syst.* **2018**.
11. Nieto-Hidalgo, M.; Ferrández-Pastor, F. J.; Valdivieso-Sarabia, R. J.; Mora-Pascual, J.; García-Chamizo, J. M. Gait Analysis Using Computer Vision Based on Cloud Platform and Mobile Device. *Mobile Inform Syst* **2018**.
12. Xu, H.; Li, L.; Fang, M.; Zhang, F. Movement Human Actions Recognition Based on Machine Learning. *IJOE* **2018**, *14* (04), 193–210.
13. Khan, A.; Janwe, M. N. Review on Moving Object Detection in Video Surveillance. *Int. J. Adv. Res. Comput. Commun. Eng.* **2017**, 664–670.
14. Colyer, S. L.; Evans, M.; Cosker, D. P.; Salo, A. I. A Review of the Evolution of Vision-Based Motion Analysis and the Integration of Advanced Computer Vision Methods Towards Developing a Markerless System. *Sports Med.-Open* **2018**, *4* (1), 24.
15. Cui, Y. Using Deep Machine Learning to Conduct Object-Based Identification and Motion Detection on Safeguards Video Surveillance (No.BNL-207942–2018-COPA). Brookhaven National Laboratory (BNL), Upton, NY, 2018.
16. Kumaran, N.; Reddy, U. S.; Kumar, S. S. Multiple Action Recognition for Human Object with Motion Video Sequence using the Properties of HSV Color Space Applying with Region of Interest, 2019.
17. Basu, A.; Petropoulakis, L.; Di Caterina, G.; Soraghan, J. Indoor Home Scene Recognition Using Capsule Neural Networks. *Procedia Comput. Sci.* **2020**, *167*, 440–448.
18. Yong, C. Y.; Chew, K. M.; Sudirman, R. Human Motion Analysis in Dark Surrounding Using Line Skeleton Scalable Model and Vector Angle Technique. *Mater. Today* **2019**, *16*, 1732–1741.
19. Jegham, I.; Khalifa, A. B.; Alouani, I.; Mahjoub, M. A. Vision-Based Human Action Recognition: An Overview and Real World Challenges. *Forensic Sci. Int.* **2020**, *32*, 200901.
20. Kececi, A.; Yildirak, A.; Ozyazici, K.; Ayluctarhan, G.; Agbulut, O.; Zincir, I. Implementation of Machine Learning Algorithms for Gait Recognition. *Eng. Sci. Technol. Int. J.* **2020**.
21. Zago, M.; Luzzago, M.; Marangoni, T.; De Cecco, M.; Tarabini, M.; Galli, M. 3D Tracking of Human Motion Using Visual Skeletonization and Stereoscopic Vision. *Front. Bioeng. Biotechnol.* **2020**, *8*, 181.
22. Hernandez, G.; Valles, D.; Wierschem, D. C.; Koldenhoven, R. M.; Koutitas, G.; Mendez, F. A. et al. Machine Learning Techniques for Motion Analysis of Fatigue from Manual Material Handling Operations Using 3D Motion Capture Data. In *2020 10th Annual Computing and Communication Workshop and Conference (CCWC).* IEEE, Jan 2020; pp 0300–0305.
23. Baldominos, A.; Cervantes, A.; Saez, Y.; Isasi, P. A Comparison of Machine Learning and Deep Learning Techniques for Activity Recognition using Mobile Devices. *Sensors* **2019**, *19* (3), 521.
24. Bulling, A.; Blanke, U.; Schiele, B. A Tutorial on Human Activity Recognition Using Body-Worn Inertial Sensors. *ACM Comput. Surveys (CSUR)* **2014**, *46* (3), 1–33.
25. Saez, Y.; Baldominos, A.; Isasi, P. A Comparison Study of Classifier Algorithms for Cross-Person Physical Activity Recognition. *Sensors* **2017**, *17* (1), 66.
26. Jobanputra, C.; Bavishi, J.; Doshi, N. Human Activity Recognition: A Survey. *Procedia Comput. Sci.* **2019**, *155*, 698–703.

27. Hara, K.; Kataoka, H.; Satoh, Y. Can Spatiotemporal 3D CNNS Retrace the History of 2D CNNS and Imagenet? In *Proceedings of the IEEE Conference on Computer Vision and Pattern Recognition*, 2018; pp 6546–6555.

28. Cho, H.; Yoon, S. M. Divide and Conquer-Based 1D CNN Human Activity Recognition Using Test Data Sharpening. *Sensors* **2018,** *18* (4), 1055.

29. Fan, L.; Wang, Z.; Wang, H. Human Activity Recognition Model Based on Decision Tree. In *2013 International Conference on Advanced Cloud and Big Data*; IEEE, Dec 2013; pp 64–68.

30. Paul, P.; George, T. An Effective Approach for Human Activity Recognition on Smartphone. In *2015 IEEE International Conference on Engineering and Technology (ICETECH)*; IEEE Mar 2015; pp 1–3.

31. Oniga, S.; Sütő, J. Human Activity Recognition Using Neural Networks. In *Proceedings of the 2014 15th International Carpathian Control Conference (ICCC)*; IEEE, 2014 May; pp 403–406.

32. Bevilacqua, A.; MacDonald, K.; Rangarej, A.; Widjaya, V.; Caulfield, B.; Kechadi, T. Human Activity Recognition with Convolutional Neural Networks. In *Joint European Conference on Machine Learning and Knowledge Discovery in Databases*; Springer: Cham, Sept 2018; pp 541–552.

33. Singh, D.; Merdivan, E.; Psychoula, I.; Kropf, J.; Hanke, S.; Geist, M.; Holzinger, A. Human Activity Recognition Using Recurrent Neural Networks. In *International Cross-Domain Conference for Machine Learning and Knowledge Extraction*; Springer: Cham, Aug 2017; pp 267–274.

CHAPTER 27

Fog-Based Intelligent Traffic Phase Timing Regulation System

SAHIL[1] and SANDEEP KUMAR SOOD[2]

[1]*Department of Computer Science and Engineering,*
Guru Nanak Dev University Regional Campus, Gurdaspur, Punjab, India

[2]*Department of Computer Applications, National Institute of Technology,*
Kurukshetra, Haryana, India

ABSTRACT

Vehicular traffic mismanagement impacts the various essential services. It causes traffic errors, massive traffic jams, and congestions on roads. The real-time automated monitoring and analysis of traffic is the key to various challenges due to traffic mismanagement. In this paper, an intelligent framework using Fog-Cloud centric Internet of Things (IoT) is proposed for traffic management in urban spaces. This system initially monitors vehicle mobility in real time at the fog layer and immediately classifies the in-schedule reachability (*ISR*) of the vehicles. This *ISR* classification determines the ability of the vehicle to reach the traffic signal point down the lane before the start of the green phase. After identifying the reachability of the vehicle, the framework predicts the traffic at the signal point before the start of the next green phase at the remote cloud servers. Based on the predicted traffic at the traffic signal point, the system adapts the green phase time at the traffic signal point of the respective lane. The framework uses the J48 decision tree for *ISR* classification at the fog layer and a proposed approach

Computational Intelligence in Analytics and Information Systems, Volume 1: Data Science and AI, Selected Papers from CIAIS-2021. Hardeo Kumar Thakur, Manpreet Kaur, Parneeta Dhaliwal, Rajeev Kumar Arya, and Joan Lu (Eds.)

for traffic prediction at the cloud layer. The result analysis acknowledges the efficiency of J48 as compared to other employed classifiers, namely, accuracy, sensitivity, specificity, and F-measure. The optimal performance of the traffic inflow prediction and subsequently the adaptation of the green phase accordingly acknowledge the utility of the proposed approach for real-time traffic regulation.

27.1   INTRODUCTION

The inclination of people toward urbanization has changed the demographic structure of the world. As a result, more people are migrating to urban spaces. According to a United Nations' report, currently, more than half of the world's human population is living in urban areas, and the number is expected to rise to 86% in the developed countries and 67% in developing countries by 2050.[1] This transition has presented various new challenges in the urban spaces, that is, water pollution,[2] air pollution,[3] increased energy consumption,[4] garbage mismanagement,[5] and vehicular traffic mismanagement.[6]

Various essential services like health, education, food, and economy are highly dependent on road-transportation. The increasing number of vehicles on the road are deteriorating the traffic management situation everywhere and harming many walks of life.[6] This scenario is even worse in urban areas, where more people are migrating to and use road transportation as the primary mode for most of their daily activities. Traffic mismanagement causes various traffic errors, massive traffic jams, and congestion and plagues the transportation system and road safety around the world.[7] This can be well depicted from a report on urban mobility that states that traffic mismanagement caused an economic loss of 2.9 billion gallons of fuel and time wastage of 5.5 billion hours in traffic jams from 2000 to 2010.[8] This paper addresses the above-stated issue by proposing a dynamic and intelligent traffic regulation system using Fog-Cloud centric Internet of Things (IoT). The system is designed to provide a ubiquitous, real-time, and area-wide traffic regulation solution based on traffic mobility on roads. It uses adaptive traffic phase time planning and helps in providing optimized and dynamic green phases for improved traffic regulation on roads.

The recent advancements in sensor technology, wireless communications, resource provisioning, and computation approaches have made it possible for vehicles to acquire and process the ubiquitous information and represent it into useful intelligence for various applications.[9] Intelligent Transport System (ITS) is the one such domain, where vehicles carry sensing capability, on-board computing facility, storage power and communication capabilities to address different transportation-related challenges.[10] The IoT is considered one of the breakthroughs in data acquisition and communication advancements.[11,12] The capability of IoT to use sensor technology and internet communication makes it the basis for various independent and cooperative services.[13] The utility of IoT can be proved from the extensive research of IoT-based systems in various domains, that is, healthcare,[14] disaster management,[15] and education.[16] The real-time monitoring capability of IoT makes it suitable for inclusion in traffic regulation. IoT offers to monitor various traffic dynamics on the road for various applications like driving behavior analysis and logistics management.

The collaboration of Cloud-Fog computing with IoT further enables the framework to monitor the traffic dynamics from remote sites in real time and provide useful insights for various analyses.[17] Cloud Computing provides scalable remote shared resources, secure communication, parallel processing, and data integration services with scalable data storage to manage and analyze enormous and continuous data.[18] The incorporation of Fog computing,[19] along with Cloud, provides delay-sensitive and location-aware computation for real-time decision-making. Furthermore, this kind of collaborative system transforms the acquired data into valuable intelligence based on various data mining approaches and supports the decision-making process.

In vehicular traffic regulation, the traffic movement phase design plays a significant role and is considered the foundation pillar. The adaptive traffic movement phase planning can accommodate the maximum possible vehicles to pass in a single green phase to avoid long waiting queues based on inflow traffic analysis. The real-time traffic dynamics interception and area-wide traffic scenario representation can make it possible for a traffic regulation system to work smartly. The proposed framework consists of four layers: sensor, fog, cloud, and communication. In the sensor layer, IoT acquires vehicle mobility data. For delay-sensitive and location-aware computation, fog computing is used at the fog layer. It avoids the communication overhead to process data in the cloud by providing localized and immediate computing.[20] The fog layer classifies the In-Schedule Reachability (*ISR*) of the vehicle to the signal point down the lane in real time. The cloud layer predicts the traffic by predicting waiting time (*waTime*), waiting queue length (*waQLen*), and the next green phase time span (*AdGPT*) for the signal point down the lane. The communication layer communicates the *AdGPT* to the signal regulating unit (SRU) of the respective lane. The SRU uses the predicted *AdGPT* to regulate the next green phase of the respective lane accordingly. The proposed framework has been designed to incorporate smart solutions in traffic regulation with the following contributions.

- The system uses Fog-Cloud centric IoT for providing real-time smart traffic regulation solutions.
- The system classifies the In-Schedule Reachability (*ISR*) of the vehicle in real time using mobility data at the fog layer of the vehicle.
- The system predicts and adapts the time duration of the next green phase of the traffic signal points at the cloud layer.

The paper is compiled into six sections. Section 27.2 reviews some significant related works to the current study. Section 27.3 discusses the system design for the proposed approach. Section 27.4 discusses the layers of the proposed framework. Section 27.5 discusses the experimental setup and performance evaluation of the proposed framework, followed by the conclusion in Section 27.6.

27.2   RELATED WORKS

In 2017, Bui et al.[21] used the synchronization theory of processes to exchange messages between connected objects (pedestrians, vehicles, and traffic regulation system) to synchronize other objects while one object is passing an intersection. This real-time traffic flow information helps the traffic regulation system to regulate traffic at intersections using the adaptive traffic phase movement. In 2017, Zambrano- Martinez et al.[22] proposed a framework to characterize the street segments by analyzing the traffic behavior based on the travel time of the vehicle using regression. Furthermore, based on the characterization of street segments and inflow traffic, the framework predicts the traffic time in a particular area of the city. In 2016, Wan et al.[23] proposed a framework for connected vehicles, where vehicles are guided by Speed Advisory System (SAS) using the traffic phase time sequences for reaching at the intersection only during the green phase. In 2017, Ahmad et al.[24] presented a study related to vehicular cloud computing-based traffic regulation. This study represents a comparison of various state-of-the-art traffic regulation systems, future challenges, and emerging technologies like the Internet of Vehicles for traffic regulation. In 2018, Perez et al.[25] presented a decentralized Fog-Cloud-based traffic regulation and forecasting model using Conditional Restricted Boltzmann Machines (CRBM). In 2019, Ning et al.[26] had designed an architecture that senses traffic jams, road surface damages, and car accidents broadcast to all vehicles using fog computing and cloud computing. This architecture uses RSUs as fog nodes to balance the computation load among cloudlets and minimize the response delay for traffic regulation message flows.

27.3 SYSTEM DESIGN

The proposed framework is based on a road network that comprises two lanes at each road with one lane for downstream traffic and one lane for upstream traffic. The road network employs Signal Regulating Unit (SRU) at each intersection, where four roads from all four directions intersect; traffic signal points for each lane, situated at the intersection down the lane; Road Side Units (RSUs) alongside each lane, situated equidistant; and loop detector for each lane situated at the intersection down the lane. The SRU regulates the duration of each traffic phase of the lanes for facilitating vehicular traffic management through their respective traffic signal points at that intersection. The loop detectors down the lane determine the count of vehicles that cross a particular cross-section of that lane, so it could provide the count for the vehicles waiting at that lane's respective intersection to move further. The proposed framework uses three traffic movement phases for regulating vehicular traffic as follows.

1. **Red Phase:** It halts vehicles' movement at the traffic signal point by flashing red light at that traffic signal point.
2. **Yellow Phase:** It indicates the halted vehicles to get ready for moving further by flashing yellow light at the traffic signal point. This phase starts after the end of the red phase at a traffic signal point.
3. **Green Phase:** It allows the vehicles to cross the traffic signal point by flashing green light at that traffic signal point. This phase starts after the end of the yellow phase, and when this green phase ends, it triggers the red phase to initiate.

In this manner, all three phases at an intersection are transitioned in a round-robin manner.

The road network of the proposed framework comprises four traffic signal points at each intersection. The framework considers each traffic signal point's initial green phase as a fixed time span, that is, G seconds. Each consecutive traffic signal point at an intersection is marked with a number in the sequence of 0, 1, 2, and 3, such that the green phase transitioned from one traffic signal to the next numbered traffic signal point in a round-robin manner, and only one traffic signal point enters into green phase at any instance, at that intersection. For regulating the next time span of the green phase at each traffic signal point (P) based on the traffic inflow, the framework collects the traffic mobility data on its respective lane during the green phase at the next two traffic signal points, that is, at $((P+1)\bmod 4)$th and $((P+2)\bmod 4)$th. This data collection phase is represented as the data collection (DatC) phase (as shown in Figure 27.1). At the end of the DatC phase, the determined traffic-inflow-based waiting time at the Pth traffic signal point for the next green phase is considered Adapted next Green Phase Time span ($AdGPT$) for the Pth traffic signal point. The framework communicates this determined $AdGPT$ to the respective SRU during the $((P+3)\bmod 4)$th green phase (as shown in Figure 27.1). Based on the received $AdGPT$, the SRU regulates the next green phase time span at the Pth traffic signal point. The activity of communicating the determined $AdGPT$ and regulating the next green phase time span is considered as the decision propagation and adaptation (DePA) phase. In this manner, the system design of the proposed framework by integrating different ICT-based paradigms facilitates the regulation of traffic phase timing for providing intelligent vehicular traffic management.

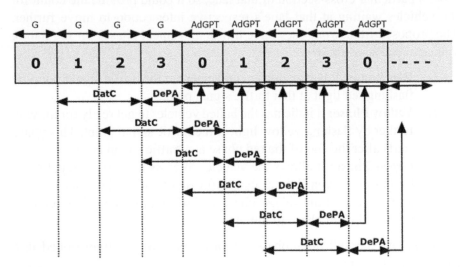

FIGURE 27.1   Traffic phase design.

27.4   PROPOSED FRAMEWORK

The proposed framework is divided into four layers: sensor, fog, cloud, and communication (as shown in Figure 27.2). In the sensor layer, the deployed sensors in the vehicles collect the mobility data of the vehicles. The fog layer is present between the sensor layer and the cloud layer. This layer bridges the computation delay of the cloud layer by bringing the computation infrastructure closer to the data origin at the edge of the network. This layer is present on each vehicle and provides delay-sensitive and location-aware computation in real time without sending the data to the cloud for computation. In the proposed framework, this layer classifies the in-schedule reachability (*ISR*) of the vehicle based on the data from the sensor layer and sends the *ISR* classification of the vehicle to the cloud layer along with other mobility data. At the cloud layer, vehicle mobility and *ISR* classified data are stored at cloud storage, so the data could be used for traffic prediction and accessed globally for various traffic-related analyses. The predicted results are also stored at cloud storage for communication to SRU. The communication layer shares the *AdGPT* of the traffic signal point with the respective SRU for adapting the next green phase time span of the respective signal point based on the traffic inflow. Each layer of the proposed framework is explained in detail as follows.

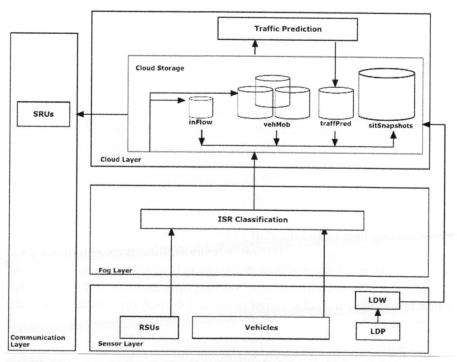

FIGURE 27.2 Proposed traffic regulation framework.

27.4.1   SENSOR LAYER

The responsibility of sensor layer in the proposed framework is to collect the mobility data of the vehicles, namely, the location (*vehL*) and velocity ($\ddot{v}$) of the vehicle. But the vehicle's OBU determines the acceleration/deceleration ($\ddot{a}$) continuously using collected mobility data, as shown in Eq. 1.

$$\ddot{a} = \frac{\ddot{v}_c - \ddot{v}_I}{T} \tag{27.1}$$

where $\ddot{v}_c$ is vehicle's current velocity, $\ddot{v}_I$ is vehicle's initial velocity, and T is the time taken by the vehicle for changing the velocity from its initial value ($\ddot{v}_I$) to current value ($\ddot{v}_c$).

The RSUs provide the lane id (*lanID*) to the OBU of the vehicle when that vehicle approaches it and trigger the OBU to relay the updated mobility data, namely, $\ddot{a}$, $\ddot{v}$, *vehL* along with *lanID* and *vehID* to the fog layer. The loop detectors for the waiting vehicles (LDW) down the lane determine the count of vehicles (*nVeh*) that cross a particular cross section of that lane and are waiting at that lane's respective intersection for moving further. LDW continuously sends the *nVeh* to the cloud layer.

27.4.2   FOG LAYER

Based on the received mobility data of the vehicle, the fog layer determines the *ISR* class by comparing the measure of Time to Reach (*T2R*) with the measure of remaining Time Before the start of Green phase (*TBG*), as shown in Algorithm 1. *T2R* represents the required time by the vehicle to reach the signal point down the lane based on the current mobility data, that is, $\ddot{v}$ and $\ddot{a}$, and the current distance between the vehicle and the traffic signal point down the lane (*dVehS*) as shown in Eq. 27.2. On the other side, *TBG* depicts the remaining time before the start of the next green phase at the *Pth* traffic signal point, for which computation is being facilitated for determining the traffic inflow-based adapted next green phase time span. The fog layer uses the difference between timestamps: starting time instance of the next green phase (t_G) at the *Pth* traffic signal point and current time instance (t_C), for determining *TBG*.

$$T2R = \frac{2 * \ddot{v} \pm \sqrt{4 * (\ddot{v})^2 - 8 * \ddot{a} * dVehS}}{2 * \ddot{a}} \tag{27.2}$$

Fog layer employs online map services to determine *dVehS* based on *vehL* and location of the traffic signal point down the lane. Foglayer uses *lanID* to locate the location of the respective lane's signal point. The fog layer employs Algorithm 27.1 during the DatC phase to determine the *ISR* class of a vehicle. In this algorithm, if it is found that the vehicle is reaching the signal point before the start of the next green phase, then its *ISR* class is set as Reaching (*RC*), and consideration for traffic prediction (*conTP*) status is set as Yes (*Y*). Otherwise, the *ISR* class is set as Not Reaching (*NRC*), and *conTP* is set as No (*N*). Once the *ISR* class and the *conTP* status are determined, these analytics and the mobility data are sent to the cloud layer.

Algorithm 27.1: In-Schedule Reachability Determination
Input: *v̈, dVehS, ä, vehID*
Output: *ISR* class and *conTP status*
Step 1: Determine vehicle's *T2R* using Eq. 2;   **Step 2:** Check if DatC phase is over, If not   **Step 2.1:** Determine *TBG* as, $TBG = t_G - t_C$;   **Step 2.2:** If *T2R* is smaller than *TBG* i.e. *T2R<TBG*   **Step 2.2.1:** Set, *ISR(vehID)=RC* and *conTP(vehID)=Y;*   **Step 2.3:** Otherwise, set *ISR(vehID)=NRC* and *conTP(vehID)=N;*

27.4.3 CLOUD LAYER

The classified traffic data, along with other mobility information from the fog layer, arrives into the cloud. At the cloud layer, the data is stored in globally accessible cloud storage. The traffic prediction component predicts the traffic at the signal points down the lanes using data from cloud storage and stores the prediction results back to the cloud storage to share with respective SRUs through the communication layer. Each component of the cloud layer is explained in detail as follows.

27.4.3.1 CLOUD STORAGE

The fog-relayed mobility-related data is stored at the cloud storage in a categorical manner in the vehMob dataset as shown in Table 27.1. It contains *ü, ä, lanID, vehID, vehL, dVehS, ISR* class, *conTP* status, and data source identity (*DSI*). *DSI* helps the framework to identify the source of data, that is, LDW, vehicle's fog layer or traffic prediction component. *lanID* identifies that to which lane the mobility data of a vehicle belongs and helps the cloud storage to maintain the mobility data lane-wise in the vehMob dataset. Similarly, *vehID* uniquely identifies the data related to a particular vehicle. On the other side, the LDW-relayed data to the cloud contains *lanID, nVeh*, and *DSI, and* it stores ininFlow dataset. There, the *lanID* identifies to which lane the traffic inflow data of the vehicles belong and helps the cloud storage maintain the traffic inflow data (*nVeh*) lane-wise. Data from the traffic prediction component of the cloud layer contains *lanID*, waiting time (*waTime*), waiting queue length(*waQLen*), *AdGPT, and DSI* and is stored in traffPred dataset. *DSI* indicates that the source of data is the traffic prediction component and *lanID* identifies that of which lane the prediction has been converged and helps in storing the related predicted *waTime, waQLen, and AdGPT* lane-wise. The data in vehMob, inflow, and traffPred datasets depicts the current situation and keeps on changing. Hence, the cloud storage maintains the snapshots of the current situations from these datasets in sitSnapshots dataset on a temporary basis.

TABLE 27.1   Traffic Mobility-Related Datasets.

S. No.	Dataset	Attributes
1.	vehMob	*ü, ä, lanID, vehID, vehL, dVehS, ISR* class, *conTP* status, and *DSI*
2.	inFlow	*lanID, nVeh*, and *DSI*
3.	traffPred	*lanID, waTime, waQLen, AdGPT, and DSI*
4.	sitSnapshots	Snapshots of the current situations from vehMob, inflow, and traffPred

27.4.3.2   TRAFFIC PREDICTION

Algorithm 27.2: Cloud-based adaptive green phase time span prediction
Input: *lanID*, vehMob and last snapshot of vehMob
Output: *waTime, waQLen* and *AdGPT*
Step 1: Set initial *waQLen* as the vehicle count indicated by LDW i.e. *waQLen =nVeh;*
Step 2: Until the end of DatC phase
Step 2.1: If *ISR(vehID)==RC*

Step 2.1.1: If *conTP(vehID)=Y* from the last snapshot of the given *lanID* in vehMob dataset

Step 2.1.1.1: No need to change the count of vehicles in *waQLen;*

Step 2.1.2: Otherwise, *waQLen + +;*

Step 2.2: Elseif *ISR(vehID)==NRC*

Step 2.2.1: If *conTP(vehID)=Y* from the last snapshot of the given *lanID* in vehMob dataset

Step 2.2.1.1: *waQLen - -;*

Step 2.2.2: Otherwise, no need to change the count of vehicles in *waQLen;*

Step 2.3: Determine *TSCT* for the entire considered set of vehicles for crossing a signal point area, as Step 2.3.1: $TSCT = \text{waQLen} * 2 \left(\dfrac{k}{\ddot{v}_S} \right);$

Step 2.4: Determine *TBG* as, $TBG = t_G - t_C;$

Step 2.5: Determine *waTime* as, *waTime = TSCT + TBG;*

Step 3: At the end of DataC phase, consider *AdGPT =waTime;*

The traffic prediction component of the cloud layer employs the *ISR* class and the *conTP* status of the vehicles, and *nVeh* count lane-wise to predict the *waTime, waQLen,* and *AdGPT,* as shown in Algorithm 27.2. In this algorithm, all vehicles which are expected to arrive before the end of DataC phase and the vehicles which are waiting at the traffic signal point indicated by *nVeh* count are considered for predicting the *waQLen* at the traffic signal point before the end of the DataC phase. Based on the determined *waQLen,* the algorithm determines the time required for the entire set of considered vehicles to cross the traffic signal point, where a certain distance (*k*) and a particular speed limit ($\ddot{v}_S$) are considered during the crossing of a traffic signal point, so it could be assured that the vehicle has passed the traffic signal point. This time is stated as Traffic at Signal Clearing Time (*TSCT*). Using *TSCT* and *TBG, waTime* is predicted continuously during the entire DataC phase for a traffic signal point (as shown in Algorithm 27.2). When the DataC phase ends, the algorithm considers the last predicted *waTime* as *AdGPT,* and stores the predicted *waTime, waQLen,* and *AdGPT* at the cloud storage. After the convergence of *AdGPT,* this component stores the *waTime, waQLen,* and *AdGPT* in the traffPred dataset.

27.4.3.3   COMMUNICATION LAYER

At the end of the DataC phase, once the traffic analytics provided by the traffic prediction component are available at the cloud storage, the communication layer provides the predicted *AdGPT* of the lane to its respective SRU. This communication and adaptation of *AdGPT* and the next green phase time span, respectively, occurred under the DePA phase. At the end of the DePA phase, the snapshot of vehMob data of the lane is saved to sitSnapshots dataset and vehMob is emptied to again get populated during its next DataC phase. The proposed framework also employs loop detectors (LDP) for determining the count of vehicles which have crossed the traffic signal point (*nPVeh*). The LDP of the respective lane at the end of the DataC phase communicates *nPVeh* to the LDW of that lane, so the *nVeh* count could be updated to depict the actual count of vehicles that are still waiting at the traffic signal point. After communicating the *nPVeh,* the LDP resets its count.

27.5   EXPERIMENTAL SETUP AND PERFORMANCE EVALUATION

Experimentation and evaluation of the proposed system are divided into three parts: (1) data generation, (2) in-schedule reachability classification efficiency, and (3) traffic prediction evaluation. Each phase of this section is explained as follows.

27.5.1   DATA GENERATION

For experimental evaluation of the adaptive traffic phase time planning, mobility data of the vehicles was required. But due to the nonavailability of the mobility data of interest, a mathematical model has been adopted to generate mobility data, where it has been assumed that the RSUs are located at every 500 m apart along the lane. The length of each lane is 5 km. The speed limit is considered a significant parameter for traffic management. Hence, it is set to 80 km/h. Acceleration/deceleration ($\ddot{a}$) is dependent on two factors: Change in velocity ($\Delta\ddot{v}$) and time taken (T). So, it is required to consider all variations in T and $\Delta\ddot{v}$ between two consecutive RSUs for acceleration/deceleration range assertion using Eq. 1 and Eq. 27.3.

$$T_{CR} = \frac{dCR}{\ddot{v}} \tag{27.3}$$

where dCR is the distance between two consecutive RSUs or two points. $\ddot{v}$ is the velocity of the vehicle. T_{CR} is the time taken to cover the distance between two consecutive RSUs or two points.

Using extreme cases of $\Delta\ddot{v}$ and time (T_{CR}) taken between two consecutive RSUs, the acceleration has been determined. Similarly, for deceleration, the range has been established in the same ways using initial velocity higher as compared to the final velocity. Using these well-defined mathematical logics, the ranges for velocity, distance, and acceleration/deceleration have been determined for data generation. For data generation, the records have been taken in such a way that no two records are matched. Based on the taken mobility data, *T2R* of every vehicle has been calculated using Eq.27.2, and the reachability class of every vehicle has been determined using Algorithm 27.1. The algorithm assigns a random *conTP* status to each vehicle and determines the effect of each vehicle's *ISR* class and *conTP* status on *waQLen* using Algorithm 27.2. The generated data has been considered the final snapshot of the mobility parameter with the classified *ISR* class and the effect on *waQLen* at the end of the DatC phase for the experimental evaluation of the employed techniques.

27.5.2 IN-SCHEDULE REACHABILITY CLASSIFICATION EFFICIENCY

The *ISR* classification at fog classifies the vehicle's on-time reachability into two classes: *RC* and *NRC*. The classification determines whether the vehicle will reach before the start of the next green phase or not. The proposed framework employs J48 decision tree to classify the inflow traffic in weka 3.8.2 on an Intel QuadCore i3 machine. It uses the ten folds cross-validation to obtain results. The J48 has been compared with three other employed baseline classifiers: K-means clustering (KMC), ZeroR, and Decision Tables (DeT) in weka. The evaluation compares the performance of J48 with the other three classifiers using four statistical measures: Accuracy (correctly classified instance rate), Sensitivity (true positive rate), Specificity (true negative rate), and F-measure. The comparison of the statistical measures from the implementation of four classifiers has been shown in Figure 27.3. The results clearly depict the utility of J48 as compared to the other classifiers. As far as the above-discussed statistical measures are concerned, J48 outperforms the other three employed classifiers. The evaluation results of the classification depict that the J48 can efficiently classify the *ISR* class of the vehicles using mobility data.

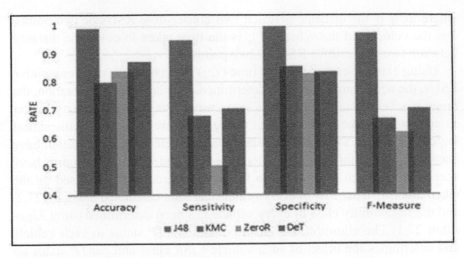

FIGURE 27.3   ISR classification performance.

27.5.3   *TRAFFIC PREDICTION EVALUATION*

The traffic prediction component predicts the traffic inflow at the traffic signal point and helps in adapting the next green phase time span of the respective signal point. Based on the simulated traffic inflow and randomness in their mobility, the proposed algorithm 2 has been employed to predict the traffic waiting time at the four signal points of a particular intersection. Based on the predicted waiting times, the green phases on those signal points have been adapted accordingly to allow the considered traffic to pass. Based on the numerical calculation of vehicle passing during the adapted green phase (*rth*_Adap) and during the fixed green phase (*rth*_Fix), for the same traffic inflow, a comparison of the number of vehicles that remained waiting on the signal point after the completion of green phase has been depicted in Fig. 27.4, for a sequence (SQ) of green phases on those traffic signal points. The results clearly depict that the *AdGPT* facilitates maximum traffic to pass and subsequently lesser waiting for the remaining vehicles. The results are the clear indication of dynamic and intelligent traffic regulation on the intersections based on the traffic inflow.

27.6   CONCLUSION

In urban areas, vehicular traffic regulation is crucial for ensuring the in-time delivery of various essential services like education, healthcare, food, and economy. In this paper, an intelligent system for traffic inflow classification and prediction at the traffic signal points has been presented by incorporating Fog, Cloud and IoT paradigms. By predicting traffic inflow, the system adapts the green phase time span on the respective signal point. The proposed system has been experimentally evaluated for traffic reachability classification and traffic prediction. The result analyses clearly acknowledge the performance of J48 for classification and the proposed approach for traffic inflow prediction. The system is open to several enhancements like the environmental conditions-based infotainment content caching and several scenarios for the electric vehicles (EV) domain. The proposed system has a vivid scope for many future studies.

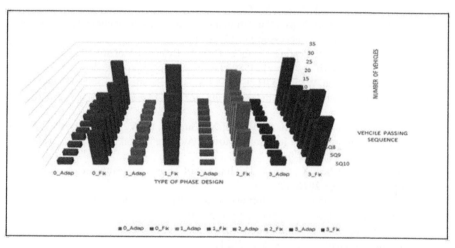

FIGURE 27.4 Performance of predicted adaptive green phase time spans.

KEYWORDS

- **fog computing**
- **intelligent traffic management**
- **intelligent transportation system**
- **cloud computing**
- **internet of things**

REFERENCES

1. World Population Prospects. https://population.un.org/wpp/Publications/Files/WPP2012_ HIGHLIGHTS.pdf (accessed Jan 15, 2021).
2. Zinia, N.; Kroeze, C. Future Trends in Urbanization and Coastal Water Pollution in the Bay of Bengal: The Lived Experience. *Environ. Dev. Sustain.* **2014,** *17* (3), 531–546.
3. Zhong, S.; Qian, Y.; Sarangi, C.; Zhao, C.; Leung, R.; Wang, H.; Yan, H.; Yang, T.; Yang, B. Urbanization Effect On Winter Haze In The Yangtze River Delta Region Of China. *Geophysical Research Letters* **2018,** *45* (13), 6710–6718.
4. Franco, S.; Mandla, V.; Ram Mohan Rao, K. Urbanization, Energy Consumption and Emissions in the Indian Context a Review. *Renew. Sustain. Energy Rev.* **2017,** *71*, 898–907.
5. Jyothi, P.; Vatsala, G.; Gupta, R. Goal Programming Model to Budgetary Allocation in Garbage Disposal Plant. *Asset Analy.* **2018,** 77–90.
6. Agyapong, F.; Ojo, T. Managing Traffic Congestion in the Accra Central Market, Ghana. *J. Urban Manage.* **2018,** *7* (2), 85–96.
7. Urban Mobility Report. https://static.tti.tamu.edu/tti.tamu.edu/documents/umr/archive/ mobility-report-2012.pdf (accessed Jan 15, 2021).
8. Litman, T. Congestion Costing Critique: Critical Evaluation of the "Urban Mobility Report". https://trid.trb.org/view/1245892 (accessed Jan 15, 2021).
9. Chen, L.; Hu, X.; Tian, W.; Wang, H.; Cao, D.; Wang, F. Parallel Planning: A New Motion Planning Framework for Autonomous Driving. *IEEE/CAA J. Automatica Sinica* **2019,** *6* (1), 236–246.
10. Sun, G.; Song, L.; Yu, H.; Chang, V.; Du, X.; Guizani, M. V2V Routing in a VANET Based on the Autoregressive Integrated Moving Average Model. *IEEE Trans. Vehicular Technol.* **2019,** *68* (1), 908–922.
11. Yin, Y.; Zeng, Y.; Chen, X.; Fan, Y. The Internet of Things in Healthcare: An Overview. *J. Ind. Inform. Integr.* **2016,** *1*, 3–13.
12. Sahil; Sood, S. Bibliometric Monitoring of Research Performance in ICT-Based Disaster Management Literature. *Qual. Quan.* **2021,** *55*, 103–132.
13. Kaur, A.; Sahil; Sood, S. Cloud-Fog Assisted Energy Efficient Architectural Paradigm for Disaster Evacuation. *Inform. Syst.* 2021.
14. Sood, S.; Sood, V.; Mahajan, I.; Sahil. Fog–Cloud Assisted IoT-Based Hierarchical Approach for Controlling Dengue Infection. *Comput. J.* 2020.
15. Neelam, S.; Sood, S. A Scientometric Review of Global Research on Smart Disaster Management. *IEEE Transa. Eng. Manage.* **2021,** *68* (1), 317–329.
16. Sood, S.; Singh, K. An Optical-Fog Assisted EEG-Based Virtual Reality Framework for Enhancing E-Learning Through Educational Games. *Comput. App. Eng. Educ.* **2018,** *26* (5), 1565–1576.
17. Sahil; Sood, S. Fog-assisted Energy Efficient Cyber Physical System for Panic-based Evacuation during Disasters. *Comput. J.* **2021.**
18. Dogra, S.; Sood, S.; Mehmi, S.; Sahil. A New Approach To Design User-Driven Security Pricing Model In Cloud Computing. In *2016 International Conference on Computing, Communication and Automation (ICCCA)*, 2016.
19. Sood, S.; Sood, V.; Mahajan, I.; Sahil. An Intelligent Healthcare System for Predicting and Preventing Dengue Virus Infection. *Computing* 2021.
20. Sahil; Sood, S. Fog-Cloud Centric IoT-Based Cyber Physical Framework for Panic Oriented Disaster Evacuation in Smart Cities. *Earth Sci. Inform.* **2020.**

21. Bui, K.-H. N.; Camacho, D.; Jung, J. E. Real-Time Traffic Flow Management Based on Inter-Object Communication: A Case Study at Intersection. *Mobile Netw. App.* **2017,** *22* (4), 613–624.
22. Zambrano-Martinez, J. L.; Calafate, C. T.; Soler, D.; Cano, J.-C.; Manzoni, P. Analysis and Classification of the Vehicular Traffic Distribution in an Urban Area. In *Ad-Hoc, Mobile, and Wireless Networks Lecture Notes in Computer Science,* 2017; pp 121–134.
23. Wan, N.; Vahidi, A.; Luckow, A. Optimal Speed Advisory for Connected Vehicles in Arterial Roads and the Impact on Mixed Traffic. *Transport. Res. C* **2016,** *69,* 548–563.
24. Ahmad, I.; Noor, R. M.; Ali, I.; Imran, M.; Vasilakos, A. Characterizing the Role of Vehicular Cloud Computing in Road Traffic Management. *Int. J. Distrib. Sens. Netw.* **2017,** *13* (5), 155014771770872.
25. Pérez, J. L.; Gutierrez-Torre, A.; Berral, J. L.; Carrera, D. A Resilient and Distributed Near Real-Time Traffic Forecasting Application for Fog Computing Environments. *Future Gen. Comput. Syst.* **2018,** *87,* 198–212.
26. Ning, Z.; Huang, J.; Wang, X. Vehicular Fog Computing: Enabling Real-Time Traffic Management for Smart Cities. *IEEE Wireless Commun.* **2019,** *26* (1), 87–89.

CHAPTER 28

Deep Learning Classification Model for the Detection of Traffic Signs

VIKAS THADA[1], UTPAL SHRIVASTAVA[2], GITIKA[3], and GARIMA[3]

[1]Amity School of Engineering & Technology, Amity University Haryana, Haryana, India

[2]Banasthali Vidyapeeth, Jaipur

[3]Amity University Haryana, Haryana, India

ABSTRACT

CNN of deep learning has become a de-facto standard for binary and multiclass image classification. To assist drivers, autonomous system classification of traffic signs is an essential component. Due to its fast execution and high testing accuracy, CNN is the first choice of most computer vision tasks. CNNs have been gaining popularity for a couple of years because of their ability to generalize and classify data with towering accuracy. In this model, we implemented a traffic signs recognition algorithm using a CNN, and it is done using python and the deep learning framework Keras. Training of 43 traffic signs was done using CNN and Keras and tested under various parameters and scenarios, such as network depth, filter size, dropout rate, preprocessing, and segmentation techniques were used for training. The research work reached test accuracies of above 95%, and the experimental results confirmed a high efficiency.

Computational Intelligence in Analytics and Information Systems, Volume 1: Data Science and AI, Selected Papers from CIAIS-2021. Hardeo Kumar Thakur, Manpreet Kaur, Parneeta Dhaliwal, Rajeev Kumar Arya, and Joan Lu (Eds.)

28.1   INTRODUCTION

Driver help systems got a lot of contemplations from each establishment and industry zones. Among DAS components, the most noteworthy modules are the traffic sign area since it offers cautions to the drivers to lessen the heaviness of driving. The revelation of traffic signs has been a retardant in sharp automobiles since the focal point of the 90s and researchers proposed myriad ways to recognize them.

Smart Transport Systems can spare a ton of time to set aside cash, spare lives, and improve our condition. ITS's can be a future business achievement. These frameworks are also firmly coupled to other significant rising advancements; the web, versatile information administrations, shrewd sensors, man-made brainpower, and topographical data frameworks (GIS). Traffic sign acknowledgment is the most critical field in the ITS. This is because of the significance of the traffic signs in day-to-day life.[2]

The ID of traffic signs is cultivated by two chief stages: disclosure and affirmation. In the area stage, the image is predealt with improved and partitioned by the sign properties like concealing or shape. The yield is a parceled picture containing potential regions as road symbols. The speed and the viability of the disclosure are two imperative factors that accept a substantial part inside the whole cycle. It lessens the chase space and shows simply likely areas. In the affirmation stage, all of the contenders are attempted against a particular course of action of features to pick whether it is in the social event of road signs or not. After that, they are described as different get-togethers. These features are picked to pressure the qualifications among the classes. A sign's condition expects a central capacity and the signs are gathered into different categories such as triangles, circles, octagons.

28.1.1   MACHINE LEARNING

Machine learning (ML) means to make machine learning by providing it with enough examples, labels, and algorithms. Machine learning takes data and labeled output and generates models (Figure 28.1). The three main branches are supervised ML, unsupervised ML, and reinforcement ML. In this research work one application of machine learning, to be precise deep learning, has been explored where the input will be images and their corresponding labels.

FIGURE 28.1   Machine learning (ML) concept.

28.1.2   *DEEP NEURAL NETWORKS*

A Deep Neural Network (DNN) is a simplification of the human brain. Instead of producing that simulated "thinking" process of the brain, a DNN crunches vast amounts of data, compares it with that stored in databases, and makes the best match, much like a human brain. Unlike the traditional Machine Learning algorithms, DNNs are far better at learning complex nonlinear mappings and produce more accurate output classification results. The term "deep" refers to the number of hidden layers stacked together in the neural network such that the first layer from left is the input layer, and the last layer will always be the output layer (Figure 28.2). Traditionally, neural networks only consisted of two or three hidden layers, but the recent deep networks may have hundreds of them. Deeper networks learn nonlinear mappings better, but could also lead to overfitting. The dimensionality of the data, its quality, the frequency and number of clusters, the representation of the data as vectors or matrices, and the method used to compute the network's activation functions are considered to be key ingredients in the different layers of the network. In the figure except for input and output, all other layers are hidden layers. It is just two layers here but can be any different number >=1.

28.1.3   *IMAGE CLASSIFICATION USING CNN*

Convolutional Neural Network (ConvNet or CNN) is a class of DNN that has become a de-facto standard widely used for the classification of images, videos, text, or sound. It works on the same principles as the DNNs. The input image is processed and classified by it. CNN is trained on a number of images ranging from a few thousands to millions. Images are made up of pixels, and each pixel has a value associated with it which defines its intensity. Each pixel is a unique feature of the image that is extracted and learned by the neurons in the CNN layers. After the weights are optimized, the neural network can then be used for image classification. The CNN is generally favored for computation efficiency, as the complexity of the network is usually minimized. Convolution, Rectified Linear Unit (ReLU), and Pooling are some of the most common layers of a CNN (Figure 28.3).[5]

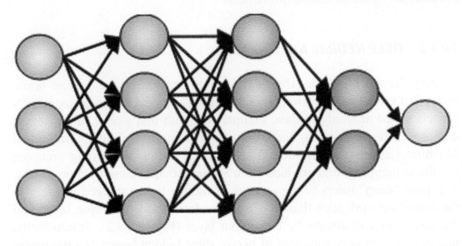

FIGURE 28.2   General model of DNN.

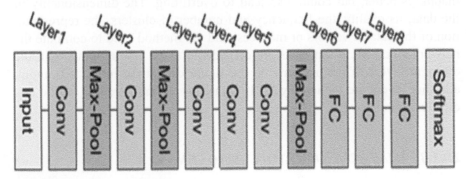

FIGURE 28.3   Basic CNN layout.

This paper is arranged as follows: Section 28.2 reviews work done in the area of traffic sign detection model, Section 28.3 explains design and execution work along with results, Section 28.4 provides concluding remarks with brief discussion about some future work.

28.2 RELATED WORK

A lot of researchers have contributed to this particular topic of the traffic sign classifier using ML. This section examines some of the work already done in this area.

In general, the traffic sign is recognized on two levels: On the first level, the process is traffic character recognition, which uses the traffic images to identify the size and location of the traffic and the second level is road sign recognition, which identifies the exact class of road signs for their classification. The traffic sign recognition is dependent on the attributes such as the color and shape of traffic signs. Traffic signs follow a fixed color scheme and white. This color helps to differentiate traffic signs from the main image. People can easily recognize road signs. Color information is an important characteristic to consider for these types of systems. Current research has shown that the simplest and most direct method is based on the color-based traffic-sign detection method.[6–9]

Recently, there has been an excellent performance in recognizing traffic signs using deep learning methods that have demonstrated excellent representational ability. Jin[10] used deep learning with a convolutional neural network with the SGD method and got high recognition rate. Dn11 achieved a recognition rate better than humans by using a multicolumn DNN for traffic classification that ran on a graphics processing unit (GPU). Qian[12] used the prior art method to achieve comparable performance. To classify traffic signs, a CNN classifier is used to learn the differentiator for max pooling positions. Ali[13] used a method based on a histogram of oriented gradients, color segmentation, and CNN. Excellent test performance and calculation speed were achieved by the author. However, real-time application in the field of traffic sign recognition requires selection of differentiators as well as a complete knowledge of the network structure. This contributes to improvement in processing time and accuracy of classification.

After a long time in 2011, the public and challenging dataset in this area was made available. A challenging database was developed by Felsberg[14] and Stallkamp.[15] They also included notes on the classification of traffic sign recognition. Prominent datasets are the Belgian dataset for traffic signs and from Germany. These are the standard database for traffic signs and have been used by many experts to review their discovered new methods.

The convolutional neural network was recently adopted for its high accuracy in object recognition.[20–22] In Ref. 20, a multilayer convolution network is proposed to improve test accuracy. This model can learn multi-level invariants of features of an image, filter bank level at each layer, a nonlinear transformation layer, and a spatial feature pool layer and classifier, test accuracy of up to 99.17% can be achieved.

28.3 METHOD AND MATERIALS

The data set used is available at Kaggle—it is a German Traffic Sign Dataset, dataset of 39,209 images (Figures 28.4, 28.5).[1]

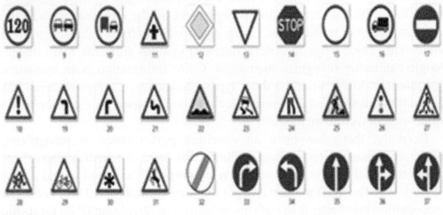

FIGURE 28.4   Traffic sign class.

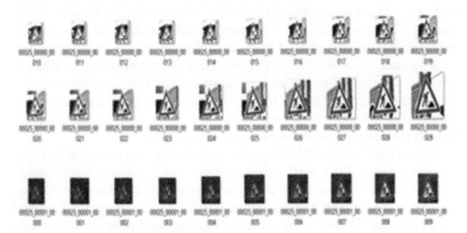

FIGURE 28.5   A single traffic sign class.

The data set contains state of information (39209, 30, 30, 3), following properties:

- Single-image, multiclass classification problem
- 43 classes ranging from 0 to 42.
- 39,209 images in total
- Size of picture 30×30 pixels
- 3 gives us information that it contains hued pictures.

Inside the training and testing directory images belonging to each class are present.

Training and testing images are present in separate directories inside the main directory.

The research work used libraries part of Anaconda 4 framework.

The steps are as follows:

- Downloading datasets
- Retrieving images and labels.
- Splitting data into test and train data
- Converting labels into One-Hot encoding
- Building a CNN model
- Compiling model by applying Adan Optimizer and categorical_ crossentropy
- Training of the model
- Plotting accuracy and loss graph
- Testing and display of the result

28.4 EXPERIMENTATION AND RESULTS

28.4.1 *EXPLORE THE DATASET*

Training data consist of 43 subdirectories, each directory representing one traffic sign class. Images are converted into NumPy array as input to the model. The train and test data are split in the ratio of 80:20. The labels were converted into One-Hot-Encoding representation as a requirement when working with keras library.

28.4.2 *BUILD A CNN MODEL*

The CNN model was used for image classification using keras. Compiling of the model is done by the Adam optimizer and loss is "categorical_cros-sentropy" as classification is multiclass.

The architecture of our model is (Figure 28.6):

```
2 X CONV2D  (FILTER=32,KERNEL_SIZE =(5,5), ACTIVATION="RELU")
MAXPOOL2D  ( POOL_SIZE=(2,2))
DROPOUT  (RATE=0.25)
2 X CONV2D  (FILTER=64, KERNEL_SIZE=(3,3), ACTIVATION="RELU")
MAXPOOL2D  ( POOL_SIZE=(2,2))
DROPOUT  (RATE=0.25)
FLATTEN
DENSE FC (256 NODES, ACTIVATION="RELU")
DROPOUT  (RATE=0.5)
DENSE  (43 NODES, ACTIVATION="SOFTMAX")
```

FIGURE 28.6   Model architecture.

28.4.3   *RESEARCH METHODOLOGY*

The methodology of the work is simple. After importing the dataset, images and their corresponding labels are retrieved. This is partitioned into train and test data. The labels are then converted into one-hot encoding. This is an essential requirement when implementing a model in Keras. This is then followed by building the model using various convolution and other layers, setting optimizer, and loss. Detailing is done in coming sections.

The convolution model summary with batch normalization is shown in Figure 28.7. The main aspect to understand is the batch normalization layer. As the name suggests, the previous layer's output batch is normalized before feeding to the next layer. The normalized input means the mean of the distribution input is o and the standard deviation is 1. The advantages of batch normalization are faster training (Figure 28.8) and better accuracy as compared to the model without it. As seen in the figure batch normalization is added after the activation of the previous layer but before the input of the next layer. The max-pooling layer is selected.

28.4.4   *TRAIN AND VALIDATE THE MODEL*

After retrieving the data and labels from the dataset and converting them into NumPy arrays with the corresponding labels, splitting is done. In the splitting process, we generally divide the data into two sets of training and testing.

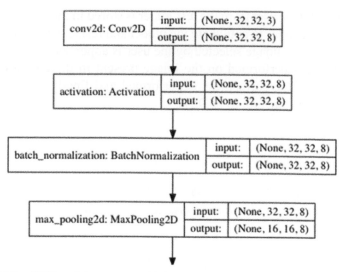

FIGURE 28.7 CNN model summary with batch normalization.

Splitting includes X_train, y_train, X_test, and y_test where X_test is the test data set. y_test is a set of labels to all the data in X_test. Similarly, X_train is the training data set. y_train is the set of labels of the data in the X_train. The test_size as 0.2 indicates that 20% of the data is being used in the testing phase and the rest is used while training the model.

After the completion of splitting the labels, that is, y_train and X_tarin are converted into one-hot encoding that is done using binary numbers and each row includes single 1 and rests low values that are 0 values which show that the particular row includes which label.

After that the building of the model takes place and finally, the training and validation phase comes into the scenario. Successive in building the model design, we train the model using a model.fit(). After 15 epochs the accuracy was stable and the model performs better with 64 batch sizes and. The model attains the accuracy of 95% on the training dataset (Figures 28.9, 28.10). After the training is done graphs for the accuracy and loss are plotted keeping epochs on the x-axis.

28.4.5 TEST THE MODEL

The dataset has a test envelope that holds a test.csv document that contains subtleties identified by the way of the picture and their class names, then the image chosen by the user from the test folder is stored in the variable images. We then utilize pandas to anticipate the model and resize the pictures to 30 × 30 pixels. Then the image selected by the user is appended in the data array and the testing is performed on the image present in the data array. Then the prediction of the correctness is performed and finally, the accuracy is calculated which came out to be 95%.

```
(39209, 30, 30, 3) (39209,)
(31367, 30, 30, 3) (7842, 30, 30, 3) (31367,) (7842,)
Epoch 1/15
981/981 [==============================] - 175s 178ms/step - loss: 2.0329 - accuracy: 0.4986 - val_loss: 0.5853 - val_accuracy:
0.8342
Epoch 2/15
981/981 [==============================] - 170s 173ms/step - loss: 0.6430 - accuracy: 0.8124 - val_loss: 0.1505 - val_accuracy:
0.9637
Epoch 3/15
981/981 [==============================] - 169s 172ms/step - loss: 0.4102 - accuracy: 0.8789 - val_loss: 0.1195 - val_accuracy:
0.9660
Epoch 4/15
981/981 [==============================] - 175s 179ms/step - loss: 0.3212 - accuracy: 0.9046 - val_loss: 0.0968 - val_accuracy:
0.9745
Epoch 5/15
981/981 [==============================] - 176s 179ms/step - loss: 0.2736 - accuracy: 0.9192 - val_loss: 0.1981 - val_accuracy:
0.9410
Epoch 6/15
981/981 [==============================] - 172s 176ms/step - loss: 0.2661 - accuracy: 0.9247 - val_loss: 0.0930 - val_accuracy:
0.9744
Epoch 7/15
981/981 [==============================] - 173s 177ms/step - loss: 0.2149 - accuracy: 0.9382 - val_loss: 0.0512 - val_accuracy:
0.9842
Epoch 8/15
981/981 [==============================] - 175s 178ms/step - loss: 0.2059 - accuracy: 0.9432 - val_loss: 0.0882 - val_accuracy:
0.9756
Epoch 9/15
981/981 [==============================] - 178s 181ms/step - loss: 0.2242 - accuracy: 0.9383 - val_loss: 0.0630 - val_accuracy:
0.9842
Epoch 10/15
981/981 [==============================] - 164s 168ms/step - loss: 0.1814 - accuracy: 0.9509 - val_loss: 0.0659 - val_accuracy:
0.9823
Epoch 11/15
981/981 [==============================] - 165s 168ms/step - loss: 0.1961 - accuracy: 0.9479 - val_loss: 0.0427 - val_accuracy:
0.9881
Epoch 12/15
981/981 [==============================] - 92s 94ms/step - loss: 0.1878 - accuracy: 0.9513 - val_loss: 0.0357 - val_accuracy:
0.9908
Epoch 13/15
981/981 [==============================] - 92s 94ms/step - loss: 0.1835 - accuracy: 0.9538 - val_loss: 0.0434 - val_accuracy:
0.9874
Epoch 14/15
981/981 [==============================] - 91s 92ms/step - loss: 0.1912 - accuracy: 0.9524 - val_loss: 0.0437 - val_accuracy:
0.9884
Epoch 15/15
981/981 [==============================] - 91s 93ms/step - loss: 0.2070 - accuracy: 0.9485 - val_loss: 0.0418 - val_accuracy:
0.9878
```

FIGURE 28.8　Training of the model.

28.5　CONCLUSION

The research work has carried out a traffic sign detection model. The model aims to attain good accuracy. We have successfully classified the traffic signs with 95% accuracy and visualized how our accuracy and loss changed. In addition to this, we have learned to train a model in such a way that the precision of the model is high and when to stop training the model once validation loss is higher than the training loss. During the development process, we studied carefully and understood the criteria for making it more effective with a high accuracy percentage. We also realized the importance of maintaining a token margin for error.

FIGURE 28.9   Graph of accuracy.

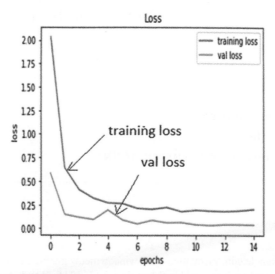

FIGURE 28.10   Graph of loss.

There are many places that we can enhance. The following are the attributes that we are about to execute in the near future.

- Real-time traffic sign recognition system.
- Multiple sign identification.
- Detection and telling of the significance of the sign.
- Improvement of the efficiency of this algorithm.

Some of the challenges we found during our research work are about low contrast of images. This low contrast of images can be enhanced using the CLAHE[23] algorithm that has been also left as future work.

AUTHOR CONTRIBUTIONS

Complete guidance and figures were provided by Dr Vikas Thada and Mr. Utpal Shrivastava. Model development and writing was done by Dr Vikas Thada, Gitika, and Garima. Proof reading was done by Mr. Utpal Shrivastava.

ACKNOWLEDGMENTS

The authors would like to thank Google for quick and efficient results on selected keywords, Google collaboratory. Sincere thanks go to mentors for guiding well and helping from the design and development of the deep learning model.

KEYWORDS

- **traffic sign detection**
- **deep learning**
- **convolutional neural networks (CNN)**

REFERENCES

1. https://www.kaggle.com/meowmeowmeowmeowmeow/gtsrb-german-traffic-sign.
2. https://www.researchgate.net/publication/29751315_Road_and_traffic_sign_detection_and_recognition
3. https://towardsdatascience.com/a-comprehensive-guide-to-convolutional-neural-networks-the-eli5-ay-3bd2b1164a53.

4. https://medium.com/ravenprotocol/everything-you-need-to-know-about-neural-networks-fcc7a15cb4.

5. https://mc.ai/a-comprehensive-guide-to-convolutional-neural-networks%E2%80%8A-2%80%8Athe-eli5-way/.

6. Soendoro, W. D.; Supriana I. Traffic Sign Recognition with Color-Based Method, Shape-Arc Estimation and SVM. In *Proceedings of the 2011 International Conference on Electrical Engineering and Informatics*; Bandung, Indonesia, 17–19 July 2011.

7. Li H.; Sun F.; Liu L.; Wang L. A Novel Traffic Sign Detection Method Via Color Segmentation and Robust Shape Matching. *Neurocomputing* 2015, *169*, 77–88. DOI: 10.1016/j.neucom.2014.12.111.

8. Bahlmann C.; Zhu Y.; Ramesh V.; Pellkofer M.; Koehler T. A System for Traffic Sign Detection, Tracking, and Recognition Using Color, Shape, and Motion Information. In *Proceedings of the 2005 IEEE Intelligent Vehicles Symposium*. Las Vegas, NV, USA, 6–8 June 2005.

9. Ardianto S.; Chen C.; Hang H. Real-Time Traffic Sign Recognition Using Color Segmentation and SVM. In *Proceedings of the 2017 International Conference on Systems, Signals and Image Processing (IWSSIP)*; Poznan, Poland, 22–24 May 2017.

10. Jin J.; Fu K.; Zhang C. Traffic Sign Recognition with Hinge Loss Trained Convolutional Neural Networks. *IEEE Trans. Intell. Transp. Syst.* 2014, *15*, 1991–2000. DOI: 10.1109/TITS.2014.2308281.

11. Cireşan D.; Meier U.; Masci J.; Schmidhuber J. Multi-Column Deep Neural Network for Traffic Sign Classification. *Neural Netw.* 2012, *32*, 333–338. DOI: 10.1016/j.neunet.2012.02.023.

12. Qian R.; Yue Y.; Coenen F.; Zhang B. Traffic Sign Recognition with Convolutional Neural Network Based on Max Pooling Positions. In *Proceedings of the 12th International Conference on Natural Computation; Fuzzy Systems and Knowledge Discovery (ICNC-FSKD)*; Changsha, China, 13–15 Aug 2016.

13. Youssef A.; Albani D.; Nardi D.; Bloisi D.D. Fast Traffic Sign Recognition Using Color Segmentation and Deep Convolutional Networks. In *Proceedings of the ACIVS 2016: Advanced Concepts for Intelligent Vision Systems*; Lecce, Italy, 24–27 Oct 2016.

14. Lecun Y.; Bottou L.; Bengio Y.; Haffner P. Gradient-Based Learning Applied to Document Recognition. *Proc. IEEE* 1998, *86*, 2278–2324. DOI: 10.1109/5.726791.

15. Krizhevsky A.; Ilya S.; Geoffrey E.H. ImageNet Classification with Deep Convolutional Neural Networks. In *Proceedings of the Advances in Neural Information Processing Systems 25*; Lake Tahoe, NV, USA. 3–6 Dec 2012; pp 1097–1105.

16. Qian R.; Zhang B.; Yue Y.; Wang Z.; Coenen F. Robust Chinese Traffic Sign Detection and Recognition with Deep Convolutional Neural Network. In *Proceedings of the 11th International Conference on Natural Computation (ICNC)*; Zhangjiajie, China, 15–17 Aug 2015.

17. Zhang J.; Huang M.; Jin X.; Li X. A Real-Time Chinese Traffic Sign Detection Algorithm Based on Modified YOLOv2. *Algorithms* 2017, *10*, 127. DOI: 10.3390/a10040127.

18. Xu Q.; Su J.; Liu T. A Detection and Recognition Method for Prohibition Traffic Signs. In *Proceedings of the 2010 International Conference on Image Analysis and Signal Processing*; Zhejiang, China, 12–14 April 2010.

19. Zhu S.; Liu L.; Lu X. Color-Geometric Model for Traffic Sign Recognition. In *Proceedings of the Multiconference on Computational Engineering in Systems Applications*; Beijing, China, 4–6 Oct 2006.

20. Sermanet, P.; LeCun, Y. Traffic Sign Recognition with Multiscale Convolutional Networks. In *Neural Networks (IJCNN), The 2011 International Joint Conference on*, 31, 2011–Aug 5, 2011; pp 2809–2813.
21. Jarrett, K.; Kavukcuoglu, K.; Ranzato, M.; LeCun, Y. What Is the Best Multi-Stage Architecture for Object Recognition? In *Computer Vision, 2009 IEEE 12th International Conference on, 29 2009*–Oct 2, 2009; pp 2146–2153.
22. Ciresan, D.; Meier, U.; Masci, J.; Schmidhuber, J. A Committee of Neural Networks for Traffic Sign Classification. In *IJCNN'11*, 2011; pp 1918–1921.
23. https://en.wikipedia.org/wiki/Adaptive_histogram_equalization#CLAHE
24. https://arxiv.org/pdf/1511.02992.pdf
25. Ioffe, S.; Szegedy, C. Batch Normalization: Accelerating Deep Network Training by Reducing Internal Covariate Shift. arXiv preprint arXiv:1502.03167, 2015.
26. He, K.; Zhang, X.; Ren, S.; Sun, J. Delving Deep Into Rectifiers: Surpassing Human-Level Performance on Imagenet Classification. arXiv preprint arXiv:1502.01852, 2015.
27. Sermanet, P.; LeCun, Y. Traffic Sign Recognition with Multi-Scale Convolutional Networks. In *Neural Networks (IJCNN), The 2011 International Joint Conference on*; IEEE, 2011; pp 2809–2813.
28. Zaklouta, F.; Stanciulescu, B.; Hamdoun, O. Traffic Sign Classification Using KD Trees and Random Forests. In *Neural Networks (IJCNN), The 2011 International Joint Conference on*; IEEE, 2011; pp 2151–2215.
29. Bahlmann, C.; Zhu, Y.; Ramesh, V.; Pellkofer, M.; Koehler, T. A System for Traffic Sign Detection, Tracking, and Recognition Using Color, Shape, and Motion Information. In *Intelligent Vehicles Symposium, 2005. Proceedings*; IEEE, 2005; pp 255–260.
30. Le, T. T.; Tran, S. T.; Mita, S.; Nguyen, T. D. Real Time Traffic Sign Detection Using Color and Shape-Based Features. In *Intelligent Information and Database Systems*; Springer: Berlin Heidelberg, 2010; pp. 268-278.

CHAPTER 29

Understanding Road Scene Images Using CNN Features

ANAMIKA MAURYA and SATISH CHAND

School of Computer and Systems Sciences, Jawaharlal Nehru University, New Delhi, India

ABSTRACT

Deep learning-based convolutional neural networks are very effective in different computer vision tasks together with semantic segmentation. Since road scene images are already very complex and unstructured traffic scenarios make it more complex and unpredictable. Numerous approaches have been suggested concerning semantic segmentation for structured road scenarios but a loss of spatial information during downsampling prevents them from segmenting small objects correctly within the image. To overcome this shortcoming, we propose to use an atrous pyramid pooling mechanism along with layers of pretrained ResNet-50 model to capture details of small objects in complex unstructured road scenarios in the encoder part. To recover spatial information from the extracted features, we use grouped convolutions that are a homogeneous multibranch mechanism that aggregates the group of convolutions and help to build a better decoder. The newly proposed approach demonstrated its superiority over state-of-art models by achieving 0.623 mean intersections over union on the validation set of the Indian Driving Dataset.

Computational Intelligence in Analytics and Information Systems, Volume 1: Data Science and AI, Selected Papers from CIAIS-2021. Hardeo Kumar Thakur, Manpreet Kaur, Parneeta Dhaliwal, Rajeev Kumar Arya, and Joan Lu (Eds.)

29.1 INTRODUCTION

Autonomous vehicle research has become an enormously burning topic in the field of transportation. Automated vehicles can significantly change urban road transportation soon. One of the most challenging problems for autonomous vehicles is navigation in urban and nonurban environments. A full global understanding of the surrounding environment is very essential for successful vehicle navigation. Deep learning-based segmentation models are very effective to train an autonomous vehicle system on how to sense its surrounding environment and make the correct decision based on this. Semantic segmentation is an important task as it provides each pixel of an image with a categorical label. With adequate advancement in deep learning, pixel-wise segmentation tasks have been brought to the next level.

For semantic segmentation, there are primarily two types of deep learning-based CNNs used: fully convolutional network (FCN) and encoder–decoder. Both types of architectures have similar layers to traditional classification models such as VGGNets, ResNets, etc., with some modifications. Encoder–decoder-based approaches achieve remarkable performance because these layers combine low-level detailed and high-ranking semantic information through skip connections to provide a better context awareness level to the decoder. A lot of work recently indicated that a deeper network would better learn the complex features. However, due to difficulties like vanishing gradients, it is not easy to train a very deep architecture. He et al.[1] suggested a deep residual learning strategy to overcome this issue, using identity mappings to facilitate training.

Recently proposed approaches such as dilated residual networks (DRNs)[2] and efficient residual factorized network (ERFNet)[3] have also exploited the residual learning for segmentation. By using dilated convolution, DRN decides to retain spatial information and prevent signal destruction of features and by using factorized residual blocks, ERFNet solves the network degradation issue. But both approaches have ignored global context and subregion information in addition to the skip connections among encoder and decoder. To resolve this, we suggest a new approach centered on the encoder–decoder paradigm for the pixel-wise prediction task. We have used the layers of the pretrained ResNet-50[1] model for feature extraction in the encoder part and grouped convolution strategy in the decoder part with skip-connections. It also employs atrous convolution in a cascade manner to acquire multiscale feature representations. Our approach is very efficient in promoting autonomous driving in Asian countries where road infrastructures are not advanced. The remaining part of this research paper is prepared as follows. Section 29.2

shortly reviews the already established segmentation works concerned with road scenarios. Next, Section 29.3 narrates the proposed technical approach in detail. The dataset and implementation details are discussed along with results in Section 29.4. Then, final remarks are conveyed in Section 29.5.

29.2 RELATED WORKS

The very first organized report[4] on deep learning-based segmentation was conveyed in 2015. In this report, a new CNN architecture was suggested for pixel-wise prediction deprived of any fully connected layers. This approach has achieved improvement over traditional machine learning approaches at that time. The segmented outputs of FCN are usually in coarse resolution due to several alternated convolution and pooling operations. To better refine the outputs, SegNet[5] was proposed based on an encoder–decoder, which uses VGG-16 as a feature extractor and also uses pooled indices from the corresponding encoder part while upsampling the feature maps. Another popular approach named DeepLab[6] enhances the coarse outputs with the help of conditional random fields (CRFs). Further, the ASPP concept was introduced in DeepLabV2[7] to capture context information at different scales. It is based on atrous convolution operations. An end-to-end semantic segmentation architecture U-Net[8] combines lower-level and higher-level feature maps which gained success for biomedical segmentation.

Recently proposed architectures[2,3,9,10] have adapted ResNets to achieve better performance. The primary contribution of ResNets is the implementation of residual connections. These connections resolve the issue of vanishing gradients and facilitate the training of deep neural networks. Another powerful framework named DRNs[2] was suggested to solve the problem of gridding artifacts and thus improve performance. In Ref. 9, a lightweight asymmetric Enet model was proposed which is faster than the SegNet model. ERFNet[3] has used residual connections with factorized convolutional to improve the Enet model. In Ref. 10, a multipath refinement approach was suggested that takes advantage of all the knowledge offered during the downsampling phase to make predictions. Another impressive approach that has utilized the deep DenseNet161 model and atrous convolutions in a cascade manner to extract multiscale contextual information.[11] Several other effective segmentation works[12–15] have been proposed for remote sensing and medical images. Most of the above-discussed works have been evaluated on well-structured road scene datasets like CityScapes.[16] Our work is centered around the recent Indian Driving Dataset (IDD) dataset[17] which mainly focuses on road scene understanding in an unstructured driving environment with greater complexities and uncertainties.

29.3 TECHNICAL APPROACH

29.3.1 ENCODER

The encoder is mainly used as a feature extractor that extracts valuable features with spatial information in encoded form. In literature, various CNN architectures have been proposed for feature extraction. It was found that merely increasing CNN's number of layers did not increase network efficiency. This is because deep CNN suffers from the issue of vanishing gradients and hinders the training process. To resolve this issue, the principle of skip or residual connections is introduced.[1] So to build a deep encoder, we use the layers of pretrained ResNet-50. This pretrained model has five downsampling paths consisting of stacked residual units. These residual units allow the feasible training of deep neural networks and improve the performance degradation problem due to the vanishing gradients. Each residual unit is described as follows:

$$\hat{y}_l = \hat{h}(x_l) + F(x_l, w_l), \tag{29.1}$$

$$x_{l+1} = \hat{a}(\hat{y}_l) \tag{29.2}$$

where x_l denotes the input and x_{l+1} denotes the output of the lth residual unit respectively, $\hat{h}(x_l)$ denotes an identity mapping function that generally equals to x_l, $F(x_l, w_l)$ represents residual mapping function, and $\hat{a}(\hat{y}_l)$ is an activation function.

29.3.1.1 CENTRAL PART

To segment objects with different sizes and ambiguous pixels that require a variety of contextual details, the multiscale features play an important role. For this, the ASPP method seems promising to extract features in various sizes.[7] In ASPP, a high enough dilation rate has to be utilized for a sufficiently large receptive field. But, as the dilation rate grows, the atrous convolution becomes gradually ineffective. So, the atrous convolution layers are arranged in a cascade manner to solve the ineffectiveness of large dilation rates.[11] In cascade mode, the atrous layer having a large dilation rate accepts the output of an atrous layer having a small dilation rate along with input features. For our network, we modify the existing DenseASPP method by using only 3, 6, 12, 18 dilation rates and removing a dilation rate set at 24, as shown in Figure 29.1. Each atrous layer can be described as follows:

$$y_1 = Z_{k,d}\left(y_{1-1} \copyright y_{1-2} \copyright \ldots \copyright y_0\right) \tag{29.3}$$

where "d" is a dilation rate of the concerned layer, "k" is a kernel size, (y_{1-1} $\copyright y_{1-2} \copyright \ldots \copyright y_0$) means concatenated feature maps from all previous atrous layers, and $Z_{k,d}(x)$ represents an atrous convolution with a dilation rate.

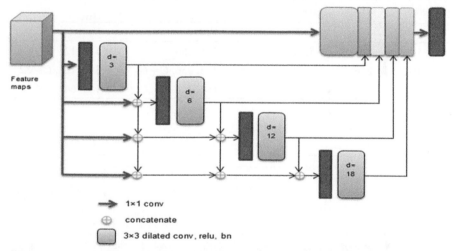

FIGURE 29.1   The detailed structure of a modified DenseASPP where the output of every atrous convolution layer is concatenated with previous atrous convolution layers and input features and then fed into the next atrous convolution layer. Note that d represents the different dilation rates.

Source: Adapted from Ref. [11].

29.3.1.2   DECODER

The decoder helps to recover the resolution of downsampled features to the original resolution for better segmented outputs. A peculiar case of grouped convolutions is channel-wise convolutions where we split the input channels into a set of groups known as cardinality.[18] This strategy not only improves accuracy but also keeps low computational costs. Firstly, final extracted features are upsampled and fused with correlated convolved features to recover the lost information during the downsampling process. After that, a processing unit that consists of three convolutional layers is used. The first layer has a 5×5 size kernel that performs convolution operation with no padding and stride 1 and the second layer performs channel-wise grouped convolution operation. The last convolutional layer is used to reduce the channel dimension. The whole process is performed four times and then features from all the previous steps are up sampled and concatenated before followed by two convolutional layers. Finally, the sigmoid classifier is used to produce outputs. The details of all four processing units are specified in Table 29.1 and the proposed approach can be envisioned in Figure 29.2.

TABLE 29.1   Summary of Processing Units of Decoder Part Where Every Layer Is Symbolized as (Kernel Size, #Output Channels).

Unit-1	Unit-2	Unit-3	Unit-4
5×5, 1024	5×5, 512	5×5, 256	5×5, 128
3×3, 1024, $C = 256$	3×3, 512, $C = 128$	3×3, 256, $C = 64$	3×3, 128, $C = 32$
1×1, 512	1×1, 256	1×1, 128	1×1, 64

Note that "C" is the cardinality.

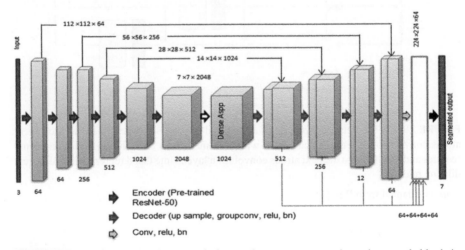

FIGURE 29.2   The proposed approach for road scene segmentation where each block is represented with its output size as (#height, #width, and #channels).

29.4   RESULTS AND DISCUSSION

We have appraised the performance of our proposed approach on a very recent IDD[17] which is made publicly available in 2018 for self-directed navigation purposes in unrestricted environments. All data are gathered from India, a developing nation, where, as in most developing countries, traffic laws are not strictly followed. The dataset tackles many problems, such as unclear road borders, the variety of participants in traffic, high-class diversity, and various weather conditions, etc. The training set has a total of 6993 images and the validation set has 981 images. The test set is a collection of 2029 images but annotated images are not offered for this set. Both the training and the validation set are finely annotated into 26 classes.

In this paper, we utilize 720×720 sized images and optimize the training loss with the AdaM optimizer. We begin the training process with a mini-batch of eight for a total of 50 epochs. The starting rate of learning is set at 0.0001 and then reduced by a factor of 0.1 in every 12 epochs. Finally, the sigmoid classifier is used for classification. All training and validation data are normalized and augmented with rotation and horizontal flips to evade the overfitting problem. We use the combined loss of binary cross-entropy and the dice coefficient as a loss function. Finally, segmented results are estimated in terms of the mean intersection over union (IoU) metric. It evaluates a proportion between the intersection (the number of TP pixels) and union (sum of the TP, FN, and FP pixels) of the given annotation and predicted mask on a per-class basis as follows:

$$IoU = \frac{TP}{TP + FP + FN} \qquad (29.4)$$

From Table 29.2, it can be witnessed that our newly proposed approach shows better accuracy than FCN-8s,[4] SegNet,[5] and ERFNet[3] models. Since FCN-8s model upsamples and fuses the different pooled features that do not contain spatial information. That is why the obtained results have rough segmented maps. The SegNet model has used VGG-16 as a backbone architecture that is not deep enough to extract complex features and also it has utilized pooled indices to recover lost information in the decoder part. ERFNet model has utilized factorized residual layers which helps in reducing computational cost but performance is not up to the mark as it overlooks multiscale contextual knowledge and lost information during the downsampling phase. But our proposed approach is better than all of them as it has used layers of deep ResNet-50 models to extract complex features and also incorporated multiscale functionality which captures small-scale information. This small-scale information helps in categorizing small objects within the image. Moreover, the grouped convolution strategy not only improves accuracy but also reduces the computational cost. Since ground truths of the test set are not freely accessible, a few images of the test set and their corresponding segmented outputs from different models are shown for comparison in Figure 29.3.

TABLE 29.2   Results Comparison in Terms of Class-Wise IoU on the Validation Set of IDD Dataset.

Model	Validation mIoU
FCN-8s[4]	0.436
SegNet[5]	0.458
ERFNet[3]	0.554
Ours	0.623

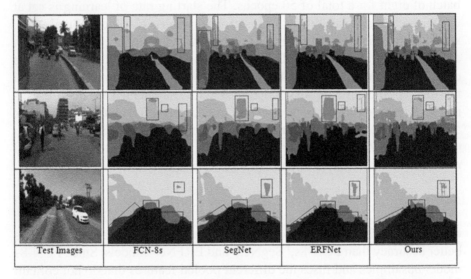

FIGURE 29.3   Results of semantic segmentation on IDD test set generated by the proposed approach and different existing models. The first column displays the random test images and the rest of the columns display predicted segmentation maps of respective models.

29.5 CONCLUSION

The road scene images are very complex as they contain various objects of different scales. We have proposed an encoder–decoder-based approach for road scene segmentation by combining the effectiveness of residual connections and grouped convolutions. The layers of pretrained ResNet-50 are utilized as a feature extractor along with the modified DenseASPP strategy. DenseASPP can segment small-sized objects without spatial loss. Moreover, we have used grouped convolutional layers in the decoder part to enhance the performance. Thus, the newly proposed approach is adapted well for unstructured traffic scenarios and achieved 0.623 mIoU on the validation set of IDD. We are also developing architecture by exploiting Xception-net and ResNet-101 as a backbone for the encoder part.

KEYWORDS

- **convolutional neural networks**
- **residual connections**
- **grouped convolution**
- **atrous convolution**

REFERENCES

1. He, K.; Zhang, X.; Ren, S.; Sun, J. Deep Residual Learning for Image Recognition. In *Proceedings of the IEEE Conference on Computer Vision and Pattern Recognition*, 2016; pp 770–778.
2. Yu, F.; Koltun, V.; Funkhouser, T. Dilated Residual Networks. In *Proceedings of the IEEE Conference on Computer Vision and Pattern Recognition*, 2017; pp 472–480.
3. Romera, E.; Alvarez, J. M.; Bergasa, L. M.; Arroyo, R. Erfnet: Efficient Residual Factorized Convent for Real-Time Semantic Segmentation. *IEEE Trans. Intell. Transport Syst.* **2017**, *19* (1), 263–272.
4. Long, J.; Shelhamer, E.; Darrell, T. Fully Convolutional Networks for Semantic Segmentation. In *Proceedings of the IEEE Conference on Computer Vision and Pattern Recognition*, **2015**, pp 3431–3440.
5. Badrinarayanan, V.; Handa, A.; Cipolla, R. Segnet: A Deep Convolutional Encoder-Decoder Architecture for Robust Semantic Pixel-Wise Labelling. *arXiv preprint arXiv: 1505.07293*, 2015.
6. Chen, L-C.; Papandreou, G.; Kokkinos, I.; Murphy, K.; Yuille, A. L. Semantic Image Segmentation with Deep Convolutional Nets and Fully Connected CRFS. *arXiv Preprint arXiv:1412.7062*, 2014.
7. Chen, L-C.; Papandreou, G.; Kokkinos, I.; Murphy, K.; Yuille, A. L. Deeplab: Semantic Image Segmentation with Deep Convolutional Nets, Atrous Convolution, and Fully Connected CRFS. *IEEE Trans. Pattern Analy. Machine Intell.* **2017**, *40* (4), 834–848.
8. Ronneberger, O.; Fischer, P.; Brox, T. U-Net: Convolutional Networks for Biomedical Image Segmentation. In *International Conference on Medical Image Computing and Computer-Assisted Intervention*; Springer, Cham, 2015; pp 234–241.
9. Paszke, A.; Chaurasia, A.; Kim, S.; Culurciello, E. Enet: A Deep Neural Network Architecture for Real-Time Semantic Segmentation. *arXiv preprint arXiv:1606.02147*, 2016.
10. Lin, G.; Milan, A.; Shen, C.; Reid, I. Refinenet: Multi-Path Refinement Networks for High-Resolution Semantic Segmentation. In *Proceedings of the IEEE Conference on Computer Vision and Pattern Recognition*, 2017; pp 1925–1934.

11. Yang, M.; Yu, K.; Zhang, C.; Li, Z.; Yang, K. Denseaspp for Semantic Segmentation in Street Scenes. In *Proceedings of the IEEE Conference on Computer Vision and Pattern Recognition*, **2018,** pp 3684–3692.
12. Wulamu, A.; Shi, Z.; Zhang, D.; He, Z. Multiscale Road Extraction in Remote Sensing Images. *Comput. Intell. Neurosci.* **2019,** *2019.*
13. Sinha, A.; Dolz, J. Multi-Scale Self-Guided Attention for Medical Image Segmentation. *IEEE J. Biomed. Health Inform.* **2020.**
14. Song, H.; Zhou, Y.; Jiang, Z.; Guo, X.; Yang, Z. ResNet with Global and Local Image Features, Stacked Pooling Block, for Semantic Segmentation. In *2018 IEEE/CIC International Conference on Communications in China (ICCC)*; IEEE, 2018; pp 79–83.
15. Wang, X.; Cavigelli, L.; Eggimann, M.; Magno, M.; Benini, L. HR-SAR-Net: A Deep Neural Network for Urban Scene Segmentation from High-Resolution SAR Data. In *2020 IEEE Sensors Applications Symposium (SAS)*; IEEE, 2020; pp 1–6.
16. Cordts, M.; Omran, M.; Ramos, S.; Rehfeld, T.; Enzweiler, M.; Benenson, R.; Franke, U.; Roth, S.; Schiele, B. The Cityscapes Dataset for Semantic Urban Scene Understanding. In *Proceedings of the IEEE Conference on Computer Vision and Pattern Recognition*, 2016; pp 3213–3223.
17. Varma, G.; Subramanian, A.; Namboodiri, A.; Chandraker, M.; Jawahar, C. V. IDD: A Dataset for Exploring Problems of Autonomous Navigation in Unconstrained Environments. In *2019 IEEE Winter Conference on Applications of Computer Vision (WACV)*; IEEE, 2019; pp 1743–1751.
18. Xie, S.; Girshick, R.; Dollár, P.; Tu, Z.; He, K. Aggregated Residual Transformations for Deep Neural Networks. In *Proceedings of the IEEE Conference on Computer Vision and Pattern Recognition*, 2017; pp 1492–1500.

CHAPTER 30

Profitable Crop Prediction for the State of Odisha Using Machine Learning Algorithms

VAIBHAV SINHA, PREETI MISHRA, and JUNALI JASMINE JENA

School of Computer Engineering, Kalinga Institute of Industrial Technology (Deemed to be University), Odisha, India

ABSTRACT

Odisha is an agrarian state. Most of the population of the state are dependent on agriculture. Disastrous changes in the climate can affect the crop production and may prompt misfortune to the farmers. This paper focuses on deriving the best possible methodology to help the farmers in choosing the most profitable crop. The dataset that has been taken on the basis of the required parameters for a particular crop like the temperature and rainfall suitable for crop growth and has been derived and integrated in from various authentic sources. After preprocessing of data, it is then classified into training and testing sets. Random forest and artificial neural networks have been used for the prediction of profitable crops and artificial neural network with Adam optimizer gives better results of 95% accuracy.

30.1 INTRODUCTION

Agriculture plays an important role in developing the economy of a state like Odisha. According to a current study, around 70% of Odisha's population

Computational Intelligence in Analytics and Information Systems, Volume 1: Data Science and AI, Selected Papers from CIAIS-2021. Hardeo Kumar Thakur, Manpreet Kaur, Parneeta Dhaliwal, Rajeev Kumar Arya, and Joan Lu (Eds.)

depend on farming for their livelihood. But due to a lack of market knowledge, farmers may not know which crops to grow for gaining more profit. Crop prediction is a significant horticultural issue. Every single farmer consistently attempts to know how much yield will get from his desire. Before, crop prediction was determined by examining a farmer's past understanding of a specific crop. The results rely upon climatic conditions and planning. The drastically changing climatic conditions in Odisha in the past few years have made a very large impact on the farmers. There are cyclones and heavy rainfalls that are ruining the crops, harming the business of the farmers, and leaving them penniless in this expensive world. This paper focuses on the application of machine learning to agrarian farming and presents a study on some of such works.

There have been various works for supporting the growth of agriculture in different regions of Odisha. Manda et al.[1] used Markov chain models and probability distribution for the planning of crops in Daspalla region of Odisha. Paltasingh et al.[2] used the aridity index for measuring the impact of weather on crop yield of Odisha. Panda et al.[3] also studied the impact of variations of climate change on the crop yield of Kalahandi, Bolangir, and Koraput. Ghosh et al.[4] used the CERES rice model for the development of rice yield prediction. Akbar et al.[5] used artificial neural network (ANN) for prediction of yield of essential oils in turmeric, collected from the state of Odisha.

From the review of literature, it was found that no such work on profitable crop prediction of Odisha exists. So in this paper, machine learning algorithms have been used for the same. Agricultural data of Odisha state have been used as a case study. We have used machine learning to develop a suitable prediction mode that is not only capable of predicting suitable crops for a particular region based upon its climatic and geographical condition but also suggesting the most profitable crop among all, by taking into account their market selling price (MSP). This information may help the farmers for beneficial decision making. The data used in this paper have been collected and compiled from various authentic sources, for all the districts of Odisha. Rest of the paper has been organized as details of techniques used, results and discussion followed by a conclusion and references.

30.2 BACKGROUND STUDY

Random forest and ANNs have been used for prediction purposes. Both the techniques have been discussed with their hyperparameter values.

30.2.1   RANDOM FOREST

Random forest is a type of supervised learning algorithm which is used for regression as well as classification. As a forest contains many trees, a similarly random forest creates decision trees for every data sample, gets the prediction from each one of them, and finally selects the best solution through voting. It is better as compared to a single decision tree because it reduces the overfitting by averaging the result.

Working of a random forest can be understood with the help of the following steps:

- Step 1—At first selection of random samples is done from the given dataset.
- Step 2—After sampling, this algorithm will construct decision trees for every sample and will obtain the prediction results from every decision tree.
- Step 3—Voting is done for every predicted result.
- Step 4—The most voted prediction result is selected to be the final prediction result.

Hyperparameter tuning : Hyperparameters are like settings of an algorithm which can be adjusted to optimize the performance of the algorithm. In the case of random forest, number of decision trees in the forest, number of features while splitting a node are considered as hyperparameters.

For hyperparameter tuning, we perform many repetitions of K-fold CV process, with different model settings. In K-fold CV, training sets are split into K numbers of subsets, called folds. Then iteratively K times, the model is fitted each time with training the data on $K-1$ of the fold and evaluation on Kth fold (validation data). At the end of the training, the average performance on each fold comes up with the final validation metrics for the model. Hyperparameters for random forest, along with their values are given in Table 30.1.

TABLE 30.1   Hyperparameters Used in Random Forest.

Hyperparameters for random forest	Values after tuning
Number of trees in a forest	200
Maximum number of levels in each decision tree	10
Minimum number of data points stored in a node before the node is split	5
Minimum number of data point allowed in a leaf node	4

30.2.2　ARTIFICIAL NEURAL NETWORK

ANN takes its name as it is based on the principle of biological nervous systems. The work network refers to the number of layers of neurons present in each system. The input is given by the neurons in the input layer, then there are one or more hidden intermediate layers present and lastly, there is the output layer which is again provided with the output via neurons.

- Step 1—The simplified dataset is provided to the input layer randomly to start the algorithm.
- Step 2—Using input and the linkages, activation rate of the hidden node is determined.
- Step 3—Using the activation rate of the hidden layer and the linkages, the output layer is determined.
- Step 4—The error rate in the output node is found. Using it, all the linkages between the hidden layer and the output layer are rectified.
- Step 5—The same weights and errors in the output layer are passed to the hidden layers and the linkages between hidden layers and input layers are also rectified.
- Step 6—This process is repeated till the desired outcome is found.

Figure 30.1 depicts the division of layers in the neural network that is used for the prediction of crops. Every layer contains 10 nodes. The source hubs are the input layer of the system depicting the input vector, which establishes the input signals applied to the neurons to the subsequent layer, which is the first hidden layer. The output signs of the subsequent layer are utilized as inputs to the third layer, that is the second hidden layer. The arrangement of output signs of the neurons in the output layer comprises the general reactions of the system to the initiation design provided by the source hubs in the beginning.

Optimizer: Optimizer is used to update the network weights in an iterative manner in the training dataset. Adadelta is an optimizer that requires no previous learning rate constant to begin with and fixes a window for the size of the past results found. While compiling the ANN model, Adadelta is used with a learning rate of 0.001 and a decay rate of 0.95. The other optimizer used is Adam which is an extension of Adadelta, under some changes in the hyperparameters. Adam is an optimization technique that is used to update the network weights in an iterative manner in the training dataset. It is used as it is adaptive to problems with large data or parameters and is computationally efficient. While using Adam optimizer, categorical_crossentropy is used in the loss function so as to find the cross-entropy metric between the labels and the predictions.

Prediction of crops

Input Layer (+34)

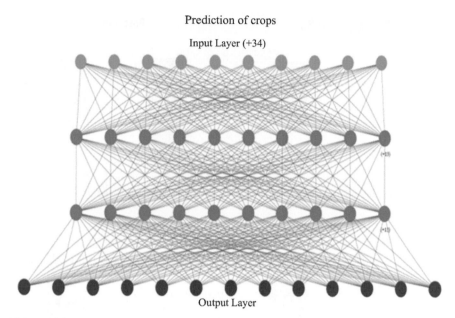

FIGURE 30.1 ANN model graph.

30.3   RESULTS AND DISCUSSIONS

30.3.1   DATASET

Crop forecast is done using RF and ANN in this work. For this, data are collected considering all the districts of Odisha over the period of years (1997–2014). Particular attributes like temperature, rainfall, month, and MSP of crops are considered for this work. The data were extracted from government sites like data.gov, farmer.gov, agricoop.nic.in and agriculture.gov, agriodisha.nic.in, orienvis.nic.in, and cseorissa.in in order to get authentic data on crops, temperature, rainfall, etc.

30.3.2   SIMULATION WITH RANDOM FOREST

Figure 30.2 depicts the performance achieved by using the random forest with hyperparameter tuning and without hyperparameter tuning. From the figure, it can be observed that a random forest with tuned hyperparameters performs better than nontuned random forest, though precision in both the cases is almost similar.

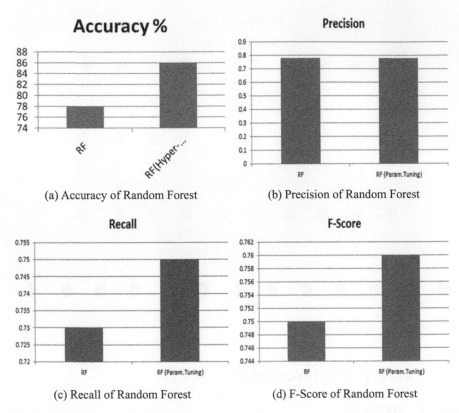

(a) Accuracy of Random Forest (b) Precision of Random Forest

(c) Recall of Random Forest (d) F-Score of Random Forest

FIGURE 30.2 Performance of random forest model.

30.3.3 *SIMULATIONS WITH ARTIFICIAL NEURAL NETWORK*

Figure 30.3 depicts the performance achieved using the ANN with Adadelta optimizer and Adam optimizer. From the figure, it can be observed that ANN with Adam optimizer performs better than ANN with Adadelta optimizer, though recall in both the cases is almost similar.

Overall, it can be observed that the ANN model performed better than the random forest model. The layered architecture of ANN learns better than the tree architecture of random forest in the case of agricultural data, but more extensive simulations with a bigger dataset are required to draw any specific conclusion. Again always the performance of the model is data-dependent, so there is no hard and fast rule on the application of learning models.

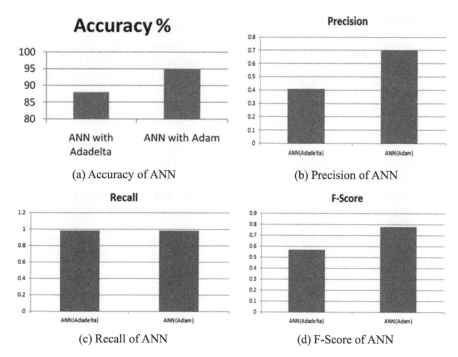

FIGURE 30.3 Performance of ANN model.

30.4 CONCLUSION

In this paper, the crop prediction is done by random forests and ANN. The data of all districts of Odisha are being collected for the past years and after analyzing the datasets from both the methods, it is clear that the result of ANN with Adam optimizer is more accurate with an accuracy rate of around 95%, than random forest. Using this, we can get the insights about the crop which will be very beneficial according to the region and climatic condition.

KEYWORDS

- **profitable crop prediction**
- **machine learning**
- **random forest**
- **artificial neural network**

REFERENCES

1. Mandal, K. G.; Padhi, J.; Kumar, A.; Ghosh, S.; Panda, D. K.; Mohanty, R. K.; Raychaudhuri, M. Analyses of Rainfall Using Probability Distribution and Markov Chain Models for Crop Planning in Daspalla Region in Odisha, India. *Theor. Appl. Climatol.* Aug 1 **2015,** *121* (3–4), 517–528.
2. Paltasingh, K. R.; Goyari, P.; Mishra, R. K. Measuring Weather Impact on Crop Yield Using Aridity Index: Evidence from Odisha. *Agric. Econ. Res. Rev.* **2012,** *25* (2), 205-216.
3. Panda, A.; Sahu, N.; Behera, S.; Sayama, T.; Sahu, L.; Avtar, R.; Singh, R. B.; Yamada, M. Impact of Climate Variability on Crop Yield in Kalahandi, Bolangir, and Koraput Districts of Odisha, India. *Climate* Nov **2019,** *7* (11), 126.
4. Ghosh, K.; Singh, A.; Mohanty, U. C.; Acharya, N.; Pal, R. K.; Singh, K. K.; Pasupalak, S. Development of a Rice Yield Prediction System Over Bhubaneswar, India: Combination of Extended Range Forecast and CERES-Rice Model. *Meteorol. App.* Jul **2015,** *22* (3), 525–533.
5. Akbar et al. Application of Artificial Neural Network Modeling for Optimization and Prediction of Essential Oil Yield in Turmeric (Curcuma longa L.). *Front. Plant Sci.* **2018,** *7,* 17, Article 1507.

CHAPTER 31

CapGAN: IoT-Based Cropping Patterns Prediction and Recommendation for Crop Cultivation

SATHYA K.[1] and RAJALAKSHMI M.[2]

[1]*Department of Computer Science and Engineering,*
Coimbatore Institute of Technology, Coimbatore, Tamil Nadu, India

[2]*Department of Information Technology,*
Coimbatore Institute of Technology, Coimbatore, Tamil Nadu, India

ABSTRACT

Agriculture, the ever-demanding field, primarily relies on healthy soils that provide nutrients and hence increase the production quality of any crop. The key components in soil features like chemical and physical properties such as moisture, climate conditions, temperature, pH are crucial in defining the crop yields. These properties can be digitally sensed, automated using an IoT device, and stored the infer data into a cloud environment for further analysis and prediction. This paper proposes CapGAN for identifying a cropping patterns recommendation system in which farmers are able to monitor the soil data, predict, and recommend suitable for cultivation resulting in high yield. CapGAN uses a generative adversarial network (GAN) for data augmentation and capsule networks for crop prediction. Furthermore, GAN is used to generate more soil features from historical cultivation and yield data. Using CapsNet architecture, the model is trained to identify the appropriate crops based on environmental factors achieving improved overall

Computational Intelligence in Analytics and Information Systems, Volume 1: Data Science and AI, Selected Papers from CIAIS-2021. Hardeo Kumar Thakur, Manpreet Kaur, Parneeta Dhaliwal, Rajeev Kumar Arya, and Joan Lu (Eds.)

accuracy of 93.6% and performance is compared with other models like multivariate logistic regression, support vector machines (SVM), and neural network, where CapsNet performed well. The proposed system implements an android-based user interface for helping the farmers to track the cropping patterns more efficiently and periodically.

31.1   INTRODUCTION

In this modern era, smart farming is considered to be an emerging technology and base for human beings. In India, agriculture is the primary source of income for most of the population and base for humans. Food production is being reinforced with smart computing technology from yield prediction, irrigation, machinery for yielding, plant genomics, environment control, and disease detection. An important section of agriculture where technology is not being fully utilized in deciding which crop to cultivate next suitable for the soil. The deciding factor in determining which crop to cultivate now mostly from the knowledge of the farmer is limited. Cropping pattern prediction is a vital feature of agriculture to help farmers increase crop production. Furthermore, machine learning techniques are championing the trend of smart farming in choosing recommended crops that learn from historical data and live data from the farm. Thus, the analysis results in suitable crops will be recommended using soil conditions, and data are sent to the farmers periodically through the mobile app. This system will help farmers to obtain better crop yield which results in maximizing profits. The key contributions of this paper are summarized as follows: (1) live soil properties like moisture, temperature, pH, and luminosity from the different regions of the farm are collected using soil sensors, and data are sent concurrently to the cloud.

(2) In cloud, data fetched from the farm are stored and monitored if there any delay or failure occurred during the transmission of data to the system. (3) Using machine learning algorithms, data from the cloud are analyzed and compared with historical data to make better decisions in choosing appropriate crops to cultivate. (4) Finally, mobile APP is developed to track the soil data and also provides suggestions to the farmers. The rest of this manuscript is structured in such a way that Section 31.2 highlights the flow of the state-of-the-art methodology for crop pattern prediction and recommendation systems. Section 31.3 discussed the proposed methods and materials, and Section 31.4 presents the experimental setup and deployment of the recommendation system. Finally, the concluding remarks and the future scope have been discussed in Section 31.5.

31.2 STATE-OF-THE-ART

31.2.1 IOT, CLOUD COMPUTING, AND MACHINE LEARNING

Recent advancements in the usage of the Internet of Things (IoT), wireless sensor networks (WSNs), and machine learning are used to increase the task automation and analysis of data within the agriculture ecosystem.[1] By applying machine learning algorithms to sensor data which enable useful information extraction and provide insights from data to take better optimal decisions. Integrating sensor networks with NNs used for the assessment of land for the cultivation of crops will help the farmers to make decisions.[1,2]

Jirapond Muangprathub et al. developed an optimal controlled system for watering crops using WSNs.[2] It includes a control box, web-based application, and mobile application and thus the system was installed in Makhamtia District, Thailand. The proposed system helps in collecting data like soil data (moisture and humidity) from sensors and temperature data from the Thai Meteorological web service. These data are periodically sent to farmer mobile devices and used for automatic watering on/off control. Besides, data analysis is also implemented to extract knowledge discovery for selecting suitable crops from environmental factors to increase the productivity of lemons.

IoT implementation for precision agriculture discusses a layered architecture for IoT and cloud communication for agricultural applications.[3] This application mainly focuses on the features of IoT and cloud communication in agricultural use cases. The analysis of soil and crop data is explained along with result visualization in the cloud. This system also helps in decision support in agricultural areas.

The WSN-based precision agriculture is referred to as a group of spatially dispersed and dedicated sensors for monitoring and recording the physical conditions of soil and the crop.[4] Certain features such as soil type, pH, moisture, region temperature, and region are considered by using these features the data can be easily collected. Macronutrients of the soil or NPK values are not considered because nitrogen, phosphorus, and potassium values may differ and are hard to compute with real-time sensing.

The cloud service-oriented architecture gives insights on things using the IoT platform based on edge and cloud computing for smart farming.[5] This provides insights on IoT with cloud for agriculture with this one can view the data that are stored in the cloud and furthermore, it can be viewed when it is needed.

31.2.2   DATA AUGMENTATION

Due to data scarcity, data augmentation techniques like generating adversarial networks are used to scale the number of new contents based on its training data which takes advantage of improving the accuracy and to avoid overfitting.[6] Distributed GAN-based intrusion distributed system can detect anomalous and internal and external attacks in every neighbor device. This proposed system maintains the privacy of user data in a few applications like health monitoring systems or financial applications.[7] Various significant GAN techniques like architecture and loss variants are surveyed for analysis of performance based on datasets.

31.2.3   DEEP LEARNING

More recently in agriculture, deep learning methods like convolutional neural networks (CNNs), recurrent neural networks have been applied for predictions like soil organic matter, crop yield, water supply, agricultural market price diseases and pest attack, etc. Neural network (NN) is inspired by the biological model of a brain which consists of a network of neurons communicating through synapses. In CNN, the number of hidden layers is deeper compared to NN and automatically detects features of a given data as scalar input and output. Capsule network (CapsNet) is an alternative to CNNs, each layer in the CapsuleNet is divided into groups of neurons as capsules with input and outputs as vectors.[8] Most popular CapsNets use a "routing by agreement" algorithm in between the layers, where they replace the CNN pooling layers with vector output. CapsuleGAN is a framework that incorporates GAN and CapsNet, in which GAN discriminators are replaced with CapsuleNet. This achieves better performance compared to CNN-based GANs.[9]

31.3   MATERIALS AND METHODS

31.3.1   SYSTEM DESCRIPTION

IoT has played a vital role in increasing momentum for smart farming. The implementation of the proposed system with sensors is deployed in the crop field and data are captured and stored on a monitor in the cloud environment. So, this work includes four components, such as data acquisition, cloud storage and monitoring, web application, deployment and mobile application, as shown in Figure 31.1.

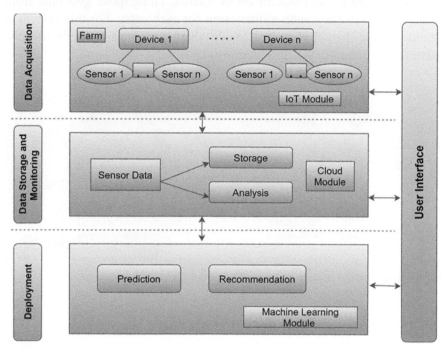

FIGURE 31.1 Overview of cropping patterns prediction and recommendation system.

31.3.2 DATA ACQUISITION

Soil features data like moisture, pH, temperature, and luminosity are captured through sensors deployed on the farm. Consider the farm with the IoT devices $(d_1, d_2, d_3, \ldots, d_n)$, and each device is connected with different sensors $(s_1, s_2, s_3, \ldots, s_n)$. This module consists of a node MCU along with sensors that are connected to the nearby WiFi hub for connection with the cloud module. It allows the node MCU to pass the sensor data to the cloud environment using an API request. The working of the IoT module is described in Figure 31.2.

31.3.3 DATA STORAGE AND MONITORING

Data acquired from IoT are stored and monitored using a cloud environment. The cloud module acts as an interface between the IoT module, machine learning module, and the user interface. The cloud used in this work is ThingSpeak. It provides HTTP APIs to send data from the IoT device and fetch data stored in the cloud in JSON format. ThingSpeak gets data from all sensors and stores it with a timestamp for each entry. For this system, a separate private channel is created, inside which there are four fields, namely, moisture, temperature, pH, and luminosity.

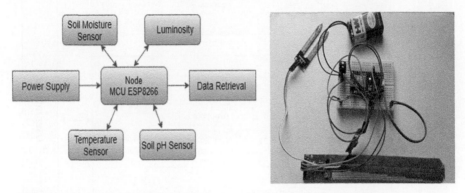

FIGURE 31.2   (a) IoT module architecture and (b) module implementation.

31.3.4   *PREDICTION AND RECOMMENDATION*

Soil data are fetched from various devices installed in the farm and updated simultaneously in the cloud. Furthermore, data retrieved from the cloud are unlabeled and are labeled with the crops name and the yield data before being used to train the machine learning module. This model is used to predict the crop to get the maximum yield for a given set of soil features. At the core, machine learning tries to classify a set of soil features to a crop with maximum yield. The trained module is also uploaded to a cloud server for access by users.

31.4   EXPERIMENTAL SETUP

31.4.1   *DATASET*

The soil dataset which comprises various features such as moisture, pH, humidity, luminosity, macro-, and micro-nutrients required for the specific crops is collected from different sources like agricultural centers, books, and web portals. This dataset holds the information to suggest the new crops for farmers based on the current soil conditions to obtain the maximum yield of the particular crop.

31.4.2 PROPOSED METHOD

31.4.2.1 GENERATIVE ADVERSARIAL NETS (GANS)

GAN is a kind of NN that helps in generating realistic data such as text, images, 3D-models, and videos. This network consists of a generator (G) and a discriminator (D). In a generation model, the objective is to create fake data similar to real data and the discrimination model acts as a binary classifier to distinguish the real and generated images. The proposed system uses GAN architecture to generate more data for soil features from the existing data, as discussed in Figure 31.3, and thus helps in increasing the dataset to avoid overfitting and underfitting problems.

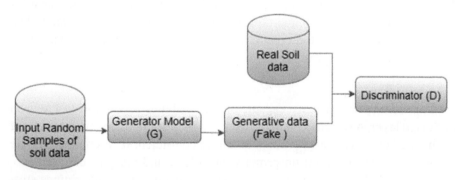

FIGURE 31.3   GAN architecture for soil data.

31.4.2.2 CAPSULE NETWORK (CAPSNETS)

Hinton et al. (2011) proposed CapsNets, a new variant of CNN that has resulted in better performance especially in computer vision and natural language processing. CapsNets architecture consists of a dedicated group of neurons that are encapsulated as every capsule.[13] Based on given inputs, a capsule computes a vector of soil features. In the proposed method uses a dynamic routing algorithm,[13] the soil data can be encoded as a vector and encapsulated with three basic layers: (1) convolutional layer (2) PrimaryCaps layer, (3) crop predict layer, as presented in Figure 31.4. Consider the input vectors u_i $(u_1, u_2, u_3, u_4, \ldots, u_n)$ from the capsules representing the soil features like temperature, moisture, pH, and luminosity are extracted using a convolutional layer.

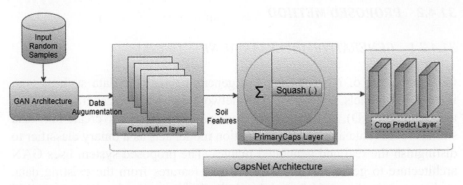

FIGURE 31.4   Overview of CapGAN architecture for crop prediction.

The output vector u_i of the capsule in the ith layer is fed to all capsules in the jth next layer $(i+1)$ and corresponding weight W_{ij} is calculated. The extracted features from the convolutional layer are fed to the primary caps layer and the prediction vector $(\hat{u}_{j|i})$ is evaluated by using eq 31.1.

$$\hat{U}_{j|i} = W_{ij}u_i \qquad (31.1)$$

This defines the primary capsule and contributes prediction to the crop predicted layer. A weighted sum (s_j) using eq 31.2 is calculated by the product of the prediction vector $(\hat{u}_{j|i})$ and a coupling coefficient (c_{ij}) representing the prediction of crops based on primary capsules i and class layer j. If the s_j value is high, then two capsules are highly relevant which determines suitable crops based on current soil conditions.

$$s_j = \sum_{i=1}^{N} c_{ij}\hat{u}_{j|i} \qquad (31.2)$$

where c_{ij} is the coupling coefficient determined by using eq 31.3.

$$c_{ij} = \frac{\exp(b_{ij})}{\sum_k \exp(b_{ik})} \qquad (31.3)$$

The weight sum s_j of each capsule in primary capsule layer i is connected to every other capsule in crop predict layer j (class layer) and is obtained to calculate the squashing function (v_j) in eq 31.4.

$$v_j = \frac{\| s_j \|^2 \, s_j}{1+ \| s_j \|^2 \| s_j \|} \tag{31.4}$$

The squashing function ensures the output from one capsule to the next layer capsule and redirects to the crop predict layer which is used to decide to choose appropriate crops and thus resulting in obtaining maximum profits.

31.4.3 PERFORMANCE ANALYSIS

This work evaluates the two different performance analyses of bandwidth speed of internet connection and various machine learning algorithms. Initially, analysis with different bandwidth for internet connection showed that the system works even if less bandwidth with good performance. The update time of live data from sensors to the mobile application is 10 s maximum. So, the intended users of the mobile application get the data from the sensors through the cloud every 10 s which is pretty fast to get the data from the soil. Also, the test with different bandwidth gave good results when tested with less bandwidth of 32 Kbps. This shows that the IoT device and mobile application can work even in low bandwidth connections up to 32 Kbps. Later, the machine learning module is tested using various algorithms like multivariate logistic regression, SVM, NN classification, CapsNets, and their corresponding performance measures are noted concerning data splitting (train and test data). The GAN network is used to create an additional dataset to train the classifiers. GAN created nearly 5000 data from the existing dataset which is identical to the data obtained from the agricultural lands. Usage of this additional data improved the accuracy of the classifiers by ~10%. The various metrics to measure the performance of the prediction systems such as accuracy, precision, recall, and F1 score are discussed in Table 31.1 and Figure 31.5.

TABLE 31.1 Performance Measures Comparison of Different Machine Learning Algorithms.

Machine learning algorithm	Performance measures			
	Accuracy	**Precision**	**Recall**	**F1 score**
Multivariate logistic regression	77.8%	73.2%	75.4%	74.6%
Support vector machines	79.1%	75.8%	74.7%	74.6%
Neural network classification	88.6%	82.7%	78.9%	80.4%
CapGAN	**93.6%**	**86.3%**	**81.7%**	**82.5%**

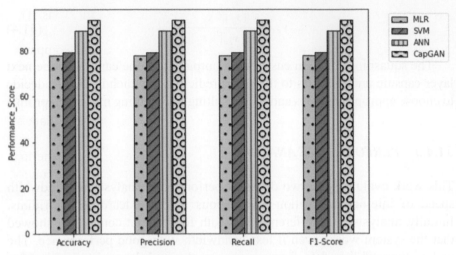

FIGURE 31.5   Comparison of machine learning algorithms for crop prediction.

31.4.4   DEVELOPMENT OF APP

The mobile application is built using react native hybrid application development library to get the live updates from the cloud. This application also has the features to enter soil features and get the crop recommendation. The intended users of this application are the farmers who can be able to get the live updates of their soil features and can get the recommendation on which crop to cultivate next. The mobile application has two major pages. One page is to get the live soil monitoring page which gives the latest soil feature measures with a delay of maximum 10 s. This page gives the last entry to the ThingSpeak and updates every 10 s. Another page is the crop prediction calculator page, which is a form with moisture, temperature, pH, and luminosity values as inputs and recommends a crop as output. These pages send the input data to the machine learning prediction module which is in the cloud and displays the recommended crops from the machine learning module. The mobile application is wholly built using React Native library which is used to create hybrid mobile applications.

31.5   CONCLUSION AND FUTURE DIRECTIONS

Agriculture plays a vital role in the Indian economy. The proposed system focuses on the farmers to obtain the maximum yield by choosing the appropriate crops to cultivate next and suitable for the soil conditions. The crop recommendation is purely based on the statistical analysis of the historic agricultural data. So, the margin for error is very minimal when compared to other conventional methods used. The maximum performance accuracy achieved by the CapGAN for the prediction of crops is 88% which is good enough to suggest the farmers use this technique. Also, the mobile application developed is a user-friendly GUI and readily provides the live data of the soil to the farmers.

In the future, the system may be added with solar cells to power the IoT device using solar power to have a longer life than the current 9V battery used. Besides, the machine learning module can also include a model that predicts fertilizer recommendations to get the maximum yield out of the cultivated crop.

KEYWORDS

- **cloud computing**
- **Internet of Things**
- **machine learning**
- **CapGAN**
- **generative adversarial networks (GAN)**
- **capsule networks**

REFERENCES

1. Mekonnen, Y.; Namuduri, S.; Burton, L.; Sarwat, A.; Bhansali, S. Review—Machine Learning Techniques in Wireless Sensor Network Based Precision Agriculture. *J. Electrochem. Soc.* **2020**, *167* (3), 037522.
2. Muangprathub, J.; Boonnam, N.; Kajornkasirat, S.; Lekbangpong, N.; Wanichsombat, A.; Nillaor, P. IoT and Agriculture Data Analysis for Smart Farm. *Comput. Electron. Agric.* **2019**, *156*, 467–474.
3. Khattab, A.; Abdelgawad, A.; Yelmarthi, K. Design and Implementation of a Cloud-Based IoT Scheme for Precision Agriculture. In *2016 28th International Conference on Microelectronics (ICM)*, 2016.
4. V., J. M. N.; R., F. F.; L., Y. M. Q. Design and Implementation of WSN for Precision Agriculture in White Cabbage Crops. In *2017 IEEE XXIV International Conference on Electronics, Electrical Engineering and Computing (INTERCON)*, 2017.

5. Zamora-Izquierdo, M. A.; Santa, J.; Martínez, J. A.; Martínez, V.; Skarmeta, A. F. Smart Farming IoT Platform Based on Edge and Cloud Computing. *Biosyst. Eng.* **2019,** *177,* 4–17.

6. Yamaguchi, S.; Kanai, S.; Eda, T. Effective Data Augmentation with Multi-Domain Learning GANs. *Proc. AAAI Conf. Artif. Intell.* **2020,** *34* (04), 6566–6574.

7. Ferdowsi, A.; Saad, W. Generative Adversarial Networks for Distributed Intrusion Detection in the Internet of Things. In *2019 IEEE Global Communications Conference (GLOBECOM),* 2019.

8. Zhao, W.; Peng, H.; Eger, S.; Cambria, E.; Yang, M. Towards Scalable and Reliable Capsule Networks for Challenging NLP Applications. In *Proceedings of the 57th Annual Meeting of the Association for Computational Linguistics,* 2019.

9. Jaiswal, A.; Abdalmageed, W.; Wu, Y.; Natarajan, P. CapsuleGAN: Generative Adversarial Capsule Network. In *Lecture Notes in Computer Science Computer Vision—ECCV 2018 Workshops,* 2019, 526–535.

10. Ayaz, M.; Ammad-Uddin, M.; Sharif, Z.; Mansour, A.; Aggoune, E.-H. M. Internet-of-Things (IoT)-Based Smart Agriculture: Toward Making the Fields Talk. *IEEE Access* **2019,** *7,* 129551–129583.

11. Zhao, C.; Shi, M.; Cai, Z.; Chen, C. Research on the Open-Categorical Classification of the Internet-of-Things Based on Generative Adversarial Networks. *Appl. Sci.* **2018,** *8* (12), 2351.

12. Yang, M.; Zhao, W.; Ye, J.; Lei, Z.; Zhao, Z.; Zhang, S. Investigating Capsule Networks with Dynamic Routing for Text Classification. In *Proceedings of the 2018 Conference on Empirical Methods in Natural Language Processing,* 2018.

13. Sahu, S. K.; Kumar, P.; Singh, A. P. Dynamic Routing Using Inter Capsule Routing Protocol between Capsules. In *2018 UKSim-AMSS 20th International Conference on Computer Modelling and Simulation (UKSim),* 2018.

14. Kang, H.; Lee, J.; Hyochan, B.; Kang, S. A Design of IoT Based Agricultural Zone Management System. In *Lecture Notes in Electrical Engineering Information Technology Convergence, Secure and Trust Computing, and Data Management 2012,* 2012; pp 9–14.

15. Jia, H.-Y.; Chen, J.; Yu, H.-L.; Liu, D.-Y. Soil Fertility Grading with Bayesian Network Transfer Learning. In *2010 International Conference on Machine Learning and Cybernetics,* 2010.

Index

Printed and bound by CPI Group (UK) Ltd, Croydon, CR0 4YY

23/10/2024

01777693-0011